Old and Dirty Go

MW01056364

Freud's collection of antiquities—his "old and dirty gods"—stood as silent witnesses to the early analysts' paradoxical fascination and hostility toward religion. Pamela Cooper-White argues that antisemitism, reaching back centuries before the Holocaust, and the acute perspective from the margins that it engendered among the first analysts, stands at the very origins of psychoanalytic theory and practice.

The core insight of psychoanalytic thought—that there is always more beneath the surface appearances of reality, and that this "more" is among other things affective, memory-laden and psychological—cannot fail to have had something to do with the experiences of the first Jewish analysts in their position of marginality and oppression in Habsburg-Catholic Vienna of the twentieth century. The book concludes with some parallels between the decades leading to the Holocaust and the current political situation in the U.S. and Europe, and their implications for psychoanalytic practice today.

Covering Pfister, Reik, Rank, and Spielrein as well as Freud, Cooper-White sets out how the first analysts' position as Europe's religious and racial "Other" shaped the development of psychoanalysis, and how these tensions continue to affect psychoanalysis today. *Old and Dirty Gods* will be of great interest to psychoanalysts as well as religious studies scholars.

Pamela Cooper-White is Christiane Brooks Johnson Professor of Psychology and Religion at Union Theological Seminary, New York, and the 2013–14 Fulbright-Freud Visiting Scholar of Psychoanalysis in Vienna. She has authored six previous books including *Braided Selves: Collected Essays on Multiplicity, God, and Persons*; and *Schoenberg and the God Idea: The Opera Moses und Aron.*

Psyche and Soul: Psychoanalysis, Spirituality and Religion in Dialogue Book Series

Jill Salberg, Melanie Suchet and Marie Hoffman
Series Editors

The *Psyche and Soul: Psychoanalysis, Spirituality and Religion in Dialogue* series explores the intersection of psychoanalysis, spirituality and religion. By promoting dialogue, this series provides a platform for the vast and expanding interconnections, mutual influences and points of divergence amongst these disciplines. Extending beyond western religions of Judaism, Christianity and Islam, the series includes Eastern religions, contemplative studies, mysticism and philosophy. By bridging gaps, opening the vistas and responding to increasing societal yearnings for more spirituality in psychoanalysis, *Psyche and Soul* aims to cross these disciplines, fostering a more fluid interpenetration of ideas.

Titles in this series:

Vol. 1: The Art of Jewish Pastoral Counseling: A Guide for All Faiths by Michelle Friedman and Rachel Yehuda

Vol. 2: Old and Dirty Gods: Religion, Antisemitism, and the Origins of Psychoanalysis by Pamela Cooper-White

Old and Dirty Gods

Religion, Antisemitism, and the
Origins of Psychoanalysis

Pamela Cooper-White

Routledge
Taylor & Francis Group

LONDON AND NEW YORK

First published 2018
by Routledge
2 Park Square, Milton Park, Abingdon, Oxon OX14 4RN

and by Routledge
711 Third Avenue, New York, NY 10017

Routledge is an imprint of the Taylor & Francis Group, an informa business

British Library Cataloguing in Publication Data
A catalogue record for this book is available from the British Library

Library of Congress Cataloging in Publication Data
A catalog record for this book has been requested

ISBN: 978-0-415-79098-7 (hbk)
ISBN: 978-0-415-79099-4 (pbk)
ISBN: 978-1-315-21268-5 (ebk)

Typeset in Times New Roman
by Wearset Ltd, Boldon, Tyne and Wear

Contents

Acknowledgments   vii
Permissions   ix

Introduction   1

PART I
Religion and Freud's Vienna circle   19

1   "So, you have seen the gang now": the Wednesday Night
    Psychological Society   21

2   "Old and dirty gods": religion and Freud's Vienna circle   56

PART II
The major contributors   91

3   The analyst pastor: Oskar Pfister (1873–1956)   93

4   "Enduring life without illusion": Theodor Reik
    (1888–1969)   125

5   Soul, will, and the search for immortality: Otto Rank
    (1884–1939)   149

6   Death and resurrection: Sabina Spielrein (1885–1942)   183

PART III
The shadow of antisemitism   215

7   "Father, don't you see I'm burning?": antisemitism as
     total context   217

8   "In the presence of the burning children": psychoanalysis,
     religion, and society—then and now   258

    Index   283

Acknowledgments

No one accomplishes a project of this scale without a great deal of help. I am grateful to so many colleagues who supported this research at every stage. It was my honor to be named the Fulbright-Freud Scholar of Psychoanalysis in 2013–14, and immense gratitude goes to the Fulbright Foundation, the Austria Fulbright office, and the Sigmund Freud Museum, Vienna—and especially to my colleague Isabelle Noth at the University of Bern, Switzerland, who first encouraged and nominated me—without whom this project would not have happened! I am grateful to Lonnie Johnson, Martina Laffer, Irene Zabarsky, and Molly Roza of Austrian Fulbright (the Austrian-American Educational Commission), who provided wise cultural orientation, networking with other American scholars in Austria, and a wonderful series of tours and *Stammtische* that gave depth and insight to my observations of Viennese culture past and present. Thanks go to Markus Öhler and the Protestant Theology Fakultät at the University of Vienna for hosting my seminar "Freud, Psychoanalysis and Religion: Critiques and Counter-Critiques," and to the wonderful students I was privileged to teach there.

I am also especially grateful to Inge Scholz-Strasser and Monika Pessler, directors of the Freud Museum spanning my time there, to Museum staff Bettina Althoff, Peter Nömaier, Simone Faxa, Moritz Hoffmann, Sandra Sparber, Robert Stepniak, Georg Thaler, visitors Annie Freud (daughter of Lucian Freud and granddaughter of Sigmund Freud) and Peter Schur (son of Max Schur), and above all to Daniela Finzi, Research Director, who oversees the Fulbright-Freud scholar program at the Museum, and has been a constant encourager, colleague, wise counselor, and friend. Finally, my deep thanks go to Christ Church Vienna (Anglican), which became a beloved international and intercultural "holding environment" in Vienna. This church's historic actions to resist the rising tide of Nazi antisemitism during World War II remain an inspiration.

I am grateful to Columbia Theological Seminary, Decatur, GA, for granting me the sabbatical leave to pursue this research, and to my pastoral theology colleagues on the doctoral faculty of the Atlanta Theological Association. Thanks also go to the colleagues at Union Theological Seminary, New York, for their ongoing support and encouragement; and to brilliant students in both cities for stimulating conversations at the intersection of psychology, theology, and social justice.

I am also grateful, three decades later, for my *Doktorvater* Christoph Wolff and the musicology faculty at Harvard University, who supported my first trip to Vienna for doctoral research on Schönberg's opera *Moses und Aron*, and inaugurated a lifelong relationship with that city's beauty and its shadows. Likewise, I express my appreciation to the faculty of the Institute for Clinical Social Work, Chicago, and to Dr. Marilyn Steele and Dr. Steven Joseph of Berkeley, California, whose in-depth teachings in psychoanalytic history, theory, practice, and research have given me the vision and the disposition to interrogate whatever lies beneath, behind, and beyond the surfaces of things.

Thanks also to my colleagues in the International Association of Relational Psychoanalysis and Psychotherapy (IARPP), the Society for the Exploration of Psychoanalytic Theory and Theology (SEPTT), the Psychology, Culture and Religion Group of the American Academy of Religion (PCR-AAR), and the Society for Pastoral Theology (SPT), for keeping rigorous scholarship and conversation alive at the intersection(s) of psychology and religion. In particular, I give thanks to SPT and the editors of the *Journal of Pastoral Theology*; my Atlanta doctoral colleagues and students; the Atlanta ThD Colloquium; the University of Chicago Divinity School; and Duquesne University's Phenomenology Center, for opportunities to present this research in its early stages and receive valuable interdisciplinary feedback.

I am deeply grateful for colleagues who took the time out of their own busy academic lives to read chapters and to give constructive critique from their considerable expertise: Dan Burston, Terry Cooper, Michael Eigen, Michelle Friedman, Christine Tind Johannessen-Henry, Jeffrey Kress, Emily Kuriloff, David Lott, Ilona Rashkow, Rami Schwartzer, Mychal Springer, and Herman Westerink—and especially my three "Psyche and Soul" Series editors Marie Hoffman, Jill Salberg, and Melanie Suchet. They have deeply enriched this project, and any errors in fact or interpretation are entirely my own. Thanks also to Adrienne Harris and Felicity Kelcourse whose shared interest in Sabina Spielrein has deepened this book; our collaboration will continue soon in another. Special thanks to Marie Hoffman whose enthusiastic support brought this project into the Routledge fold. I am also grateful to Kim Levert and Michael Cooper-White for eagle-eye editing, to Jan Rehmann for helping me take my German language skills to the next level, and to my editors at Routledge, Kate Hawes, Charles Bath, and Steve Turrington, for shepherding this book from initial concept to completion.

Finally, as always, love and gratitude to Michael and Macrina and our family, *sine quo nihil*.

Permissions

Draft portions of Chapter 2 were previewed as a Work in Progress at the Society for Pastoral Theology annual study conference, June 16, 2014, published in the *Journal of Pastoral Theology*, *27* (1) (2017). Adapted by permission, editors of JPT/Taylor & Francis, July 10, 2017.

A section of Chapter 3, "Why didn't Freud reject Pfister?" adapted from Cooper-White (2014), "Why Didn't Freud Reject Pfister?" *Pastoral Psychology 63* (1): 91–95, used by permission, Springer, March 9, 2017.

A section of Chapter 6, "Destruction as a cause of coming into being," adapted from Cooper-White (2015), "'The Power that Beautifies and Destroys': Sabina Spielrein and 'Destruction as a Cause of Coming into Being'," *Pastoral Psychology 64* (2): 259–278, used by permission, Springer, March 9, 2017.

The epigraph to Chapter 8 quoted from Irving Greenberg (2000), "The Shoah and the Legacy of Antisemitism: Judaism, Christianity, and Partnership after the Twentieth Century," in Tivka Frymer-Kensky, David Novak, Peter Ochs, David Fox Samuel, and Michael A. Singer (Eds.), *Christianity in Jewish Terms* (pp. 25–48). Boulder, CO: Westview/Perseus, used by permission, Perseus Books Group/CCC Republication, February 22, 2017.

All photographs featured in this book were taken by the author Pamela Cooper-White. The photo of Freud's waiting room in Vienna was taken with the kind permission of the Sigmund Freud Museum, Vienna, March 28, 2017.

Introduction

The year is 1902. Five men sit in a close circle on a red velvet upholstered couch and matching square-backed chairs, around a Victorian turn-legged table bearing papers and journals, black coffee and cake. The air is thick with tobacco smoke. There is an urn that contains ballots with all the members' names, so that speakers can—and must—speak, in random order.[1] A meticulously dressed, bearded man sits in a chair a few inches apart from the rest of the group, drawing on his cigar, appraising them all with gimlet eyes. He is biding his time to speak until all the others have weighed in. A floor-to-ceiling ceramic coal heater chuffs somewhat ineffectually in the corner; it is the discussion that is generating the heat. The topic is religion.

The bearded man is Freud, of course, and this is his waiting room.

Here and in the next room—his consulting room proper, with its carpet-draped couch—the walls are covered with pictures, and every surface is filled up with ancient archaeological figurines. With affectionate irony, he calls them "my old and dirty gods"—"*meine ... alten und dreckigen Götter.*"[2] These figures represent both an intellectual interest in classical and Egyptian antiquity common among educated men and women of letters[3] and, as well, are a metaphor for psychoanalysis itself—digging for long-buried evidence of powerful but often unacknowledged truths. Freud recognizes the compulsive nature of his collecting of these objects as an addiction second only to his cigars.[4] That they are gods presents an even deeper mystery, never plumbed directly by Freud himself, but suggesting the simultaneous fascination and aversion characteristic of a neurotic symptom.

Freud's insistent atheism—and his somewhat contradictory, obsessional return to the topic of religion throughout his cultural writings—are both well documented. In a letter dated October 9, 1918 to the Swiss pastor-analyst Oskar Pfister, he described himself as "a completely godless Jew."[5] This phrase was not merely a double negation (as both godless and Jew) of the dominant Roman Catholic religion of fin-de-siècle Vienna, but also served as a more complex signifier: in childhood an identity formed in a humanistic Judaism, and a growing identification with its intellectual and racial heritage against the backdrop of increasing antisemitism.[6] Freud's cultural writings on religious themes are well known: First, the essay "Obsessive Actions and Religious Practices" in 1907,[7] and then, more famously, *Totem and Taboo* in 1913,[8] *The Future of an Illusion* in 1927,[9] and *Moses and Monotheism* in 1939,[10] as well as a host of lesser known essays, speeches, and correspondence mentioning both religion in general, and his own Jewish heritage in particular.[11]

Less well known, however, are the attitudes toward religion among the men—and eventually women—who joined him once a week to reflect on a wide range of implications of the new psychological science: psychoanalysis. There has been no in-depth exploration of the treatment of religion by this "Wednesday Night Psychological Society"—Freud's immediate circle of psychoanalysts in Vienna—with the exception of Otto Rank and Theodor Reik whose work is still familiar to some specialists.[12] In general, there has been much less scholarly interest in Freud's Viennese circle as a whole than in Freud himself,[13] and statements about the group have tended toward generalizations.[14] Peter Gay in his comprehensive critical biography of Freud concluded that "Freud's view of religion as the enemy was *wholly shared* by the first generation of psychoanalysts. The attempts of some later psychoanalysts to reconcile psychoanalysis with religion would never have found the *slightest sympathy* in Freud and his colleagues" (emphasis added).[15]

In the present book, I investigate this premise based on my research as a senior Fulbright scholar at the Sigmund Freud Museum in Vienna in 2013–14, beginning with the research question: What religious themes appear in discussions and writings of Freud's Wednesday Night Psychological Society? I began with the recorded minutes of this group and the journal *Imago*—their journal for cultural psychoanalytic writings—followed by an examination of other published works by members of Freud's Viennese circle prior to World War II. Part I will focus on Freud's Wednesday Night Psychological Society through its vicissitudes, conflicts, and expansions from its founding in 1902 in that small waiting room at Berggasse 19 to the year of its dissolution in the face of the Nazi terror of 1938 in Austria—and the ways in which their views on religion played a part in this all-too-often neglected history.

Part II will explore the contributions of four figures who explored religious themes and ideas the most among Freud's inner circle. Swiss pastor and psychoanalyst Oskar Pfister's prolific contributions to the psychology of religion and his pioneering integration of pastoral and psychoanalytic clinical methods will be examined in Chapter 3. Although not a member of the Vienna circle per se,[16] he kept up a close correspondence with Freud and some of its members, and the attitudes of Freud's followers toward religion can hardly be considered without including him. The discovery and publication of additional correspondence between Freud and Pfister revealed further depth to this unlikely but warm relationship.[17]

Two of the better known members of the Vienna Society, Theodor Reik and Otto Rank, also made extensive forays into the psychoanalytic study of religion. Reik, who remained a loyal foot soldier in the movement, and Rank, who broke with Freud after years of intimacy, both wrote many volumes engaging questions of religion, mythology, ritual practices, and the nature of spirit. Their writings on religious themes will be examined in Chapters 4 and 5, respectively.

Sabina Spielrein has also recently been recognized as an important pioneer of psychoanalysis following the discovery of her letters and diaries[18]—amplified more recently by the somewhat sensationalized Hollywood film *A Dangerous Method* focusing on her romantic relationship with Jung (her analyst and dissertation advisor in Zürich) and her subsequent migration to Freud and the Vienna Society. Scholarly accounts of her life and her own distinctive contributions as a psychoanalyst (often foreshadowing formulations of better known theorists including Anna Freud, Jean Piaget, and Freud himself) have led to wider dissemination of her works. Her writings on religious themes will be explored in detail in Chapter 6.

Much is already well known, of course, about the Swiss psychiatrist Carl ("C.G.") Jung and his prolific writings on religion, mythology, symbolism, and his theories of the collective unconscious and of archetypes. Jung was never a member of the Viennese group per se, although he was in very close communication with Freud from 1907 to 1913, and sat in on one of the Wednesday night meetings in 1907. Fascinated with religion, spirituality, and the occult well before meeting Freud, Jung never renounced this interest in the face of Freud's atheism during the period of their closest association. After their traumatic schism in 1913 (which had ripples throughout all the centers of psychoanalysis at that time), Jung felt even more free to pursue his interests in the deep significance of religious and cultural symbols. He founded his own separate organization for his "analytical psychology," which has grown far beyond its roots in Zürich and remains a vibrant worldwide movement today.[19]

Because Jung was not a member of the Vienna Society, which is the focus of this book, and there is already a vast amount of literature devoted to Jung and his analysis of religious themes, I will not try to summarize all of his many writings on religion,[20] nor the related scholarship. Jung's *Red Book*, released for publication by Jung's heirs in 2009,[21] is a fascinating document of Jung's own internal, spiritual journey beginning around the same time as his split with Freud.[22] More will be said in Chapter 1 about Jung's rise in favor with Freud as an "heir apparent," their subsequent falling out, and the impact of this relationship on the Viennese group.

Another prominent foreigner, Ernest Jones, also deserves a brief mention here for his selected essays on religion.[23] While not an official member of the Vienna Psychoanalytic Society, Jones did visit their meetings beginning in 1908, lived in Vienna for several months in 1912, and was a regular correspondent from his home in Britain.[24] As the eventual founder of the British Psychoanalytical Society in 1919 and the *International Journal of Psychoanalysis* (from 1920 to 1939), Jones was Freud's most devoted standard bearer in Britain. His writings on religion hew closely to Freud's own explorations, especially in *Totem and Taboo*. He read widely in anthropology and psychology, with special attention to the works of the British anthropologist James Frazer.[25] While a few of his writings made original contributions to the field of psychology and religion in the early twentieth century, notably his essay on the "God-complex,"[26] his primary contribution was as an interpreter of the psychoanalytic study of religion to an English-speaking audience.

The tragic murders of Spielrein and at least ten other first-generation psychoanalysts in the Holocaust[27] enhance the poignancy and importance of investigating their attitudes as subjects caught at the intersection of ethics, religion, culture, and political subjugation. Moreover, in the course of this research, antisemitism became apparent as an over-arching theme, without which none of the individual contributions of the Viennese analysts can be fully understood. This realization evolved as a second and perhaps even more compelling thesis of this book, to be addressed in Part III. More will be said shortly about the two theses of the book, and this view from a more panoramic lens.

Beginning the research: the primary sources

My initial research question took me directly into the thought, and also the world, of the early analysts around Freud in Vienna. One wonders upon entering these rooms, "What would it have been like to be a fly on the wall and listen to the discussions that took place here?" In a sense, we can do that, filtered through the perceptions of Otto Rank, who was tasked by Freud with recording the minutes of the Vienna Psychological Society from 1906 until Rank's departure from Vienna in 1915 for military duty during World War I.[28]

The minutes of the Wednesday Night Society

Rank kept detailed *Protokolle* not only of topic headings and business matters, but of the actual substance of the group's discussions during those years. Unfortunately, the records after Rank's departure consist only of brief records of business matters, attendance lists, and abbreviated titles of presentations.[29] The published source contains a few fragmentary notes of meetings in 1915–18, and then one terse entry in 1938, describing the decision to disband in light of the Nazi takeover of the psychoanalytic society, its training institute and publishing house, and of psychiatry in general. Because so much of this material was originally in the form of a group conversation, I took an ethnographic approach to a reading of the Society's minutes in both English and German—first culling any mentions of religion, then transcribing and compiling these into broad themes and sub-categories.[30] Reading the group's published writings with the backdrop of these less formal discussions reveals more of the temperament, biases, and overall interests of the authors, and the minutes allow the reader to place the published materials in the larger context of their ongoing discourse.

The journal Imago

A second set of primary materials consists of the writings of these same analysts on the topic of religion. A particularly valuable resource for these writings is the journal *Imago*, founded by the Society in 1912 and, like the Society itself, suspended with the *Anschluss* in 1938.[31] Sachs suggested the journal's name based on a term first coined by Jung to convey both the idea of an "erotic impression" in the transference from earliest childhood, e.g., the Father-Imago, and its associations to "the masculine creative deity" found in ancient religion and mythology.[32] *Imago* was thus intended as a periodical of "applied psychoanalysis," where cultural themes could be developed that had no obvious place in the scientific and clinical *Jahrbuch für Psychoanalyse und Psychologische Forschungen*.[33] *Imago* was the group's outlet for the kind of wide-ranging and interdisciplinary writings that Freud and his circle often engaged in during their Wednesday meetings, including further forays into history, biography, anthropology, archaeology, philosophy, the paranormal, and—especially of interest for this project—the study of religion across time and culture.

While some of the group's ideas about these fields would now be regarded as spurious, based on faulty evidence or faulty interpretation, the authors made an effort to read and cite known experts of their time. They read widely and ecumenically—but it should be noted that they themselves did not have direct expertise in many of the fields they explored in these cultural writings, and their ideas (including Freud's own) must be understood as the often speculative efforts of experts in one field to apply its principles to other fields without an equally intimate knowledge of those fields' methods. A critical reading of the articles in *Imago* enhances one's understanding of the discussions of the Society, and vice versa. The minutes do not extend significantly past the year 1915, but later articles in *Imago* and related monographs suggest a continuing shape and content to their interest in religion as a topic.

Monographs, collected essays, memoirs, and correspondence

Beyond *Imago*, several early analysts who were either members of Freud's Vienna circle or had a close relationship to it, published monographs and volumes of collected essays on religion. The works of Pfister, Reik, and Rank are prime examples of this literary productivity. A third, more informal but similarly revealing source is the personal letters and memoirs of members of the Vienna circle, and reminiscences of those who visited briefly or were analyzed by Freud before 1939. Relevant details from those memoirs and correspondences will be cited throughout the volume.

The early context: Berggasse 19

The Sigmund Freud Museum in Vienna occupies the home and consulting offices at Berggasse 19,[34] where from 1891 Freud conducted his private practice of psychoanalysis,[35] wrote, taught, supervised, and convened discussions until the family was forced to escape Vienna after the Nazi *Anschluss* in 1938. This location is of symbolic interest in relation to the position of the early psychoanalysts themselves—situated physically but also culturally between the *Tandelmarkt*, a "jumble of junk shops ... owned by poor Jewish shopkeepers"[36] on the eastern hilltop, and the *Votivkirche* ("dedication church"—an opulent architectural symbol of the Catholic-imperial bond), the university, the *Rathaus* (city council) and other palatial buildings along the *Universitätsring*. It was in this setting, between the old *Ostjuden* culture and Habsburg-Catholic power, that Freud first convened his "Wednesday Night Psychological Society."[37]

Initially this was a very small group—just five specially invited, like-minded inquirers.[38] It grew and eventually was reorganized as the Vienna Psychoanalytic Society in 1908.[39] By 1910 the group had outgrown Freud's waiting room and began to convene in the Café Korb in the *Innere Stadt* nearby—virtually in the shadow of both the Roman Catholic Church of St. Peter and the imposing *Stephansdom* (St. Stephen's Cathedral). Soon after, the Society moved again to a more official and spacious venue, the *Doktoren Collegium* ("College of Physicians").[40] Individual members nevertheless continued to meet with Freud in his consulting rooms for conversation, supervision, and analysis—formal and informal. Berggasse 19 remained the inner sanctum of psychoanalysis until its seizure by the Nazis in 1938.

Two theses: the expected result and the return of the repressed

The first thesis: complexity in the Viennese analysts' views on religion

As noted above, I entered the project with one research question in mind: What religious themes appear in the discussions and writings of Freud's Wednesday Night Psychological Society? My hypothesis was that their views might be more complex and less strictly conforming to Freud's ideas than was assumed by previous scholars. The primary sources did, in fact, confirm a rich and often more complex view of the attitudes toward religion among Freud's early followers than has generally been recognized (detailed in Chapter 2). Capturing well the mix of orthodoxy and creativity that characterized psychoanalysis from its beginnings with the Wednesday Night Psychological Society, Paul Federn—one of the earliest and longest-standing members of the Vienna Society—shared the following recollection in tribute to Freud at the New York Psychoanalytic Institute in 1948:

> Freud … foresaw that many shades and deviations and derivations necessarily would develop.… Only in this respect, are we "orthodox"; but we are open to every change which is progress without abandoning the established truth and the principles confirmed by our scientific method.[41]

A second thesis: antisemitism and the return of the repressed

These first findings would have been more than enough to say "mission accomplished" based on my initial research aims. A second, unanticipated thesis emerged, however, that I believe in the long run may prove even more significant as a result of this study: that the surrounding atmosphere of antisemitism, even before the rising horror of the Nazi movement, stands at the *fons et origo* of psychoanalysis. Antisemitism shaped the first analysts' ethical sense, and was formative in their theory as a desire to analyze (from the underside) what lay beneath every surface of the human psyche. Obviously there is no one impetus behind the development of psychoanalysis, and to claim antisemitism as a singular root cause would be reductionistic. Yet, with its curling tentacles, it was one of the most pervasive—as well as sometimes denied—social forces in twentieth-century Vienna, and could not have failed to suffuse the thinking of Freud's circle in some ways, both consciously and unconsciously.

Antisemitism constituted an ancient ocean of hatred in which the first psychoanalysts (almost all of whom were Jewish[42]) had to swim, throughout their entire lives. It took constant vigilance to survive, much less succeed, in its dangerous waters. Above and beyond all the other themes discovered in the Wednesday

Night Society's discussions of religion, then, antisemitism stands as a "total context,"[43] an ineradicable, overarching reality that could not have failed to influence these first analysts' discoveries and explorations—and without which their ideas, especially concerning religion itself, cannot be fully understood.

I came to this realization in a visceral way while walking from my apartment in Leopoldstadt to the Freud Museum in the more affluent neighborhood of Alsergrund. I became aware that symbolically I was tracing Freud's footsteps across the Danube Canal, from the eastern European Jewish ghetto to the upwardly mobile 9th district. These two neighborhoods had contained two of the largest proportions of Jewish inhabitants in Vienna since the waves of immigration from eastern Europe in the nineteenth century and before (see Chapters 1 and 7), but they were very different Jewish populations with differing cultural and spiritual lives.

Of course the Holocaust itself was the culminating event—or, more accurately, process—by which longstanding religious and cultural hatred and envy toward the Jews as "Other" became systematized as a "science" of racial inferiority and ultimately extermination (see Chapter 7). Concentrated in the historically Jewish neighborhoods, one can find today—especially when looking for them—small brass plaques commemorating individuals and families who lived at a specific locale and then were deported to their deaths in the Holocaust. These plaques, called "*Stolpersteine*" ("Stumbling Blocks"), were first created by German artist Gunter Demnig in 2009 as calls to remembrance. Demnig quotes from the Talmud: "A person is only forgotten when his or her name is forgotten." The engravings generally begin with the words "*Hier wohnte…*" ("Here lived…") and end with "*gemordet*" ("murdered"), the place if known (usually a concentration camp) and year.[44] The idea of stumbling stones is also a reminder of an old slur that if a person stumbled on the street, a Jew must be buried there. This slur has been re-appropriated to signify the importance of being stopped in our tracks, to notice, and to remember.

All over Vienna there are memorials to the victims of the Holocaust. Their sheer ubiquity is a statement of the horrific extent to which entire Viennese neighborhoods were impacted not only by the final genocidal months and years, but also by the centuries-old pervasiveness of the antisemitism that allowed the Nazis to flourish and the evil to spread like a wildfire through both Vienna and the Austrian countryside. Perhaps to walk the city as a foreigner myself allowed me to search out these many monuments with less ambivalence because my eyes were not covered by blinders of familiarity—or (as much?) denial. Or perhaps because of the endemic racism in my own North American context, combined with personal observations of antisemitism in my childhood and young adulthood, I was primed as a Christian of partial German descent to see these visible memorials, and to seek them out, either as an act of righteous remembrance, an act of penance, or both. In any case, the palpable sense of Viennese antisemitism as a climate, an atmosphere, was something that I no longer just knew from reading *about* it in books, but came to *know* (both anew and again, like Freud's "return of the repressed"[45]) at a visceral level. I had seen its not-so-subtle signs with my own eyes, and I felt its miasma on my own skin.

Nor is antisemitism unique to Austria; it is likely worse today in some other central and eastern European countries.[46] But keeping the focus on Vienna, it became clear to me (both through reading history but also reading the newspaper, the culture, and the comments of acquaintances), the Holocaust is a memory that throughout Austria is still fraught with social denial, amid public calls for remembrance. Until as recently as 1991, when in a speech to Parliament Austrian Chancellor Franz Vranitzky publicly called the Austrian people to responsibility for the atrocities of the Holocaust, the official and popular view tended to coincide in a concerted effort to deflect all blame onto Germany.[47] Images of Austria as an occupied state, and Austrians as victims themselves of Nazi aggression, were repeated, mantra-like, in an effort to absolve Austria from its own violence toward the Jews and other groups slated for expatriation—and then, extermination.

Today there are laws against a former Nazi party member serving in the government, and Holocaust-denial speech, neo-Nazis, and hate crimes are officially banned. There have been official efforts at restitution and remembrance. However, a "soft" denial, coupled with ongoing antisemitism, persists in the general culture at large. I have met a number of older Austrians whose families were here during the war, and the usual response to any query about the Nazis or the Holocaust is an acknowledgement that yes, the Austrians were complicit, but: "Not everyone approved. My family certainly did not!" If so many families "did not," then who were all those people in the cheering throngs on the Heldenplatz giving Hitler a triumphal entry into Vienna? One sardonic (typically Viennese) joke that circulates about this rewriting of history is the saying, "Oh no, they weren't cheering. On that day on the Heldenplatz, they were just all waving their hands and shouting at Hitler 'Go away!'."

A friend who moved to Vienna from Germany over thirty years ago commented that in those earlier days she sat next to an older woman on a park bench, and after exchanging polite greetings, the woman grumbled that there were too many "*Ausländer*" ("foreigners"). My friend replied, "*I'm* actually an Ausländer—I'm from Germany." The woman stated flatly, "Oh, I don't mean you. I mean the Jews." While such comments are probably made less readily to strangers these days, people I know and trust acknowledge that antisemitism and racism (mostly referred to as xenophobia) persist. There is a strong anti-immigration and anti-Islamic mood (as well as fairly small counter-protests which I saw around the university).

Since the October election in 2013, the far-right political party the "Freedom Party of Austria" (FPÖ),[48] led by a charismatic speech-maker who stays just this side of illegal hate speech, Heinz-Christian Strache, gained even further ground, rising to first place among Austrians from 23 to 25 percent in a Gallup poll with a strong anti-immigration campaign.[49] In 2016, the FPÖ candidate Norbert Hofer led with 36 percent in the first general election. In the delayed runoff election in December,[50] the independent candidate Alexander van der Bellen won by a margin of 350,000 votes (53 to 47 percent)—but the far-right still captured close to 50 percent of Austrians' popular support. A slogan of this right-wing, anti-immigration movement, "*Pummerin statt Muezzin*" ("the cathedral bell, not the Islamic call to prayer"), echoes the sentiments expressed in the nationalist movement at the turn of the twentieth century: Keep Austria white, German-speaking, and Catholic.

Memento mori

My morning and evening walks took me past two contrasting monuments. One, planted in a narrow park along the east side of the canal, was a soot-darkened and apparently untended but very ornate miniature chapel dedicated to the memory of Johann Nepomok Hummel. A plaque indicates that it was placed there by the then *Bürgermeister* (mayor), Karl Lueger. As will be discussed later in this book, Lueger was elected in 1895 by the first explicitly antisemitic political party, the Christian Socialists, and installed in 1897; Hitler regarded him as a model leader. He is considered a symbol of the rising antisemitism at the turn of the century in Vienna, and his name was (mostly) removed in 2012 from the portion of Vienna's most public street, the *Ringstrasse*. Once called the "Karl Lueger Ring," it is now the *Universitätsring*. Yet at least one subway entrance to the busy Schottentor station near the university still bore his name in January 2014, while I was living in Vienna. His statue still stands in the Dr. Karl-Lueger Platz on the other end of the Ring.[51]

In his desire to create a modern German city, Lueger planted over a dozen structures throughout Vienna, with his name prominently displayed. The largest monument is an enormous Baroque-style church, the *Dr.-Karl-Lueger-Gedächtsniskirche* ("commemoration church") dedicated to St. Karl Borromäus, and still serving as an active Roman Catholic place of worship. It is planted squarely in the center of the *Zentralfriedhof,* or central cemetery, where numerous luminary Viennese musical, literary, and historic figures are buried. So Lueger casts a large shadow over Vienna to this day. His name and presence are still widely tolerated, without critical reflection on the antisemitism he represents. The little chapel I passed daily embodies the darkness and obscurity of this shadow. With its dingy stucco walls covered with graffiti, its interior locked behind heavy wrought iron gates and strewn with dirt and litter, it looks less like a monument to a saint or a statesman than a haunted house: a *memento mori*.

Across the canal from Leopoldstadt, in the 9th district at the top of Berggasse, stands a very different monument in the small courtyard of a well-kept Catholic Church, the *Servitenkirche*. This monument commemorates all the victims of the Holocaust who lived on the adjoining street, Servitengasse. The memorial consists of a collection of skeleton keys, each with a name tag for one of the Servitengasse victims. The keys represent both the mundane business of daily life, and its violent disruption—as well as serving as symbols of homes inhabited and wrenched away.

Walking daily between Lueger's uncanny chapel and the Servitengasse memorial, as well as all the other Holocaust memorials throughout Vienna, it became utterly clear to me that even if the first analysts had never written a word about antisemitism, their work, their sense of identity, and their very lives, were marinated in this bitter reality, and it could not have failed to have an impact on their creative thinking. Although there is, in fact, very little actual discussion of antisemitism recorded in the minutes of their meetings (see Chapter 2), their writings and memoirs as a whole—taken together with historical accounts of Austrian political and cultural history (see Chapter 7)—tell a more complete story.

My research at the Freud Museum and on the Vienna Psychoanalytic Society's early thoughts on religion, has certainly raised antisemitism and the Holocaust to the forefront of my own consciousness in new ways. Although I was raised in Episcopal and Methodist churches, and currently serve as an ordained Episcopal priest, my hometown on the north shore of Boston has a large Jewish community. I had friends whose grandparents still bore tattooed numbers on their arms. For me, therefore, the Holocaust has never been abstract. I have perpetually been drawn to study Freud and his circle because the history of psychoanalysis is a perspective from which one can try to make sense of the irrational—both personally and in social and political movements. It is also a perspective haunted by religion as a much-contested subject. The rise of overt antisemitism and the fusion of church and state at the turn of the twentieth century in Austria, together with Freud's adamant embrace of his Jewish heritage while utterly rejecting religious belief, make for fascinating research. And it is research that troubles the waters.

Notes

1 Freud instituted the urn as an old rabbinic tradition to prevent the teacher from monopolizing the discussion, but the obligation to speak was soon resented by the members, feeling exposed to scrutiny whether they were prepared to address a topic or not. See Strozier and Offer, 2011: 15. The urn was abolished by vote of the members in 1908 (Nunberg and Federn, 1967, Vol. II: 352).
2 Letter of Freud to Wilhelm Fließ, August 1, 1889 (Masson, 1985: 363), as translated in Marinelli, 2009. For an overview of the collection, see Gamwell and Wells, 1989. In his Introduction to the volume (p. 19), Gay cautions,

> We have not yet penetrated the full meaning of Freud's antiquities for him, although this assembly of objects helps us to make significant strides toward such an understanding.... These small objects meant much to him.... Although sometimes, as we dissect Freud, using his antiquities as so many surgical knives to probe his mysteries, we might remember the sheer pleasure he took in those pieces. Sometimes a statue is just a statue.

Cf. Gay, 2006: 170–173: "his antiquities seemed reminders of a lost world to which he and his people, the Jews, could trace their remote roots" (ibid., 172). Freud reportedly told the Wolf Man that they also represented to him the whole process of psychoanalysis as an archaeological excavation of each patient's psychic depths (ibid., 171).
3 Roazen, 1975: 177.
4 Schur, 1972: 247; Gay, 2006: 170–171.
5 Meng and Freud, 1963: 63.
6 Throughout this book, following Ostow, 1996, I will use the spelling "antisemitism." As Ostow (p. 14) has argued,

> other terms that have been proposed, such as Jew-hatred or anti-Judaism, have not replaced it. In this book I shall spell the term without capitals and without a hyphen, thus indicating my rejection of the racial implications of the term.

Ostow acknowledges, "It is a poor compromise, adopted only in order to comply with general usage." Ostow defines antisemitism most basically as "prejudice against Jews," (p. 13) but notes the complexity of anti- and philosemitism often co-existing as two "vectors" of the same prejudice, and the reality that many people's attitudes (citing Luther and Wilhelm Marr) change over time (p. 15). The problematics of defining Judaism and Jewishness—which can encompass religion, culture, and heritage—make a precise definition of antisemitism equally problematic. This issue will be further discussed in Chapters 2 and 7.
7 Freud, 1959a/1907.
8 Freud, 1955a/1913.
9 Freud, 1961/1927.
10 Freud, 1964/1939.
11 E.g., Freud, 1959b/1926. On Freud and religion, see Hewitt, 2014.
12 E.g., Merkur, 2013.
13 Mühlleitner and Reichmayr, 1997: 74.
14 Ibid., 73.

15 Gay, 2006: 533.
16 Pfister did petition once to join the Vienna Psychoanalytic Society—letter Pfister to Freud, July 9, 1914, in Noth 2014: 101–102 (see Chapter 3).
17 Noth, 2014; Noth, *et al.*, 2014.
18 Carotenuto, 1982.
19 See http://iaap.org. Accessed October 28, 2016.
20 E.g., Jung, 1960/1933, 1970, 1999.
21 Jung, 2009.
22 Ulanov, 2000; Tacey, 2013; Paulist Press "Jung and Spirituality" series, edited by Robert L. Moore (e.g., Moore and Meckel, 1988); Shamdasani, 'Introduction' to Jung, 2009.
23 Jones, 1964.
24 Roazen, 1975: 356, citing Jones 1959: 197.
25 Frazer, 1911–15.
26 Jones, 1964: 244–265 (orig. publ. 1913, *Internationale Zeitschrift*); cf. "The Madonna's Conception through the Ear" (in Jones, 1964: 266–357, orig. publ. 1914, *Jahrbuch*).
27 Mühlleitner and Reichmayr, 1997: 79–80, 94–102. See also Chapter 8.
28 Nunberg and Federn, 1962, Vol. I: xvii.
29 Nunberg and Federn, 1962, Vol. I: xviii, 1972, 1975, Vol. IV: 288–304.
30 Questions of translation include, for example, the English words "spirit," "soul," "mind," "psyche," in relation to *Geist, Seele, Wesen, Sinn, Charakter*, etc., which carry different connotations and usages, some religious and some not. *Seele* can mean both "soul" (spiritual), and "self" (psychosocial), and there is also *Selbst* ("self"—making a noun out of the reflexive form, as in English). *Das Ich*, Freud's term for the ego, refers to mainly rational, mainly conscious subjectivity. Contemporary theorists debate the terms "ego," "self," and more recently, "subject." *Geist* is equally ambiguous, as "spirit" and "mind" or "intellect"—or "ghost"! Context, then, is crucial in translating these terms.
31 Reconstituted in 1939 by Freud and Hanns Sachs (one of the original editors of *Imago*), under the name *American Imago*, initially with writings by analyst émigrés.
32 Rose, 1998: 124.
33 Founded in 1909 with Freud and Bleuler as general editors, Jung as editor.
34 For more on Berggasse 19, see Leupold-Löwenthal *et al.*, 1994; Scholz-Strasser, 1998.
35 Freud first began private consultations in 1886, the year of his marriage to Martha Bernays: www.freud-museum.at/freud/chronolg/1886-e.htm.
36 Bettelheim, 1991: 15. Cf. Sachs' description in 1944: 50.
37 For more on this group, see Federn and Wittenberger, 1992 and Graf, 1942: 470.
38 Gay, 2006: 174.
39 About the history of the group, Gay, 2006: 173–179; Roazen, 1975 (based on personal interviews with early analysts).
40 Sigmund Freud Museum, n.d.: 1908; Nunberg and Federn, 1962, Vol. I: xix; Wiener Psychoanalytische Vereinigung, n.d.
41 Federn, 1948.
42 Mühlleitner and Reichmayr, 1997: 85–88.
43 Term from sociolinguistics and anthropology, as the encompassing surround of a culture, its practices and language(s), which may appear only partially in the subjective consciousness of individuals.
44 Demnig, n.d.
45 E.g., Freud, 1955b/1919: 249.
46 Personal travel 2013–14, 2015; cf. Mikanowski, 2012.
47 Demokratiezentrum Wien/Vienna Democracy Center, 2015.

48 *Freiheitliche Partei Österreichs.*
49 Cf. Ehl, 2013.
50 www.bbc.com/news/world-europe-38202669. Accessed December 5, 2016.
51 A pressure group from the University for Applied Arts and the Jewish Museum, Vienna, has organized to transform the Dr. Karl-Lueger Platz into a monument against antisemitism and racism in Austria: http://en.luegerplatz.com/impressum.php. Accessed October 25, 2016.

References

Bettelheim, Bruno (1991). *Freud's Vienna and other essays.* New York: Vintage.

Carotenuto, Aldo (1982). *A secret symmetry: Sabina Spielrein between Jung and Freud.* Arno Pomerans, John Shepley, and Krishna Winston (Trans.). New York: Pantheon.

Demnig, Gunter (n.d.). *Stolpersteine.* Online at www.stolpersteine.eu/en. Accessed October 25, 2016.

Demokratiezentrum Wien/Vienna Democracy Center (2015). *Der "Opfermythos in Österreich: Entstehung und Entwicklung."* Online at www.demokratiezentrum.org/wissen/timelines/der-opfermythos-in-oesterreich-entstehung-und-entwicklung.html Accessed October 28, 2016.

Ehl, Martin (2013). Populists in the fast lane. *Vienna Review,* November 18. Online at www.viennareview.net/news/europe/populists-in-the-fast-lane. Accessed October 28, 2016.

Federn, Ernst and Wittenberger, Gerhard (Eds.) (1992). *Aus dem Kreis um Sigmund Freud: Zu den Protokollen der Wiener Psychoanalytischen Vereinigung.* Frankfurt-am-Main: Fischer.

Federn, Paul (1948). Notes. *Psychoanalytic Quarterly, 16:* 595–597.

Frazer, James (1911–15). *The golden bough,* 12 vols. London: Macmillan.

Freud, S. (1955a). *Totem and taboo.* In J. Strachey (Ed.), *Standard edition of the complete works of Sigmund Freud,* Vol. 13: 1–162. (Orig. publ. 1913.)

Freud, Sigmund (1955b). The Uncanny. In J. Strachey (Ed.), *Standard edition of the complete works of Sigmund Freud,* Vol. 17: 217–256. (Orig. publ. 1919.)

Freud, Sigmund (1959a). Obsessive actions and religious practices. In J. Strachey (Ed.), *Standard edition of the complete works of Sigmund Freud,* Vol. 9: 115–127. (Orig. publ. 1907.)

Freud, Sigmund (1959b). Address to the Society of B'nai B'Rrith. In J. Strachey (Ed.), *Standard edition of the complete works of Sigmund Freud,* Vol. 20: 271–274. (Orig. publ. 1926.)

Freud, Sigmund (1961). *The future of an illusion.* In J. Strachey (Ed.), *Standard edition of the complete works of Sigmund Freud,* Vol. 21: 5–56. (Orig. publ. 1927.)

Freud, Sigmund (1964). *Moses and monotheism.* In J. Strachey (Ed.), *Standard edition of the complete works of Sigmund Freud,* Vol. 23: 3–138. (Orig. publ. 1939.)

Gamwell, Lynn and Wells, Richard (1989). *Sigmund Freud and art: His personal collection of antiquities.* Binghamton, NY: SUNY Press and London: Freud Museum.

Gay, Peter (2006). *Freud: A life for our time.* New York: W. W. Norton.

Graf, Max (1942). Reminiscences of Professor Sigmund Freud. *Psychoanalytic Quarterly, 2* (4): 465–476.

Hewitt, Marsha Aileen (2014). *Freud on religion.* New York: Routledge.

House of Terror Museum (2015). History of the museum. Online at www.terrorhaza.hu/en/museum. Accessed October 25, 2016.

Jones, Ernest (1959). *Free associations: Memories of a psychoanalyst*. New York: Basic Books.

Jones, Ernest (1964). *Essays in applied psychoanalysis, Vol. 2: Essays in folklore and religion*. London: Hogarth.

Jung, C. G. (1960). *Psychology and religion*. New Haven, CT: Yale University Press. (Orig. publ. 1933.)

Jung, C. G. (1970). Psychology and religion: West and east. *The Collected Works of Carl G. Jung*. R. F. C. Hull (Trans.), Vol. 11. Bollingen Series 20. Princeton, NJ: Princeton University Press.

Jung, C. G. (1999). *Jung on Christianity*. Murray Stein (Ed.). Princeton, NJ: Princeton University Press.

Jung, C. G. (2009). *The Red Book*. Sonu Shamdasani (Ed.), Mark Kyburz, John Peck, and Sonu Shamdasani (Trans.). New York: W. W. Norton. (Orig. unpubl. manuscript 1914–30, 1959.)

Leupold-Löwenthal, Harald, Lobner, Hans, and Scholz-Strasser, Inge (1994). *Sigmund Freud Museum: Berggasse 19, Vienna—Catalogue*. Vienna: Brandstädter.

Lin, Lana (2015). Lost objects: Berggasse 19 and absence in the space of psychoanalysis. *The Canadian Network for Psychoanalysis and Culture, 1: The Freudian legacy today* (pp. 11–32). Online at www.academia.edu/23211830/Lost-Objects-Berggasse-19-and-Absence-in-the-Space-of-Psychoanalysis. Accessed September 3, 2017.

Marinelli, Lisa (2009). "My old and dirty gods": An exhibition on Freud's archaeological collection. J. Titherige (Trans.). *American Imago, 66* (2): 149–159. Notes online at www.freud-museum.at/online/e/inhalt/museumausstellungenGoetter.htm. Accessed October 29, 2016.

Masson, Jeffrey Moussaief (1985). *The Complete letters of Sigmund Freud to Wilhelm Fliess, 1887–1904*. Cambridge, MA: Belknap/Harvard University Press.

Meng, Heinrich and Freud, Ernst L. (Eds.) (1963). *Psychoanalysis and faith: The letters of Sigmund Freud and Oskar Pfister*. Eric Mosbacher (Trans.). New York: Basic Books.

Merkur, Dan (2013). *Relating to God: Clinical psychoanalysis, spirituality, and theism*. Lanham, MD: Jason Aronson.

Meyer, Michael A. and Brenner, Michael (1996). *German-Jewish history in modern times, Vol. 1: Tradition and Enlightenment 1600–1780*. New York: Columbia University Press.

Mikanowski, Jakob (2012). The frightening politics of Hungary's House of Terror. Online at https://theawl.com/the-frightening-politics-of-hungarys-house-of-terror-a421981fa2e3#.efech22x0. Accessed October 25, 2016.

Moore, Robert L. and Meckel, Daniel J. (Eds.) (1988). *Jung and Christianity in dialogue*. Jung and Spirituality Series. Mahwah, NJ: Paulist Press.

Mühlleitner, Elke and Reichmayr, Johannes (1997). Following Freud in Vienna. *International Forum of Psychoanalysis, 6*: 73–102.

Muxeneder, Therese (2009). Ethik des Bewahrens: Exil und Rückkehr des Schönberg-Nachlasses. Vienna: Arnold Schönberg Center. Online at www.schoenberg.at/images/stories/bilder_statische_artikel/archiv/ethikbewahrens.pdf. Accessed January 20, 2014.

Noth, Isabelle (Ed.) (2014). *Sigmund Freud-Oskar Pfister Briefwechsel 1909–1939*. Zürich: TVZ Theologischer Verlag.

Noth, Isabelle, Morgenthaler, Christoph, Cooper-White, Pamela, and Westerink, Herman (2014). Forum on the friendship between Sigmund Freud and Oskar Pfister. *Pastoral Psychology, 1* (63): 79–100.

Nunberg, Herman and Federn, Ernst (Eds.) (1962–75). *Minutes of the Vienna Psychoanalytic Society*, Vols. I–IV. M. Nunberg (Trans.). New York: International Universities Press.

Nunberg, Herman and Federn, Ernst (Eds.) (1976–81). *Protokolle der Wiener Psychoanalytischen Vereinigung*. Bd. I–IV. Frankfurt am Main: S. Fischer. (Neuausgabe: Gießen: Psychosozial-Verlag, 2007.)

Ostow, Mortimer (1996). *Myth and madness: The psychodynamics of antisemitism*. New Brunswick, NJ: Transaction Publishers.

Roazen, Paul (1975). *Freud and his followers*. New York: Alfred A. Knopf.

Rose, Louis (1998). *The Freudian calling: Early Viennese psychoanalysis and the pursuit of cultural science*. Detroit: Wayne State University Press.

Sachs, Hanns (1944). *Freud: Master and friend*. Cambridge, MA: Harvard University Press.

Scholz-Strasser, Inge (1998). Introduction and legends. Lonnie Johnson (Trans.). In Edmund Engelman, *Sigmund Freud: Vienna IX. Berggasse 19* (pp. 7–22). Vienna: Christian Brandstätter.

Schur, Max (1972). *Freud, living and dying*. New York: International Universities Press.

Sigmund Freud Museum Wien (n.d.). *Vita Sigmund Freud*. Online at www.freud-museum.at/en/sigmund-and-anna-freud/vita-sigmund-freud.html. Accessed September 29, 2015.

Strozier, Charles B. and Offer, Daniel (2011). Freud and his followers. In C. B. Strozer, D. Offer, and Oliger Abdyli (Eds.), *The leader: Psychological essays* (pp. 13–30). New York: Springer Verlag.

Tacey, David (2013). *The darkening spirit: Jung, spirituality, and religion*. New York: Routledge.

Ulanov, Ann Belford (2000). *Religion and the spiritual in Carl Jung*. Mahwah, NJ: Paulist Press.

Wiener Psychoanalytische Vereinigung (n.d.). *Geschichte der Wiener Psychoanalytische Vereinigung*. Online at www.wpv.at/verein/geschichte. Accessed November 15, 2013.

Part I

Religion and Freud's Vienna circle

"So, you have seen the gang now"
The Wednesday Night Psychological Society

Freud's Wednesday Night Psychological Society initially was comprised of four members in addition to Freud himself, all physicians: Alfred Adler, Max Kahane, Rudolf Reitler, and Wilhelm Stekel. They quickly grew in number, handpicked from the larger public circle around Freud—who regularly attended his lectures at the university and demonstrated a desire to study more deeply. These first analysts became a close-knit "circle of friends."[1] Early members (prior to the reorganization of the Society in October, 1908) included physicians Paul Federn, Eduard Hitschmann, Rudolf Reitler, Maximilian Steiner, and Isidor Sadger (the latter two being the earliest to actually practice psychoanalysis). Freud was eager to expand the group to non-medical intellectuals as well, including the music critics David Bach and Max Graf (the father of "Little Hans"),[2] Hugo Heller (Freud's publisher), and the anti-establishment columnist Fritz Wittels (Sadger's nephew, and close associate of the acerbic cultural critic Karl Kraus).[3]

By 1910 the membership included Sándor Ferenczi (a brilliant Hungarian who straddled the worlds of Budapest and Vienna), Victor Tausk and Hanns Sachs (both lawyers who had turned to writing), Carl Furtmüller (a socialist city school inspector and friend of Adler's),[4] Margarete Hilferding (a general practitioner of medicine and the first woman analyst), and Baron Alfred von Winterstein (a philosopher).[5] Distinguished international visitors included psychiatrists Carl ("C. G.") Jung, Ludwig Binswanger, Max Eitingon, and Karl Abraham[6] from Zürich; Ernest Jones from London; and Abraham ("A. A.") Brill from the United States.[7]

For all of them, psychoanalysis had become "*die Sache*" ("the cause").[8] As Louis Rose points out, many of the early members had begun as students caught up in the *Jung Wien* movement—characterized by disillusionment and outrage toward the inertia of the Viennese establishment and its lip service to liberalism and democracy. Rose writes:

> Moral outrage at the world provided them with a dissenting consciousness and a sense of mission. It did not, however, endow them with a critical method or a positive commitment. The psychoanalytic movement channeled

their personal mission into a collective cause, and their moral rage into intellectual radicalism. At the furthest reaches of moral criticism, their explorations and questioning led to Freud's circle, and the science of psychoanalysis.[9]

Therefore, culture—including religion—was from the beginning a subject of investigation, however counterintuitive it might seem now through a lens of twenty-first-century empirical psychology.

No topic was considered out of bounds: "biology, animal psychology, psychiatry, sociology, mythology, religion, art and literature, education and criminology, even the association and psychogalvanic experiments."[10] This had been Freud's attitude from the beginning, and in his 1926 pamphlet *The Question of Lay Analysis*, he continued to view psychoanalysis as more than a clinical theory, but also as *Kulturwissenschaft* (a "science of culture")[11]: "[A]nalytic instruction would include branches of knowledge which are remote from medicine and which the doctor does not come across in his practice: the history of civilization, mythology, the psychology of religion and the science of literature."[12]

While absolute conformity was not required, their discussions have the ring of a seminar of students who are all sparring to get the "right" interpretation of the teacher's lecture. In his autobiography, Stekel referred to himself (following a brief analysis with Freud for some sexual difficulties)[13] as "the apostle of Freud who was my Christ!"[14] Graf compared the group's reverence for Freud with religious devotion, and the early years as a period of unity and commitment:

> There was an atmosphere of the foundation of a religion in that room. Freud himself was its new prophet who made the theretofore prevailing methods of psychological investigation appear superficial. Freud's pupils—all inspired and convinced—were his apostles. Despite the fact that the contrast among the personalities of this circle of pupils was great, at that early period of Freudian investigation all of them were united in their respect for and inspiration with Freud.[15]

This was not hyperbole. Freud at least once referred to himself in a 1910 letter as a "*Menschenfischer*"—a "fisher of men" (echoing the Gospel of Matthew 4:19).[16] Karl Abraham, also, after visiting the Vienna group for the first time in December, 1907, made a comparison to religious devotion in a letter to Max Eitingon: "Sadger is like a Talmud-disciple; he interprets and observes every rule of the Master with orthodox Jewish severity."[17] Freud himself attributed this to Sadger's character, saying in a letter to Jung that Sadger was a "congenital fanatic of orthodoxy, who happened by mere accident to believe in psychoanalysis rather than in the law given by God on Sinai-Horeb."[18] Even Jones, for all his admiration of Freud, seems to have had the master's authoritarian streak in mind when writing his article "The God Complex"—noting characteristics of aloofness and "solitary grandeur," and concluding with the observation that "as a rule they are atheists, and naturally so because they cannot suffer the existence of any other God."[19]

The impression of deference to Freud's views is reinforced by the typical flow of the evening's conversation.[20] The group would gather over coffee and cake, and have a smoke. There might be a brief business meeting. A speaker (either one of the group or a guest) would usually present a paper, and then the group would go after the speaker with hammer and tongs. As noted in the Introduction, the order of speakers was decided (until 1908) by drawing lots from an urn.[21] Finally, after enough heat had been generated and the fog of cigar smoke was impenetrable,[22] Freud would conclude the evening with his own remarks, evaluating both the speaker's presentation and the other members' comments. In Nunberg's words, "It was a process of give-and-take which took place in these discussions. Naturally, Freud gave more than the others could take."[23] Graf recalled that "the last and decisive word was always spoken by Freud himself."[24] It was an atmosphere of devotion to the master, made tolerable for such professional men by the heady intellectual excitement of new and daring ideas.

Rising tensions: 1907–08

At the same time, there were also infamous ruptures in the group's cohesion. Some quarrels, Freud, believed, were a result of resistance to the psychoanalytic ideas he proposed:

> [T]hey could not breathe in the sticky atmosphere of the dark underground, of the "sewers," as it were, but longed to bask in the bright sunshine on the surface. Of course, all of us would prefer to breathe fresh air, were it possible for the psychoanalyst to indulge in surface psychology. As was to be expected, those who preferred surface psychology soon abandoned psychoanalysis altogether.[25]

The term "surface psychology" was leveled at Sadger (by Stekel),[26] and eventually at Adler and anyone else who did not strictly adhere to the Freudian shibboleths of unconscious conflict, infantile sexual development and the oedipal crisis, and the role of psychoanalysis in uncovering them. Around 1908, a combination of personal and theoretical disputes led to irreconcilable differences, beginning with Adler, and soon thereafter with Stekel.

All too often as fissures developed, members of the group, including Freud himself, would attribute the opposing point of view to that member's psychopathology, using the tools of "wild analysis" as a weapon.[27] At the same time, there was some real pathology among the members, some of whom may have joined, at least in part, to seek their own therapy. As Nunberg wrote in his introduction to the minutes,

> We have learned from our analyses that in order to heal inner conflicts it is necessary first to bare their sources and thus to understand them. We have also learned that we often project our own conflicts onto the external world.

It seems safe to assume that the urge of these men to understand and heal their fellow men reflected to a great extent their own need for help.[28]

And there were suicides.[29] This was not so uncommon among German-speaking European intellectuals, and in highly cultured circles suicide was not regarded with the same stigma that we often view it today.[30] Some of the suicides among the group were courageously taking the choice of when and how to die into their own hands as a moral choice. After the *Anschluss*, and again in 1941 with the start of the deportations, there were waves of suicides as Austrian Jews faced shock, despair, and terror.[31] When Anna Freud was arrested in 1938, Max Schur, the family's doctor, gave her and her brother Martin strong doses of barbiturate to take in case of torture.[32] Anna and her father discussed suicide as a serious option.[33] After enduring tremendous pain and hardship both from his cancer and from fleeing the Nazis, Freud finally attained his wish to rejoin his family in London and "to die in freedom."[34] He committed physician-assisted suicide, telling his beloved doctor Max Schur that "now it's nothing but torture and makes no sense any more."[35] Federn shot himself in his analytic office a decade after Freud's death when faced with incurable cancer of the bladder.[36]

Yet some of the suicides, notably Viktor Tausk's in 1919, seem to have been more psychopathologically driven, and were, at least in part, dramatic reactions to rejection by Freud from his inner circle.[37] According to Roazen, many members of "that tiny subculture readily believed that if Freud dropped a man it could lead to his self-extinction. Exclusion from the revolutionary community was an annihilation greater than any physical death."[38]

Tensions increased over the years as the Society grew and certain members— depending on one's interpretation—asserted their independence of thought, or strayed from the foundational teachings and methods of Freud, their founder and ego-ideal. Wittels was a frequent target of opprobrium due to his vehement and often misogynistic views on women, and on sexual matters.[39] The more serious tensions were between Freud and Adler on the primacy of the sexual drive versus aggression. In a close mirroring of theory with their personality dynamic, they engaged in a pitched battle between Freud's theory of childhood sexuality and oedipal hatred toward the father versus Adler's growing insistence on the role of an "inferiority feeling" in pathology and the "will to power" as the primary uncon-scious source of motivation. There was also animosity between Adler and Stekel, Stekel and Tausk, and Wittels and Stekel.[40] In a letter to the colleagues written from Rome on September 22, 1907 during their summer hiatus, Freud attempted to palliate the conflicts by dissolving the group and inviting each member to decide individually if they would like to rejoin, or depart without recrimination.[41]

Jung: the heir apparent and sibling rivalry

Jung first appeared on the scene in Vienna early in March, 1907, when, with his wife Emma and younger Swiss colleague, Binswanger, he visited Freud and his family. He had begun reading Freud at the suggestion of his superior at the Burghölzli psychiatric hospital soon after the publication of *The Interpretation of Dreams*, and decided to test out Freud's theories for himself with his own clinical patients (among them, eventually, Sabina Spielrein). He first cited Freud in a paper in 1906, and soon after struck up a correspondence with him. During his 1907 visit, Jung enjoyed numerous conversations with Freud, one in which they talked "virtually without a pause for thirteen hours."[42]

Jung and Binswanger also sat in as guests of the Wednesday Night Society that week. On that particular evening, Adler was presenting the case of a wealthy Russian Jewish patient who had a compulsion when bathing to remain submerged entirely under water until he had counted to certain Jewish mystical numbers 3, 7 or 49. "If one looks at the matter as a whole, the patient says, then it looks like a baptism."[43] Adler noted that "as a Jew, he had studied in an antisemitic Gymnasium; altogether, his 'Jewish complex' was very much in the foreground."[44] The ensuing discussion involved assigning sexual symbolism to the patient's numerology as relative sizes of Christian and Jewish penises.

Jung was invited to speak. With some deference to his being a newcomer to psychoanalysis and a newcomer to the group, he commented on the frequency with which numbers would appear in his association experiments. Then, perhaps without understanding the growing tension between Freud and Adler, or simply joining in with what he experienced as the general tone of energetic debate, Jung opined without any apparent reticence that the group's criticism of Adler's concept of organ inferiority was too harsh. He noted, "It is a brilliant idea which we are not justified in criticizing because we lack sufficient experience."[45] Freud ended the discussion by returning to sexual symbolism: "The contents of the symptoms have the nature of a compromise: It is as if the patient said, 'I want to be baptized—but the Jewish penis is still larger. (Thus I remain a Jew.)' "[46]

That Jung's first discussion with the Viennese circle centered on questions of Jewish identity, neurosis, and antisemitism is all the more striking given that much of Jung's appeal for Freud—and consternation for the Viennese—was precisely his status as a Gentile inheritor of psychoanalysis, with all that that implied both positively and negatively for the psychoanalytic movement. While it may not be possible to know for sure, it would be interesting to speculate whether this case of a "Jewish complex" was chosen by Adler (with or without a tip-off from Freud) in advance of the meeting with Jung's upcoming visit in mind.[47] Adler had already converted to Protestantism three years earlier,[48] and unlike Freud, did not identify strongly with his Jewish heritage.[49] He was certainly aware of antisemitism, however.[50] Whatever Adler's motives, a case presentation of a Jewish patient tormented by religious compulsions on the occasion of a visit from the group's most famous Gentile rival, however unconsciously motivated, could not have been entirely coincidental.

Jung's reaction to being immersed in such a Jewish milieu was one of culture shock. He later recalled in an interview with Kurt Eissler: "I felt so foreign before this Jewish intellectual society…. That was something completely new to me.... I found it very difficult to adjust, to adopt the right tone." Eissler observed that "the coffee house atmosphere was 'so foreign' to Jung, the conversations all contained 'a certain cynicism,' and Jung felt like a country bumpkin in the face of so much sophisticated banter."[51] "You wouldn't be an anti-Semite now, would you?" Freud asked. "No, no!' Jung replied, "Anti-Semitism is out of the question." Jung's biographer Deirdre Bair comments,

> Not for Freud, however, who continued to level such charges in subsequent meetings and throughout the several years of their collaboration. Jung countered the first accusation by saying that if Freud insisted on branding him as such, he would call him "Anti-Christian" because his "every second word was always a quote from Voltaire." Freud dismissed it, preferring his own interpretation of Jung as an "anti-Semite."[52]

Bair notes that when Freud called his own group "those damn Jews" Jung felt "independent" enough to contradict Freud, praising the "virtues" of the Jews, who he said were famous for their sense of family unity. "There you are mistaken," Freud insisted. "They only stick together by their common hatred."[53] Freud's comment has the ring of irony as well as derision, an irony that may have been lost on Jung at the time.

For a period of years following this intense week-long visit, Freud and Jung entered into a mutual fascination and an intense, even traumatic transference-countertransference enactment from the beginning. From Jung's side, as Jung confessed to Freud in a letter in October, 1907, it was a "veneration" in the "character of a 'religious' crush," which "because of its undeniable erotic undertone" was at once "disgusting and ridiculous."[54] Jung goes on to confess that

> this abominable feeling comes from the fact that as a boy I was the victim of a sexual assault by a man I once worshipped.... This feeling, which I still have not quite got rid of, hampers me considerably.... I therefore fear your confidence.[55]

Freud was somewhat more circumspect in his avowal of feelings toward Jung in August, 1908: "I'm fond of you; but I have learned to subordinate that factor."[56]

On Freud's part, it was with relief that he believed he had found a worthy disciple who could carry psychoanalysis on into the future, and as a Gentile, bring it into the mainstream of psychiatric respectability. As Gay has put it, Jung was "not Viennese, not old, and best of all, not Jewish, three negative assets that Freud found irresistible."[57] Freud believed that Jung not only had the intellectual capacity to lead psychoanalysis into the future, but also hoped that Jung's Gentile background would provide a foothold into mainstream psychiatry.[58] Freud wrote to Binswanger in 1911, amid a series of letters lamenting the conflicts in Vienna and his theories being misunderstood elsewhere, "When the empire I founded is orphaned, no one but Jung must inherit the whole thing. As you see, my politics incessantly pursues this aim, and my behavior toward Stekel and Adler fits into the same scheme."[59] And to Ferenczi he wrote, "I had intended to thank Jung for the feeling that the children are being taken care of, which a Jewish father needs as a matter of life and death."[60]

Ambivalence, even to the extent of an intense love-hate relationship, characterized the relationship from the beginning, but the tensions between Freud and Jung only surfaced directly after some time. Freud was initially eager to forgive what he perceived as a culturally "alien"[61] and even "uncanny" sense from the Swiss psychiatrists, especially Bleuler.[62] He wrote to Abraham as a fellow Jew that

> I nurse a suspicion that the suppressed antisemitism of the Swiss that spares me is deflected in reinforced form upon you. But I think that we as Jews, if we wish to join in anywhere, must develop a bit of masochism, be ready to suffer some wrong. Otherwise there is no hitting it off.[63]

Decades later, Sachs also reflected on Freud's failure to fully recognize the oedipal dynamics at play between Freud and Jung—that "of all persons who are likely to get into sharp opposition to the reigning monarch, the likeliest is the crown prince."[64] But Freud's "passionate desire to leave the future of psychoanalysis in trustworthy hands was strong enough to get the better of his theoretical knowledge and hard-won experience."[65] Freud and Jung continued on cordially for about two years, with both men withholding their reservations and differences, buoyed by the hope of what a partnership could achieve for both of them. For Freud, it was the ardent desire to ensure a legacy for psychoanalysis (as he defined it); for Jung, it was the desire to create and achieve. This synergy was potent, and—at least for a time—kept disagreements at bay.

1908–10: expansion and rivalries

As Freud and his theories gained more international acclaim, in contrast to both the irritations he felt with his Vienna circle and the ongoing opprobrium of the conservative Viennese psychiatric establishment outside their group, he began to gravitate more and more toward international colleagues. The Vienna Society was especially impacted by Freud's growing enthusiasm for his relationship with Jung and the Zürich psychiatrists. This internal conflict occurred during the same years when dissension was arising internally within the group. From 1907, when Jung first visited Freud and the Vienna Society, until the final exchange of letters in January, 1913 in which they agreed to sever ties, the group viewed Jung as a dangerous outsider. Referring to Jung in his memoirs, Stekel wrote, "The former harmony among the Freudians was gone; there was an heir-pretendency and a secret rivalry among the pupils."[66] Wittels jealously compared Freud's devotion to Jung with God's pronouncement to Jesus at his baptism as told in the Gospels: Freud's "face beamed whenever he spoke of Jung: 'This is my beloved son, in whom I am most pleased.' "[67]

As the numbers of Freud's international adherents grew, he also began venting his frustrations about the members of the Society in colorful terms to his correspondents outside Vienna. When Binswanger visited from Zürich alongside Jung in 1907, Freud remarked disparagingly, "So, you have seen the gang now?"[68] By 1910, Freud wrote that he had a "long pent up aversion to the Viennese" and could "no longer get any pleasure" from them. "I have a heavy cross to bear with the older generation, Stekel, Adler, Sadger."[69] Freud even wrote to Jung, "I sometimes get so angry at my Viennese that I wish you/they had a single backside so I could thrash them all with one stick."[70]

In addition to his comments about the group in general, Freud quite freely expressed condescension and contempt for individual members. He wrote to a student that "tactlessness and unpleasant behavior of Adler and Stekel make it very difficult to get along together. I am chronically exasperated with both of them."[71] And in several letters to Jones, Ferenczi, and Jung in 1909–12, Freud variously called Stekel an "impudent liar," a "*mauvais sujet*,"[72] and a "perfect swine"[73] who was overcome with "moronic petty jealousies" ("*schwachsinnige Eifersüchteleien.*")[74] One of Freud's American analysands, Joseph Wortis, reported that even in an analytic session Freud told him that Stekel was a "man of no scruples," with "petty" (pea-sized—"*erbsengross*") fantasies of grandeur.[75] Jones recounted how

> [Stekel] was fond of expressing this estimate of himself half-modestly by saying that a dwarf on the shoulder of a giant could see farther than the giant himself. When Freud heard this he grimly commented: "That may be true, but a louse on the head of an astronomer does not."[76]

The members were well aware of Freud's disdain. In April, 1910, when much conflict was bubbling to the surface, Stekel lamented to the group that Freud "seems to harbor deep hatred toward Vienna."[77] At the same meeting, Tausk "expresses his feeling that something very saddening is taking place," and Sadger also "thinks that he has observed that Freud has been fed up with the Viennese for the last two years now. However, the fact is that we need him."[78]

The years 1908 through 1910 were a watershed for psychoanalysis, in which the growth of the movement required more formal structure and international collaboration. Rank's Minutes for February 5, 1908, begin with a lengthy discussion about the need for some reorganization of the meetings. Peter Gay writes:

> The meetings grew testy, even acrimonious, as members sparred for position, vaunted their originality, or voiced dislike of their fellows with a brutal hostility masquerading as analytic frankness.... By 1908 such acerbic meetings were far from rare. All too often, vehemence made up for lack of penetration.... The rubbing up of sensitive, often labile, individuals against one another was bound to produce sparks of hostility. What is more, the provocative subject matter of psychoanalytic inquiry, rudely touching on the most

heavily guarded spots in the human psyche, was taking its toll and generating a pervasive irritability.[79]

Graf is recorded in the minutes as stating,

> proposals to reorganize stem from a feeling of uneasiness. We no longer are the type of gathering we once were. Although we are still guests of the Professor, we are about to become an organization. Therefore, he suggests the following motion: To move the meeting from the Professor's apartment to another place.[80]

In the interests of freedom of thought, Adler and Federn further argued for discontinuing the group's previous practice of "intellectual communism"—i.e., holding all theorizing in common. The group adopted an amendment in which "every intellectual property set forth in this circle may be used as long as it has not explicitly been claimed by the author as his property."[81] Although congenial in finding this compromise, the group was asserting a new level of intellectual independence. On the issue of acrimonious debate, Freud refused to be conscripted into the role of disciplinarian, and proposed that a small subcommittee draft some proposals for procedures going forward.[82]

At the next meeting a week later, that committee (Freud, Adler, Hitschmann, and Wittels) made its recommendations: no-one henceforth would be obligated to speak (changing the function of the urn), one monthly meeting should be devoted to book and article reviews (assigned to one member each time), papers should be announced in advance so others could prepare on the topic, four unexcused absences would prompt Freud to ask that person if he wanted to resign. No changes in rules for accepting new members would be instituted yet, but Rank did record some discussion about making "more stringent requirements for admission."[83] Adler wrote, "This assembly is something in between a group invited by Professor Freud and a society; therefore, whoever is acceptable to the Professor must also be acceptable to the others."[84] He proposed the creation of a second, larger society that could meet in a more public location, with a select subgroup continuing to meet more intimately in Freud's waiting room.[85] This "minority motion" engendered a "vigorous debate," and, in the end, the group adopted a compromise proposed by Freud, in which a larger group would be formed, but would "take place entirely independently from the Wednesday circle."[86]

Meanwhile, amidst conflict, the organization continued to grow. Membership almost doubled in a single year (1909–10), increasing from twenty-three to forty-three, with sixteen more members added in 1911.[87] As Freud's reputation grew internationally, nearly all new members in Vienna (ten out of twelve) in one year alone (1911) came from other countries.[88] After Adler's conflictual departure with several sympathizers, a large number of other members departed before World War I—not in protest, but on the contrary, to form offshoot societies in other countries.[89] The Viennese, who considered themselves the inner circle, felt their sense of primacy increasingly threatened, and jealousies increased.

Freud convened the first international congress of "friends of psychoanalysis" in Salzburg on Easter Sunday in 1908. Although the meeting was not large (forty-two attendees), there were representatives from all the centers of psychoanalysis—Vienna, Zürich, Berlin, Budapest, London, and New York.[90] The speakers were the early luminaries from the major cities: Freud himself, Jung, Ferenczi, Abraham, and Jones. The participants agreed to formally create an International Society for Psychoanalysis (IPA), and inaugurated the first psychoanalytic journal, *Jahrbuch für Psychoanalytische und Psychopathologische Forschungen* (*"Annual for Psychoanalytic and Psychopathological Research"*).[91] The "directors" were to be Bleuler, a high-profile international choice as director of the Burghölzli Hospital in Zürich (Jung's superior), and Freud, himself, with Jung as the "editor."[92] The balance of power in favor of the Swiss could not have been more clear.[93]

Two years later, at Freud's behest, Ferenczi organized the next international congress in Nürnberg, at which the IPA was officially founded. Ferenczi nominated Jung as its first president, with another Swiss psychiatrist (and Jung family relation), Franz Riklin, as secretary.[94] This also meant that the IPA offices would be located not in Vienna, but in Zürich.[95] This in itself would have been enough of an affront to the Viennese, who still considered Vienna to be the birthplace and center of psychoanalysis. But Ferenczi, who had not been involved with psychoanalysis for very long, further insulted them in his opening "Memorandum" with "derogatory remarks about the quality of the Viennese analysts," while advocating for Zürich as the future center of psychoanalysis, with Jung at its head.[96]

The Vienna group called a secret meeting in Stekel's hotel room.[97] Freud got wind of it and came unannounced to plead with the Viennese about the necessity of expanding psychoanalysis beyond their local Jewish circle:

> "Most of you are Jews, and therefore you are incompetent to win friends for the new teaching. Jews must be content with the modest role of preparing the ground. It is absolutely essential that I should form ties in the world of general science. I am getting on in years, and am weary of being perpetually attacked. We are all in danger...." Seizing his coat by the lapels, he said "They won't even leave me a coat to my back. The Swiss will save us all—will save me, and all of you as well."[98]

Sobered and no doubt a bit shocked by Freud's fervor, the group forged a compromise. The presidency would have a term limit of two years. But they deeply resented having so much international control over an enterprise that had been their own from its earliest years.

At the meeting of the Vienna Society on April 6, immediately following the first international congress, there was a tense debriefing of the events in

Nürnberg.[99] At this meeting, Freud returned to the point that, in the beginning, they were all his guests, but a larger international organization required that they now operate more formally.[100] He proposed that Adler become the president of the Vienna Society, and exhorted them to cultivate better relations among one another and with the international groups.[101] Adler went on to encourage the group to "give up our seclusion," while proposing that the Vienna Society begin its own monthly journal, the *Zentralblatt für Psychoanalyse*,[102] to be edited by Adler and Stekel. Freud further proposed having an executive committee of three to four members.[103]

The group reacted to all these changes, not surprisingly, with hurt and dismay. They had been sidelined, and no one was pretending otherwise, as noted above. Stekel mourned the loss of Freud, who now seemed to "harbor deep hatred toward Vienna."[104] Federn disingenuously professed no dislike of the Swiss, but assigned the blame to the Zürich members' own "aloof behavior."[105] Tausk, Sadger, Wittels, Friedjung, and Reitler all expressed grief over the change that was upon them. But Hitschmann continued to protest the new alliance with the Swiss, saying

> the Zürichers, as a breed, are totally different people from us in Vienna. But for all of that we do not underestimate our inner qualities. As far as the reconstitution [of the Society] is concerned, we have nothing against that form so long as, with this change, we do not have to do without Freud's personal influence.[106]

Freud, for his part, had obviously given some forethought to raising Adler and Stekel to such positions of prominence within the group. Anticipating the deepening conflict in his relationships with each of them, he was hoping to hold them in the Society. Freud wrote to Ferenczi of his hope that "possibly in that position [of president, Adler] will feel an obligation to defend our common ground."[107]

Having vented their frustration and mourning, the group recognized they had little choice, and buckled down to the business of making plans. Federn, Hitschmann, Rank, Steiner, and Stekel were nominated by Adler to be the executive committee. Oppenheim, Furtmüller, Reitler, and Sadger were nominated to be the editorial committee for the new journal. In an attempt to hold onto "the old patriarchal relationship" at least in part, Federn, Stekel, and others pressed Freud to remain the leader as an "honorary president."[108] Freud refused, reiterating the importance of passing the torch to a younger man who would be "unhampered" in maintaining the freedom of Vienna from other groups, and insisting that "his resignation [was] not only a nominal one."[109] Perhaps reluctant to give up too much of his authority, he then suddenly proposed that he would accept the new title of "scientific chairman"—a compromise that had all the earmarks of a neurotic symptom: simultaneously withholding and granting the group's wish for him to remain in place as their father.

The reorganization was formally accomplished at the next meeting on April 14. Bylaws were officially approved. Some of the same issues raised in 1908 resurfaced, namely, procedures for admitting new members, giving more power to the executive committee, and altogether abolishing the hated urn. A library was established, and it was decided that a more appropriately formal meeting place (not a café) would be rented.

Women in the Vienna society

In the midst of this unsettling reorganization, a debate over women's candidacy also boiled over at the April 6 meeting. Women's membership, like so many other issues, was contested in the early years, with Sadger and Wittels predictably lining up against,[110] and Freud, Adler, and Federn in favor. In 1910, following a heated discussion and a secret side meeting convened by Freud among those in agreement, Maria Hilferding was admitted as the first woman member.[111] A test ballot to admit women "in principle," held on April 14, resulted in eleven to three in favor. "Professor Freud would take it as a gross inconsistency, were we to exclude women on principle."[112] This meeting occurred in an atmosphere of increasing animosity and insecurity on the part of the Vienna society, and a general mood of melancholy prevailed. Hilferding's candidacy was referred to the executive committee,[113] and on April 27, Hilferding was elected by a vote of twelve to two, with one abstention.[114] Sadger requested that a letter from Wittels be read aloud before balloting, but Adler opposed this, and "after a rather long debate" the letter—presumably opposing women's membership—was deferred to an "unofficial session."[115]

The first International Psycho-Analytic Congress in Salzburg, 1908, had only included one woman—Frieda Gross, the wife of Otto Gross.[116] By the third Congress in 1911, Swiss women swelled the female ranks, and there were eight women present altogether, including Lou Maria Moltzer, Mira [Oberholzer-] Gincburg, Lou Andreas-Salomé, Beatrice Hinkle, Emma Jung, M. von Stach, Toni Wolff, and Martha Böddinghaus.[117] A trickle of women were admitted to the Vienna Society in succeeding years, including Sabina Spielrein in 1911 (again, over Sadger's objections),[118] Hermine Hug-Hellmuth in 1913 (also the first woman doctoral candidate at the University of Vienna), Helene Deutsch in 1918,[119] and (of course) Anna Freud in 1922.[120] The percentage of women never reached 10 percent at its height.[121]

Nevertheless, psychoanalysis did attract many women adherents, especially internationally, because of its inherent opposition to "repressive codes and received knowledge."[122] Russell Jacoby writes,

> Apart from traditional professions assigned to women, such as teaching and nursing, it is likely that no other profession counted among its ranks as many women as did psychoanalysis in its early years. These women were not quiet and demure; they frequently bucked family and tradition to study

psychoanalysis; they also were often cultural and political radicals. With a single exception, Fenichel's circle of political psychoanalysts was exclusively female.[123]

1911: the excommunication of Adler

Organizational decisions did not end internal feuding among the members, but merely postponed a deeper conflict from boiling over. Adler began to express his theoretical independence more aggressively, no doubt emboldened by his new leadership role. The minutes of the meetings, as well as Freud's increasingly frustrated letters to his foreign correspondents, tell a story of Adler's increasing departure from Freud's insistence on the role of the sexual drive as the primary unconscious motivation. For Adler, power, not sex, was at the core of the unconscious. As early as 1909, Adler was developing his own ideas of "organ inferiority"[124] and the will to power as the cause of neurosis, especially in men. The popular term "inferiority complex" stems from Adler's theorizing that a neurotic desire for power stemmed from inner feelings of inadequacy.[125]

At the first meeting of the group in January, 1911, Adler presented a paper starkly delineating his differences with Freud's theories, particularly regarding what he called "the masculine protest"—the perception of organ inferiority is prior to sexual libido, and is an expression of a compensatory ego need to be powerful.[126] Adler further saw the qualities of masculinity and femininity as a cultural "valuation" but not a foundational "motive force"[127] by which "woman is devalued by man—[as] is clearly expressed in our culture; indeed, it can even be regarded as being a driving force in our civilization."[128] Anticipating Freud's own working out of an aggressive drive by almost a decade,[129] Adler asserted the "instinct of aggression" as primary,[130] and on February 1, in a second paper, he directly downgraded the centrality of the Oedipus complex as merely one component of the masculine protest—"the point of departure from which it is possible to gain *more significant* insights into the characterology of the neurotic" (emphasis added).[131] Autobiographical motives were clearly in play when Adler took this shot across the bow, but his theories also cohered with his philosophical and political commitments as a socialist interested in power relations and societal justice.

Freud is not recorded as saying anything at the January meeting, but on February 1, he came prepared with a harsh and detailed critique, attacking Adler's propositions as "reactionary and retrograde."[132] He dismissed Adler's theories as "unsound"[133] and "no more than the usual misunderstandings on the part of the ego ... the denial of the unconscious, of which the ego is guilty."[134] Freud saw himself as defending not only the theory of libido, but the whole theory of the unconscious.[135] Because of Adler's "significant intellect with a great gift of presentation," his ideas were all the more dangerous: "[T]hey will make a deep impression and will, at first, do great harm to psychoanalysis."[136] This regression to "surface psychology," Freud feared, would appeal to other analysts' latent resistance to the theory of sexuality, and "consequently, this doctrine will at first do harm to the development of psychoanalysis; on the other hand, as far as psychoanalytic findings are concerned, it will remain sterile."[137]

Adler resigned from the presidency of the Society later the same month. After a little more pressure from Freud, he resigned as co-editor of the *Zentralblatt* and quit the Society altogether. In spite of final protestations that his theories were not in opposition to Freud's,[138] his last recorded attendance at a meeting of the Society was at the end of May.[139] His closest colleagues—Bach, Maday, and Hye[140]—followed him into a new society, which he pointedly named "The Society for Free Psychoanalysis."[141]

The following autumn, Freud told Ferenczi he was determined to "force out" the rest of the "Adler pack."[142] At a "special plenary session" at the Café Arkaden, which by its unofficial location suggests a certain clandestine atmosphere, Freud declared that business could nonetheless be conducted.[143] Then, as Rank furtively recorded, the unnamed "Chairman" (Freud) raised the issue of joint membership in the Vienna Society and in Adler's "circle" which bore "the character of hostile competition … [T]he board regards their present position as being contradictory."[144] The resolution to ban dual membership was passed eleven to five, with five abstentions, after a sketchily recorded but obviously emotional discussion.[145]

Furious at the ambush, Furtmüller, Oppenheim, Hilferding, Franz and Gustav Grüner, and Klemperer immediately resigned.[146] Rank wrote, "The Chairman then evolves a programme of work for the immediate future and, in closing, invites those who wish an explanation about the Adler affair to [come to] his apartment Monday at nine o'clock."[147] The entire event smacked of palace intrigue and autocratic rule. In the ensuing years, Freud would denounce Adler in the most searing terms possible. To Abraham he labeled Adler paranoid, and to Jones he wrote, "It is the revolt of an abnormal individual driven mad by ambition, his influence upon others depending on his strong terrorism and sadismus."[148] In Gay's words, "This was denunciation as diagnosis."[149]

Freud and Jung: growing tensions

Cracks had already begun to develop in the relationship between Freud and Jung by the time of their famous voyage in 1909 with Ferenczi to Clark University in Massachusetts. Freud was the invited lecturer, and all three guests were highly regarded among the American psychologists. But Jung and Ferenczi had already felt mutual jealousy,[150] and at the same time, Jung was feeling restive about Freud's paternal stance toward him. Shipboard on the SS *George Washington* from Bremen to New York, the three colleagues strolled the deck and analyzed each other's dreams. When Freud held back, saying that to reveal more about a particular dream would be "to risk my authority,"[151] Jung went on to write that "at that moment [Freud] lost it [his authority] altogether. That sentence burned itself into my memory."[152] Jung had had enough.

For a while, Freud continued to hold out hopes for Jung as his successor. When Jung was elected president of the International Psychoanalytic Society in Nürnberg,[153] Freud wrote to Ferenczi in 1910, "Now don't be jealous, but take Jung into your calculations. I am more convinced than ever that he is the man of the future."[154] Nevertheless, the fissures were growing. Jung increasingly had doubts about the centrality of the oedipal crisis and the definition of libido as exclusively sexual as opposed to a more general life energy. Religion itself also became a wedge. Freud began to encroach on what Jung regarded as his own arena of research, namely ancient religions and culture. Jung was beginning to formulate his idea of the collective unconscious and archetypes of human behavior that could be discerned in the symbolism of ancient myths and legends. When Freud wrote to both Ferenczi and Jung that he was beginning to turn his interest to prehistoric religion—which would eventually become his first major monograph on religion, *Totem and Taboo*[155]—Jung immediately felt threatened by Freud's newly kindled interest in ancient religions.

Freud, continuing his triangular relationship with Ferenczi and Jung, reported to Ferenczi that it was "storming and raging again in some corner of Jung, erotically and religiously," and that Jung was writing to Freud only "with visible displeasure."[156] Jung had already bridled at Freud's suggestion that others might be recruited to the psychoanalytic study of religion,[157] and in late 1911 he made known to Freud that he felt his turf was being invaded:

> The outlook for me is very gloomy if you too get into the psychology of religion. You are a dangerous rival—if one has to speak of rivalry. Yet I think it has to be this way, for a natural development cannot be halted, nor should one try to halt it. Our personal differences will make our work different.[158]

Freud's atheism was another increasingly difficult sticking point. For Freud, especially after he began investigating religion diagnostically (e.g., his first published essay on religion, "Obsessive Actions and Religious Practices," written in 1907),[159] religious experience was an expression of infantile wish fulfillment. Its rituals were forms of obsessive-compulsive neurosis. While Freud's negative assessment of religion hardened considerably in the ensuing years, in the name of scientific truthfulness, Freud had early in his life rejected not only the idea of belief in God, but any notion of transcendence whatsoever.

For Jung, this was intolerable. While Jung had rejected his father's strict and depressive Calvinist beliefs, he had had from childhood a sense of the numinous, and he was not prepared to sacrifice all his intuitions for the sake of pure science. Neither man would accept the doctrines of their inherited religions. Freud— surrounded all his life by an oppressive Catholic regime and influenced by a free-thinking liberal Judaism—saw only neurosis and oppression in traditional religious observance. But Jung, who recognized at a young age his liberation from an oppressive church by way of a significant dream (of God letting loose an "enormous turd" to shatter a glittering cathedral),[160] eventually envisioned not atheism, but the potential for an individual spiritual quest, freed from institutional constraints. Jung later wrote, "The neurotic is ill not because he has lost his old faith, but because he has not yet found a new form for his finest aspirations."[161] In a February, 1912 letter, Freud accused Jung of hiding "behind a religious-libidinal cloud."[162]

The exchange of letters between Freud and Jung during this period are extraordinary for their admixture of intimacy bordering on the erotic, and mutual suspicion and complaint. Self-analysis and mutual analysis are sprinkled throughout the correspondence in an effort perhaps to try, by understanding their underlying emotional dynamic, to heal their widening rift. Their theoretical differences were not so much increasing as becoming more deeply elaborated and openly expressed. In their published writings and public lectures, they had moved quite a bit beyond disputes over details of a shared theory. Rather, they were beginning to set forth demonstrably different systems of thought.

1912: Stekel and the ugly scene

In the midst of the growing hostilities between Freud and Jung, another internal battle was brewing within the Vienna Society. Stekel had been an embarrassment to some of the Vienna members from the very beginning. According to Jones, Stekel was known to fabricate clinical material to justify his opinions, so much so that "Stekel's 'Wednesday patient' became proverbial."[163] Binswanger, on his second visit to Vienna early in 1910, commented, "I was struck by his strong mania for generalizations."[164] Even on limited acquaintance, Jung thought Stekel's "mania for indecent confessions" bordered on "exhibitionism."[165] As Roazen describes him, Stekel

> was one of the more undisciplined people to join Freud's early group ... a talented and prolific writer, as well as a poet and an excellent musician, and some of his clinical descriptions had great merit. But his work was somewhat journalistic, and his interest in sexuality remained quasi-pornographic; to some in the movement he seemed a dubious character with a dirty-minded interest in case material.[166]

For many years Freud, who had first known Stekel as a patient and seemingly cured him of a "sexual perversion,"[167] defended Stekel and found his talent at interpreting dream symbolism instructive. Freud had ceased to view Stekel as merely an eccentric, and began to see him as an insightful analytic adherent. As Binswanger noted in 1910 after Stekel presented a paper on doubt and anxiety, at that time Freud was still defending him to the group, even while offering strenuous critique.[168]

But Freud, too, eventually found Stekel irritating, and often complained of him to others outside Vienna. (It was Stekel to whom Freud referred as a "louse on the head of an astronomer.")[169] Stekel still held the reins as the editor of the *Zentralblatt*, which made Freud increasingly uneasy because of the growing consensus about Stekel's lack of judgment and intellectual integrity. Stekel's voluble participation in a long series of meetings on the topic of masturbation was the beginning of the end.[170] Stekel (together with Ferenczi) advocated for viewing the practice as non-pathological, going against Freud and most of the other Viennese who maintained the traditional psychiatric idea that it was unhealthy, both physically and psychologically. Multiple meetings of the Society in 1911 were devoted to resolving this ongoing debate.[171]

The final blowup occurred over a conflict between Stekel and Tausk, who "hated each other."[172] At the final meeting in Spring, 1912,[173] Freud nominated Tausk as book review editor for the *Zentralblatt*. Stekel refused, and as Freud wrote to Ferenczi the same night, it turned into an "ugly scene."[174] Freud took Stekel to task for presuming to hold his personal conflicts above his duty as an editor to represent the International Association. Freud pressed Stekel to resign from the editorship. Stekel refused. Freud forced Stekel's hand, asking Jung to call together all the regional presidents of the IPA in Munich, and as well, requesting everyone else to withdraw from the journal. Thus, the *Zentralblatt* died of starvation. A new *Internationale Zeitschrift für Psychoanalyse* subsequently took its place, with Ferenczi, Rank, and Jones as editors. Stekel resigned entirely from the Vienna Society on November 6, 1912.[175]

Freud expressed relief at Stekel's imminent departure, writing to Abraham on November 3 that he was weary of defending Stekel "against the whole world. He is an unbearable fellow."[176] Freud later referred to him in a letter to Ferenczi as "a case of 'oral insanity'."[177] Unlike the ruptures with Adler and Jung, Freud apparently felt no personal distress at Stekel's separation from the Society. In later years, Stekel believed that Jung had set Freud against him.[178]

Freud's and Jung's divorce: the end of "Aryan patronage"

During the same period, a tipping point came in the breakdown of Freud's and Jung's relationship. Freud went hastily to Switzerland in May, 1912, to visit Binswanger, who had undergone surgery for appendicitis during which a malignancy was discovered and removed. In spite of theoretical differences of their own, mostly revolving around Binswanger's continuing interest in philosophy, Freud and Binswanger had developed a very warm, even familial relationship. Their letters are full of mutual assurances of loyalty and affection. Binswanger, on the authority of current medical experts, thought he had at most only three years to live. Freud's letter to Binswanger conveys that he was stricken by this news from another potential Swiss Gentile heir: "one of my flowering young men—one of those who were supposed to continue my own life."[179]

Freud arranged to visit Binswanger as soon as possible, while keeping the younger man's news confidential, as requested. He made a hurried weekend visit, during which Binswanger recounted enjoying family time with Freud near Lake Konstanz. Binswanger was feeling better. They took walks together and talked at length about psychoanalysis, discussing theoretical disagreements without rancor.[180] Freud departed back to Vienna without stopping to see Jung at Küsnacht.[181] The visit meant a great deal to Binswanger, a sure sign of Freud's sincere friendship. But when Jung learned about it, he took it as a malicious slight against himself.[182]

A flurry of letters followed between Jung and Freud, containing mutual reproaches laced with psychoanalytic interpretations of their own and each other's unconscious intentions. Freud, as usual, complained to other correspondents about the conflict, and began to write about the possibility of a break. Freud blamed Jung's paranoia and oedipal strivings. And the specter of Jewish–Gentile conflict rose again. To Ferenczi he wrote that it was futile to try to bring together "Jews and goyim in the service of ΨA.... They are separating like oil and water."[183] One month later, however, he wrote to Rank that he still hoped for the "integration of Jews and anti-Semites on the soil of ΨA."[184]

On the heels of Adler's departure and the other internal conflicts in Vienna, Freud's complaints prompted a suggestion by Jones that they create a secret committee that would function as guardians of psychoanalytic orthodoxy. The ground had already been laid for unofficial meetings at the Café Arkaden when Freud conspired to expel Adler's friends from the Vienna Society. Now, there was the potential for a real Star Chamber, a society within the IPA that would ensure a kind of theoretical purity. The founders who conspired to make the proposal were Jones, Ferenczi, and Rank. Abraham and Sachs were also invited. Gay observed that "[t]he plan says much about the besetting insecurity of these first psychoanalysts. Freud thought that 'perhaps it could be adapted to meet the necessities of reality,' but frankly recognized a boyish, perhaps a romantic element, too, in this conception."[185] Jones had used the same charged language: "The idea of a united small body, designed, like the Paladins of Charlemagne, to guard the kingdom and policy of their master, was a product of my own romanticism." The Committee was formed, and for at least a decade functioned as a private "band of brothers."[186] If Freud thought that Jung was going through a paranoid patch, this turn of events certainly did nothing to alleviate it.

More determined than ever to assert his own ideas, Jung accepted an invitation to speak at Fordham University during the fall of 1912. He reported to Freud that his expanded definition of libido as a general life force was well received. Provocatively, he indicated that he had disputed all the Freudian shibboleths— infantile sexuality, the Oedipus, and repression of sexual wishes as the basis of pathology. After a further exchange of letters full of mutual accusations and misunderstandings, Freud suggested that they meet in person in Munich to resolve their differences. Now it was Freud who perceived a slight, when Jung and Riklin published essays on psychoanalysis in Swiss journals without citing him. Freud still thought that Jung was unstable, and that the younger man harbored an oedipal death wish toward him. In their meeting, by Jones' account, "Suddenly, to our consternation, [Freud] fell on the floor in a dead faint. The sturdy Jung swiftly carried him to a couch in the lounge, where he soon revived."[187] Upon waking, Freud reportedly said, "How sweet it must be to die."[188]

Any rapprochement achieved in Munich was short-lived. The two resumed their mutual accusations of hostile slips and insults, and using "wild analysis," each framed himself as the victim of the other. Finally, just before Christmas, 1912, Jung let loose in a letter, excoriating Freud for "treating your pupils like your patients ... in that way you produce slavish sons or impudent rascals (Adler-Stekel and the whole impudent gang that is now giving itself airs in Vienna)."[189] Jung declared himself finished with a relationship of "such servility."[190] Although Freud must have been stricken by Jung's tone of finality, he continued to blame Jung's outburst on an episode of madness: "He seems all out of his wits, he is behaving quite crazy."[191] Freud confessed to Jones that Jung's letter evoked in him a feeling of shame.[192] One more exchange of letters between Freud and Jung, however, and the relationship was at an end. Freud lobbed one more accusation of neurosis at Jung and proposed "that we abandon our personal relations entirely."[193] Jung sent a typewritten postcard with the words, "The rest is silence."[194]

The divorce took a bit longer within the IPA, however. Jung was still president and editor of the *Jahrbuch*. Freud and his continuing followers were nervous and again mobilized to eject a former star—no doubt deriving some vengeful satisfaction in this after their long period of jealousy. The 1913 International Congress in London witnessed a near-brawl with flying mutual accusations of antisemitism and anti-Christian prejudice.[195] After a political struggle lasting many months, Jung resigned as editor of the *Jahrbuch* and, in April, 1914, also resigned as president of the IPA.[196] Fifteen of the sixteen Zürichers left the IPA a few months later.[197] Most members of the Swiss psychoanalytic society remained loyal to Jung (Binswanger and Pfister were exceptions) and constituted the first organization for Jung's new analytical psychology. Freud later conceded that "this may be a school of wisdom; but it is no longer analysis."[198]

During the denouement, Freud wrote to Ferenczi, advising him on how to respond to the Swiss analyst Maeder's assertions that Jewish–Aryan differences had caused the breakup. Freud wrote familiarly in a mix of German and Yiddish, "Our dear Swiss have gone crazy [*meschugge*]."[199] In a more serious tone, he went on to acknowledge, "On the matter of Semitism: there are certainly great differences from the Aryan spirit. We can become convinced of that every day. Hence there will surely be different world views [*Weltanschauungen*] and art here and there."[200]

Freud repudiated Jung's statements, ostensibly made during the latter's American lectures, that "ΨA was not a science but a religion,"[201] and reiterated to Ferenczi his allegiance to a purely scientific worldview. "There should not be a particular Aryan or Jewish science. The results must be identical; and only their presentation may vary.... If these differences occur in conceptualizing objective relations in science, then something is wrong."[202] Where biographer Gay interpreted this as Freud's backpedaling from a racial reading of the split, Freud's words—written from one Jewish insider to another—might just as easily be seen as a reckoning with antisemitism permeating the Swiss school,[203] from which Freud was now anxious to disassociate. He was finished with any desire for "Aryan patronage."[204]

Freud published *On the History of the Psychoanalytic Movement* shortly thereafter (1914), a declaration of what constituted true psychoanalysis, and an unmitigated screed against both Adler and Jung and their adherents.[205] Jung's "attempting to correlate the neuroses with religious and mythological phantasies" was chief among Freud's many complaints.[206] Freud acknowledged that both he himself and Pfister had drawn parallels between religious rituals and neurotic symptoms, and that in his *Totem and Taboo* he had addressed "problems of social anthropology in light of analysis."[207] But Freud saw Jung's analysis to be a reversal of priorities, using religious themes as a tool to analyze neurosis, rather than using psychoanalysis to scientifically investigate religious ideas.[208]

Conformity, creativity, and unconscious group dynamics

The splits with Adler, Stekel, Jung, and later with Rank and Ferenczi can certainly be understood in oedipal terms, as the combatants themselves largely viewed the struggles as father-son rivalries (with the exception of Adler, who saw sociopolitical power struggles rather than unconscious erotic conflicts).[209] As many scholars have observed, it was precisely the most brilliant and the most independent analysts—Adler and Jung, Rank (see Chapter 5) and Ferenczi—whom Freud drove away most painfully. Roazen wrote, "Freud was such a great man that his followers had to struggle to be original, and sometimes they were led thereby to reject what was valuable in Freud."[210] Stekel wrote that Freud suffered from the same "primitive horde complex" he described in *Totem and Taboo*: "He is the Old Man, afraid of his disciples."[211] Adler's defection was based in large part on this feeling, before any substantive debate, that he could not develop theory along his own lines. And Jung protested Freud's refusal to allow him to rise from the status of an oedipal son to an equal.

Freud, himself, acknowledged that he always needed "an intimate friend and a cordially detested enemy."[212] As Reik later recalled, "He was capable of much love, but he was also a good hater."[213] He could exercise considerable patience with talented followers' disagreements, but once he decided they had crossed the line into heresy, it was as though their theoretical differences were betrayals, and their transgressions became unforgiveable. Once he excommunicated someone, Freud was unsparing in his enmity. The long parade of acolytes-turned-enemies throughout Freud's career gave rise to a not-unfounded general impression among Freud's biographers that Freudian orthodoxy was the prevailing requirement of discourse within the Viennese Society, and that dissent was usually fatal to one's membership in the group.

This must be viewed somewhat more complexly, however, as a dynamic of dissension that evolved over time. With the gradual institutionalization of the Vienna Society and its inevitable power struggles, the Viennese felt envy and insecurity. The pressure to conform to a Freudian orthodoxy grew in proportion to the number of Freud's followers, but in the early days there was less uniformity of thought.[214] In his memoir as a lifelong loyalist of the Vienna Society and member of Freud's Committee, Hanns Sachs tried to split the difference between total agreement and total freedom to disagree in relation to Freud's sharing of his own works in progress with the group. Sachs affirmed that Freud tolerated criticism well from those he respected, but had no time for those whose opinions he felt were based either on non-psychological foundations or on their own need to pontificate. His allergy to moralizing was particularly intense:

> The criticism of others, who he considered more or less competent judges, was welcome and when he read his papers in manuscript either to his close friends or to the group in Vienna or at the meetings of the I.P.A. an animated discussion followed; he would carefully enter into the spirit of every objection and endeavor to assess its weight and strength accurately. Yet he was hardly ever so far convinced by anything that was said that he felt it necessary to make any change. These arguments were not new to him.... The great patience which Freud showed in listening to arguments and answering them, even if they were a bit stale, was reserved exclusively for honest opponents who kept the discussion of the basis of an objective search for truth. For those who used declamations and high sounding words instead of arguments he showed no indulgence at all.... [W]hen ... a professor on the faculty of philosophy, mounted the high horse of a moralistic harangue (this man's permanent hobby horse as well as milking cow), Freud picked up his hat and overcoat and left the room without a word.[215]

Wortis later recalled expressing dismay to Freud about "so much animosity" among psychoanalysts, to which Freud replied that "it is unavoidable.... But it is not the scientific differences that are so important, it is usually some other kind of animosity, jealousy or revenge, that gives the impulse to enmity. The scientific differences come later."[216]

In part, the hierarchical nature of the relationships among Freud and his followers should be understood in the larger historical context of Vienna itself. It is probably most difficult for Americans, with our independent-minded tendencies, to understand this mindset. In Austria, and in the convoluted society of Vienna, no-one advanced in any social or professional endeavor without a patron, and more than traces of this persist to this day. As Sachs wrote of Vienna,

> the famous Viennese Gemütlichkeit was a form of self-indulgence which tried to avoid sharp conflicts and harsh convictions.... Austria was a constitutional monarchy with all the usual trappings: a charter of liberties, two

houses of parliament, responsible ministers, independent law courts, and usual machinery of government. Yet it was an open secret that none of all these institutions possessed a scrap of real power, not even the bureaucracy. This power was in the hand of the Austrian "eighty families"; these formed an absolutely stabilized upper crust which automatically excluded everyone from influence who tried to oppose them.... Their influence was so firmly established that it was beyond all questioning. To get anywhere it was necessary to have backing from "above." ... The style of life of the privileged class became, as a matter of course, the pattern after which the middle class tried to model its conduct, imitating it down to the slightest mannerisms. (The rich Jews, after they had surmounted the religious barrier, were easily in the forefront.)[217]

Especially in the early days when choosing to be a psychoanalyst was taking a rebellious leap away from the medical and academic establishment, Freud was the new father with revolutionary ideas who would nevertheless provide his "sons" with protection and a degree of professional assistance—even monetary assistance in the form of referrals and sometimes even cash.[218] Of course their involvement with the group also gave them a heady sense of belonging to an enterprise that was at once deliciously counter-cultural, and intellectually exciting. This further bound them toward their leader. Sachs recalled that "[c]onsciousness of being an exception gave these nonconformists extraordinary energy, and they approached their problems with a personal fervor which toward the end of the century was often absent in the strictly organized science of Germany."[219] To leave Freud's aegis after having already burned bridges with the establishment, and to strike out on one's own, meant being exposed to the elements in a city that functioned almost entirely beneath the surface on favors, patronage, and access to power. The most brilliant defectors in many cases had their own separate networks—or had built up a following of their own—while some of the less talented early analysts probably felt they had few alternatives but to stay.

In spite of all these dynamics, some dissent was not only tolerated but encouraged by Freud, especially in the earlier years. Binswanger recalled that "conflicting opinions were voiced freely, and that no one pulled his punches—Freud himself, for all the respect shown him, was often contradicted."[220] And some debate did continue even into the later years, as well. In 1912, after the traumatic departure of Adler and his allies, Freud prounounced (somewhat disingenuously):

It is never the aim of the discussions in the Vienna Psychoanalytic Society to remove diversities or to arrive at conclusions. The different speakers, who are held together by taking a similar fundamental view of the same facts, allow themselves to give the sharpest expression to the variety of their individual opinions without any regard to the probability of converting any of their audience who may think otherwise. There may be many points in these discussions which have been misstated and misunderstood, but the final outcome, nevertheless, is that every one has received the clearest impression of views differing from his own and has communicated his own differing views to other people.[221]

Many years later, Helene Deutsch recalled,

> All … created the same atmosphere about the master, an atmosphere of absolute and infallible authority on his part. It was never any fault of Freud's that they cast him in this role and that they—so rumor has it—became "yes men." Quite the contrary, Freud had no love for "yes men" and so it fell out that the very ones who proved to be the most loyal and the more reliable adherents were not the recipients of a warmer sympathy on his part.[222]

How can such contrasting views of the group's conformity versus diversity be reconciled, and how much conformity or diversity was tolerated by the group in its theories about religion? Kenneth Eisold, in an analysis of the Vienna Society's group dynamics following Wilfred Bion's unconscious group theory, suggests an admixture of conscious and unconscious motives on Freud's part—consciously intending to support "the personal freedom of each individual"[223]—but "his deferential tactfulness also had the effect of reminding members that only Freud himself had the power to take such a step; it was his group."[224] Eisold makes the case that in addition to the oedipal dynamics between Freud and individual followers, there was a multi-layered group dynamic, both conscious and unconscious.

As a "work group,"[225] the Society had as its conscious task the mission of expanding Freud's psychoanalytic theorizing beyond the consulting room and the clinic, and promoting psychoanalysis as an intellectual movement. However, the group oscillated unconsciously between two "basic assumptions" (using Bion's terminology[226]) to ward off group anxieties. On the one hand, the group operated out of a "fight or flight" assumption, more at the surface level of awareness. This mode was repeatedly reinforced by Freud's own role as "fight leader," framing psychoanalysis as a cause besieged by multiple enemies, and his view of himself as a Hannibal or Moses leading an unpopular struggle for truth. On the other hand, as Eisold argues, the group operated at a deeper level out of a "dependency" assumption, in which they feared Freud's abandonment as their indispensable leader (in classical terms, their father/ego ideal), and often displaced onto one another the jealousies they felt toward their outside rivals. Eisold makes the point that casting Freud in "the unwelcome role of the aging despot who prevents young men from getting ahead"— Freud's own words in a letter to Jung[227]—was as much the *group's* responsibility and unconscious manipulation as it was due to Freud's own failures as a leader.[228]

Regarding Freud's role as leader and the group's response, Strozier and Offer have observed more positively,

> Nor were the members of the group wholly naïve regarding the tyranny of Freud's role.... Many presentations sharply diverged from Freud's ideas, and so much remained unexplored that neither Freud nor his followers could easily define a single, orthodox line to follow. Stekel, for example, in these early years, was always refreshingly odd. The group process, whatever else it did, also fostered a remarkable creativity in the group.[229]

Reik's recollections affirmed Freud's receptivity to new thinking:

> Until ripe old age Freud was receptive to all new ideas and original thought in psychoanalysis. He met them without prejudice, even when he did not agree; but he required a long time to feel at home in new views. Although he always evinced a lively and open-minded interest in all intellectual changes, he left it to the younger generation to extend psychoanalysis beyond the specific limitations that he had set himself.[230]

The very intimate nature of the group's subject fostered individuals' identification with their theories, which were sometimes frankly mingled with autobiography. Debate, then, often felt like personal criticism, and at times may have threatened members' very sense of psychic equilibrium. Yet, they were not unaware of the dangers, and had the determination to persevere in their debates, believing—whether they ultimately stayed in Freud's circle or moved on—that the subject of psychoanalysis was of the deepest psychological and social importance. Lou Andreas-Salomé (whose muse-like friendships ranged from Nietzsche and Rilke to Freud and his doomed disciple Tausk) wrote in her diary decades later regarding the nature of the group's struggles. Reading through her gendered lens, it is possible to see an account of courage and intellectual excitement as well as conflict:

> [Psychoanalysis] subjects life to insight—just as, on the other hand, psychoanalysis has bent to life the narrow, withered knowledge of academic psychology, thus laying the foundations of its pre-eminent scientific achievement. This is the very reason why, within this circle and beyond, splits arise and disputes—and it is more difficult to settle these than any others, without endangering the continuity of results and methods. Yet at the same time, it is beautiful to see men facing one another in honest battle. So much more is it my, the woman's part to thank. To thank all these evenings, even the dull ones, for the sake of the One who chaired them and gave them of his time.[231]

Religion: a continuing arena for creative thinking

The topic of religion was not exempt from debate by members of the group throughout its history, nor was it wanting for creativity. As will be seen in the following chapter, in spite of the most famous conflicts and splits, *both* fealty toward Freud *and* freedom to dissent—within limits—held true for the group's discourse on religion. Nor can any of the splits among Freud and his immediate Vienna circle be attributed primarily to differences concerning religion, although Jung's openness to religious and spiritual themes was certainly one aspect of the crisis between himself and Freud. At the same time, Pfister, the most unwavering religious believer, was never rejected (see Chapter 3), nor did Pfister ever renounce his loyalty to Freud and psychoanalysis, even when the majority of Swiss analysts followed Jung into a separate school of analytical psychology.[232]

In the end, Graf's recollections, comparing the evolution of the Vienna circle to the founding of a religion—from initial inspiration and excitement, to competitiveness and struggles against authority, to concern with matters of both structure and dogma—seem apt:

I have compared the gathering in Freud's home with the founding of a religion. However, after the first dreamy period and the unquestioning faith of the first group of apostles, the time came when the church was founded. Freud began to organize his church with great energy. He was serious and strict in the demands he made of his pupils; he permitted no deviations from his orthodox teaching. Subjectively, Freud was of course right, for that which he worked out with so much energy and sequence, and which was as yet to be defended against the opposition of the world, could not be rendered inept by hesitations, weakenings, and tasteless ornamentations. Good-hearted and considerate though he was in private life, Freud was hard and relentless in the presentation of his ideas. If we do consider him as a founder of a religion, we may think of him as a Moses full of wrath and unmoved by prayers, a Moses like the one Michael Angelo [*sic*] brought to life out of stone—to be seen in the Church of San Pietro in Vincoli in Rome. After a trip to Italy, Freud never tired of talking to us about this statue; the memory of it he kept for his last book [referring to *Moses and Monotheism*, 1939].... The original circle of the Viennese apostles began to lose its significance for Freud, particularly because his most gifted pupil turned away to follow a path of his own—Alfred Adler, who in a series of excellent discussions of his own views quietly and firmly defended [his] point of view ... Freud would not listen. He insisted there was but one theory, he insisted that if one followed Adler and dropped the sexual basis of psychic life, one was no more a Freudian. In short, Freud—as the head of a church—banished Adler; he ejected him from the official church. Within the space of a few years, I lived through the whole development of a church history: from the first sermons to a small group of apostles to the strife between Arius and Athanasius.[233]

Yet in spite of Graf's evident admiration, and his gratitude for Freud's treatment of a phobia in his son (the case of "Little Hans"),[234] he, too, eventually left the group in 1913—two years after Adler, one year after Stekel, and around the same time as Jung departed.[235] As Graf notes,

> Freud's best pupil cannot be compared to this creative imagination and real genius.... But I was unable and unwilling to submit to Freud's "do" or "don't"—with which he once confronted me—and nothing was left for me but to withdraw from his circle.[236]

Graf's perception of the Vienna circle as a quasi-religious body conforms well to Freud's own views on the progression of religion from primal struggles between sons and fathers, to the development of rituals to expiate guilt over such betrayal of the father. The members of Freud's inner circle are most often referred to in both contemporaneous and modern accounts as "followers," "pupils," or even "disciples," but never "colleagues"—even though many joined the Wednesday night meetings with well-established careers and reputations. Resentments were inevitable.

Thankfully, the Vienna Society never decapitated its father-leader, but some of its most creative thinkers could not tolerate their originality being so constrained and left, often to found their own schools of psychoanalysis. Others remained and many others joined. Theodor Reik summed up the tension between fealty toward Freud and independent thought as follows:

> We have made [the cause of psychoanalysis] our own. We pledged ourselves to it when it was still unpleasant and ill-advised to do so. We protected it in its development both from its enemies and from its friends—which last was often far more difficult.... Not so long ago psychoanalysts were called a sect. Even today they are reproached for their faith in authority, for the narrow-mindedness and dogmatism with which they follow their teacher through thick and thin. But we have not been blinded by loyalty to any error or omission. Our love for the man [sic] and our admiration for his achievements *have not precluded our criticism of details* . They have simply made it *impossible for us to offer this criticism irreverently* [emphasis added].[237]

Over time it was Freudians, and not Freud himself, who most attempted to ossify "classical psychoanalysis." As Roazen noted,

> Jones made a great display of the extent of whatever doctrinal [Freudian] differences there were between him and Freud, in an effort to establish how tolerant Freud could be. It is true that Freud's openness sometimes horrified Jones; late one night Freud got into a "superstitious" enough mood even to talk about the possible existence of the Almighty.[238]

In conclusion, it cannot be said that the members' views on any topic, either before 1908, in the years surrounding World War I, or in the heady days of "Red Vienna" leading into the steady rise of more overt antisemitism, were ever entirely monolithic. Their appraisals of religious themes were varied and wide-ranging, and now deserve a more thorough investigation.

Notes

1 Rose, 1998: 56, citing Graf and Sadger.
2 Freud, 1955a/1909.
3 Nunberg and Federn, 1962–75, vol. I: xxxiii–xxxvii. For ease of reference, hereafter the Minutes will be cited as *Minutes* by volume and page number only (e.g., *Minutes* I: 1). For a complete listing of members from 1902 to 1938, including changes, see Mühlleitner and Reichmayr, 1997: 75. About their backgrounds, see Rose, 1998: 15, 25–35.
4 Bronner, 2008: 31.
5 Mühlleitner and Reichmayr, 1997: 73–102.
6 Abraham later founded the Berlin Institute.
7 Gay, 2006: 178; "Dr. A. A. Brill Dies," *New York Times*, March 3, 1948. Brill was born in Austrian Galicia (like Freud) in 1874, but at age fifteen emigrated to New York. He founded the New York Psychoanalytic Society in 1911.
8 Rose, 1998: 11; Fichtner, 2003: xxxiii; Jacoby, 1983: 46.
9 Rose, 1998: 27.
10 *Minutes* I: xxii.
11 Rose, 1998: 20.
12 Freud, 1959c: 246.
13 Roazen, 1975: 212.
14 Stekel, 1950: 106.
15 Graf, 1942: 471.
16 Stekel, 1950; Gay, 2006: 179.
17 Gay, 2006: 178.
18 McGuire, 1974: 130; Roazen, 1975: 351n.
19 Jones, 1964, excerpted in Roazen, 1975: 351–352.
20 Sterba's (1978) description comes from a later time in which Freud had withdrawn from the Society meetings due to illness, and again convened a select group in his Berggasse waiting room.
21 *Minutes* I: 1, II: 352. First recorded meeting October 10, 1906; resolution by Adler to abandon the practice of the urn February 12, 1908.
22 M. Freud, 1957: 110. Freud's son, Martin, recalls that

> the room was still thick with smoke and it seemed to me a wonder that human beings had been able to live in it for hours, let alone to speak in it without choking. I could never understand how father could endure it, let alone enjoy it, which he did. It is possible that to some of his guests the smoke-charged atmosphere was an ordeal, but it is certain they thought the price low in exchange for the high privilege of a close personal contact with a great teacher.

23 Ibid., xxii.
24 Graf, 1942: 471.
25 *Minutes* I: xxiii.
26 Ibid., 255.
27 Gay, 2006: 235.
28 *Minutes* I: xxi.

29 Including Paul Federn, Max Kahane, Monroe Meyer, Tatjana Rosenthal, Herbert Silberer, Eugenia Sokolnicka, Wilhelm Stekel, and Viktor Tausk (Bronner, 2008).
30 Gay, 2006: 166. Suicide and preoccupation with death were prominent themes in Romantic literature, and often led sensitive young adults in late eighteenth–early twentieth-century Europe to self-destruction. One of Freud's favorite writers, Goethe, set off a wave of suicides with his *Sorrows of Young Werther* in 1779. Hume's essay "On Suicide," (publ. posthumously in 1783), contra the Christian prohibition, elevated suicide to a noble moral choice.
31 Yahil, 1990: 571.
32 Schur, 1972: 498.
33 Ibid., 499.
34 Ibid. Quoting a letter from Freud to his son, Ernst.
35 Ibid., 529.
36 Roazen, 1975: 307.
37 Enumerated by Roazen, 1975: 338–339, 347, 358, 420; 1969: 120–160, 331n, 339n, 435; Wittels, 2014: 241.
38 Roazen, 1975: 322.
39 Writing for Kraus' journal *Die Fackel* ("The Torch"), Wittels accosted the hypocrisy of Viennese sexual mores, while characterizing women as natural sexual servants of men (Rose, 1998: 58–59).
40 Wittels, 1995/1940: 112–118, 122.
41 *Minutes* I: 203; Jones, 1955: 9–10.
42 Jung, 1989/1961: 149. For others' recollections of the visit, see Gay, 2006: 202.
43 *Minutes* I: 140.
44 Ibid., 139–140.
45 Ibid., 145.
46 Ibid.
47 Jung, letter to Freud, March 31, 1907 (McGuire, 1974: 24–27). There is no comment to this effect (at least that I could find) in any of the relevant correspondence from the period. In his letter to Freud immediately after the visit, Jung argues for a broadening of the concept of libido, mentioning Rank in support, but makes no mention of Adler's case. Jung's co-traveler, Binswanger, twice mentions attending the Wednesday night meeting—once in his memoir, and once years later in a letter to Freud, but makes no comment on Adler's presentation (Fichtner, 2003: xxxiv, 105). Hoffman (1994) does not mention the evening in his Adler biography.
48 Hoffman, 1994: 52. Two of Adler's siblings also formally left Judaism to become Catholic, and *Konfessionslos* (unaffiliated).
49 Ibid., 52–54, 110–111. See Chapter 2.
50 Ibid., 14–15, 54–55. Likely motivated by career advancement.
51 Unpublished interview, Library of Congress (Bair, 2003: 118).
52 Bair, 2003: 119.
53 Eissler interview in Bair, 2003: 119, citing Roazen, 1975: 290.
54 McGuire, 1974: 95; Gay, 2006: 204.
55 McGuire, 1974: 95.
56 Ibid. ("Habe ich Sie ja auch lieb; aber dieses Moment habe ich unterzuordnen gelernt.") Cf. Gay, 2006: 201. Gay translates this passage perhaps more intimately as "I also have love for you." The statement is not equivalent to "I love you," however (Jan Rehmann, personal communication).
57 Gay, 2006: 202.
58 Roazen, 1975: 228.
59 Binswanger, 1957: 31.
60 Freud letter to Ferenczi, July 9, 1913 in Brabant *et al.*, 1993: 500.

61 Falzeder, 2002: 62.
62 Ibid., 54.
63 Ibid., 53–54. Letter to Abraham, July 23, 1908.
64 Sachs, 1944: 120.
65 Ibid. Sachs (1944) saw this as a rare instance of Freud's being "a victim of his wishful thinking" (p. 118). Sachs prided himself on having seen early on "the signs in the sky" (ibid.).
66 Stekel, 1950: 125; Roazen, 1975: 215.
67 Wittels, 2014: 138.
68 Fichtner, 2003: xxxiv, 105.
69 Jones, 1955: 130; Roazen, 1975: 216.
70 Gay, 2006: 213; McGuire, 1974: 260n2. Gay notes Freud's ambivalence toward Jung in this statement: he was referring to the Viennese, but wrote "*Ihnen*" (you) where he meant "*ihnen*" (them)!
71 Roazen, 1975: 215.
72 Gay, 2006: 214, 681n.
73 McGuire, 1974: 259.
74 Gay, 2006: 214.
75 Wortis, 1984: 30.
76 Jones, 1955: 136; Roazen, 1975: 215.
77 *Minutes* II: 466.
78 Ibid., 467.
79 Gay, 2006: 176–177.
80 *Minutes* I: 301.
81 Ibid., 303. Cf. pp. 299, 302–303.
82 Ibid., 301–302.
83 Ibid., 315.
84 Ibid.
85 Ibid., 315.
86 Ibid., 317.
87 Mühlleitner and Reichmayr, 1997: 78.
88 Ibid.
89 Ibid. Most returned to their homelands, e.g., Sándor Ferenczi (Hungary), Ludwig Binswanger (Switzerland), and George Morgenthau (United States).
90 Gay, 2006: 215.
91 Gillespie, 1982: n.p.
92 Gay, 2006: 215.
93 Eugene Bleuler, unpublished letter to Freud, 1911, in Gay, 2006: 215. Bleuler eventually protested Freudian orthodoxy, and resigned from the IPA: "This 'who is not for us is against us,' this 'all or nothing' is in my opinion necessary for religious communities and useful for political parties ... but for science I consider it harmful."
94 Gay, 2006: 218.
95 Gillespie, 1982: n.p.
96 Jones, 1955: 69.
97 Wittels, 2014: 140; Stekel, 1950: 128–129; Roazen, 1975: 182–183; Gay, 2006: 218–219.
98 Wittels, 2014: 140; Gay, 2006: 218.
99 *Minutes* II: 463–471.
100 Ibid., 463.
101 Ibid., 464.
102 Ibid., 466, 471.
103 Ibid., 466.

104 Ibid.
105 Ibid.
106 Ibid.
107 Letter to Ferenczi, April 3, 1910, in Jones, 1955: 78.
108 Ibid., 467–468.
109 Ibid., 469.
110 Wittels, 1995: 51. Much later, Wittels said he had "changed my mind completely
     and for many years have been in favor of them…. My article against medical women
     was a 'masculine protest' dictated by fear."
111 *Minutes* II: 477.
112 Ibid.
113 Ibid., 478.
114 Ibid., 499.
115 Ibid., 498.
116 Maddox, 2006: 64.
117 Freud Museum, London, n.d.
118 *Minutes*, III: 281, 284.
119 Roazen, 1969.
120 Gay, 2006: 436–437. For more on women's participation in the Society, see
     Balsam, 2003.
121 Mühlleitner and Reichmayr, 1997: 75; cf. Appignanesi and Forrester, 1992; Roazen,
     1975: 420–488.
122 Jacoby, 1983: 12.
123 Ibid., 12–13.
124 *Minutes* II: 260–265; Freud, 1959b/1925: 52–53.
125 On the split with Adler, see Gay, 2006: 216–224.
126 *Minutes* III: 102–105, 102n3, 104n5; later published in the *Zentralblatt*.
127 Ibid., 109–110.
128 Ibid., 141.
129 Freud, 1955c/1920.
130 *Minutes*, III: 111.
131 Ibid., 145.
132 Ibid., 147.
133 Ibid., 148.
134 Ibid., 149.
135 Ibid., 151.
136 Ibid., 147.
137 Ibid.
138 Ibid., 268.
139 Ibid., 279. Minutes of the final June, 1911 meeting "have not been preserved."
140 Ibid., 281.
141 Roazen, 1975: 185. Later renamed the Society for Individual Psychology.
142 Gay, 2006: 223.
143 *Minutes* III: 280.
144 Ibid., 281.
145 Ibid., 283.
146 Ibid.
147 Ibid.
148 Unpublished letter to Jones, August 9, 1911, Library of Congress, in Gay, 2006: 223.
149 Gay, 2006: 223.
150 Jung, letter to Ferenczi, January 6, 1909, in Gay, 2006: 204, 679n.
151 Jung, 1989/1961: 158.

152 Ibid.
153 Gay, 2006: 217.
154 Letter to Ferenczi, December 29, 1910, in Brabant *et al.*, 1993: 246.
155 Freud, 1955b/1913.
156 Ibid., 137.
157 McGuire, 1974: 279.
158 Ibid., 460.
159 Freud, 1959a/1907.
160 Jung, 1989/1961: 36–39.
161 Ibid., 289; Roazen, 1975: 252.
162 McGuire, 1974: 485.
163 Jones, 1955: 153.
164 Binswanger, 1957: 5.
165 McGuire, 1974: 517.
166 Roazen, 1975: 211.
167 Ibid., 212.
168 Binswanger, 1957: 5.
169 Ibid., 215.
170 This was the end of a longstanding debate from at least as early as 1908. Jones, 1955: 272, 275n6, 335, *et passim*.
171 *Minutes* III: 320–328, 336–346, 357–367; IV: 20–27, 35–42, 57–62, 68–74, 75–81, 92–96.
172 Jones, 1955: 154.
173 Ibid. Jones reports this anecdote, but there is no record of it on that date in Nunberg's and Federn's compilation of the minutes of the Vienna Psychoanalytic Society (p. 102n).
174 Ibid.
175 Ibid., xviii.
176 Ibid.
177 Ibid., 155, citing a 1924 letter from Freud to Ferenczi.
178 Stekel, 1950: 142.
179 Binswanger, 1957: 39.
180 Ibid., 42.
181 Küsnacht was about two hours away from Kreuzlingen by the very best modes of transportation at the time, but in the opposite direction from Vienna.
182 For Jung's perspective on this, see Bair, 2003: 226–228, *et passim*; McLynn, 1997: 194–196.
183 Brabant *et al.*, 1993: 399.
184 Letter from Freud to Rank, August 18, 1912, Rank Collection, Columbia University, in Gay, 2006: 231, 683n.
185 Gay, 2006: 230.
186 Jones, 1955: 172–184; cf. Grosskurth, 1991.
187 Jones, 1972: 348. This was the second time Freud had fainted in Jung's presence, the first being three years earlier, shortly before they boarded their ship for America, concerning Freud's suspicion that Jung harbored a death wish against him (Jones, 1955: 61, 166).
188 Jones, 1972: 348. Freud later acknowledged "there is some piece of unruly homosexual feeling at the root of the matter" (ibid.).
189 McGuire, 1974: 534–535; Gay, 2006: 234.
190 Ibid.; Gay, 2006: 235.
191 Gay, 2006: 235. Sigmund Freud, letter to Ernest Jones, December 26, 1912, Freud Collection, Library of Congress, cited in Gay, 2006: 684n.
192 Ibid., 236.

193 McGuire, 1974: 539; cf. Gay, 2006: 236.
194 McGuire, 1974: 540. A few more letters were exchanged regarding *Jahrbuch* and IPA business; ten years later, out of the blue, Jung respectfully referred a patient to Freud (ibid., 553).
195 Bair, 2003: 240.
196 Gay, 2006: 241; Stevens, 1994: 15.
197 Bair, 2003: 247.
198 Freud, 1964/1933: 143. Cf. Roazen, 1975: 278.
199 Freud, letter to Ferenczi, June 8, 1913, in Brabant *et al.*, 1993: 490.
200 Ibid.
201 Ibid., 491.
202 Ibid.; Gay, 2006: 684n.
203 For a balanced and fair reflection on Jung's alleged antisemitism, his motives for cooperating with the Nazis during World War II, and the implications of this controversial dimension of Jung's history for analytical psychology, see Stevens, 1994: 113–128. Jung did harbor more than a trace of generalized racism against Jews, which he imbibed from Swiss-German culture at the time—e.g., his love of Wagner—but his cooperation with Nazi psychologists was, in part, intended (however misguidedly) to protect certain Jewish colleagues; he never condoned Hitler's genocidal program.
204 Sigmund Freud, letter to Ferenczi, May 4, 1913, Freud–Ferenczi Correspondence, Library of Congress, cited in Gay, 2006: 684n.
205 Freud, 1957/1914: 1–66.
206 Ibid., 36.
207 Freud, 1957/1914: 37.
208 Ibid.
209 Freud's painful earlier split from Wilhelm Fliess was likely a similar dynamic in reverse. On Fliess, see Gay, 2006: 55–59.
210 Roazen, 1975: 179.
211 Stekel, 1950: 192–193; Roazen, 1975: 215; a view shared by Wittels, 2014/1924: 193.
212 Wittels, 2014/1924: 44.
213 Reik, 1940: 6.
214 Burston, 1994: 213.
215 Sachs, 1944: 99.
216 Wortis, 1984: 163.
217 Sachs, 1944: 25–26, 28.
218 Roazen, 1969: 26.
219 Ibid., 38.
220 Binswanger, 1957: 7.
221 Freud, 1958/1912: 243.
222 Roazen, 1975: 300.
223 Ibid., 203.
224 Eisold, 1997: 91.
225 Ibid., 89, citing Bion, 1967.
226 Ibid.
227 McGuire, 1974: 373; Eisold, 1997: 88.
228 Eisold, 1997: 89.
229 Strozier and Offer, 1985: 25.
230 Reik, 1940: 19.
231 *Minutes* I: xxxi.
232 *Minutes* II: 243, 245, 461; III: 289; IV: 10, 213.
233 Graf, 1942: 471–473.

234 Freud, 1955a/1909.
235 Mühlleitner and Reichmayr, 1997: 77.
236 Graf, 1942: 475.
237 Reik, 1940: 36.
238 Roazen, 1975: 353.

References

Appignanesi, Lisa, and Forrester, John (1992). *Freud's women*. New York: Basic Books.
Bair, Deirdre (2003). *Jung: A biography*. Boston: Little, Brown.
Balsam, Rosemary (2003). Women of the Wednesday Society: The presentations of Drs. Hilferding, Spielrein, and Hug-Hellmuth. *American Imago, 60* (3): 303–342. Online at https://muse.jhu.edu/journals/American_imago/v060/60.3balsam.pdf. Accessed September 19, 2015.
Binswanger, Ludwig (1957). *Sigmund Freud: Reminiscences of a friendship*. New York: Grune and Stratton.
Bion, Wilfred (1967). *Experiences in groups*. New York: Basic Books.
Brabant, Eva, Falzeder, Ernst, and Giampieri-Deutsch, Patrizia (Eds.) (1993). *The correspondence of Sigmund Freud and Sándor Ferenczi, Vol. I, 1908–1914*. Cambridge, MA: Belknap/Harvard University Press.
Bronner, Andrea (Ed.) (2008). *Vienna Psychoanalytic Society: The first 100 years*. Vienna: Christian Brandstätter.
Burston, D. (1994). Freud, the serpent and the sexual enlightenment of children. *International Forum of Psychoanalysis, 3*: 205–219.
Eisold, Kenneth (1997). Freud as leader: The early years of the Viennese society. *International Journal of Psycho-analysis, 78* (1): 87–104.
Falzeder, Ernst (Ed.) (2002). *The complete correspondence of Sigmund Freud and Karl Abraham, 1907–1925*. Caroline Schwarzacher *et al.* (Trans.). London: Karnac.
Fichtner, Gerhard (Ed.) (2003). *The Sigmund Freud–Ludwig Binswanger correspondence, 1908–1938*. Arnold J. Pomerans (Trans.). New York: Other Press.
Freud, Martin (1957). *Glory reflected: Sigmund Freud—man and father*. London: Angus and Robertson.
Freud, Sigmund (1955a). *Analysis of a phobia in a five year old boy* ["Little Hans"]. In J. Strachey (Ed.), *Standard edition of the complete works of Sigmund Freud*, Vol. 10: 1–150. (Orig. publ. 1909.)
Freud, Sigmund (1955b). *Totem and Taboo*. In J. Strachey (Ed.), *Standard edition of the complete works of Sigmund Freud*, Vol. 13: 1–255. (Orig. publ. 1913.)
Freud, Sigmund (1955c). *Beyond the pleasure principle*. In J. Strachey (Ed.), *Standard edition of the complete works of Sigmund Freud*, Vol. 18: 1–64. (Orig. publ. 1920.)
Freud, Sigmund (1957). *On the history of the psycho-analytic movement*. In J. Strachey (Ed.), *Standard edition of the complete works of Sigmund Freud*, Vol. 14: 1–66. (Orig. publ. 1914.)
Freud, Sigmund (1958). *Contributions to a discussion on masturbation*. In J. Strachey (Ed.), *Standard edition of the complete works of Sigmund Freud*, Vol. 12: 239–254. (Orig. publ. 1912.)
Freud, Sigmund (1959a). *Obsessive actions and religious practices*. In J. Strachey (Ed.), *Standard edition of the complete works of Sigmund Freud*, Vol. 9: 115–127. (Orig. publ. 1907.)

Freud, Sigmund (1959b). *An autobiographical study*. In J. Strachey (Ed.), *Standard edition of the complete works of Sigmund Freud*, Vol. 20: 1–74. (Orig. publ. 1925.)

Freud, Sigmund (1959c). *The question of lay analysis*. In J. Strachey (Ed.), *Standard edition of the complete works of Sigmund Freud*, Vol. 20: 183–250. (Orig. publ. 1926.)

Freud, Sigmund (1964). *New introductory lectures on psycho-analysis*. In J. Strachey (Ed.), *Standard edition of the complete works of Sigmund Freud*, Vol. 22: 1–182. (Orig. publ. 1933.)

Gay, Peter (2006). *Freud: A life for our time*. New York: W. W. Norton.

Gillespie, William (1982). History of the IPA. Online (adapted) at www.ipaworld/en/FrStaging/IPA1/history_of_the_ipa.aspx. Accessed September 3, 2017.

Graf, Max (1942). Reminiscences of Professor Freud. *Psychoanalytic Quarterly, 11*: 465–476.

Grosskurth, Phyllis (1991). *The secret ring: Freud's inner circle and the politics of psychoanalysis*. Reading, MA: Addison-Wesley.

Hoffman, Edward (1994). *The drive for self: Alfred Adler and the founding of individual psychology*. Reading, MA: Addison-Wesley.

Jacoby, Russell (1983). *The repression of psychoanalysis: Otto Fenichel and the political Freudians*. New York: Basic Books.

Jones, Ernest (1955). *The life and work of Sigmund Freud, Vol. 2: Years of maturity 1901–1919*. New York: Basic Books.

Jones, Ernest (1964). The God complex. In *Essays in applied psychoanalysis, Vol. 2: Essays in folklore and religion* (pp. 244–264). London: Hogarth.

Jones, Ernest (1972). *The life and work of Sigmund Freud, Vol. 1: The young Freud 1856–1900*. New York: Basic Books.

Jung, C. G. (1989). *Memories, dreams, reflections*, rev. ed. Aniela Jaffé (Ed.), Richard and Clara Winston (Trans.). New York: Vintage. (Orig. publ. 1961.)

Maddox, Brenda (2006). *Freud's Wizard: Ernest Jones and the transformation of psycho-analysis*. Cambridge, MA: Da Capo Press.

McGuire, William (Ed. and Trans.) (1974). *The Freud/Jung letters*. Cambridge, MA: Harvard University Press.

McLynn, Frank (1997). *Carl Gustav Jung: A biography*. New York: St. Martin's.

Mühlleitner, Elke and Reichmayr, Johannes (1997). Following Freud in Vienna. *International Forum for Psychoanalysis, 6*: 73–102.

Nunberg, Herman and Federn, Ernst (Eds.) (1962–75). *Minutes of the Vienna Psychoanalytic Society 1902–1918*, 4 vols. M. Nunberg (Trans.). New York: International Universities Press.

Reik, Theodor (1940). *From thirty years with Freud*. Richard Winston (Trans.). New York: Farrar & Rinehart.

Roazen, Paul (1969). *Brother animal: The story of Freud and Tausk*. New York: Alfred Knopf.

Roazen, Paul (1975). *Freud and his followers*. New York: Alfred Knopf.

Rose, Louis (1998). *The Freudian calling: Early Viennese psychoanalysis and the pursuit of cultural science*. Detroit: Wayne State University Press.

Sachs, Hanns (1944). *Freud: Master and friend*. Cambridge, MA: Harvard University Press.

Schur, Max (1972). *Freud, living and dying*. New York: International Universities Press.

Stekel, Wilhelm (1950). *The autobiography of Wilhelm Stekel*. Emil Gutheil (Ed.). New York: Liveright.

Sterba, Richard (1978). Discussions of Sigmund Freud. *Psychoanalytic Quarterly, 47*: 173–191.

Stevens, Anthony (1994). *Jung.* Oxford, UK: Oxford University Press.

Strozier, Charles B. and Offer, Daniel (1985). The heroic period in psychohistory. In *The leader: Psychohistorical essays* (pp. 21–39). New York: Springer Verlag.

Wittels, Fritz (1995). *Freud and the child woman: The memoirs of Fritz Wittels.* Edward Timms (Ed.). New Haven: Yale University Press. (Orig. unpubl. manuscript "Wrestling with the man: The story of a Freudian," *c.*1940.)

Wittels, Fritz (2014). *Sigmund Freud: His personality, his teaching, and his school.* Edan and Cedar Paul (Trans.). New York: Routledge. (Orig. publ. 1924.)

Wortis, Joseph (1984). *My analysis with Freud.* Northvale, NJ: Jason Aronson.

Yahil, Leni (1990). *The Holocaust: The fate of European Jewry, 1932–1945.* Ina Friedman and Haya Galai (Trans.). Oxford, UK: Oxford University Press.

Chapter 2

"Old and dirty gods"
Religion and Freud's Vienna circle

Religion was a more significant—and complex—topic of discussion for the Viennese analysts than has been formerly recognized in the psychoanalytic literature. Viewed as a matter of cultural, anthropological, and archaeological interest, religion was investigated alongside every other possible topic within the broad rubric of applied psychoanalysis. Transcripts of comments on religion just in the minutes of the Vienna Psychoanalytic Society alone run to sixty-one single-spaced typed pages, and the members' associated published writings are even more extensive. It would be a mistake, then, to think of the group's commentary on religious themes—or on cultural matters more generally—as peripheral to their work or to their theorizing.

Why did they pursue religion in particular as a field for exploration? As Nunberg wrote in his introduction to the minutes,

> The members of the group saw far more in psychoanalysis than a psychopathology and a method of treating sick people. They knew that man [sic] is a social being as well as a biological entity. They recognized that the relations of man with his environment are expressed not only in his behavior but also in works of art and literature, in religion, and in social institutions. Therefore, they found it necessary to concern themselves not only with the sick human being but also with literature, religion, philosophy, anthropology, sociology, and so forth.... In those early years it was difficult to obtain suitable case material for psychoanalytic study. But this material was easily available from nonclinical sources. This may explain the striking fact that at the outset, and even later, problems of art, literature, mythology, religion, education, were discussed more than were problems of psychiatry.[1]

Rank and Sachs also noted in their introductory essay to the first issue of *Imago* in 1912 that the study of cultural phenomena in general, and religion in particular, was the logical extension of psychoanalysis from the diagnosis and treatment of neurosis to the realm of normality, and the ways in which humans could collectively sublimate the antisocial libido-drives. Religion had an especially significant role to play as "the first and most powerful guardian of all cultural achievement, because the gratification which every individual must renounce [for the sake of civilization] is projected outwards toward God, as 'union with God' by means of identification."[2]

It is also important to note that, unlike much of modern Europe, fin-de-siècle Vienna was saturated with religion. The Catholic Church and the Habsburg monarchy were entwined to a degree that every institution (including government and education) and every person was regulated by the Church's decrees. Just as the spire of the *Stephansdom* (St. Stephen's Cathedral) dominated the skyline of Vienna, Catholicism established its hegemony over religious beliefs and practices, and all non-Christians were forced to live in its shadow.

In the U.S., where the separation of church and state is written into the Constitution (however much contested), it is difficult to fathom the thorough intertwining of church, law, and education in twentieth-century Vienna. The Catholic Church had a direct influence over accepted sexual and social norms (leading as well to a culture of hypocrisy and concealment of actual sexual behavior that would have been labeled as dissolute or degenerate, well chronicled in the plays of Arthur Schnitzler).[3] This hypocrisy was an innate paradox in Viennese cultural life. In Hanns Sachs' words, "It has ever been a tricky business to understand Vienna; she was neither *jeune cocotte* nor *vieille pieuse*, but young and old, lascivious and pious at the same time."[4]

Further, it was (and remains to this day in many respects) a society of aristocratic patronage and *Protektion*.[5] "Official gaiety" masked political cynicism and apathy toward the lower classes.[6] Laxity in following rules or *Shlamperei* ("slovenliness"),[7] while at the same time referring officiously to rules as an expedient for saying "no," cloaked the reality of behind-the-scenes maneuvering. Without a sponsor, as Sachs commented in his memoirs (see Chapter 1), it was difficult for anyone—but especially a Jew—to advance in the ranks of officialdom.[8] Freud learned this lesson over the course of sixteen long years of waiting bitterly while being passed over time and again for promotion to the title of Professor, until he swallowed his pride and sought a well-connected Gentile advocate.[9]

The extent to which Viennese culture was saturated with Christian symbolism and imagery is even reflected in Freud's and his followers' own correspondence. Christian holidays were observed as national holidays (a practice continued in Austria today), so mentions of "Christmas," "Easter," "Pentecost," etc., in the group's correspondence were commonplace, and many Jews, including those in Freud's own social circle, celebrated Christmas.[10] Freud more than once referred to his "cross to bear" (e.g., in a letter to Fliess, "No one can help me in the least with what oppresses me; it is my cross, I must bear it, and God knows that in adapting to it, my back has become noticeably bent"),[11] and following an old peasant superstition would add three crosses after references to sex in his correspondence (a sign to ward off witches)![12] Such phrases, though frequent, should not be interpreted to mean that Freud or his Jewish followers had a lifelong unconscious wish to be Christian,[13] although a constant, low-level resentment and envy of Christian privilege must have been part and parcel of Jewish psychic life in Vienna. The use of Christian expressions testifies to the pervasiveness and utter normalizing of Catholicism throughout Austrian culture and society.

Religion was therefore "overdetermined" as a multi-valent topic of investigation to which the early analysts returned again and again. As noted in the Introduction, my initial research question was "What religious themes appear in discussions and writings of Freud's Wednesday Night Psychological Society?" This chapter will present my findings, using an ethnographic approach, organized into themes and sub-themes according to the amount of attention paid to each: The first and most discussed theme was religion in general as a cultural phenomenon and its psychodynamic origins. This section concludes with discussions regarding anthropological studies of religion beyond Judaism and Christianity (following Freud's precedent in *Totem and Taboo*[14]), including symbols of the human condition, prehistoric religion, and the status of women in the evolution of religions. Next followed the theme of Christianity, with sub-themes including oedipal interpretations of scripture and beliefs, and analyses of the Church's teachings on sin, sex, and death. After this comes a brief section on religion in the context of clinical case material. The last theme was Judaism and Jewishness—as notable for what was omitted (the experience of antisemitism) as it was for what the analysts, almost all Jews themselves, permitted themselves to think and say to one another.

My conclusion in this chapter is that, contrary to previous generalizations in the scholarly literature about the homogeneity of attitudes toward religion among Freud's followers, an examination of the primary sources gives evidence for considerable complexity and creativity in their thoughts on religious and existential subjects.

General references to religion: symptoms, symbols, and defense

Religion was never explicitly defined by the group per se, but following Freud's implicit usage, the term generally meant adherence to the worship of a transcendent God or gods—a cultural development viewed as "higher" than animism and totemism.[15] Religion was generally classified by the group as falling within the realm of affect rather than what they valued more highly—rational thought. Stekel observed,

> There are two kinds of persons who cannot fall ill with a neurosis: the absolutely devout and the typically amoral. Skeptics most often fall prey to neurosis. In most people piety is not based on logic, but is an affect.[16]

Religion was considered to be most accessible to psychoanalytic study in the form of its rituals and practices.[17] Subjective religious experience was rarely discussed, except as symptomatic of neurosis. For most of the group, the classification of religion as an affective phenomenon meant that it could not be evaluated as a scientific system equivalent to psychoanalysis, and for some this also meant that it could not be taken as seriously, except as an example of pathology—as in Furtmüller's flat statement that "Religious need can always be only one thing: a flight from reality."[18]

Yet nuances can be observed in the group's debates about specific religious practices and phenomena. Freud's own most polemical writings on religion did not appear until the late 1920s (e.g., *The Future of an Illusion* in 1927,[19] *Civilization and Its Discontents* in 1930,[20] and the highly speculative *Moses and Monotheism* in 1939[21]). That is to say, although Freud was certainly formulating his strongly anti-religious ideas by the early 1920s, there was still a good deal of flux in both Freud's and his Viennese colleagues' thinking about religion especially before that time. Freud later became more vehement about religion always serving the function of an infantile wish fulfillment—a vision of bliss that had to be projected into a fantasized Heaven (a way to preserve the pleasure principle) in order to repress the inevitable suffering entailed by the human condition (represented by the reality principle).[22] But in the earlier days at the beginning of these minutes, he seems to have viewed it more as a projection of parental imagoes—which might be either good *or* bad psychologically.[23] In reviewing an essay by Pfister,[24] he also suggested without apparent reproach that religion is a form of sublimation (which made the therapeutic role of the pastoral counselor easier than that of the non-religious analyst):

> Religion is the most convenient form of sublimating, easily achieved by many people. The pastor turns toward God the love that is tendered him; and this path has long since been smoothed out. With the physician, on the other hand, the patient often fails when it comes to resolving the transference, since the physician cannot offer him any substitute for it. In this context it seems plausible [to assume] that the increase in neuroses is connected with the decrease in religiosity.[25]

Even as some of Freud's ideas in *Totem and Taboo*, first published serially in *Imago* during 1912, influenced the group's discourse that year, Federn—who sometimes appears to be the strictest "Freudian" of the group even in disagreement at times with Freud himself—said,

> the religion people receive and accept as it is, *does no harm* [emphasis added]; it is those who, from the very beginning founder on the parental complex, and who must therefore recreate their religion on the basis of this complex, that do suffer severely from it.[26]

Federn, although Jewish, "was taken with the Christian ideal of charity, and was always on the verge of converting to Protestantism (as his two brothers did; his wife was a Protestant and his children were raised as such)."[27]

It was about five years into the Wednesday night gatherings that Freud began to publish writings specifically on religion, first noting similarities between religious rituals and the compulsions associated with obsessional neurosis.[28] Freud had already distinguished obsessional "psychoses" from hysteria as early as 1894 while still working with Fliess, and by 1896, Freud had made note of behavioral defenses including "penitential measures" and "burdensome ceremonials" (*"Maßregeln der Buße, lästiges Zeremoniell"*).[29] In his *Psychopathology of Everyday Life* in 1901, he noted that "a large part of the mythological view of the world which reaches far into the most modern religions, *is nothing other than psychological processes projected into the outer world.*"[30] In "Obsessive Actions and Religious Practices" (published in the first issue of a new *Zeitschrift für Religionspsychologie* in 1907), he elaborated,

> while the minutiae of religious ceremonial are full of significance and have a symbolic meaning, those of neurotics seem foolish and senseless. In this respect an obsessional neurosis presents a travesty, half comic and half tragic, of a private religion. But it is precisely this sharpest difference between neurotic and religious ceremonial which disappears when, with the help of the psycho-analytic technique of investigation, one penetrates to the true meaning of obsessive actions.[31]

Following Freud, then, many of the group, therefore, classified religion *itself* as a form of obsessional neurosis.

By 1921, Freud himself had come to recognize religion as the "most powerful protection against the danger of neurosis," but viewed it as a "crooked cure" based on an illusion.[32] Social consensus held the illusion in place and protected it. As early as 1908, Freud led one discussion beyond neurosis into the realm of psychosis and delusion:

> Paranoia can be studied very well in nonmorbid cases. The reformer, as long as he is alone, is considered a paranoiac (lately Richard Wagner). The fact that he has followers protects an individual against being declared ill. Thus, the founding of the Christian religion, for example, is a paranoia of twelve men (the vision of the resurrection, etc.). Had the religion not found so many adherents, it would certainly have been judged a morbid fantasy of a few men.[33]

It was considerably later, in 1933, that he declared outright that "[o]f the three powers which may dispute the basic position of science [i.e., art, philosophy, and religion], religion alone is to be taken seriously as an *enemy*,"[34] precisely because of its allure as a defense against neurotic guilt.

Nevertheless, religion could also be seen by the group more benignly as a protective form of sublimation—in Freud's own words, "easily achieved by many people,"[35] and even giving some advantage in resolving the transference to the pastoral counselor, as noted above. Federn repeated Freud's assertion that "the increase in neuroses is connected with the decrease in religiosity,"[36] adding that "the frequency of suicide is related to the decline in religiosity." Stekel chimed in to state that "statistics show that fewer suicides are recorded in very religious countries."[37] Some of this, the group agreed, was because of religious institutional injunctions prohibiting suicide.[38] In later discussions, however, some members posited religion as a means through which unbearable guilt and anxiety (hallmarks of neurosis) could be managed (i.e., through rituals of expiation, and also projections of redemption and heavenly reward).[39]

Guilt was a prominent, related theme. In a typical statement, "Häutler repeats that the scientific law of causality was taken over from religious life, which links guilt and punishment."[40] Based on his interest in criminology, Stekel even asserted in 1910 (on the basis of what evidence is unclear) that

> a peculiar mechanism is shown by another group of men, among whom the reaction to the criminal takes the form of a flight into piety. We know that everyone goes through a pious period; in the neurotic this does not ever come to an end. It is impossible to discover a neurotic who is really impious. Certainly, many have overcome religion intellectually, yet affectively they are still deeply rooted in faith, which is expressed in fits of superstition, spiritualism, and transcendentalism. A number of ministers, monks, and nuns have come to piety by way of criminality. It is in expiation of their own criminal fantasies that they have carried through the flight into piety.[41]

In one lengthy discussion in 1912, amid the many discussions on masturbation in the years 1911–12, Stekel reiterated that "the sense of guilt is social from the start; it refers to inhibitions that were created by higher agencies (e.g., by religion). The sense of guilt arises in those cases where children believe in God or fear him." Freud, however, replied that he himself would "not speak of religious feelings of guilt, because the sense of guilt has been proven historically to have existed at times when there was no question of religion."[42]

On a more positive note, there were occasional hints among the group that religion could be respected as a cultural product, functioning in society at least as a civilizing channel—much like art—for the sublimation of instinctual drives. As previously noted, Freud's observation in 1911 credited "old Jewish religion" with the origins of civilization "by guiding all libidinal currents into a bed of propagation."[43] Returning to the subject of moral prohibition and reward, he further elaborated the following year in a presentation "On the Two Principles of Psychic Happenings,"

> [T]he pathogenic process in the neuroses begins with the repression of unconscious fantasies. How difficult this substitution is for psychic life can be judged from the fact that the endopsychic perception of this psychic catastrophe is cast outward in the form of mythological projection and appears

as man's religious postulate of a *reward in the world to come*. At the root of this postulate lies the principle that one is compensated for a renunciation of pleasure (what "the world to come" means, if one reads back from it, is: This is how it was, once upon a time, in the unconscious psychic life.) The further developments of this myth are well known. *Religion* has made use of it for its own purposes—in order to achieve the complete renunciation of the pleasures of this world—in so far as it demands asceticism; it has not, of course, overcome the pleasure principle. Objective *science* alone succeeds in overcoming that, and even it is not altogether independent, since on the one hand it provides the pleasure of intellectual investigation and recognition, and on the other hand it contributes in the end to the improvement of our living conditions.[44]

Occasional mention was made in a more anthropological vein of prehistoric and non-western religions, usually in passing, and with the same approach as Freud's *Totem and Taboo*,[45] in which Freud sought to demonstrate the universality of the oedipal dynamic in his surmise that an actual historical act of parricide existed at the very foundations of human civilization. In this vein, Wittels asserted that primal religion had its origins in the veneration of women as bearers of children. In a paper entitled "The Natural Position of Women" he engaged in a flight of evolutionary psychological speculation on his favorite subject, women's primordial nature:

> Women may also have been the cause of primordial religion: she was venerable, originally occupied a regal position, and she feels happy in this role even today. For woman, in contrast to eternally changing man, is the most conservative creation.... Woman was the object of adoration only until property was invented. Wanting to leave his possessions to his own progeny, man locked woman in a cage of monogamy ... now she no longer needs to be beautiful, but chaste; it is no longer sufficient that she give pleasure, she must also be faithful; she now must adorn herself. The result of this state of affairs is our accursed present-day culture in which women bemoan the fact that they did not come into the world as men; they try to become men (feminist movement). People do not appreciate the perversity and senselessness of these strivings; nor do the women themselves.[46]

Freud responded that the paper "amused and stimulated him," while noting John Stuart Mill's statement regarding child rearing as an impediment to women's working for a living.[47] Adler argued most strongly against the "attitude that a woman is a possession," and envisioned a near future in which changing roles of men and women would liberate women to "take up a profession."[48] Nunberg and Federn note "how Adler's attention was attracted by the social and political aspects of the problem, whereas Freud thought of it in psychological and anthropological terms."[49] Explaining the Marxist roots of Adler's feminism, they note that such liberal ideas "were much discussed among the educated of Vienna in those days, and the members of the Wednesday circle were, of course, familiar with them."[50]

References to Christianity: Oedipus and the devil

Comments on Christianity were somewhat more uniform, mostly falling into two categories—first, oedipal and characterological interpretations of Christian beliefs and doctrine (as the group perceived them, mostly as outsiders) and second, psychosocial comments on the role of the institutional church as an enforcer of sexual repression.

Oedipal interpretations

Religious images and biblical stories were generally interpreted from early days in terms of sexual symbolism.[51] Conversely, Stekel also pronounced that "all these sexual symbols are at the same time religious symbols."[52] A more substantive connection was made repeatedly between religion in general and the oedipal struggle between sons and fathers for the mother's love, and for power.[53] For example, Sadger stated,

> Religious laws are, in the last analysis, precepts given by the father. Principle of causality: to the child, one individual is the cause of everything and everybody, and that is the father. The feeling of "harmony" appears when the child has taken on the father's role.[54]

And in a general discussion,

> [Reik] touches upon the connection between the father complex and religion, and points out that the extent to which infantile curiosity affects religious doubt, and how the latter, as well as atheism, is rooted in the father complex.... This glorification of the mother is true also of the "Madonna type" in which mother and pure virgin are combined.... Reitler finds a contradiction in the thesis that when the father's authority suffers, then "God the father" springs into action. It is the other way round: if the father's authority suffers, then the child loses his faith in God.... Luther is named as an example of the parent complex that is significant from the point of view of cultural history (pope–antichrist=devil; disbelief in the Virgin Mary).[55]

Sadger, in a 1912 armchair analysis of the poet Christian Hebbel, remarked that

> The child accepts religion because he does not exercise any criticism. He does not have to be an obsessional neurotic for this, just as he does not have to be an obsessional neurotic to identify with Christ—something that any believing Catholic can achieve.[56]

He went on to suggest what had by then become a taboo idea (for which Ferenczi was later ostracized)[57]—the issue of actual child abuse:

> The real problem with sadism was not broached: the problem of whether it originates in the fact that the child has been ill treated, or goes back to an independent *Anlage*. As an etiological factor, one often encounters an early combination of precocious sexual sensations with corporal punishment, even if it was not these persons themselves who were beaten.[58]

Freud's response to this was swift and harsh, saying that Sadger had ignored the entire psychic superstructure underlying both neurosis and character formation (i.e., the oedipal struggle).[59] In a pithy rebuttal, he stated, "Even without analysis we know that poets, like other human beings, have had parents and therefore also a parental complex."[60] Regarding religion and the unconscious, Freud delivered one of his characteristically mordant aphorisms: "What Sadger has said about religion is not valid; if religion were to be used as proof for the existence of the unconscious, animals, who work almost exclusively with the unconscious, would have to be more religious than men."[61]

Other religious motifs were brought up by the group from time to time, for example, references to biblical texts as evidence of ancient corroboration for psychoanalytic ideas about the human condition, and the interpretation of certain religious images as psychological symbols (the devil, the Virgin Mary, Heaven, and Hell, etc.). On rare occasions, these ideas became topics for an entire evening. For example, when Hugo Heller (Freud's publisher) presented a review of an 1869 book, *On the History of the Devil*,[62] he took a psycho-historical perspective—the devil as a personification of the suppressed sexual phallic drive and of cruelty, standing in contrast to the purity and goodness of the Father-God.[63] The group's oedipal line of thinking can be summed up in Stekel's pithy statement, "It is not Christianity that has burdened sexuality with the sense of guilt; it is the sense of guilt that has created Christianity. In this, the attitude toward the father must, of course, be taken into account."[64]

Sex, sin and death: the Catholic Church

The theme of sin, guilt, and oedipal struggle often led the group into a discussion of the repressive teachings of Christianity, connecting sexuality with sin and death. Baron Winterstein, a philosopher by training, presented a paper in 1911, "On the Feeling of Guilt." As reported in the minutes,

> [The] inner feeling of guilt comes to be materialized in the concept of God; with this as a start, Baron Winterstein tries to develop an understanding of certain phenomena of religious thinking, especially of the Christian religion, by showing how some of the concepts can be explained as projections of mental facts (need for expiation, omniscience, omnipotence of God.)

Thus, the feeling of guilt is preserved in the concept of Original Sin; the deed itself, however, no longer belongs to the realm of consciousness. One could term this tendency toward unburdening oneself of one's own responsibility "historical retrojection." It is supplemented by the doctrine of justification and redemption. In the Virgin Mary as mother, we see the wish of every child to dissociate his own mother from things sexual.

Traits similar to those of Jesus can be shown to be present, in a certain sense, in Otto Weininger,[65] in whom the feeling of guilt played an enormous role. What we feel as guilt is our instinctual life, the unconscious. Both faith and superstition arise out of the same psychic disposition; faith is an advanced, sublimated safeguarding measure that has been adopted by the subject, whereas in superstition even more fear is comprised. Both are reactions to the neurotic uncertainty about whether or not one has committed a sin.

The speaker concludes with the suggestion that we have to overcome the mass neurosis of the Christian church, too, for there is still far too much feeling of guilt and fear in men.[66]

Stekel, in a discussion about anxiety resulting from masturbation, remarked, "[T]he feeling of guilt seems to be more severe in Catholic children, because they are taught the concept of sin at an early age."[67] Freud's own comment about Catholicism was,

[Wittels'] case ... shows distinctly in what way religious instruction acts upon the lives of Catholic children. How many a germ of psychosis enters the child's brain along this path! The Christ-fantasy that is clearly present in this case also goes back to that. It is this that gives the attack its character of ecstasy.[68]

There was a fairly lengthy general discussion in 1908 about the harm caused by the (Catholic) Church's teachings to children concerning sin and confession:

For most children communion constitutes a very severe trauma. It is unbelievable to what traumata seven-year-olds are thereby exposed. Hitschmann can confirm this: he mentions an obsessional neurotic who had spent her childhood in a convent boarding school where she had to go to confession every week, but had to bathe only once a year; sexual dreams were also regarded as a sin there. She had the fantasy that the Host would be put not into her mouth, but into her vagina.... Tausk, too, knows a woman suffering from an obsessional neurosis whose actual content was communion and confession; behind these, however, stood father and mother—Christ and the Church.[69]

Christianity was also frequently characterized by the group as masochistic. Earlier, in 1908, Rank had asserted in a critique of a paper by Wittels (on

venereal disease) that "the masochistic character of the whole Christian movement, particularly in its beginning, should have been stressed."[70] A year later,
Wittels himself stated, "The fact that the state does not interfere with masochism
may have as its reason the fundamentally masochistic character of Christianity."[71] In 1911 Reik also stated,

> The reaction against the joy of life in antiquity, a reaction that reached its
> culmination in Christianity, conceives of all worldly pleasure as sin, and St.
> Augustine designates death as the punishment for original sin. Thereby the
> ideational connection [between death and sexuality] becomes very much
> apparent.[72]

A somewhat more positive evaluation of Christianity's role in socialization
vis-à-vis sexuality—although still understood as repressive—was also made by
the group, mainly with regard to the early development of Christianity in antiquity. In 1911 Federn declared,

> Christianity was a reaction against the enormous exaggeration of sexuality
> (orgies) at the end of antiquity, a reaction that was necessary for the preser-
> vation of mankind. Christianity's psychological mistake lies, as Nietzsche
> and Freud have shown, only in its failure to recognize the fact that no sup-
> pression can be completely successful, and that in the case of a strong
> instinct it has to lead to just such excesses in fantasy as the original
> unbridled instinct did.[73]

This was echoed in Freud's published statement one year later,

> that the ascetic current in Christianity created psychical values for love
> which pagan antiquity was never able to confer on it. This current assumed
> its greatest importance with the ascetic monks, whose lives were almost
> entirely occupied with the struggle against libidinal temptation.[74]

Freud (apparently without irony) also observed that the Reformation once again
saved western civilization from sexual dissipation: "[T]he Catholic Church was
at the brink of dissolution at the time of the Renaissance; it was saved by two
factors: syphilis and Luther."[75]

Finally, regarding the group's attitudes toward Christianity in general, Furtmüller offered a caveat against simplistic interpretations. Objecting to elements
of over-generalization in Winterstein's presentation quoted above, he said:

> With regard to religious ideas, too, the result would have been richer and
> more firmly established had the speaker not worked with such terse, concen-
> trated concepts. *Nor can the concept of the Christian religion be grasped in
> such a simple way* [emphasis added].[76]

Religion in the clinical case material

In addition to abstract theoretical discussions of religion and religious phenomena, the members of the Society periodically made reference to religious practices and beliefs that appeared in some of their case histories. Adler's early case of the Jewish patient who suffered from obsessional symptoms regarding waters and counting (see Chapter 1) is one such example.[77] In 1908, Freud discussed a case of psychosis published by the Viennese-American analyst A. A. Brill while Brill was studying in Zürich. The patient saw himself as a "free-thinker and a friend of the Jews," but his father was "tyrannical, bigoted, and anti-Semitic."[78] The patient had been to Pennsylvania for a visit, and upon returning, had turned to mysticism in a revolt against the father—who had become "God the Father." Freud praised Brill for his deft interpretation of a number of religious and mythological symbols (such as the Egyptian gods Isis and Osiris, and the saintly "pure fool" Parsifal) as disguises for the patient's wishes in his everyday life.[79] Jung's influence on Brill's analysis is apparent; Freud, still nurturing his hopes for Jung, did not object.

Early in 1909, Stekel described a "saintly" rabbi would lose his voice whenever the word "Jehovah" was to be spoken, due to unconscious associations between the letters for the name of God in a book belonging to his father and his "voluptuous" sexual fantasies.[80] That fall, Freud mentioned a "Christ fantasy" in a psychotic individual as an example of how Catholic religious instruction could introduce "a germ of psychosis [into] the child's brain"[81] (possibly referring to the Schreber case, which preoccupied him the following summer).[82] In October 1910, Reitler suggested that "only children" (from a "single-child marriage"), as well as first-born children, "ought to be particularly prone to becoming the 'savior type' described by Freud."[83]

The same year, Hitschmann presented two cases of obsessional prayer rituals. The first involved a man who prayed compulsively to keep his father alive, and to protect himself from the danger of compulsive masturbation. Hitschmann described the man's love for his father as "excessive" and "grotesque," and the resolution of this and other similar cases of obsessional neurosis revolved around uncovering the oedipal wish for his father actually to die.[84]

Hitschmann's second case involved a ten-year-old girl who exhibited signs of a split in her personality between childlike cheerfulness and brooding obsessional neurosis. In her history was a beating "for stubbornness" at the age of five, and a pattern of sleeping with her mother in the parents' bed. She developed a number of compulsive rituals, shortness of breath, and preoccupation with death. Eventually, when saying her bedtime prayers,

> she was suddenly overcome by anxiety, began to scream, continually repeated the prayer for hours on end and could be calmed down only with difficulty. She states the following: When I am praying and thinking of Father, then something like a black veil comes over me, and I am afraid that

I must die. Then at another time she does not believe that she has to die. She never repeats her prayer without thinking of her father.[85]

In both cases, Hitschmann argued that preoccupation with death—both one's own and that of a supposedly beloved father—actually stemmed from a death wish toward the father and the desire to possess the mother for him/herself.[86] Hitschmann clearly supported the idea of a neurotic symptom as compromise formation between denial and gratification: the torment of the symptoms provided the punishment for the unbidden wishes—in these cases religiously infused punishment—while a masturbatory element in every case simultaneously provided a forbidden pleasure. Stekel praised Hitschmann for demonstrating "the importance of the religious factor for the exploration of neuroses, and, secondly, that all obsessional fears are linked with the 'death clause'."[87] In a remark aimed more at Stekel than Hitschmann, Freud thought this too obvious "to enrich us with any new insight; we already know that religion is the universal obsessional neurosis."[88]

References to Judaism and Jews as a group: oppression and obsession

With the exception of some clinical case material, Judaism and Jewishness were mentioned much less often than Christianity or religion in general (which often were conflated). The idea of an inverse proportion of religiosity and neurosis did not seem to hold true for the group when it came to discussing Jews. Many of the group seemed to accept uncritically the then common antisemitic stereotype of Jews as more prone to neurosis—both sexual and obsessional—an assumption going back in Freud's own training to Charcot.[89] When Max Eitingon asked "whether it is quite necessary to assume a predisposition.... Whether the frequency of [obsessional] neurosis is greater among Jews?"[90] Rank noted, "Most participants answered 'yes' to this question."[91] Sadger cited numerous cases of obsessional neurosis among the Polish Jews, and later again stated, "The Jew's disposition to obsessional neurosis may be related to his addiction to rumination [Grübelsucht]."[92]

Drawing on Freud's connection between the castration complex and circumcision, Wittels stated,

> Mockery seems to be linked with physical deformity, and in that way to be suitable as a special domain of the Jews, in accordance with a remark Freud made in the analysis of the phobia of a five year old boy [Max Graf's son, "Little Hans"].[93]

Federn also mused,

> A strong father-complex alone is not sufficient to explain the disposition of Jews toward neurosis, because among the [Gentile] peasants, too, the father

complex is usually pronounced, and yet it is only comparatively rarely that they fall ill with a neurosis.[94]

Stereotypical characterizations of Jews as greedy and money-hungry, embedded in European culture since the middle ages, were also expressed without much critique. For example, in 1911,

> Dr. Hilferding relates a passage from Werner Sombart's book on Judaism, *The Jews and the Economy*, in which, referring to Freud's doctrine, Sombart asserts that in the sexual life of the Jews a displacement has occurred of sexuality onto money-making as a social activity.[95]

A general discussion of Jewish sexual repression and neurosis ensued. Occasional objections were lodged against such over-characterizations, but these were often followed by other generalizations: "Federn believes that the Jews were not originally ascetics, but became so only to the same extent as they became Christianized. Sombart's wrong premise demonstrates how correct Freud was when he derived the money-making complex from anal eroticism."[96]

The by-then generally accepted "scientific" assumption that Jews constituted a race also found its way into the group's discourse. For example, Sadger pronounced that "[i]n certain races (Russian and Polish Jews) almost every man is hysterical."[97] The group voted in 1908 to purchase a subscription to *Archiv für Rassenbiologie*,[98] a journal devoted to the study of "racial biology." Notably, Freud had carefully read the neurologist Leopold Löwenfeld's 1894 textbook, in which Löwenfeld (an early supporter of Freud) rebutted a racial explanation for the apparent prevalence of neurasthenia among the Jews in favor of a socio-economic interpretation: "physical poverty ... moral pressure ... early marriage, and the great number of children.... Historically, there is no trace of such a predisposition to be shown."[99] Perhaps in line with this objection, Federn also stated, "Neuroses ... are more frequent among Jews because the preconditions for it are found more frequently in that group."[100] Yet Freud himself is not recorded as interrupting pathologizing generalizations during the Wednesday night meetings. The predisposition of Jews to mental illness was understood as a scientific fact at the time based on supposedly scientific racial taxonomies, as described in detail by Gilman.[101] It is striking, then, but not surprising given the prevailing professional consensus on race characterization, that negative stereotypes filtered so easily into the group's discourse—even as Ostow suggests, unconsciously in the form of internalized racism.[102]

Assimilation—and internalized antisemitism?

Was this internalized antisemitism? There was certainly more complexity to the analysts' self-understanding as Jews than their sometimes offhand anti-Jewish comments suggest. The phenomenon of Jewish *Selbsthass* ("self-hatred") was already known in Jewish circles in the early twentieth century well before Theodor Lessing popularized the term.[103]

It is important not to over-generalize about this or any other aspect of the complex, multiple identifications, allegiances, and aspirations that characterized the Jewish analysts of Vienna—nor to assume their views were entirely uniform. As analyst and historian Thomas Kohut stated in an interview about his father Heinz Kohut, an émigré from Vienna, much younger than Freud, and the later founder of Self Psychology in Chicago, "Heinz Kohut was deeply and pro-foundly Viennese.... My father did not identify as a Jew. If there was any God in our house, it was Goethe."[104] Thomas Kohut refuted the suggestion that his father intentionally lied about his Jewish background:

> The accusation that my father was lying, or being deliberately misleading about who he was represents a failure to understand what it meant to be Jewish in Vienna in the decades before the Nazi Anschluss, or to appreciate the deep psychological wounds inflicted by anti-Semitic persecution and flight. Indeed, those who insist that people who are "racially Jewish" must either identify themselves as Jewish or be dismissed as "self denying" or "self hating" Jews are essentializing Jewishness in profoundly troubling, indeed racial, ways.[105]

Often, however, the group's characterizations of Jews referred in particular to eastern European Jews, as if they were an entirely different ethnic group. Even allowing for some irony that may have escaped translation into the professional minutes of the meetings, however—occasional knowing nods or raised eyebrows indicating some sense of recognition among themselves—the Viennese circle was vigorously jumping on the bandwagon to essentialize those other Jews as "Other." Sadger commented, for example, "that he had the opportunity of observing numerous obsessional neuroses—impotency, onanism—among the Polish Jews."[106]

One explanation of the tendency of the analysts to speak in derogatory terms about "Jews" was in an effort to dis-identify themselves with their own roots among the *Ostjuden*—poor immigrants who were still very visible on the streets of Vienna, and a frequent subject of ridicule in "cultured" Viennese circles. As Gay noted in *Freud, Jews, and Other Germans*, an element of anxious disdain allowed German Jews to differentiate themselves from the *Ostjuden* by way of demeaning jokes and snide characterizations:

> Like other feelings, hatred is over-determined; it has more sources than the hater himself knows.... [H]e might single out for special vituperation those whom he uncomfortably, perhaps unconsciously, identified as his own kind.... Whatever the proper moral response to such opinions, the term *Selbsthass* in no way encompasses their meaning. There is social snobbery in its disclaim-ers and generalizations, there is a measure of German chauvinism in them;

there is even, however misguided, something of a didactic intention: to pillory the noisy, the vulgar, the sharp dealers might purify the behavior of other Jews and thus undermine the case for anti-Semitism. But the element that came to dominate, by the 1920s, this Jewish embarrassment at the spectacle of other Jews was a renewed fear. For centuries Jews had learned to be inconspicuous.... The old fear returned, but under new conditions and hence under incomprehensible guises. The long ascent of Jewish integration into German culture was, if not exactly over, certainly imperiled.[107]

This repudiation of the uncouth ghetto Jew was borne of the analysts' desire to assimilate into a pan-German Austrian cultural elite. Sociologist Steven Beller writes,

It proved almost impossible for Jews who had once been in love with Germany ever to break the spell completely. Even Freud, who recognized early on the dangers of German nationalism, could not totally destroy the love of things German which he had acquired as a student nationalist. The irony of the situation was that by the early twentieth century German high culture was strongly Jewish.... [T]his was especially true in Vienna and it was resentfully recognized by the non-Jewish population.[108]

Almost all of the earliest analysts—like Freud himself, whose parents moved to Vienna in 1860 from Freiberg, Moravia[109]—were sons or grandsons of Jewish immigrants who had sacrificed much to resettle in Vienna from other territories of the Habsburg Empire in eastern Europe. About half had started as tradesmen in the 2nd district of Vienna—historically the Jewish ghetto since the reign of the Emperor Leopold for whom the district is still named (Leopoldstadt). Still others' fathers had already established themselves as doctors, lawyers, and bankers. Hitschmann, for example, had a grandfather who was a medical doctor, a father who was a banker and accountant, and two brothers in banking and the legal profession, respectively.[110] The most affluent among them, the Baron von Winterstein, was the son of a titled privy councillor and vice-governor of the Austro-Hungarian Bank.[111]

Eventually, as many as one-third of the members of the Vienna Society came from homes with fathers that had already achieved assimilation into academic and professional careers.[112] Regardless of their own economic status, however, the analysts' fathers sent their sons to the best *Gymnasien* (rigorously academic high schools),[113] in the hopes that the boys would matriculate at the university, and via intellectual mastery of the professions would be admitted—or follow them—into the professions. Freud's move across the Danube Canal from the 2nd district to the ninth is a physical embodiment of this move up from the narrow streets of the still Yiddish-speaking, religiously Orthodox *Ostjuden* from whom most professional-class Jews in Vienna preferred to distinguish themselves.

By the late 1890s, with the accession of the Austrian nationalist, pro-Catholic Christian Social Party, and in 1897 the election of the antisemitic mayor, Karl Lueger, the dream of Jewish assimilation began to crumble (see Chapter 7).[114] Emperor Franz Josef I had overturned Lueger's election as mayor of the city four times between 1895 and 1897, but finally bowed to the will of the electorate—and Pope Leo XIII—and confirmed Lueger's election in 1897.[115] After this turn of events, feeling betrayed by the liberal Christian electorate comprised mostly of civil servants, the Jewish intelligentsia were deeply disillusioned.[116] Many, as historian Carl Schorske noted, turned toward art,[117] and some joined the literary *"enragés"* writing critical *fueilletons* (the op-ed pieces of the day).[118]

Rose describes the disillusionment of the Vienna analysts following the reactionary withdrawal of nineteenth-century reforms under Franz Josef:

> The anger of future psychoanalysts can be traced to the impact on them of political and social changes in late nineteenth-century Austria. The Austrian Constitution of 1867 had offered support and protection to the middle class, especially its Jewish members, and had furthered the Liberal agenda for political and cultural reform. Constitutional guarantees of individual rights, together with steps toward greater secularization of education and the appointment of a Liberal ministry, promised conditions for complete freedom of conscience, an opportunity of unusual significance in clerical and aristocratic Austria. Forces of reaction, however, suppressed that promise, and in the aftermath members of the middle class quietly abandoned faith in it. Instead, they pursued cultural assimilation with the Catholic aristocracy.[119]

At the same time, the psychoanalysts mostly rejected conversion as a means to social acceptance. Wittels, in his 1904 pamphlet *Der Taufjude* ("The Baptized Jew"), expressed scathing contempt for those who converted for the sake of "social ambition" (*Strebertum*). He saw such compromise as a breach of integrity and an act of moral perjury.[120] Freud himself urged Max Graf not to baptize his son ("Little Hans"). In Graf's words,

> On the occasion of some of his visits the conversation would touch upon the Jewish question. Freud was proud to belong to the Jewish people which gave the Bible to the world. When my son was born, I wondered whether I should not remove him from the prevailing anti-Semitic hatred, which at that time was preached in Vienna by a very popular man, Doctor Lueger. I was not certain whether it would not be better to have my son brought up in the Christian faith. Freud advised me not to do this. "If you do not let your son grow up as a Jew," he said, "you will deprive him of those sources of energy which cannot be replaced by anything else. He will have to struggle as a Jew, and you ought to develop in him all the energy he will need for that struggle. Do not deprive him of that advantage."[121]

Nor did Freud's views against conversion ever change, except to increase in vehemence against all religious adherence: Two years after Hitler's accession to power in Germany, Freud told his American patient Joseph Wortis that Jewish conversion to Christianity was

> essentially dishonest, and the Christian religion is every bit as bad as the Jewish. Jew and Christian ought to meet on the common ground of irreligion and humanity. Jews who are ashamed of their Jewishness have simply reacted to the mass suggestion of their society.[122]

Soon after Hitler's annexation of Austria (the *Anschluss*) in 1938, of course, conversion to Christianity offered no protection, since Jews were scientifically classified as an inferior race, not a religion.

Antisemitism—omission or deletion?

With the exception of a few comments on clinical cases of patients who were disturbed in some way about antisemitism, the group remained silent on the topic—or at least nothing of the kind was recorded in the minutes. Psychoanalysis of course involves paying attention to gaps and omissions as well as what is said. It would be hubris to assume that one can know with certainty what the gaps mean, without exploring them with the speaker—and even then, there are no certain, final meanings. In the case of the Wednesday Night Psychological Society, we can only speculate, based on other sources, what such a gap might mean, when clearly this was a topic that affected them all so personally as well as professionally.

First, we must ask whether the minutes are an accurate record on this subject. Did the group in fact speak of antisemitism, and did Rank as secretary edit such comments out? This is entirely possible, especially at the level of brief, offhand comments. We know, for example, as noted above, that Freud discussed "the Jewish question" with the Grafs.[123] The minutes were a professional record of a scientific meeting, and personal asides would not be considered appropriate. Brief, seemingly throwaway comments were recorded on all manner of other topics—but upon examination, these always had to do with some theoretical point, however speculative. Speculation was welcome (to a point). Even quite intimate personal self-disclosure, for example about matters of sexual fantasy and neurosis, was tolerated if not always encouraged. Yet every discussion had a theoretical or diagnostic focus, or both. Antisemitism simply was not admitted as a subject for diagnosis. Why not? As Ernst Federn proudly noted in his introduction to the minutes, no topic was out of bounds.[124] Yet antisemitism, apparently, was.

One reason might be that it fell into the realm of contemporary political life. It is well known that Freud did not like political discussions. Although the group did occasionally discuss Judaism, their approach was either historical and/or anthropological, or diagnostic in terms of oedipal dynamics. For Freud and his followers, contemporary persecution of Jews seemed to pertain to politics, not science. Adler's insistence on bringing a socialist perspective into psycho-analysis itself, investigating the role of power and powerlessness both in the individual psyche and in society, was precisely what brought about his eventual rift with Freud and his expulsion from the group. While many of the Society's members were liberal in their private political outlook, members who looked and acted too much the part of the leftist Jew could not be tolerated.

Given the prevailing level of discrimination, and what the early analysts had endured to reach their current professional positions as physicians, lawyers, philosophers, and writers, there was also likely a strong sense that to speak about antisemitism—even among themselves—was dangerous. Assimilation required accommodation and adaptation.[125] To the extent that they identified as German intellectuals, to admit to themselves, much less to bring into professional con-versation the very fact of antisemitism, would have broken through some of their carefully tended façades as cultured persons who had escaped the ghetto. Such conversation, even if possible, would never have been considered appropriate for professional minutes, although these only circulated among the membership.

Nor was *being* Jewish a topic for publication, with Freud himself being the major exception to the rule.[126] Notably, it was Freud who published the most comments about antisemitism, some quite early—albeit in footnotes. As noted above, he speculated early on that antisemitism had its origins in the fear of cas-tration, related to the practice of circumcision, noting this as a cause of persecu-tion common to both Jews and women.[127] This was an idea he retained to the end of his life.[128]

In his last major work, *Moses and Monotheism*, Freud finally published his thoughts on the psychological dynamics of antisemitism in some detail. With the *Anschluss* a fact, and writing from exile, he gave voice to convictions (however much we might disagree with them today) that echo themes from his *Totem and Taboo* years before, and that were doubtless in his mind for many decades:

> The poor Jewish people, who with their habitual stubbornness continued to disavow the father's murder, atoned heavily for it in the course of time. They were constantly met with the reproach "You killed our God!" And this reproach is true, if it is correctly translated.[129]

This, he explained, refers to the primal horde's murder of the father, described in *Totem and Taboo* years earlier—although in that work he barely referred to Judaism per se.[130] He thought the Christians had it only half right—humans killed their first God, and had been making up religions to atone for it ever since. But the murder of Christ was only a late re-enactment.

He went on in a more sociological vein to comment how "A phenomenon of such intensity and permanence as the people's hatred of the Jews must of course have more than one ground," and that one factor was Jews' different ethnic origins and their scapegoated existence over many centuries as an embedded minority culture. What was to account, however, for the hatred of Jews and not other ethnic minorities? He proposed that there was another reason that

> has a still greater effect: namely, that they defy all oppression, that the most cruel persecutions have not succeeded in exterminating them, and, indeed, that on the contrary they show a capacity for holding their own in commercial life and, where they are admitted, for making valuable contributions to every form of cultural activity.[131]

Thus *envy*, not merely difference, was also fuel for antisemitism. Returning to his primeval religious theory, but following the train of association from envy, he concluded that the deepest jealousy was toward the Jews' identity as the Chosen People of God. Invoking both envy and castration (again), he wrote,

> The deeper motives for hatred of the Jews are rooted in the remotest past ages; they operate from the unconscious of the peoples, and I am prepared to find that at first they will not seem credible. I venture to assert that jealousy of the people which declared itself the first-born, favourite child of God the Father, has not yet been surmounted among other peoples even to-day: it is as though they had thought there was truth in the claim. Further, among the customs by which the Jews made themselves separate, that of circumcision has made a disagreeable, uncanny impression, which is to be explained, no doubt, by its recalling the dreaded castration and along with it a portion of the primaeval past which is gladly forgotten. And finally, as the latest motive in this series, we must not forget that all those peoples who excel to-day in their hatred of Jews became Christians only in late historic times, often driven to it by bloody coercion. It might be said that they are all "mis-baptized." They have been left, under a thin veneer of Christianity, what their ancestors were, who worshipped a barbarous polytheism. They have not got over a grudge against the new religion which was imposed on them; but they have displaced the grudge on to the source from which Christianity reached them. The fact that the Gospels tell a story which is set among Jews, and in fact deals only with Jews, has made this displacement easy for them. Their hatred of Jews is at bottom a hatred of Christians, and we need not be surprised that in the German National-Socialist revolution this intimate relation between the two monotheist religions finds such a clear expression in the hostile treatment of both of them.[132]

One of Freud's very last writings was "A Comment on Anti-Semitism," published posthumously in a newspaper for German émigrés in Paris. In it, he praised a Gentile author, Count Coudenhove-Kalergi, for his book *Das Wesen des Antisemitismus* ("The Essence of Antisemitism"), reprinted in 1929 by the count's son. Freud paraphrased from memory:

[T]he truth is that for long centuries we [non-Jews] have treated the Jewish people unjustly and that we are continuing to do so by judging them unjustly. Any one of us who does not start by admitting our guilt has not done his duty in this.... So let us cease at last to hand them out [mere] favours when they have a claim to *justice* [emphasis added].[133]

Freud concluded tersely, "has the work of the two Coudenhoves had no influence on our contemporaries?"[134]

Jewish identity

It is all the more important, then, in light of the political context, that as the founder of psychoanalysis Freud continually proclaimed his identity as a Jew, separating this from his vehement religious stance as an atheist. As early as 1908, Freud told the group, "we are far too little aware of the difference that exists between our emotional life and that of a Christian."[135] After the painful split with Jung, he asserted this difference even more starkly in a letter to Spielrein:

I am, as you know, cured of the last shred of my predilection for the Aryan cause, and would like to take it that if [your] child turns out to be a boy he will develop into a stalwart Zionist.... We are and remain Jews. The others will only exploit us and will never understand or appreciate us.[136]

Both of these comments are consistent with Freud's statement made much later, in a 1926 presentation to the B'nai Brith lodge—a Jewish fraternal society that Freud attended regularly from 1897 to 1907: "That you were Jews could only be agreeable to me; for I was myself a Jew, and it had always seemed to me not only unworthy but positively senseless to deny the fact."[137] In 1927 he said in an interview, "My language is German. My culture, my attainments are German. I considered myself German intellectually, until I noticed the growth of anti-Semitic prejudice in Germany and German Austria. Since that time, I prefer to call myself a Jew."[138]

Scholars have debated whether psychoanalysis was distinctively Jewish in origin,[139] or could have arisen elsewhere than among the Jewish intelligentsia of fin-de-siècle Vienna. Certainly some of the components of Freud's theory pre-existed his "discovery" of the unconscious (*das Unbewusste*), albeit with varying definitions (e.g., in the philosophical writings of Franz Brentano)[140] whom Freud admired greatly while in *Gymnasium* (briefly flirting with conversion to Catholicism, or at least some form of theism, at the time).[141] But as Freud matured, he differentiated himself from the "Christian views" of the Viennese medical establishment.[142]

Freud's vehemence in rejecting religion, especially Christianity, has been occasionally queried by some as just the kind of defensive fervor that analytically signals its opposite in the unconscious realm.[143] Given their milieu of pervasive societal antisemitism, however, it is difficult to assign repressed or ulterior motives to Freud's and his followers' suspicions toward Christianity, particularly oppressive Catholicism.

Freud clearly believed it was no accident that the majority of his circle of analysts were Jewish by heritage. While he thought science in general was blind to so-called "Aryan" or Jewish differences, he did share the then-conventional view of Jews as a distinct race with distinctive characteristics that enabled them to embrace the radicalism of psychoanalytic theory. Among these traits, he thought, were a long history of valuing intellectual work, the capacity to work from a position of marginalization (so that it was easier as social outcasts to also be intellectual outcasts), a rejection of mysticism in favor of abstraction (as in the refusal to depict G-d in images), and an emphasis on the ethical life.[144]

Just as "religion" itself was never explicitly defined by the group, when speaking about Judaism—or perhaps more accurately, Jewishness—the group seems always to have assumed (as mostly insiders) that they knew what they meant by "Jew" and "Jewish." As Eliza Slavet points out, the word *Judentum* in German encompasses more than the English word "Judaism," which mainly refers to the Jewish religion. *Judentum* incorporates religion, tradition, and ethnic heritage all in one term.[145] Even as Freud himself steadfastly proclaimed his Jewish identity, it was something that could not be precisely pinned down—an "essence" (*Hauptsache*) as he put it,[146] inherited as a memory of ancient ancestors, historically created, reshaped, and handed down over the centuries. It was genetic in the Lamarckian sense, not (as Lamarck could be read[147]) the antisemitic designation of an inferior race, but a heritage of deeds and kinship, violence and expiation[148]—repressed, remembered, re-repressed, and re-formed over the generations, creating over time a distinctive blend of characteristics, cultural practices, and sense of clan.

As Gay, Slavet, Sander Gilman, and others have pointed out, Freud maintained his Lamarckian version of evolution throughout his life, believing in the heritability of traits acquired through historical experiences. He was convinced that Jews, as a race, had inherited many characteristics through supposed experiences of prehistoric parricide and expiation, and many subsequent centuries of persecution.[149] Beller notes that Lamarckism was not an uncommon idea among Jewish intellectuals *c.*1900, because a "theory of the inheritance of acquired characteristics offered the prospect, among humans, that the Jewish race would one day become just like the German, that it would change for the better."[150] Many Jewish progressives would have diluted Jewish identity into extinction, but Freud himself resisted this. He wrote,

> Above all, I found that I was expected to feel myself inferior and an alien because I was a Jew. I refused absolutely to do the first of these things. I have never been able to see why I should feel ashamed of my descent or, as people were beginning to say, of my "race."[151]

This begs the question of what it actually meant to be a Jew in fin-de-siècle Vienna, in a context of mass assimilation and, to a lesser degree, conversion to Christianity, which was a requirement for holding any official clerical or teaching position. To complicate matters further, Jews themselves differed on such matters then as now. This also includes debates within historiography, as Geller points out: "How one translates *Judentum* into English betrays one's agenda."[152] Even to reduce the complexity to a division between the *Ostjuden* and the German-identified Jewish bourgeoisie is to overlook the great variety of attitudes and aspirations among Jews in any century.[153] Beller writes,

> Indeed *any* system which starts with the premise that there is one Jewish mind, which can explain all manifestations of the Jews in western culture, will fall down in the face of the huge variety of Jewish experience. If put in this way, it could be said that *the* Jewish mind does not exist, that it is a myth.[154]

The early psychoanalysts, predominantly atheists or agnostics, followed Freud in rejecting orthodox religious belief while maintaining their sense of Jewish heritage. At the same time, bourgeois Jews mostly lived and socialized in the same few neighborhoods, both because they were for the most part shunned socially by Gentiles of the same class, and because they sought the ease of a common background and cultural perspective. Martin Freud noted that there were almost daily visitors in the Freud household, "most of them Jewish and members of the upper middle classes."[155] In identifying the various players in Freud's dream of Irma's injection,[156] Marthe Robert shows the deep personal and professional entanglements among Freud's household, his Viennese colleagues, his patients, and their families.[157] This web of relationships is only one example of the many intersecting ties, both familial and professional, that held the bourgeois Jewish society together in the 9th district, which Freud and his family inhabited. It was a maze of affiliations.

While these professionally accomplished Jews adhered to an ethnic or even racial identification with *Judentum*, they failed to envisage the most extreme potential for violence in such racializing taxonomies. Relatively few Jews, in general (even those who had converted to Christianity out of expediency), and none of the analysts in particular, sought to forswear their Jewish heritage. There were positive as well as negative aspects to this sense of Jewish identity, including cultural pride and ethnic solidarity, which at its height helped to constitute the Zionist movement.[158]

There were personal antecedents to Freud's own defiant, non-pacifist assertion of his Jewishness, including his recollection of his father Jakob's "unheroic conduct" when Sigmund was about twelve years old: Jakob recounted how a Christian had knocked off his new fur cap, likely the fur-trimmed dress *Streiml* of the Hasidim.[159] Rather than fight back, Jakob simply "went into the roadway and picked up [his] cap."[160] Freud's youthful identification with the Semitic hero Hannibal, and later with Moses, was of a piece with his determination to resist antisemitic discrimination. But beyond any personal or historical events, by age seventy, Freud also saw Jewish identity as something ineffable, which had made for him

> the attraction of Jewry and Jews irresistible—many obscure [or "dark"] emotional forces [*dunkle Gefühlsmächte*] which were the more powerful the less they could be expressed in words, as well as a clear consciousness of inner identity, the safe privacy of a common mental construction.[161]

The B'nai Brith *in Vienna and the first analysts*

The bonds of Jewish pride led to another significant tie among many of the members of the wider Viennese psychoanalytic circle, the *B'nai Brith* ("Sons of the Covenant")—part of an international network of lodges begun in New York in 1843 and established in Vienna in 1895 in direct response to the rise to power of the Christian Socials.[162] Its mission—the promotion of equal rights for Jews, and an Enlightenment vision of unity and "brotherhood among men"—was humanitarian and idealistic, not religious.[163] Invited to join by fellow physician Edmund Kohn, among others, Freud became a member of the "Wien" branch in September, 1897, shortly after Lueger's confirmation as mayor, and attended almost every week throughout the following decade.[164]

The year 1897 is a well-known marker in Freud's autobiography, as he publicly disclosed in *The Interpretation of Dreams*.[165] It was the year his father died, and he subsequently began his self-analysis. But the direct connection to political events and the rise of an explicitly antisemitic government in Vienna is often not noticed in accounts of Freud's intellectual biography. In his analysis of a dream about Rome, he wrote,

> The Jewish problem is concern about the future of one's own children, to whom one cannot give a country of their own, concern about educating them in such a way that they can move freely across frontiers. "By the waters of Babylon we sat down and wept."[166]

Freud had already resigned from the Society of Physicians in 1887, citing their inflexible "Christian views,"[167] and ceased lecturing at the university between 1898 and 1903 in protest against the institution's antisemitic policies.[168] It was in the years 1895–96 that Freud turned away from the "seduction theory" of hysterical neurosis, perhaps (at least in part) not just because he was unwilling to believe the pervasiveness of sexual abuse among good bourgeois Viennese fathers and uncles in general,[169] but because he was unwilling to believe—or to air publicly—this truth about *Jewish* fathers and uncles, thereby giving ammunition to the antisemites.[170]

It was also in 1897 that Hermann Nothnagel nominated Freud for promotion, with no immediate success. Over half the teaching faculty in medicine in 1910 were of Jewish descent; yet as Freud well knew, to achieve promotion to full-time status, conversion was required.[171] As noted at the beginning of this chapter, his own promotion from *Privatdozent* ("tutor," the lowest rung of unpaid lecturer) to *ausserordentliche Professor* ("extraordinary professor"—a more prestigious titled adjunct position, though still unpaid) was long delayed while many Gentiles leapfrogged over him.[172] Through his self-analysis during this time, Freud overcame his virtually phobic love-hate fantasy about Rome as the seat of Catholicism, and after traveling there (identifying with his hero Hannibal's siege of the city), he returned with a new determination to work the system. He finally made the necessary connections, setting in motion the process of *Protektion* to achieve his promotion in 1902, where merit alone had not succeeded.[173]

In 1897 Freud also enlisted several close friends into the circle of the Vienna B'nai Brith, who would eventually join the Wednesday Night Psychological Society, including Hitschmann and Oskar Rie.[174] His first public lectures on his work-in-progress on dream interpretation were given to the brotherhood that same year, and to another Jewish society, the *Jüdische akademische Lesehalle*. Freud presented twenty lectures in all to the B'nai Brith over two decades (1897–1917).[175] He had become vehemently and publicly Jewish. Truly, as Freud told the B'nai Brith many years later, they were his first intellectual supporters:

> Because I was a Jew I found myself free from many prejudices which restricted others in the use of their intellect; and as a Jew I was prepared to join the Opposition and to do without agreement with the "compact majority." So it was that I became one of you, took my share in your humanitarian and national interests, gained friends among you and persuaded my own few remaining friends to join our society. There was no question whatever of my convincing you of my new theories; but at a time when no one in Europe listened to me and I still had no disciples even in Vienna, you gave me your kindly attention. You were my first audience.[176]

The B'nai Brith was in many ways, then, the direct forerunner of the Wednesday Night Psychological Society[177]—an oasis of safety and a haven for free intellectual exploration with a passion for social justice and humanitarian reform, free from the surrounding antisemitic climate.

Conclusion

The foregoing exploration of the early analysts' attitudes toward religion demonstrate that there was, indeed, considerable variety and complexity in their thinking about religious themes. As early as Freud's famous visit to America with Rank and Ferenczi, the eminent American Harvard psychologist William James, author of *The Varieties of Religious Experience*,[178] had questioned "the Freudians' programmatic, obsessive hostility to religion."[179] But as described above, that hostility was not monolithic, nor can it be understood apart from the oppressive

Catholic hegemony over Viennese cultural life. The diversity of their interests within the wide umbrella of religion as a topic of research, and even their own personal attitudes toward religious affiliation, demonstrates the elasticity of Freud's expectations of conformity. Clashes, as seen in the previous chapter, were "over-determined" not only by threats to the central tenets of psycho-analytic theory, but also by the clashes of personalities and loyalties in the unconscious group dynamics of the Society itself. Religion was not exempt from debate and polemic. It remained an arena where speculation, competition, and creativity was still possible, and managed to flourish. The following chapters in Part II will extend this discussion through the work of four theorists whose contributions further illuminate the variety and creativity among the first generation of analysts' approaches toward psychology and religion.

Moreover, antisemitism, which seemed to be curiously neglected by Freud's Vienna circle, emerged as a theme for deeper exploration. The seeds of internalized antisemitism are already apparent if one looks with a psychoanalytic lens at what was said, but also, importantly, what was not said, minimized, or glossed over. The group's vehement rejection of the repressive teachings of the Austrian Catholic Church already represents one form of protest, while their often uncritical acceptance of racialized Jewish caricatures and distancing of themselves from the *Ostjuden* (eastern European Jewry) from whose families they themselves came represents a complex and largely subliminal form of internalized antisemitism, racism, and classism that also cannot be ignored. Antisemitism emerges from the thicket of details of their discussions as an overarching context and reality without which none of their comments on religion can be fully understood. It is perhaps a question of seeing the forest for the trees. If the details of the group's discussions about religion were the trees, antisemitism constituted the forest canopy. And the forest would soon catch on fire.

Notes

1 Nunberg and Federn, 1962–75, Vol. 1: xxxviii. For ease of reference, hereafter the Minutes will be cited as *Minutes* by volume and page number (i.e., *Minutes* I: 1). For original German, see Nunberg and Federn, 1976–81.
2 Rank and Sachs, 1912: 15 (Transl. PC-W).
3 Cf. in Germany the plays of Wedekind (e.g., 2015).
4 Sachs, 1944: 36.
5 Beller, 1989: 175.
6 Johnston, 1972: 115.
7 Beller, 1989: 175; Johnston, 1972: 22.
8 Sachs, 1944: 25–26, 28.
9 E.g., Gay, 2006: 136–139.
10 M. Freud, 1957: 11. Blum (2010: 82) notes that Christmas figures prominently in the timing of "Anna O's" symptoms, stimulated by "intense conflicts concerning Christian and Jewish observance," unnoticed by Breuer and Freud. (Cf. Breuer, 1955/1893–95.)
11 Masson, 1985: 406.
12 Grosskurth, 1991: 21.
13 Contra Vitz, 1993.

14 Freud, 1955b/1913.
15 Ibid., e.g., xiv, 77, 92, 100.
16 *Minutes* II: 288.
17 Reik, 1951: 14–15.
18 *Minutes* II: 32.
19 Freud, 1961a/1927.
20 Freud, 1961b/1930.
21 Freud, 1964b/1939.
22 Freud, 1958b/1911.
23 *Minutes* II: 149–150.
24 *Minutes* II: 149.
25 Ibid.
26 *Minutes* IV: 11.
27 Roazen, 1975: 306.
28 Freud, 1959a/1907. Freud's (1961a/1927) characterization of religion as an illusion based on infantile wish fulfillment came later, although it can be glimpsed early on.
29 Freud, 1962/1896: 173.
30 Freud, 1960/1901: 258, emphasis original.
31 Freud, 1959a/1907: 118–119.
32 Freud, 1955c/1921: 142.
33 *Minutes* I: 295.
34 Freud, 1964a/1933: 160.
35 *Minutes* II: 149.
36 Ibid.
37 *Minutes* II: 500.
38 *Minutes* II: 506.
39 *Minutes* III: 29, 42, 137.
40 *Minutes* I: 151.
41 *Minutes* III: 42.
42 *Minutes* IV: 61–62.
43 *Minutes* III: 273.
44 *Minutes* III: 29, emphasis original. Revised and published as Freud, 1958b/1911.
45 Freud, 1955b/1913.
46 *Minutes* I: 349–350.
47 *Minutes* I: 351.
48 *Minutes* I: 352.
49 Ibid., 352n8.
50 Ibid.
51 For example, *Minutes* I: 142–143, 154, 162, 164; IV: 50–56; Levy, 1917; Reik, 1917, 1919, 1951: 165–332.
52 *Minutes* IV: 9.
53 Re: oedipal theory, see Gay, 2006: 112–113, 329.
54 *Minutes* I: 152.
55 *Minutes* IV: 52–53.
56 *Minutes* IV: 50–56.
57 Ferenczi, 1949: 225n1, 2.
58 *Minutes* IV: 16.
59 *Minutes* IV: 16–17.
60 *Minutes* IV: 16.
61 Ibid.
62 Gustav Roskoff, 1869, noted in *Minutes* II: 117n1.
63 *Minutes* II: 117–124.

64 *Minutes* IV: 37.
65 Viennese philosopher (1880–1903), author of *Sex and Character* in 1903 (an earlier draft of which Freud had read and rejected). A Jewish convert to Protestantism, Weininger's writings were antisemitic and misogynistic, but gained greater notoriety after he committed suicide at age twenty-three. Fliess later accused Freud of disclosing Fliess' theories on bisexuality to Weininger, who plagiarized them (Gay, 2006: 154–156; Roazen, 1975: 93–94).
66 *Minutes* III: 133–137.
67 *Minutes* III: 359.
68 *Minutes* II: 285–286.
69 *Minutes* II: 272.
70 *Minutes* I: 240.
71 *Minutes* II: 62.
72 *Minutes* III: 311.
73 *Minutes* III: 313.
74 Freud, 1957a/1912: 187.
75 *Minutes* III: 239.
76 *Minutes* III: 139.
77 *Minutes* I: 139–145.
78 *Minutes* II: 78.
79 *Minutes* II: 78–79.
80 *Minutes* I: 142.
81 *Minutes* II: 285–286.
82 Freud, 1958a/1911 (begun summer 1910).
83 *Minutes* III: 11.
84 *Minutes* II: 406–407.
85 *Minutes* II: 407–409.
86 Ibid.
87 *Minutes* II: 412.
88 *Minutes* II: 413.
89 Gilman, 1993: 93–168; 2010: 70–71.
90 *Minutes* I: 94.
91 Ibid.
92 *Minutes* I: 98.
93 *Minutes* II: 387, citing Freud, 1955a.
94 *Minutes* IV: 179.
95 *Minutes* III: 272–273.
96 *Minutes* III: 273.
97 *Minutes* I: 44.
98 *Minutes* I: 362.
99 Quoted in Gilman, 2010: 73. Gilman (1993) argues that the then common symptom *globus hystericus*, or hysterical choking, was connected not only to repressed childhood sexual wishes, but also a cultural symptom connected to the attempted suppression of the Jewish voice amidst pressure to appear "cultured" (p. 72). Cuddihy (1974) similarly interprets Anna O's hydrophobia and "strangulated anger" as "a psychological expression of the socio-cultural 'ordeal of civility'" (pp. 41–42).
100 *Minutes* II: 46–47.
101 Gilman, 1993: 17; Robert, 1976: 95. Freud himself observed what he viewed as "neuropathological taint" in his own family gene pool—letter to Martha Bernays, 1882.
102 E.g., Ostow, 1996. As noted by Ostow, the term "anti-Semitism" does not appear in the index, cf. *Minutes* IV: 343.

103 Lessing, 1930. Cf. Gay, 1978: 195. Lessing himself was a Jew who converted to Lutheranism and became a vocal anti-Semite. He recanted once World War I was underway and was shot as a traitor by Nazi assassins in 1933 (Gay, 1978: 195, 197). Gay cites a vicious exchange of letters between Lessing and Freud. "Don't you think," Freud asked, "that self-hatred like Th. L.'s is an exquisite Jewish phenomenon?" (letter from Freud to Kurt Hiller, February 9, 1936, in ibid., 195.)

104 Kuriloff, 2014: 12.

105 Ibid., 12–13.

106 *Minutes* I: 94.

107 Gay, 1978: 198–200. McCagg (1989) prefers the term "'self'-denial" over "self-hatred," arguing that in order to rise socially and economically, assimilation was the price that had to be paid (pp. 27–43).

108 Beller, 1989: 162–163; cf. Klein, 1985: 54–57.

109 Now Příbor, Czech Republic.

110 Rose, 1998: 29.

111 Ibid.

112 Mühlleitner and Reichmayr, 1997: 91.

113 All but thirteen members of the Society had such educations (Mühlleitner and Reichmayr, 1997: 88). Close to half (sixty-eight) attended the University of Vienna, and over 80 percent were college educated—82 percent in medicine; others in philosophy and law (ibid., 88). Jewish enrollment in the University of Vienna reached its peak in 1881–91 (one-third of the student body and 48 percent of the medical school). Jewish students still comprised 34 percent in 1926 (Beller, 1989: 33–34).

114 Rozenblitt, 1983; Klein, 1985.

115 Klein, 1985: 70.

116 Beller, 1989: 45–47.

117 Schorske, 1981.

118 Rose, 1998: 26, 35.

119 Ibid., 26–27.

120 Ibid., 34; Klein, 1985: 138–139.

121 Graf, 1942: 473.

122 Wortis, 1984: 144.

123 Graf, 1942: 473.

124 *Minutes* I: xxii.

125 Ostow (1982) notes a similar "gentleman's agreement" among the émigré analysts in America that "one does not discuss Jewishness" (p. 150, cited in Prince, 2009: 190; Kuriloff, 2014: 11).

126 Vienna-born Fenichel wrote about antisemitism, but only in the 1940s in America. Fenichel briefly joined the Vienna Society, but moved to Berlin in 1922 and became a vocal Marxist. At great personal risk, he organized an international underground *Rundbrief* among Marxist analysts during World War II. His political ideas were downplayed for the émigré American psychoanalytic establishment (Fisher 2004: 60). His dynamic analysis was that "the Jew is a projection, a displacement substitute for the homicidal, dirty, and voluptuous tendencies concealed in the Jew-haters" (ibid., 6). On Fenichel and his activism, see Jacoby, 1983; cf. Kuriloff, 2014: 7–9.

127 Freud, 1955a/1909: 36n1; cf. 1957b/1910: 95n3, footnote added 1919.

128 Freud, 1964b/1939.

129 Ibid., 90.

130 Freud, 1955b/1913: 152n1. Westerink asks: "Why is Judaism [so] absent from *Totem and Taboo*?" Personal communication, February 18, 2017.

131 Freud, 1964b/1939: 90–91.

132 Ibid., 91.

133 Freud, 1964c/1938: 292.
134 Ibid., 293.
135 *Minutes* II: 31.
136 Carotenuto, 1982: 120–121; Kerr, 1994: 458–459. Note that here, as elsewhere, Freud used the term "Aryan" (a racial designation), not "Gentile" (a religious one) (Brickman, 2010: 27–28; Gilman, 1993).
137 Freud, 1959c/1926: 273.
138 Quoted in Gay, 1987: 139. The journalist was George Viereck, a German-American, who in later correspondence begged Freud "as a brother physician" to reconsider his atheism and allow God to reveal God's truth to him. Freud recalled,

> I sent a polite answer, saying that I was glad to hear that this experience had enabled him to retain his faith. As for myself, God had not done so much for me. He had never allowed me to hear an inner voice; and if, in view of my age, he did not make haste, it would not be my fault if I remained to the end of my life what I now was— "an infidel Jew."
>
> (Freud, 1961c/1928: 170)

Cf. Strachey's ed. note, ibid., 169).
139 For example, Gay, 1987: 117–122.
140 For example, Brentano, 2014/1874: 59–62, *et passim*.
141 Ibid., 38. Ellenberger (1970) exhaustively researches the historical antecedents of the concept of the unconscious.
142 Freud to Fliess, cited in Klein, 1985: xiv.
143 Most conspicuously Vitz, 1993: 5.
144 For example, Gay, 1987: 127–134.
145 Slavet, 2009: 20. The term *Judenschaft* ("Jewry") was sometimes used in the late eighteenth century in public discourse on emancipation of the Jews in Germany. This term identified Jews as a "nation" or "colony," but not yet a racialized group (Cuddihy, 1974: 46, citing Chancellor Helmut Schmidt).
146 Freud, 1955b/1913: xv (Preface to the Hebrew translation, 1934).
147 For example, Gilman, 1993.
148 Freud, 1955b/1913, 1964b/1939.
149 Gay, 1987, 2006; Slavet, 2009; Gilman, 1993, 2010. For a detailed discussion of "Freud's 'Lamarckism' and the politics of racial science," as well as Ernest Jones' suggestion that Lamarckism was a Jewish idea, see Slavet, 2009: 68–97. Cf. Gilman, 1993, pp. 12–48 on "Freud and the epistemology of race."
150 Beller, 1989: 139.
151 Freud, 1959b/1925: 9.
152 Jay Geller, "*Atheist Jew or atheist Jew*," 2006: 1, cited in Slavet, 2009: 21.
153 Beller, 1989: 81.
154 Ibid., 82, emphasis original.
155 M. Freud, 1957: 34.
156 Freud, 1953/1900; cf. *Minutes* IV: 106–121.
157 Robert, 1976: 86.
158 Lessing (1930) argued that assimilation was *Selbsthass*. He urged fellow Jews to throw off the shackles of German culture and return to the "blood and soil of the homeland" (Palestine) (Beller, 1989: 79).
159 Salberg, 2007: 201.
160 Freud, 1953/1900: 197.
161 Freud, 1959c/1926, to the B'nai Brith. Cf. Gay, 1987: 133; Gay, 2006: 597–604.
162 On "the prefiguring of the psychoanalytic movement: Freud and the B'nai Brith," see Klein, 1985: 69–102.

163 Ibid., 78.
164 Ibid., 72, 74, 76, 97n13.
165 Freud, 1953/1900.
166 Ibid., 442.
167 Klein, 1985: 71.
168 Ibid.; Billig, 1999: 232.
169 Masson, 1984.
170 Billig, 1999: 252n161. On the seduction theory, cf. Gilman, 1993: 89–90.
171 Beller, 1989: 33–34.
172 Letter to Fliess, March 11, 1902, in Masson, 1985: 455–457. Cf. Schorske, 1981: 203. For more on the delayed promotion, antisemitism, and Freud's festering ambition, see Robert, 1976: 73–74.
173 Granted in March, 1902 (ibid.; Jones, 1972: 372–374; Gay, 2006: 136–139; Sachs, 1944: 78). Eissler (1974) and Sulloway (1992) minimize antisemitism as the reason, but this argument is not supported by a comprehensive review of the evidence.
174 Klein, 1985: 74, 98n23–25.
175 Klein, 1985. Cf. Grollman, 1965: 41.
176 Freud, 1959c/1926: 274.
177 Cf. Klein, 1985: 74.
178 James, 2015/1902.
179 Gay, 2006: 211.

References

Beller, Steven (1989). *Vienna and the Jews 1867–1938: A cultural history.* Cambridge, UK: Cambridge University Press.

Billig, Michael (1999). *Freudian repression: Conversation creating the unconscious.* Cambridge, UK: Cambridge University Press.

Blum, Harold P. (2010). Anti-Semitism in the Freud case histories. In Arnold D. Richards (Ed.), *The Jewish world of Sigmund Freud: Essays on cultural roots and the problem of religious identity* (pp. 78–95). Jefferson, NC: McFarland.

Brentano, Franz (2014). *Psychology from an empirical standpoint.* London: Routledge. (Orig. publ. 1874.)

Breuer, Josef (1955). Fräulein Anna O. In *Freud, Studies on hysteria,* in J. Strachey (Ed.), *Standard edition of the complete works of Sigmund Freud,* Vol. 2: 19–47. (Orig. publ. 1893–95.)

Brickman, Celia (2010). Psychoanalysis and Judaism in context. In Lewis Aron and Libby Henik (Eds.), *Answering a question with a question: Contemporary psychoanalysis and Jewish thought* (pp. 25–54). Brighton, MA: Academic Studies Press.

Carotenuto, Aldo (1982). *A secret symmetry: Sabina Spielrein between Freud and Jung.* New York: Pantheon.

Cuddihy, John Murray (1974). *The ordeal of civility: Freud, Marx, Levi-Strauss and the Jewish struggle with modernity.* New York: Basic Books.

Eissler, Kurt R. (1974). Ein zusätzliches Dokument zur Geschichte von Freuds Professur. *Jahrbuch für Psychoanalyse, 7*: 101–113.

Ellenberger, Henri F. (1970). *The discovery of the unconscious: The history and evolution of dynamic psychiatry.* New York: Basic Books.

Ferenczi, Sándor (1949). Confusion of tongues between adults and the child: The language of tenderness and of passion. Michael Balint (Trans.). *International Journal of Psycho-analysis, 30*: 225–230. (Orig. publ. 1933.)

Fisher, David James (2004). Towards a psychoanalytic understanding of fascism and anti-semitism: Perceptions from the 1940's. *Psychoanalysis and History, 6* (1): 57–74. Online at www.hagalil.com/2009/12/fisher. Accessed January 15, 2017.

Freud, Martin (1957). *Glory reflected: Sigmund Freud—Man and Father.* London: Angus and Robertson.

Freud, Sigmund (1953). *The interpretation of dreams.* In J. Strachey (Ed.), *Standard edition of the complete works of Sigmund Freud*, Vol. 4–5 (entire). (Orig. publ. 1900.)

Freud, Sigmund (1955a). Analysis of a phobia in a five-year old boy ["Little Hans"]. In J. Strachey (Ed.), *Standard edition of the complete works of Sigmund Freud*, Vol. 10: 1–150. (Orig. publ. 1909.)

Freud, Sigmund (1955b). *Totem and taboo.* In J. Strachey (Ed.), *Standard edition of the complete works of Sigmund Freud*, Vol. 13: 1–255. (Orig. publ. 1913.)

Freud, Sigmund (1955c). *Group psychology and the analysis of the ego.* In J. Strachey (Ed.), *Standard edition of the complete works of Sigmund Freud*, Vol. 18: 65–144. (Orig. publ. 1921.)

Freud, Sigmund (1957a). *On the universal tendency to debasement in the sphere of love.* In J. Strachey (Ed.), *Standard edition of the complete works of Sigmund Freud*, Vol. 11: 177–190. (Orig. publ. 1912.)

Freud, Sigmund (1957b). *Leonardo da Vinci and a memory of his childhood.* In J. Strachey (Ed.), *Standard edition of the complete works of Sigmund Freud*, Vol. 11: 57–138. (Orig. publ. 1910.)

Freud, Sigmund (1958a). *Psycho-analytic notes on an autobiographical account of a case of paranoia (dementia paranoides)* ["The Schreber Case"]. In J. Strachey (Ed.), *Standard edition of the complete works of Sigmund Freud*, Vol. 12: 3–82. (Orig. publ. 1911.)

Freud, Sigmund (1958b). *Formulations on the two principles of mental functioning.* In J. Strachey (Ed.), *Standard edition of the complete works of Sigmund Freud*, Vol. 12: 213–226. (Orig. publ. 1911.)

Freud, Sigmund (1959a). *Obsessive actions and religious practices.* In J. Strachey (Ed.), *Standard edition of the complete works of Sigmund Freud*, Vol. 9: 115–128. (Orig. publ. 1907.)

Freud, Sigmund (1959b). *An autobiographical study.* In J. Strachey (Ed.), *Standard edition of the complete works of Sigmund Freud*, Vol. 20: 1–74. (Orig. publ. 1925.)

Freud, Sigmund (1959c). *Address to the Society of B'Nai B'Rith (1926).* In J. Strachey (Ed.), *Standard edition of the complete works of Sigmund Freud*, Vol. 20: 271–274. (Orig. publ. 1941.)

Freud, Sigmund (1960). *The psychopathology of everyday life.* In J. Strachey (Ed.), *Standard edition of the complete works of Sigmund Freud*, Vol. 6 (entire). (Orig. publ. 1901.)

Freud, Sigmund (1961a). *The future of an illusion.* In J. Strachey (Ed.), *Standard edition of the complete works of Sigmund Freud*, Vol. 21: 5–56. (Orig. publ. 1927.)

Freud, Sigmund (1961b). *Civilisation and its discontents.* In J. Strachey (Ed.), *Standard edition of the complete works of Sigmund Freud*, Vol. 21: 59–146. (Orig. publ. 1930.)

Freud, Sigmund (1961c). *A religious experience.* In J. Strachey (Ed.), *Standard edition of the complete works of Sigmund Freud*, Vol. 21: 167–172. (Orig. publ. 1928.)

Freud, Sigmund (1962). *Further remarks on the neuro-psychoses of defence.* In J. Strachey (Ed.), *Standard edition of the complete works of Sigmund Freud*, Vol. 3: 157–185. (Orig. publ. 1896.)

Freud, Sigmund (1964a). *New introductory lectures on psycho-analysis.* In J. Strachey (Ed.), *Standard edition of the complete works of Sigmund Freud,* Vol. 22: 1–182. (Orig. publ. 1933.)

Freud, Sigmund (1964b). *Moses and monotheism: Three essays.* In J. Strachey (Ed.), *Standard edition of the complete works of Sigmund Freud,* Vol. 23: 1–138. (Orig. publ. 1939.)

Freud, Sigmund (1964c). *A comment on anti-Semitism.* In J. Strachey (Ed.), *Standard edition of the complete works of Sigmund Freud,* Vol. 23: 287–294. (Orig. publ. 1938.)

Gay, Peter (1978). *Freud, Jews and other Germans.* Oxford, UK: Oxford University Press.

Gay, Peter (1987). *A godless Jew: Freud, atheism, and the making of psychoanalysis.* New Haven: Yale University Press.

Gay, Peter (2006). *Freud: A life for our time.* New York: W. W. Norton.

Gilman, Sander L. (1993). *Freud, race, and gender.* Princeton, NJ: Princeton University Press.

Gilman, Sander L. (2010). Sigmund Freud and electrotherapy. In Arnold D. Richards (Ed.), *The Jewish world of Sigmund Freud: Essays on cultural roots and the problem of religious identity* (pp. 66–77). Jefferson, NC: McFarland.

Graf, Max (1942). Reminiscences of Professor Freud. *Psychoanalytic Quarterly, 11:* 465–476.

Grollman, Earl A. (1965). *Judaism in Sigmund Freud's world.* New York: Appleton-Century/Bloch.

Grosskurth, Phyllis (1991). *The secret ring: Freud's inner circle and the politics of psychoanalysis.* Reading, MA: Addison-Wesley.

Jacoby, Russell (1983). *The repression of psychoanalysis: Otto Fenichel and the political Freudians.* New York: Basic Books.

James, William (2015). *The varieties of religious experience.* New York: Routledge. (Orig. publ. 1902, 1906, 1929.)

Johnston, William M. (1972). *The Austrian mind: An intellectual and social history 1848–1938.* Berkeley: University of California Press.

Jones, Ernest (1972). *The life and work of Sigmund Freud, Vol. 1: The young Freud 1856–1900.* New York: Basic Books.

Kerr, John (1994). *A most dangerous method: The story of Jung, Freud, and Sabina Spielrein.* New York: Vintage.

Klein, Dennis B. (1985). *Jewish origins of the psychoanalytic movement.* Chicago: University of Chicago Press.

Kuriloff, Emily A. (2014). *Contemporary psychoanalysis and the legacy of the Third Reich.* New York: Routledge.

Lessing, Theodor (1930). *Der jüdische Selbsthass.* Berlin: Jüdischer Verlag.

Levy, Ludwig (1917). Sexualsymbolik in der biblischen Paradiesgeschichte. *Imago, 5:* 16–30.

Masson, Jeffrey Moussaief (1984). *The assault on truth: Freud's suppression of the seduction theory.* New York: Farrar, Straus & Giroux.

Masson, Jeffrey Moussaief (Ed. and Trans.) (1985). *The complete letters of Sigmund Freud to Wilhelm Fliess 1887–1904.* Cambridge, MA: Belknap/Harvard University Press.

McCagg, William O., Jr. (1989). *A history of Habsburg Jews, 1670–1918.* Bloomington: Indiana University Press.

Mühlleitner, Elke and Reichmayr, Johannes (1997). Following Freud in Vienna. *International Forum of Psychoanalysis, 6*: 73–102.

Nunberg, Herman and Federn, Ernst (Eds.) (1962–75). *Minutes of the Vienna Psychoanalytic Society*, Vols. I–IV. M. Nunberg (Trans.). New York: International Universities Press.

Nunberg, Herman and Federn, Ernst (Eds.) (1962–75). *Protokolle der Wiener Psychoanalytischen Vereinigung.* Bd. I–IV. Frankfurt am Main: S. Fischer. (New edition: Psychosozial-Verlag, Gießen 2007.)

Ostow, Mortimer (Ed.) (1982). *Judaism and psychoanalysis.* New York: KTAV.

Ostow, Mortimer (1996). *Myth and madness: The psychodynamics of anti-semitism.* New Brunswick, NJ: Transaction Publishers.

Prince, Robert (2009). Psychoanalysis traumatized: The legacy of the Holocaust. *American Journal of Psychoanalysis, 69* (3): 179–194.

Rank, Otto and Sachs, Hanns (1912). Entwicklung und Ansprüche der Psychoanalyse. *Imago, 1* (1): 1–16.

Reik, Theodor (1917). Das Kainszeichen: Ein psychoanalytischer Beitrag zur Bibelerklärung. *Imago, 5* (1): 31–42. (Presented to the Vienna Psychoanalytic Society, December, 1914.)

Reik, Theodor (1919). Psychoanalytische Studien zur Bibelexegese. I. Jaákobs Kampf. *Imago, 5* (5/6): 325–363. (Presented to the Vienna Psychoanalytic Society February, 1918.)

Reik, Theodor (1951). *Dogma and compulsion: Psychoanalytic studies of religion and myths.* New York: International Universities Press.

Richards, Arnold D. (Ed.) (2010). *The Jewish world of Sigmund Freud: Essays on cultural roots and the problem of religious identity.* Jefferson, NC: McFarland.

Roazen, Paul (1975). *Freud and his followers.* New York: Alfred Knopf.

Robert, Marthe (1976). *From Oedipus to Moses: Freud's Jewish identity.* Ralph Manheim (Trans.). New York: Anchor Books.

Rose, Louis (1998). *The Freudian calling: Early Viennese psychoanalysis and the pursuit of cultural science.* Detroit: Wayne State University Press.

Roskoff, Gustav (1869). *Geschichte des Teufels*, 2 vols. Leipzig: F.A. Brockhaus.

Rozenblitt, Marsha (1983). *The Jews of Vienna, 1867–1914: Assimilation and identity.* Albany, NY: SUNY Press.

Rozenblitt, Marsha (1992). The Jews of Germany and Austria: A comparative perspective. In Robert Wistrich (Ed.), *Austrians and Jews in the twentieth century* (pp. 1–18). New York: St. Martin's Press.

Sachs, Hanns (1944). *Freud: Master and friend.* Cambridge, MA: Harvard University Press.

Salberg, Jill (2007). Hidden in plain sight: Freud's Jewish identity revisited. *Psychoanalytic Dialogues, 17* (2): 197–212. (Reprinted in Arnold D. Richards (Ed.) (2010). *The Jewish world of Sigmund Freud: Essays on cultural roots and the problem of religious identity* (pp. 5–21). Jefferson, NC: McFarland.)

Schorske, Carl E. (1981). *Fin-de-siècle Vienna: Politics and culture.* New York: Vintage.

Slavet, Eliza (2009). *Racial fever: Freud and the Jewish question.* New York: Fordham University Press.

Sulloway, Frank (1992). *Freud, biologist of the mind*, 2nd ed. Cambridge, MA: Harvard University Press.

Vitz, Paul C. (1993). *Freud's Christian unconscious.* Grand Rapids, MI: Eerdmans.

Wedekind, Frank (2015). *Spring awakening.* Tom Osborn (Trans.). Richmond, UK: Alma Classics. (Orig. publ. 1891.)

Wortis, Joseph (1984). *My analysis with Freud.* Northvale, NJ: Jason Aronson.

Part II

The major contributors

Chapter 3

The analyst pastor
Oskar Pfister (1873–1956)

Oskar Pfister is best known today for his long and amicable correspondence with Sigmund Freud (from 1909 until Freud's death in 1939).[1] Pfister initiated the correspondence in 1909 when he was 35. In an unpublished autobiographical sketch he wrote, "[w]hen I read Freud I felt as if old dreams and premonitions had suddenly become reality."[2] Writing to Pfister at the beginning of their correspondence, Freud stated (quite generously, considering his staunch atheism),

> You know our eroticism includes what you call "love" in your pastoral care—*Seelsorge*[3] ... in itself psychoanalysis is neither religious nor the opposite, but an impartial instrument which the minister may employ as much as the layman [provided that] the liberation of sufferers is the aim.[4]

Pfister likewise viewed the love found in liberal Protestantism "starting from its religious-ethical feeling" (and over-against both Catholic and Calvinist repressiveness) to be a close parallel for the love made possible through enlightened sublimation in psychoanalysis.[5] His ability to maintain a collegial and positive relationship with Freud, in spite of their serious difference over faith vs. atheism, is somewhat remarkable in light of the many defections and evictions from Freud's inner circle throughout Freud's career. However, the two were committed to maintaining their friendship and agreeing to disagree on matters of religion. They exchanged well over 215 letters[6] including over 80 that were newly discovered in the last decade,[7] now published in a complete critical edition.[8] Freud encouraged Pfister's expanding of the scope of psychoanalytic inquiry, and in turn, Pfister wholeheartedly adopted Freud's method of psychoanalysis as the best and deepest approach to pastoral care and counseling. He remained a loyal champion of Freud's theories all his life.

In addition to his publications on theological and religious topics, Pfister contributed numerous essays and monographs on the subject of psychoanalysis in general, and he had a particular interest in reforming education. He wrote two early case studies demonstrating his method of analytic pastoral care,[9] as well as psychobiographies of important historical religious figures, such as Count Ludwig von Zinzendorf (the founder of the Moravian church movement),[10]

Margaretha Ebner (a saint and mystic),[11] the apostle Paul,[12] and John Calvin.[13] He also wrote several pieces on trance states and altered states of consciousness such as glossolalia, automatic writing,[14] and religious hysteria.[15] Many of his monographs were intended as textbooks, including a quite early volume, *The Psychoanalytic Method*, first published in 1913.[16] His writings in the 1920s showed his wide range of interests, for example, conflicts in psychoanalysis,[17] expressionism in art,[18] psychology and philosophy,[19] and books on love in children[20] and in marriage.[21]

Pfister's most comprehesive textbook on *Analytische Seelsorge* ("Analytic Soul-care")[22] appeared in 1927 after he had been engaged in his counseling practice for nearly two decades.[23] "The Illusion of a Future,"[24] Pfister's bold answer to Freud's atheist manifesto *The Future of an Illusion*,[25] stands as a milestone in the development of pastoral theology, care, and counseling, incorporating both a psychoanalytic and a faith perspective. He continued to be a prolific writer throughout his life, producing a book or major article nearly every year until his death, on topics as varied as juvenile delinquency,[26] Buddhism,[27] the Navajos,[28] various forms of unbelief,[29] narcissism,[30] freedom and compulsion in Judeo-Christian history,[31] Christianity and fear,[32] a critique of Calvin's anxiously aggressive and "unchristian" character in light of his involvement in a witchcraft trial,[33] the ethical foundations of Freud's psychoanalysis,[34] and his final pitting of Freud against the existential philosopher Karl Jaspers.[35] In all, he published twenty full-length monographs, 244 articles and pamphlets, fifty-five book reviews, and served as editor or co-editor of six different journals.[36]

Replying in 1918 to Freud's question why the world had to wait for a completely godless Jew (*"auf einen ganz gottloser Jude"*[37]) to invent psychoanalysis, Pfister wrote to Freud,

> You are not godless, for he who lives the truth lives in God, and whoever strives for the freeing of love "dwelleth in God."[38] If you raised to your consciousness and fully felt your place in the great design, which is to me as necessary as the synthesis of the notes is to a Beethoven symphony, I should say of you: *A better Christian never was* [emphasis added].[39]

This well-known passage is preceded in Pfister's letter by a lesser known and perhaps even more presumptuous comment: "You are no Jew, which to me, in view of my unbounded admiration for Amos, Isaiah, Jeremiah, and the author of Job and Ecclesiastes, is a matter of profound regret."[40] Freud graciously refrained from making a direct reply.[41]

Pfister became known throughout Europe as the *Analysenpfarrer*—the "analyst pastor,"[42] and in his pastoral theology of love, he regarded Jesus as the first psychoanalyst. Although Pfister is scarcely known in American psychoanalysis or psychiatry, the American Psychiatric Association together with the Association of Professional Chaplains awards an annual Oskar Pfister prize for "significant contributions to the field of religion and psychiatry."[43]

Biography[44]

Pfister is considered by many historians to be the first pastoral counselor and pastoral theologian.[45] He was born, the youngest of four sons, in Wiedikon (now part of Zürich), Switzerland, in 1873. His father, Johannes, died of tuberculosis when Pfister was just three years old. Johannes himself was a Reformed pastor, and was studying medicine at the time of his death.[46] Johannes was strict and dogmatic in his Protestant beliefs.[47] Oskar's mother, Luise, a piano teacher, was more pietistic—tending toward the more emotional and practice-oriented faith of her family in Königsfeld im Schwarzwald—a Moravian community since the early 1800s (seventy miles north of Zürich in the Black Forest region of southern Germany).[48] After Johannes' death, the family was beset by illness and poverty, and Luise took them back to Königsfeld where they lived for four years with her parents and sister. Pfister's years in Königsfeld with his mother, brothers, aunt, and grandparents would have imbued in him a belief in a loving God who could be experienced subjectively through prayer and community. At both pre-oedipal and oedipal stages, when individuals' own God-*imagoes* are planted in the unconscious, modeled on one's parents in early childhood,[49] Pfister might well have struggled internally with a stern father-God of judgment versus a more accessible mothering God of love. All these factors would have predisposed him to reject the abstractions and rigors of doctrine in favor of a practice of pastoral care and social work grounded in godly love.

When Pfister was seven, the family returned to Wiedikon, where he began his formal schooling. He excelled as a student, and, following in his father's footsteps, he went on to study theology at the University of Zürich and the University of Basel. After graduation he pursued further training in philosophy for two semesters in Zürich and Berlin. He was taught by some of the "greats" at the time, including Adolf von Harnack and Wilhelm Dilthey. After completing his *Vikariat* (pastoral internship) he was ordained in the Swiss Reformed Church and began serving a parish in Wald, near Zürich, in 1897. During his first year of ministry he received his PhD, writing a dissertation on the Swiss liberal theologian and philosopher of religion Alois Emanuel Biedermann.[50] As Herman Westerink has noted, Biedermann gave credence to the idea that psychology and religion could be joined:

> Pfister believed that Biedermann should be praised for having brought forward the importance of the analysis of subjective religious experiences, and for having attached great value to Schleiermacher's idea of religious development and edification as an inner process in a religious person.[51]

Thus Pfister began his long career embracing psychology and personal subjectivity as essential to religion, and opposing academic dogmatic theology which he condemned as "speculative, scholastic, and dead."[52]

Pfister married Erika Wunderli the same year, and an only son, Oskar Robert (who would grow up to be a psychiatrist), was born a year later in 1898.[53] In

1902 Pfister was called to serve as pastor of the Zürich *Predigerkirche*,[54] a post he kept until 1939. The congregation was located in an old section of Zürich with many social problems.[55] This setting prompted Pfister to look to both psychology and pedagogy as a means of helping his community. He also continued to pursue his intellectual interests, immersing himself in philosophy and systematic theology. In 1904 he received an award for his first monograph, *Die Willensfreiheit* ("Free Will"),[56] in which he put forth an anti-deterministic theological argument in favor of a natural freedom of the will, in spite of the forces of socialization and internal drives.[57] He was tiring of purely abstract questions, and given his pastoral context, was drawn more and more toward practical theological concerns—*Seelsorge*—and enlightened education.

In 1903, several years before meeting Freud, he published *Die Unterlassungssünden der Theologie gegenüber der modern Psychologie* ("Sins of Omission of Theology Compared to Modern Psychology")[58]—a plea for the application of scientific knowledge to individual and group therapy. By 1906 he was also deeply involved in education and eventually developed a psychoanalytic method of pedagogy he termed *Pädanalyse*.[59] He spent thirty years as a religion teacher in the state high school (*Kantonsschule*), and from 1908 through 1918 he also taught a teachers' seminar in Jung's home village of Küsnacht. Delving further into the realm of social welfare, in 1907 he published *Die soziale Entwicklung als Kampf um die Menschenwürde: Ein Mahnwort*[60] ("Social Development as Struggle for Human Dignity: An Exhortation").

As he began to encounter difficulties with individual patients in his practice of *Seelsorge*, he sought supervision at the Burghölzli Clinic with Binswanger and Jung. (Binswanger also stayed in the Pfisters' home for a period of time.) It was Jung who introduced Pfister to psychoanalysis in 1908—the period of Jung's own closest involvement with Freud. Pfister, always a man of action, arranged a visit to Berggasse 19 the following April, 1909. Pfister delighted the whole family with his attention to the children and his friendly, unpretentious manner. Freud later wrote to Ferenczi that Pfister was "a charming fellow" who "flattered everyone to death, a warm-hearted dreamer, half Saviour, half Pied Piper. We parted good friends."[61] Anna Freud later remembered,

> In the totally non-religious Freud household Pfister, in his clerical garb and with the manners and behavior of a pastor, was like a visitor from another planet. In him there was nothing of the almost passionately impatient enthusiasm for science which caused other pioneers of analysis to regard time spent at the family table only as an unwelcome interruption of their theoretical and clinical discussions. On the contrary, his human warmth and enthusiasm, his capacity for taking a lively part in the minor events of the day, enchanted the children of the household, and made him at all times a most welcome guest, a uniquely human figure in his way.[62]

Pfister held two strong attractions for Freud at the time: First, he was a philo-sophically trained researcher with a passion for psychology and a critical eye toward religion, even as a practitioner. Freud was cultivating lay analysts at the time, whom he thought could expand the reach of psychoanalysis into non-medical fields of research. And second, Pfister was involved with Jung and the progressive wing of Swiss psychiatry. If Jung was rapidly fulfilling Freud's fantasy of a Gentile heir apparent, Pfister would surely be one of his lieuten-ants—adding credibility in Protestant religious circles. On Pfister's side of the equation, having lost his father at a very young age, he would have likely been glad, as were many of Freud's next generation of followers (see Chapters 4 and 5), to have a man he so deeply admired play a fatherly role in his professional and personal life.[63] Pfister's biographer Eckart Nase interprets Pfister's need for Freud as part of a compromise formation in which Pfister—as the narcissistically wounded son—discovered/created a new Mother Church, a Father Freud, and a Brother Jesus.[64]

Upon returning to Zürich, Pfister took on more psychoanalytic patients, and began to employ Freudian theory and technique with great enthusiasm. He generally practiced a form of brief analysis, especially with his parishioners, but also accepted referrals from Freud and conducted longer-term, more formal psychoanalyses with these patients.[65] Two case studies in the newly published letters of Freud and Pfister also show how patients were referred back and forth between the two men (and other colleagues)—for example, Freud's little known but frequently referenced analysis with Elfriede Hirschfeld[66]—with Freud sup-plying supervision to Pfister from afar.[67]

Pfister attended the 3rd International Congress in Weimar and was active in helping to found the Zürich psychoanalytic society. In 1911 he entered training analysis with Riklin.[68] Riklin was also interested in applied psychoanalysis, having published a book of his own on Freudian symbolism in fairy tales in 1908.[69] Like Jung, Spielrein, and others at the Burghölzli, Riklin did not limit psychoanalysis to the treatment of neurotic patients, but was also interested in the apparent links between psychosis, symbolism, and dreams.[70]

It was during this time that Pfister began to publish his own case studies, as well as the psycho-biographical essays noted above—applying an oedipal ana-lysis to the creative output of such historical figures as Count Ludwig von Zinzendorf,[71] the founder of his mother's Moravian church who taught Christi-anity as a "religion of the heart."[72] While Pfister's conscious intention was prob-ably to apply a neutral, scientific approach, identifying sublimated sexual neuroses underlying Zinzendorf's ideas, other theologians and clergy saw this as pure disparagement and their reaction was severe.[73] The prominent Reformed theologian Eduard Thurneysen was incensed.[74] Freud, on the other hand, praised Pfister's clarity and open-mindedness in contrast with his critics' "saccharine underhandedness."[75]

By 1913, the growing conflict between Jung and Freud forced a crisis in Pfister's own identity and vocation as an analyst. Pfister made his declaration of allegiance to Freud with the publication of *The Psychoanalytic Method*.[76] The book was written primarily for non-medical therapists and educators, and was one of several more popular explanations of psychoanalytic theory that made Freud's ideas accessible to the wider public.[77] In it, Pfister distinguished between illusory religious experiences, borne of neurosis, versus the "true and healthy religion" made possible through psychoanalytic treatment. As Westerink notes, "religion," according to Pfister, had "the ethical mission to 'convert,' to sublimate feelings of anxiety, hate and guilt into a religiosity of love."[78] Westerink continues,

> [A]t the same time, true religion does not only unveil religious illusions, which he also calls religious errors, as invalid, but it also defends against regression into neurotic forms of religiosity.... This did not necessarily mean that true religion was completely without anxiety or a sense of guilt, but true (healthy) religion was not determined by these feelings.[79]

Pfister's continuing loyalty to Freud alienated him from the rest of the Swiss analytic community, and he was the target of attacks fueled by anti-Freudian hostility.[80] After the final acrimonious split between Freud and Jung in 1913, most of the original Swiss psychoanalysts remained loyal to Jung and seceded from the International Psychoanalytic Association. Pfister was forced out of his teaching role as an analytic *Dozent*. Now in exile in his own country, he wrote to Freud asking if he could join the Vienna Psychoanalytic Society.[81] Pfister is not listed in the official records of the Society, but for many years he was an ardent participant via correspondence, publishing numerous articles in *Imago* as well as many monographs.

After some turmoil, Pfister, together with his analysand Emil and Mira Oberholzer, founded a new Swiss Society for Psychoanalysis in 1919.[82] Pfister could not follow Jung's path in declaring the unconscious to be the source of ultimate existential truth.[83] Jung's enduring influence can still be seen, however, even in one of Pfister's later cases in 1927.[84] In one dream analysis Pfister interpreted a rank of soldiers in the dream as the patient's own strength, waiting to emerge. It might be argued that Pfister also influenced Jung, for example, regarding the libido as the life force, underlying the creative aspects of sublimation.[85]

Following the upheavals within the Swiss analytic community, Pfister embarked on a new period of creative productivity. He lectured widely in Germany, Scandinavia, and England[86] as a kind of circuit rider for psychoanalysis. He wrote a popular book grounded in both psychoanalysis and pedagogy entitled *Love in Children and Its Aberrations: A Book for Teachers and Parents*.[87] He followed this with a book on love in marriage in 1925: *Die Liebe von der Ehe und ihre Fehlentwicklungen: Eine Tiefenpsychologie Untersuchungen im Reiche des Eros* ("Marital Love and Its Developmental Failure: A Depth Psychological Investigation in the Realm of Love").[88] The latter brought a Christian love ethic into dialogue with psychoanalytic sexual theory as a way of strengthening what he saw as inevitable problems in marriage after the first flush of romantic love had passed. This was in part autobiographical, reflecting emotional strains in his own marriage to Erika,[89] culminating in his being "in danger of committing adulteries" (*Thorheiten*) as Freud put it to him years later.[90] In the 1920s, Pfister can be seen advocating passionately for the use of a psychoanalytic perspective combined with Christian ethics to bring relief to suffering families—something for which he himself was grasping, to maintain his integrity. Pfister continued to emphasize children and families in context, with a view toward alleviating unjust social conditions. Thus, in addition to being one of the first pastoral psychotherapists, Pfister may also have been the first Christian social worker.

During the same period, he also wrote several critical investigations of the converted Indian Christian missionary, Sadhu Sundar Singh.[91] Singh was a popular sensation at the time, "causing a considerable rustling of leaves in the Christian forest."[92] Following Freud's reality principle, Pfister considered Singh to be a spiritual charlatan, and he used his argument against the prophet's miracles and mysticism as a platform to promote "reality thinking" applied to religion. Like the theologian Rudolf Bultmann, whom he admired, Pfister set forth a demythologized Christian faith, shorn of superstition, and rooted in the historical-critical biblical research of his time.[93] Even so, Pfister admitted that some people "could be deeply edified by Sundhar's religious talk in spite of all objections."[94]

For Pfister, *Seelsorge* was at the heart of the pastor's mission, and psychoanalysis was in his view simply the deepest and richest source for effective practice.[95] One of his most important contributions to the practice of pastoral care, in 1927, was *Analytische Seelsorge: Einführung in die praktische Psychoanalyse für Pfarrer und Laien* ("Analytic Pastoral Care: Introduction to Practical Psychoanalysis for Pastors and Laypersons")[96] Pfister did not intend for pastoral care and counseling to be the exclusive purview of ordained clergy. Just as he himself was a "lay" (non-medical) analyst, so he also believed that the work of pastoral counseling could be conducted by "lay" (non-ordained) Christians—insisting that they had both the right and also the responsibility to obtain sound psychological training.[97]

In this volume, Pfister tied the mission of pastoral care to Christ's own merciful care for those in need, and his ministry of healing. Well aware of the perils of trying to relate Christian *Seelsorge* with Freud's psychoanalytic method (with both its Jewish and atheistic connotations), Pfister took a methodological turn in defense of his practice. Psychoanalysis, he said, was not in itself a worldview, but rather a method—a "plow" that would prepare the ground for spiritual and moral healing. Christianity was the worldview, which psychoanalysis could assist suffering believers in attaining. "Sowing follows after the plow—'as a sower, Jesus walked across the fields of the world'."[98] With this as his overarching framework, Pfister went on to address a variety of pastoral concerns which a minister might be called upon to address,[99] framed in terms of the sufferings and distorted ways of living caused by sin and evil, and the redemptive power of care to restore faith and relieve psychic suffering. Modes of suffering included "moral" (*sittliche*) impairments[100]—"compulsions to evil" such as stealing, alcoholism, sexual perversions, "Don Juanism," and pedophilia, as well as the pain of ruptured relationships, uncontrolled anger, and self-defeating unconscious life plans—and "religious" (*religiöse*) impairments[101] such as ghost hauntings and visions, and falling prey to religious clichés and "horizontal" reductions of faith to purely secular matters. He took up the necessity of confession within the purview of pastoral care, and showed tender concern for parishioners troubled by doubt, "wanderings from faith," and partial or total unbelief. He saw psychoanalysis as equally effective whether applied to behavioral or spiritual matters—the same "plow" would prepare the ground for healing in all types of fields.

Freud expressed general agreement with this in a letter to Pfister very early in their relationship:

> In itself psycho-analysis is neither religious nor non-religious, but an impartial tool which both priest and layman can use in the service of the sufferer. I am struck by the fact that it never occurred to me how extraordinarily helpful the psycho-analytic method might be in pastoral work, but that is surely accounted for by the remoteness from me, as a wicked pagan, of the whole system of ideas.[102]

Pfister's clinical technique, however, was certainly one of which Freud and his strictest followers in both Vienna and Zürich did not entirely approve. Pfister believed in the efficacy of psychoanalytic techniques of dream analysis, free association, management of resistances, and transference interpretation. But he believed equally in a "synthesis" of drive theory (uncovering the unconscious motivations that caused individuals neurotic distress), with the higher aim of "salvation by love" ("*Erlösung der Liebe*").[103] To that end, he appears to have been quite active in the therapeutic process, viewing his role not with the "emotional coldness of the surgeon" recommended by Freud (when Freud was at his most nervous about boundaries).[104] He evinced the warm and loving attitude of the Christian pastor, while his job as he saw it was not only to probe unconscious motives to alleviate neurotic suffering, but to teach, to exhort, and to pronounce absolution for the sake of salvation.

Pfister regarded the parishioner-patient's idealization of the pastor as a positive aid to care, mobilizing the energy of love (Pfister's interpretation of *libido*) as a shield against fear.[105] Interestingly, Freud never rejected Pfister on the grounds of expanding the definition of libido beyond sexuality, as he had quarreled with Jung. On the contrary, in his *Group Psychology*, Freud cited Pfister directly in expanding the definition of libido to the "love-force":

> We are of opinion, then, that language has carried out an entirely justifiable piece of unification in creating the word "love" with its numerous uses, and

that we cannot do better than take it as the basis of our scientific discussions and expositions as well. By coming to this decision, psycho-analysis has let loose a storm of indignation, as though it had been guilty of an act of outrageous innovation. Yet it has done nothing original in taking love in this "wider" sense. In its origin, function, and relation to sexual love, the "Eros" of the philosopher Plato coincides exactly with the love-force, the libido of psychoanalysis, as has been shown in detail by Nachmansohn and Pfister; and when the apostle Paul, in his famous epistle to the Corinthians, praises love above all else, he certainly understands it in the same "wider" sense.[106]

For Pfister, the libido was also a matter of will and character-building, so that freedom through psychoanalysis from neurotic preoccupations and anxieties would facilitate a healthy form of sublimation that was directed and empowered by faith toward the good.[107] Just as psychoanalysis was a tool of natural science to aid in achieving mental health, Pfister saw a further need for the inculcation of morals to achieve spiritual wellbeing. People of all ages, he thought (opposing the Calvinist doctrine of "total human depravity"), "very frequently have an inner need of positive values of a spiritual nature, of ethics and a philosophy of life, and these ... psychoanalysis cannot supply."[108]

Freud, of course, rejected any form of moralizing out of hand as having no place in the scientific role of the analyst. As early as 1909, Freud reported to the Wednesday Night Society that an essay by Pfister (in fact, Pfister's first published article describing analytic pastoral care[109]) was "interesting in several respects," with the one caveat that the transference was not fully grasped. Freud attributed that to

the fact that it is easy for Pfister to manage this transference. Religion is the most convenient form of sublimating, easily achieved by many people. The pastor turns toward God the love that is tendered him; and this path has long since been smoothed out.[110]

It was more difficult, Freud thought, for "the physician," because he did not have any substitutionary love to offer. It was in this precise context that Freud suggested that neurosis and religiosity might exist in inverse proportion (see Chapter 2).[111]

Freud continued to grant Pfister a certain waiver with regard both to the resolution of the transference (or its lack of resolution in a kind of "crooked" cure through love[112]), and to the activity of the analyst beyond interpretation. Writing to Pfister as late as 1927, he declared, "It should not be concluded ... that analysis should be followed by synthesis."[113] Freud left it up to the patient to integrate the insights from analysis into his or her own conduct of life. However, in the same letter, he conceded that "analytic passivity" was also an error, and that

You as a minister naturally have the right to call on all the reinforcements at your command, while we as analysts must be more reserved, and must lay the chief accent on the effort to make the patient independent, which often works out to the disadvantage of the therapy. Apart from that I am not so far from your point of view as you think.[114]

Sadly, the Swiss Psychoanalytic Society, which Pfister had worked so hard to establish after the schism with Jung, split again just a decade later in 1928–29, with a movement to purge the Society of lay analysts. In this, the psychiatrists were taking their cue from the psychoanalytic branches of the International Psychoanalytic Association in Berlin and New York. As will be seen in the chapter on Theodor Reik, this divisive issue had just driven Reik out of Vienna, and prompted Freud to publish a vigorous defense, *The Question of Lay Analysis*.[115] Pfister once again found himself bitterly embattled, this time as the target of the medical analysts' opprobrium. His method of brief analysis was also a point of contention. Pfister's former analysand and Society co-founder Emil Oberholzer now marshalled forces to compose a twenty-seven-page complaint against him.[116] Pfister's letters to Freud document a painful rift.

Pfister still had his pastoral post, however, from which he was able to continue to practice, teach, and write. Perhaps it was in part due to Freud's knowledge of these painful conflicts that he wrote to Pfister in October, 1927 that he had held back publishing his *Future of an Illusion*:[117]

> I had been wanting to write it for a long time, and postponed it out of regard for you, but the impulse became too strong. The subject-matter—as you will easily guess—is my completely negative attitude to religion, in any form and however attenuated, and, though there can be nothing new to you in this, I feared, and still fear, that such a public profession of my attitude will be painful to you. When you have read it you must let me know what measure of toleration and understanding you are able to preserve for the hopeless pagan. Always your cordially devoted Freud.[118]

Pfister wrote back graciously saying, "There is nothing new to me in your rejection of religion. I look forward to it with pleasurable anticipation. A powerful-minded opponent of religion is certainly of more service to it than a thousand useless supporters."[119] Pfister gave notice, however, that he would feel free to reply—and to do so publicly: "You have always been tolerant towards me, and am I to be intolerant of your atheism? If I frankly air my differences from you, you will certainly not take it amiss. Meanwhile my attitude is one of eager curiosity."[120] Freud replied in turn that he looked forward to Pfister's rebuttal to his self-avowed "declaration of war." He declared that it would give him "positive pleasure, it will be refreshing in the discordant critical chorus for which I am prepared."[121]

In spite of their mutual assurances of friendship, this could not have come at a worse time for Pfister. Isolated and rejected by many of his colleagues in Zürich, he fell ill for several weeks, and he set himself the task of writing his

"Friendly Disagreement with Prof. Sigmund Freud: The Illusion of a Future"[122] from his sickbed. He sent a draft to Freud in advance of submitting it for publication, and was gratified at the "non-partisan" review it received from Freud and the editorial board of *Imago*. The essay was quickly published the same year (1928), and Pfister subsequently incorporated it into a book, *Psychoanalyse und Weltanschauung*.[123]

Shortly thereafter, in 1929, Pfister's first wife Erika died. The following year he remarried, and enjoyed a happy relationship with his second wife Martha Zuppinger-Urner, a second cousin.[124] Martha had two children from a previous marriage, and the Pfister household once again was a home for children. In 1930, not long after his marriage, Pfister took a seven-month leave in America, beginning with a 4,000-attendee World Congress for Spiritual Hygiene in Washington, D.C. He went on to lecture at the universities of Berkeley, Stanford, Chicago, and Columbia in New York City. The University of Chicago offered him a professorship, which he declined. Pfister, though an accomplished scholar, had already turned down offers of university professorships in Zürich[125] and in Riga, Latvia,[126] always preferring direct practical work with parishioners, patients, and students over "paper theology."[127]

But Pfister kept writing. In the 1930s he produced numerous articles, and two more books on pastoral counseling. The first of these, in 1931, *Der Innerste Richter und seine Seelsorgliche Behandlung* ("The Inner Judge and its Pastoral Treatment"),[128] has a contemporary pastoral ring to it—confronting the overweaning inner critic through a caring and non-judgmental application of depth psychotherapy. The second book, in 1934, *Neutestamentliche Seelsorge und psychoanalytische Therapie* ("New Testament Pastoral Care and Psychoanalytic Therapy"),[129] addressed a turn in Protestant practical theology at the time to align pastoral care more closely with Reformed theology,[130] but with his own liberal emphasis on the love of Christ as the overarching message of the Gospel rather than doctrines regarding sin, judgment, and justification. That year, Pfister was awarded an honorary doctorate from the University of Zürich for his work in pastoral care and child psychotherapy.

His last visit with Freud occurred in 1936.[131] Their correspondence tapered off to just a few letters—perhaps not entirely coincidentally following Pfister's critique of Freud's *Future of an Illusion*. But Freud's pain and illness would also have been a factor in this, and both men continued to declare their friendship to the end of Freud's life. When Hitler invaded Austria in 1938, Pfister was one among several friends in Switzerland and elsewhere[132] to discreetly offer the Freud family refuge, but Freud chose to emigrate to London instead. Increasingly hard of hearing,[133] Pfister retired from his pastorate in Zürich in 1939, the year of both Freud's and Bleuler's deaths.

In retirement, in spite of advancing health problems, Pfister continued to write, publishing his book *Christianity and Fear*.[134] In it, he summarized his life-long emphasis on the damaging effects of repression and neurotic anxiety, while elaborating on the Johannine theme of love and its therapeutic significance:

"perfect love casts out fear,"[135] which had been the cornerstone of his pastoral theology. Continuing in a more argumentative mood again a few years later he produced *Calvins Eingreifen in die Hexer- und Hexenprozesse von Peney 1545 nach seiner Bedeutung für Geschichte und Gegenwart: Ein kritischer Beitrag zur Charakteristik Calvins und zur gegenwärtigen Calvin-Renaissance* ("Calvin's Intervention in the Peney Witch Trial in 1545, According to its Significance for History and the Present: A Critical Contribution on Calvin's Character and the Present-day Calvin-Renaissance").[136]

In retirement, he continued to condemn the element of cruelty he saw in the strict, uncompromising doctrinal writings of the Reformed church in Switzerland. He was, moreover, disputing Thurneysen, who in 1928 had applied Karl Barth's neo-orthodox Reformed theology to his own work on *Seelsorge*.[137] In general, Pfister had always felt that educators were more receptive to his work than theologians.[138] This was a long-festering complaint. "Above all, it grieved him that his much-admired Eduard Thurneysen dismissed him so quickly, called his lifework theologically questionable, and regarded its Christian substance as shriveled to a few rudiments of ethics."[139] To Thurneysen, Pfister's equation of Freud's psychoanalytic method with Christian love as "natural hygiene" seemed theologically naïve, and unacceptably pietistic.[140]

Fear and guilt were significant themes for both Pfister and Thurneysen, but their approaches were utterly different. Thurneysen rejected psychological approaches to pastoral care, and following Barth, saw healing exclusively in the assurances of justification for sin in the redeeming of an utterly transcendent, sovereign God. Barth himself had no use for psychoanalysis. Bundled together with his reaction against liberal theology, he saw theology descending into "the gruesome morass of the psychology of the unconscious."[141] Pfister's whole life, on the other hand, was dedicated to helping people overcome anxiety through a combination of understanding the neurotic origins of their anxiety and an experience of the loving acceptance of an immanent God.

Pfister's last book, published four years before his death, was another lengthy argument, bringing him full circle back to his original doctoral studies in philosophy and the psychology of religion: *Karl Jaspers als Sigmund Freuds Widersacher: Eine kritische Apologie* ("Karl Jaspers as Sigmund Freud's Adversary: A Critical Apologia").[142] Jaspers had recently moved to Basel from Heidelberg, Germany, which put him in Pfister's crosshairs. His monumental work *Von der Wahrheit* ("Of Truth") had just been published.[143] Jaspers is best known today as an existentialist philosopher whose articulation of the "limit situation" of existence led him to embrace a Kierkegaardian "leap of faith" toward the transcendent, while rejecting the anthropomorphic God of Judaism and Christianity.[144] Earlier, Jaspers had trained as a psychiatrist before becoming known as a philosopher, and his *General Psychopathology*[145] became a standard diagnostic text. Jaspers rejected any psychoanalytic view of the content of psychotic patients' hallucinations and delusions, believing that psychosis was an organic disease process impervious to analytic interpretation.

Pfister, in sharp disagreement with both the psychiatric and philosophical dimensions of Jaspers' *oeuvre*, reasserted his own synthesis of a psychoanalytic hermeneutic with the loving care of an immanent Christ. Jaspers was writing from a very different context, however, having been dismissed from his professorship in Heidelberg in 1937 for his outspoken sympathy toward the Jews. His wife was Jewish, and they lived under the continual threat of deportation to the camps. Jaspers was above all making a plea for rationality in the face of the Nazi threat. Pfister may not have fully appreciated Jaspers' situation, since as a Christian pastor in neutral Switzerland he did not fear for his own personal safety. Pfister certainly knew, through Freud's ordeal, of the dangers that others faced, however. He was overcome with revulsion (*Ekel*) for the Nazis during a visit to Germany in May, 1933—who with their stench of "Proletarian militarism" and "unspeakable stupidity" (*würdeloser Dummheit*) took out their wrath against the "defenceless" (*wehrlosen*) Jews.[146]

Pfister's last work was an article, "Gesundheit und Religion" ("Health and Religion"),[147] in a journal devoted to spiritual health, published the year before his death, of uremia, in 1956.[148] He had already suffered an embolism of the lung in 1944 shortly after completing *Christianity and Fear*,[149] and his health had been declining. At the time of his death, he was planning another volume on psychoanalysis and existentialism.[150] Once again in argumentative mode, he wanted to re-emphasize the foundations of *Seelsorge* in Freudian drive theory and Christian love (as depicted in research on the historical Jesus by his friend Albert Schweitzer),[151] over against the appropriation of existential philosophy and so-called "*Daseinanalyse*" into psychotherapy.[152]

Pfister: the loyal opposition

One feature of Pfister's character becomes clear from his biography. Although he was a devout Christian whose spiritual and social compass was Christ's love, he was never afraid of conflict. In fact, to the end of his life, he engaged vigorously in intellectual combat, and in many cases instigated it. His lifelong allergy to rigid Protestant dogmaticism, and his willingness to put up a fight, placed his pastorate in jeopardy at times,[153] just as his adamant adherence to Freud's theories had alienated him from the Swiss circle around Jung. His early writings were admonitions to the theological and ecclesial establishments to put more energy into practical theology—social work, psychotherapy, enlightened pedagogy, and care for the poor. He pitted scientific evidence against the abstractions of theology and philosophy. Having discovered Freud, he remained with him even when nearly everyone with whom he had built his life as an analyst turned against him (in the process, perhaps, neglecting to credit the legacy of Jung and the Swiss school in his own development). When his own classical analytic society turned against him and other non-medical practitioners, he persisted in his vocation and founded his own school for lay analysis.

Even with Freud, however, he was by no means a doormat, as will be seen in his reply to Freud's *Future of an Illusion*,[154] entitled "Friendly Disagreement with Prof. Sigmund Freud: The Illusion of a Future," "*Die Illusion einer Zukunft*" and published in *Imago* in 1928.[155] Faith was the ground he would not cede to any opponent. When it came to his relationship with Freud, he was a devoted friend and follower, but when it came to matters of religious faith, he was also Freud's most loyal opposition.

"The Illusion of a Future"

Pfister's "Illusion of a Future" is one of his most illuminating writings regarding his working out of a vocation that embraced both psychoanalysis and pastoral theology. In a letter to Freud accompanying the draft of that essay for Freud's review, he rationalized their differences, saying, "When I reflect that you are much better and deeper than your disbelief, and that I am much worse and more superficial than my faith, I conclude that the abyss between us cannot yawn so grimly." He stated—perhaps disingenuously, perhaps passive-aggressively?[156]— that he pictured Freud "smiling indulgently" at him upon receiving his critique, and possibly even deriving "a little bit of pleasure from it." He proffered,

> Our difference derives chiefly from the fact that you grew up in proximity to pathological forms of religion and regard these as "religion," while I had the good fortune of being able to turn to a free form of religion which to you seems to be an emptying of Christianity of its content, while I regard it as the core and substance of [the Gospel].[157]

In this very long article, Pfister summarized his own decades-long reconciliation of his vocation as a Protestant pastor with his vocation as a devoted Freudian analyst. He did not pull any punches when it came to defending religious belief, while maintaining Freud's method as a critical contribution to the practice of *Seelsorge* and the enlightened education of children. Because of its importance in the literature of psychology and religion, this essay warrants a detailed summary.

Pfister began with a letter to "Dear Professor" at the outset of the essay:

> Your book was for you an inner necessity, an act of honesty and of a confessional mood. Your colossal life's work would have been impossible without the smashing of false gods, whether they stood in universities or church halls.... To be frank about it: I have a strong suspicion that you do battle against religion—out of religious feeling.[158]

He noted that Christ spoke of liberation, which he also saw in Freud's work:

> And yet I turn decisively against your judgement of religion. I do it with the modesty appropriate to an inferior, but also with the joyfulness with which

one defends a holy and loved object and with a serious approach to truth that your strict school has encouraged. Yet I also do it in the hope that many a person who is frightened away from psychoanalysis by your rejection of religious belief will then take kindly to it again as a method and a sum of empirical insights.[159]

In the first section, "Freud's Criticism of Religion," Pfister followed Freud's own logical method of stating the arguments against his thesis and then putting them down. He enumerated Freud's critiques of religion, and then went about systematically countering them:[160]

1   "*The accusations.*"[161] Pfister first summarized Freud's critique of religion as akin to obsessional neurosis stemming from the Oedipus complex, and as infantile wish fulfillment. He then set out to address these critiques in turn.

2   "*Religion as neurotic compulsion.*"[162] Pfister suggested that the "instinctual renunciations" required by civilization precede religion, but that religion as well as society could do away with excessive repression:

> [E]ven if it is difficult to deny this burden of compulsion in religion's very first stages, one must still ask if it belongs to religion's essence. Couldn't this collective neurotic trait very well fall away without harm, and even to the advantage of the whole, just as the tadpoles give up their tails so that as frogs they can hop about the world that much more comfortably?[163]

He distinguished between the early totem cult's origins in repression of the sexual drive, and the later development of "social-ethical monotheism" in Judaism (a distinction Freud viewed more in terms of a seamless development rather than a break), pointing to Christianity as a further development of liberation from "compulsively neurotic nomism": "Must compulsive structures really always be inherent in religion? I believe that, on the contrary, the highest religious developments in fact abolish coercion."[164] He went on to cite similar movements toward freedom, conscience, and love in "the religion of Akhenaton and ... of Buddha."[165]

3   "*Religion as a wishful construct.*"[166] Pfister cited a parallel to Freud in Feuerbach's writing almost a century earlier: "That ideas of God and the beyond are often painted with colours from a wish palette is something I have always known."[167] Pfister, however, perceived renunciation of infantile wishes in both the strenuous morality of the Israelite prophets, and again in the New Testament:

> [I]n the Gospel, we see instinctual wishes fought against in a powerful way and this becomes all the stronger as the development of Jesus proceeds in a steady battle with the tradition. We see the idea of reward,

the idea of race, and the idea of the next life, with its colouration of
sensuality all repressed, and the idea of reward, according to the view
of psychoanalysis, is in fact repressed far more skillfully and wisely
than in the rigorous philosophy of [Kant's] categorical imperative, with
its misguided pouring aside of love.... Jesus stresses explicitly that
sensual expectations for the life after death are to be ruled out (Matt.
22:30). His highest ideal, the kingdom of God, has the earth as its
setting and ideal ethical and religious values that have nothing to do
with instinctual wishes as its content.[168]

4   *"Religion as hostile to thought."*[169] Pfister flatly rejected the idea that rationality and religion were incompatible, stating that Protestants "criticize the
Bible and dogmas as radically as did Homer or Aristotle."[170] Catholics, he
asserted, practice apologetics from a rational stance, and the Reformers were
scientific in their thinking: "Even the gloomy Calvin, Geneva's sinister
grand inquisitor, made his juridical thinking accessible to his fortress-like
theology."[171] He went on to name many brilliant scientists and mathemati-
cians whose intellect was not impeded by their faith in God (Descartes,
Newton, Darwin, Pasteur, Pascal) as well as philosophers (Kant, Fichte,
Hegel, Bergson). As an educator, Pfister also argued that religious thought
could enrich rather than limit children's intellectual development.

5   *"Religion as a guardian of civilisation."*[172] Here Pfister found himself agreeing with Freud's critique that religion has gone too far at times in functioning as "civilisation's police."[173] Yet, he asserted, Christianity functions at its
best as it "must strive toward the most fundamental changes in our culture,
which is alienated and stunted in its inner values, especially emotional
ones."[174] Religion when "taken most seriously" can stand "as a leader and
beacon toward true civilisation from our sham civilisation" characterized by
"war, the spirit of Mammon, love of pleasure, the poverty of the masses,
exploitation, oppression, and innumerable other wrongs."[175] "Thy kingdom
come" in the Lord's Prayer, for Pfister, was a call to social change and
enrichment of human life through "truth, beauty, love," and intellectual
achievement.[176]

In a second section entitled "Freud's Scientism," Pfister took up Freud's claim
that science, in contrast to religion, is what can "make people happy":[177]

1   *"The belief in a science that makes people happy."*[178] Pfister praised Freud's
scientific positivism, but disputed as too optimistic Freud's final assertions
in *The Future of an Illusion* that science would ultimately triumph and the
reality principle would provide true consolation. Here, in my view, Pfister
misread Freud, whose pessimism is clear in the last page of *The Future of
an Illusion*—we can be disillusioned and in that sense become mature, but
nothing can make us "happy," the desire for which is itself an infantile wish.

2   *"Historical examination."*[179] Pfister briefly suggested that *The Future of an Illusion* "diverges" from Freud's usual rational positivistic stance, coming close to philosophy, but then he re-established Freud as one who "towers over the materialists of the 18th century."[180]

3   *"Freud's optimism about science."*[181] Here Pfister examined Freud's claim that science represented pure progress. Using psychoanalytic thinking to counter Freud's (supposed) confidence in science, he wrote, "Couldn't there be a wish hidden behind Freud's belief in the ultimate victory of the intellect, and couldn't his prophecy of the end of an illusion include the parade of a new illusion, namely a scientific one?"[182]

4   *"Freud's belief in the adequacy of science."*[183] Pfister refuted Freud's empiricism more firmly, stating,

> [A]s joyfully and enthusiastically as I follow Freud on the wonderful paths of his empirical science, at this point it is impossible for me to keep step with him. Here Freud's brilliant intellect soars to an intellectuality that, intoxicated by its successes, forgets its limits. We human beings are not only thinking devices; we are living, feeling, desiring beings. We need goods and values; we have to have something that satisfies our emotions, that stimulates our aspirations.[184]

He lifted up art as "the herald, blessed with a prophetic gift, of deep secrets and the revealer of costly treasures that now, and in the future, escape the scholar's spectacles; it is a wonder of nourishment for hungry souls."[185] Pfister then returned to his emphasis on the moral-ethical importance of religion: "And even less can ingenious science replace for us the realm of moral values and strengths,"[186] especially as represented by "the ethics of Jesus" (distinct from rigid moralistic strands of Christianity which Pfister critiqued for regressing "into the puritanical").[187] He concluded this section with the statement "Under belief ... we understand not only an idea but rather the stirring of the entire inner human being. How poor science seems to us in contrast to this abundance!"[188]

Pfister believed that he and Freud shared a passion for the truth. Citing his own article on psychoanalysis and worldview,[189] he asserted that science could in fact give rise to both a new metaphysics and a moral framework. Pfister did not want to throw out the baby of religion with the bathwater of scientific inquiry, but rather, to forge a synthesis: "[a] balanced religion can result only from the harmonious combination of belief and knowledge, from the interpenetration of wishful and realistic thinking."[190] For Pfister, superstitious belief in miracles was obsolete, but the Bible itself "has become not smaller for us, but more splendid, since we no longer suspect it of being a paper pope and infallible oracle." As a free Protestant believer, Pfister saw the Bible as a continuing source of "moral commitment" and "a hygienics that gives information about the dangers threatening individual and social health and, thereby points to a lawfulness that makes decisions about happiness and suffering and is decisive for the shaping of life."[191] This lawfulness, he stated, is an expression of "the highest cosmic evolutionary striving and, as the result of a relation to the will of the creator ... [is] sacred."[192]

"Can we dispense with this religious deepening?" he asked. "Will the advance of the exact sciences make it superfluous?"[193] Rejecting conservative orthodox beliefs, Pfister declared, "I must, in opposition to Freud's prophecy of the future of an illusion, posit the no longer prophetic, but psychologically-based assertion of the illusion of such a future." Pfister, led by the "god Logos" of the Gospel of John, believed that Freud, "led by his god Logos," ultimately had the same goal of "divine wisdom and love":[194]

> It is not the religious creed that is the true criterion for a Christian; in John 13:35 another is given. "By this love you have for one another, everyone will know that you are my disciples." At the risk of being mocked by loose tongues, I dare to assert again that Freud, in the light of these words, with his view of life, and his life's work has pre-eminence over many a certified church-Christian who considers him a heathen, as he does himself.[195]

"And thus," Pfister announced, making his boldest synthesis of all, "*The Future of an Illusion* and 'The Illusion of a Future' unite in the strong belief whose credo is: 'The truth shall make you free!'."[196]

Freud's reply as the article was making its way through the publishing house was cordial, although he could not resist a barbed retort to the effect that analysts should leave the work of granting forgiveness to the priests, and that priests should not be analysts: "I should like to hand [psychoanalysis] over to a profession which does not yet exist, a profession of *lay* curers of souls who need not be doctors and should not be priests."[197] This remark stung Pfister, who declared that he himself had conducted treatments "without ever mentioning a word about religion," as appropriate. However, ethics and moral guidance was not something he was willing to abandon, and he begged Freud to

> ... forgive a long-standing enthusiast for art and humanitarianism and an old servant of God.... At heart you serve exactly the same purpose as I, and act "as if" there were a purpose and meaning in life and the universe, and I with my feeble powers can only fit your brilliant and analytical discoveries and the healing powers into that gap. Do you really wish to exclude from analytical work a "priesthood" understood in this sense? I do not believe that that is what you mean.

Freud replied a week later on a conciliatory note, admitting that excluding priests "does not sound very tolerant," and although he imagined a future in which neither priests nor a "pious illusion of providence" would be necessary, he agreed that "patients' demands for ethical values" should not cause difficulties. He protested that Pfister was flattering him with "an excessively friendly thought," that he behaved "as if there were 'one life, one meaning in life'," and that it always reminded him of the rabbinic tale of "the monk who insisted on regarding Nathan [a Jew] as a thoroughly good Christian. I am a long way from being Nathan, but of course I cannot help remaining 'good' towards you. Cordially yours, Freud." With that last exchange, the two friends ended their most strenuous debate.

Why didn't Freud reject Pfister?[198]

There is no doubt that Freud valued Pfister as a loyal remnant of psychoanalytic orthodoxy in Switzerland after Jung departed with many other Swiss analysts in his wake. But Freud's loyalty toward Pfister transcended the maxim "The enemy of my enemy is my friend." The correspondence between Freud and Pfister is in some sense an *Urtext* for the most friendly debate imaginable between the "godless Jew"[199] and the liberal Swiss pastor who was drawn to the invigorating ideas and insights of psychoanalysis, but nevertheless retained his belief in a loving, provident God.

Freud wrote to Pfister that his continuing belief in God was the one thing he could not forgive him[200]—yet, this "transgression" was not enough for Freud to break off the relationship. Why was this unforgivable belief on Pfister's part nonetheless so forgivable, in the sense that Freud continued to express admiration and even kindness toward Pfister? Ana-Maria Rizzuto's book *Why Did Freud Reject God? A Psychodynamic Interpretation*[201] may offer some clues to the question: Why *didn't* Freud reject Pfister?

Rizzuto's initial analysis in answer to her question "Why did Freud reject God?" should be familiar to scholars of psychology and religion—that in spite of a more religious upbringing than Freud later admitted, and an early attraction toward both the God of his liberal Jewish father and the God of his rather hysterical Roman Catholic nanny, early childhood losses and traumas (including the move from Freiberg to the poor Jewish ghetto of Vienna, the shameful and public arrest of an uncle for embezzlement, the precipitous dismissal of his nanny who also molested him, and his mother's constant preoccupation with new babies and bouts of tuberculosis), this sensitive and intelligent boy's childlike faith was shattered, and replaced with an at times defensive intellectual quest to conquer both the "higher … and infernal regions" via the "discovery" of the unconscious.[202] Freud's eventual insistence on infantile sexuality and the centrality of the drives of sex and aggression no doubt further poked a stick in the eye of nineteenth-century Viennese religion, which was so moralistically avoidant of both.

But under rebellion lay tragedy, beginning in early childhood and compounded by decades of war, violence, and antisemitism. These experiences engendered a profound pessimism in Freud about any inherent goodness in humanity, as he wrote in *Civilization and Its Discontents*: "Man is wolf to man."[203] In a fictional encounter between Freud and C. S. Lewis in the play

"Freud's Last Session," the playwright Mark St. Germain captures the heart of Freud's angry rejection of God.[204] Lewis says, "If pleasure is [God's] whisper, pain is his megaphone." Freud rises out of his chair and spits out, "So cancer is God's voice. If I tell him today I believe, my tumor would rejoice and vanish." Lewis demurs, but Freud continues,

> We carry self-destruction within us.... Original sin? ... Just the hubris of it! That mere men could incense a god by eating an apple! That God would then reward them by delivering his Son to be sacrificed, a vicious murder that redeems them? ... I'm sure Hitler, the little altar boy who served at church every Sunday, agrees with you. But I cannot.

Here the stage note reads: "He is in pain and out of patience." Freud's character continues,

> We speak different languages. You believe in revelation. I believe in science, the dictatorship of reason. There is no common ground.... My daughter Sophie died of Spanish Flu at twenty-seven. A mother, a wife, snatched from her family! But this was God's plan if only I was smart enough to understand it? My grandson Heinele was killed by tuberculosis at five years old! Five! What a brilliant plan of God to murder him! I wish cancer attacked my brain instead. Then, perhaps, I could hallucinate there is a God, and seek vengeance.[205]

Rizzuto goes further, showing a link between Freud's relationship with his father Jakob and his (Sigmund's) faith in God (not surprising, given that Rizzuto's important first book, *The Birth of the Living God*,[206] was concerned with the origins of individuals' God-imagoes in early object relations). She discusses at length the Philippson Bible that Jakob gave Sigmund on the latter's thirty-fifth birthday to mark his entrance into mature middle age.[207] The Bible is an illustrated parallel-text German-Hebrew Bible with extensive historical and archaeological commentary—an Enlightenment-inspired liberal project aimed at invigorating Judaism among German Jewish intellectuals. Jakob had originally given it to Sigmund when the boy was about age seven, and he presented it to him again in adulthood inscribed with a plea, cleverly redacted from biblical quotations, that he return to the faith. Rizzuto shows how Freud's rejection of God was bound up with his disillusionment with his father (summed up in the story of the anti-Semite knocking his father's hat off, and his father simply stepping into the street to retrieve it rather than fighting back or vowing revenge),[208] but, as well, shows how much he loved both his father and that Bible as a child. He spent hours poring over its pages, and even colored many of the illustrations by hand. Although he disavowed its importance as a sacred text later in his life, Freud wrote in the 1935 revised edition of his *Autobiographical Study*, "My deep engrossment in the Bible story (almost as soon as I had learnt the art of reading) had, as I recognized much later, an enduring effect upon the direction of my interest."[209] This familiarity with the biblical text provided the backdrop for his fluency in debating both psycho-analytic and religious ideas with Pfister.

Rizzuto further shows a link between the Philippson Bible and Freud's addic-tion to acquiring antiquities. Rizzuto points out a close resemblance between these objects and the illustrations in the Philippson Bible, especially the prepon-derance of Egyptian objects in Freud's collection. There were several ancient Jewish artifacts as well.[210] Notably, Freud began collecting these antiquities immediately after the death of his father. Rizzuto makes the claim that these objects served as "transitional objects" to his lost father. The Bible itself had to be disavowed as part of Freud's conscious overturning of his father's author-ity—paralleling the oedipal theory, which he was developing while grieving his father's death.[211] But with that grief, the repressed also returned in the form of a hypomanic defense—surrounding himself with the very images that his father's Bible displayed—in three dimensions, eventually crowding every corner of his consulting room and study.[212]

These figures, most of them representing ancient gods, were the first audience for his work—a comfort which, like cigars (a vice he inherited from his father), he claimed he could not do without—in Peter Gay's words, "his silent, loyal, immensely rewarding companions."[213] They functioned as the perfect neurotic symptom—at once fulfilling the forbidden wish to return to the naïve, childhood love and protection of the father, and the more conscious disavowal of the father's power. Now God/the gods were reduced to objects that Freud could control and domesticate. He would sometimes bring them to the family dinner table,[214] display them to patients and friends, and even pet them[215] like his beloved Chow dog, Jofi. Yet, he regarded at least some of them as having a kind of talismanic value—he regarded a particular Venus figure as protective, and was most anxious that she arrive safely in the move to London when he and his family fled the Nazis. This calls to mind, as well, Diane Jonte-Pace's,[216] Madelon Sprengnether's,[217] and, to some extent, also Rizzuto's work[218] associating Freud's rejection of religious experience (especially what his contemporary, the anthropologist Romain Rolland, had called the "oceanic feeling"[219]) with his fear and rejection of the maternal—at the same time as he depended heavily on the care and protection of women, from his wife and sister-in-law, to his benefactor Marie Bonaparte (who helped to get both him and his antiquities out of Vienna), and of course, his daughter Anna.

So what does all this have to do with Oskar Pfister? And why, if Freud rejected God, did Freud *not* reject Pfister? My theory—admittedly speculative—is that Pfister functioned much in the same way for Freud as did his collection of ancient gods and goddesses. At the conscious level, Pfister was a good disciple with a notable quirk—his retention of religion. But Pfister never contested Freud's sexual theory, the Oedipus, or the drives. Pfister's challenges were of the kind that Freud encouraged. Freud seemed to think that they were more likely to expand the insights of psychoanalysis than to undermine them. Pfister "gave good son" in a way that Jung and others did not. And perhaps all the more significantly for Freud after Jung's defection, he had in Oskar Pfister not only a Gentile disciple, but a super-Christian one—a pastor!

Like all good neurotic symptoms, Freud's attachment to Pfister also fulfilled his forbidden wishes. Pfister "gave good son," but he also "gave good father." Pfister, as a liberal and intellectual man of faith, invoked Freud's childhood memories of his father—but not the father who once traumatized Freud (1900) with the scathing words, "This boy will amount to nothing!"[220] Pfister was an admiring protector. In this way he also invoked Freud's adoring mother, who believed that her "*goldener Sigi*"[221] would one day be a great man. Pfister's intelligent discourse about both psychology and religion perhaps carried reminiscences of the Phillipson Bible—which not only presented the ancient sacred text, but provided thoughtful commentary about its *Sitz-im-Leben*—a kind of psychosocial history of the Jewish people, and in form, a kind of depth-analytic hermeneutical guide.

Most speculatively, as a Christian, might Pfister even have represented belief in the Resurrection, or an afterlife? Writing to Fliess immediately following his father's death, Freud explicitly disavowed any interest in life after death.[222] Yet he surrounded himself with Egyptian organ-jars, sarcophagi, and figures of gods who ferried souls to the afterlife, weighed their moral substance on golden scales, and provided magical entry into the underworld of the dead!

My conclusion is that Freud didn't reject Pfister because he couldn't. Pfister was the return of the repressed for Freud. Freud's conscious ego had thrown God out, along with his disappointing and disapproving father and his supposedly infantile reliance on faith. Freud's god "Logos" required facing up to the reality principle as an adult who had "put away childish things" (I Cor. 13:11)—or, in words from *The Future of an Illusion*: "Men cannot remain children forever; they must in the end go out into 'hostile life'."[223] But the desires of Freud the boy could not be so neatly put to rest. Pfister was for Freud, in Rizzuto's words, a "rebirth of the living father/God"[224]—an "antiquity" (as one who clung to ancient beliefs) who not only provided an audience like the "old and dirty gods" on Freud's desk, but who actually talked back, kindly, respectfully, intelligently. The Freud-Pfister relationship becomes a window not only into Freud's conscious ideas and theories and his rebuttal of religion, but perhaps also into his repressed desires—for a God and father who would admire and love him, and carry his name forward in the Book of Life.

Notes

1 Meng and Freud, 1963; Noth, 2014.
2 Hoffer, 1958: 616, citing Pfister, 1953; Noth, 2014: 9, 359.
3 Lit. "soul care."
4 Meng and Freud, 1963: 12–13, 16–17; Gay, 1987: 73.

5 Gay, 1987: 84. Cf. Noth, 2014: 24.
6 There are 215 in Noth, 2014, plus a few family correspondences; we know that Freud destroyed some additional letters by Pfister upon the latter's request (Noth and Morgenthaler, 2014: 85).
7 Noth and Morgenthaler, 2014: 85.
8 Noth, 2014.
9 Pfister, 1909a, 1909b.
10 E.g., Pfister, 1910, 1911b, 1912b.
11 Pfister, 1911a.
12 Pfister, 1920a.
13 Pfister, 1947, 1948a.
14 Pfister, 1912a, 1913.
15 Pfister, 1911–12.
16 Pfister, 1917/1913, 1924b.
17 Pfister, 1920b.
18 Pfister, 1922.
19 Pfister, 1911–12.
20 Pfister, 1924a/1922.
21 Pfister, 1925.
22 Pfister, 1927a.
23 See also Pfister, 1943.
24 Pfister, 1993/1928.
25 Freud, 1961a/1927.
26 Pfister, 1931c.
27 Pfister, 1931a.
28 Pfister, 1932.
29 Pfister, 1935a.
30 Pfister, 1935b.
31 Pfister, 1940, 1944.
32 Pfister, 1948b/1944.
33 Pfister, 1947, 1948a.
34 Pfister, 1949.
35 Pfister, 1952.
36 See Nase, 1993: 575–595 for complete bibliography.
37 Meng and Freud, 1963: 63; Noth, 2014: 105.
38 I John 4:16.
39 Meng and Freud, 1963: 63, cf. orig. German in Noth, 2014: 106–107.
40 Ibid.
41 Cf. Gay, 1987: 81. Decades later, Anna Freud found the remark "A better Christian never was" incomprehensible, and offensive (unpubl. 1954 letter to Jones—Gay, 2006: 192n).
42 Hoffer, 1958.
43 APA, 2016.
44 No critical biography of Pfister is published in English. Details can be gleaned from his correspondence, his obituary, two autobiographical essays (Pfister, 1927b, 1953), and other primary sources. Brief English summaries include Noth and Morgenthaler (2014), Zulliger (1966), and Lee (2005). The best source (in German) is Nase, 1993: 568–574, which includes an annotated timeline of Pfister's life and works.
45 The Emmanuel Movement in Boston was roughly contemporaneous (Holifield, 1983: 201–209).
46 Nase, 1993: 568; Noth and Morgenthaler, 2014: 82.
47 Nase, 1993: 568.

48   Pfister introduced Albert Schweitzer, its most famous resident, to Freud (Noth, 2007; Noth and Morgenthaler, 2014: 82).
49   Rizzuto, 1979.
50   Pfister, 1898.
51   Westerink, 2009: 52–53.
52   Ibid., 53. As Westerink notes, his interest in psychology predated his reading of Freud's *Interpretation of Dreams* in 1908, largely due to the influence of Schleiermacher and Biedermann (p. 51).
53   Nase, 1993: 568.
54   Literally, "Preachers' church," from its origins as a Dominican abbey—the "Order of Preachers" (Isabelle Noth, personal communication).
55   Nase, 1993: 568.
56   Pfister, 1904.
57   Nase, 1993: 567; Westerink, 2009: 55.
58   Pfister, 1903.
59   Pfister, 1923, 1924b; cf. Noth, 2014: 24.
60   Pfister, 1907.
61   April 26, 1909, in Brabant *et al.*, 1993: 55; Gay, 2006: 191.
62   Anna Freud, Preface to Meng and Freud, 1963: 11.
63   Cf. Nase, 1993: 151–166.
64   Ibid.
65   Noth, 2014: 15, 18–19.
66   Falzeder, 1994; Noth, 2014: 371.
67   Noth and Morgenthaler, 2014: 85; Noth, 2014: 15.
68   Shamdasani, 2012: 35–37.
69   Riklin, 1915/1908.
70   Gollnick, 1992: 36–39.
71   Pfister, 1911b, 1912b.
72   Atwood, 2004: 256.
73   Cf. Westerink, 2009: 57.
74   Noth, 2010: 79–81.
75   "süssliche Hinterhältigkeit" (PC-W transl.) (Freud, letter to Pfister, May 28, 1911, in Noth, 2014: 80, 81n3; cf. Meng and Freud, 1963: 50: "fulsome reserve." Freud had already praised Pfister's Zinzendorf research on June 17, 1910; Freud found Zinzendorf quite sympathetic, if foolish (Noth, 2014: 67; Meng and Freud, 1963: 40–41)).
76   Pfister, 1917, 1924b. Freud considered this Pfister's most important work (Meng and Freud, 1963: 95).
77   Gay, 2006: 458, 461.
78   Westerink, 2009: 59, citing Pfister, 1924b: 355.
79   Ibid., 59–60, citing Pfister, 1924b: 356.
80   Nase, 1993: 568.
81   Letter from Pfister to Freud, July 9, 1914, in Noth, 2014: 101–102.
82   Moser, 2011; Noth, 2014: 8; Nase, 1993: 136.
83   See Nase, 1993: 195–198, 2000: 70.
84   Noth, 2014: 17, citing Pfister, 1927a.
85   Westerink, 2009: 55, 58.
86   Gay, 2006: 458; Lee, 2005.
87   Pfister, 1924a/1922.
88   Pfister, 1925.
89   Noth and Morgenthaler, 2014: 87.
90   Freud, letter to Pfister, June 1, 1927 (Noth, 2014: 230–231, PC-W transl.; bowdlerized in Meng and Freud, 1963: 108 as "in danger of committing stupidities"). See

    also Falzeder, 1994: 307; Noth, 2014: 230–231; Freud–Jung letters 1911–12, in
    McGuire, 1974: 448–493.
 91 E.g., Pfister, 1926. Cf. Nase, 1993: 581–583.
 92 Scharfenberg, 1988: 5.
 93 Ibid.
 94 Ibid.
 95 Cf. Noth, 2010: 62–109.
 96 Pfister, 1927a.
 97 Ibid., 121–144.
 98 Ibid., 139, as cited in Noth, 2014: 27. Cf. Noth, 2010: 84–94.
 99 Ibid., 25–115.
100 Ibid., 61.
101 Ibid., 62–115.
102 Freud to Pfister, February 9, 1909, in Meng and Freud, 1963: 17.
103 Meng and Freud, 1963: 4.
104 Freud, 1958/1912: 115.
105 Nase, 2000: 80.
106 Freud, 1955b/1921: 91, citing Pfister, 1921.
107 Cf. Westerink, 2009: 55.
108 Letter from Pfister to Freud, February 9, 1929, in Meng and Freud, 1963: 127
109 Pfister, 1909a.
110 Nunberg and Federn, 1976–81, II: 149.
111 Ibid.
112 Freud, 1955b/1921: 142.
113 Meng and Freud, 1963: 113.
114 Ibid.
115 Freud, 1959b/1926.
116 Noth and Morgenthaler, 2014: 85.
117 Freud, 1961a/1927.
118 Meng and Freud, 1963: 109–110. Letter from Freud to Pfister, October 16, 1927.
119 Ibid., 110. Letter from Pfister to Freud, October 21, 1927.
120 Ibid.
121 Ibid., 112. Freud to Pfister, October 22, 1927.
122 Pfister, 1993/1928.
123 Pfister, 1928.
124 Nase, 1993: 156n100, 572.
125 Noth and Morgenthaler, 2014: 83.
126 Nase, 2000: 67.
127 Hoffer, 1958.
128 Pfister, 1931b.
129 Pfister, 1934.
130 E.g., Thurneysen, 1988/1928.
131 Nase, 1993: 572.
132 E.g., Binswanger, 1957: 100, and Jones, 1972: 233–237.
133 Nase, 1993: 572.
134 Pfister, 1948b/1944.
135 I John 4:18.
136 Pfister, 1947. Cf. Pfister, 1948a.
137 Thurneysen, 1988/1928.
138 Meng and Freud, 1963: 104.
139 Scharfenberg, 1988: 8.
140 Thurneysen, 1988/1928: 73.

141 Scharfenberg, 1988: 12.
142 Pfister, 1952.
143 Jaspers, 1947.
144 Jaspers, 1971/1935.
145 Jaspers, 1972/1913.
146 Noth, 2014: 289; Meng and Freud, 1963: 139.
147 Pfister, 1955.
148 Nase, 1993: 572. His second wife Martha survived him, living on until 1989.
149 Ibid.
150 Ibid., 573.
151 Schweitzer, 2001/1910–50; cf. Noth, 2007.
152 Nase, 1993: 573. "*Daseinanalyse*" began with Binswanger's turn toward existential philosophy (e.g., 1942).
153 Gay, 2006: 191.
154 Freud, 1961a/1927.
155 Pfister, 1993/1928.
156 Reijzer, 2011: 64.
157 Pfister letter to Freud, February 20, 1928, in Meng and Freud, 1963: 122. "*Evangeliums*" (cf. Noth, 2014: 256) means "Gospel," not "evangelism" as per Meng and Freud.
158 Ibid., 559.
159 Ibid.
160 Contra Reijzer (2011), who sees Pfister's essay as "inconsequential" and "not touch[ing] the main points of Freud's argument" (p. 61).
161 Ibid., 560.
162 Ibid.
163 Pfister, 1993/1928: 561.
164 Ibid.
165 Ibid., 562.
166 Ibid., 563.
167 Ibid.
168 Ibid., 564.
169 Ibid., 567.
170 Ibid.
171 Ibid., 568.
172 Ibid., 569.
173 Ibid.
174 Ibid.
175 Ibid.
176 Ibid.
177 Ibid., 570.
178 Ibid.
179 Ibid., 571.
180 Ibid., 572.
181 Ibid.
182 Ibid., 574.
183 Ibid.
184 Ibid.
185 Ibid., 575.
186 Ibid.
187 Ibid.
188 Ibid., 577.

189 Pfister, 1920b.
190 Pfister, 1993/1928: 577.
191 Ibid.
192 Ibid.
193 Ibid., 578.
194 Ibid.
195 Ibid.
196 Ibid.
197 Meng and Freud, 1963: 126.
198 This section adapted from Cooper-White, 2014. Used by permission, Springer Press.
199 Meng and Freud, 1963: 64.
200 Noth and Morgenthaler, 2014.
201 Rizzuto, 1998.
202 Freud, 1953/1900.
203 Freud, 1961b/1930: 111n3.
204 St. Germain, 2011: 25–26.
205 Ibid., 26.
206 Rizzuto, 1979.
207 Rizzuto, 1998: 105–133.
208 Freud, 1953/1900: 197; see Chapter 2.
209 Freud, 1959a/1925: 8.
210 Yerushalmi, 2013/1991.
211 Freud, 1955a/1914: 244, cited in Rizzuto, 1998: 244.
212 Gamwell and Wells, 1989.
213 Gay, 1989: 15.
214 Jones, 1955: 393, cited in Rizzuto, 1998: 18.
215 Salisbury, 1989, cited in Rizzuto, 1998: 19.
216 Jonte-Pace, 2001.
217 Sprengnether, 1992.
218 Rizzuto, 1998.
219 E. Freud, 1960: 389.
220 Freud, 1953/1900: 16.
221 Jones, 1972: 3, cited in Rizzuto, 1998: 194.
222 Freud, letter to Fliess, December 4, 1896, in Masson, 1985; cf. Rizzuto, 1998: 2.
223 Freud, 1961a/1927: 49.
224 Cf. Rizzuto's (1979) title: *The Birth of the Living God.*

References

APA (American Psychiatric Association) (2016). Oskar Pfister award. Online at www.psychiatry.org/psychiatrists/awards-leadership-opportunities/awards/oskar-pfister-award. Accessed August 21, 2016.

Atwood, Craig (2004). Zinzendorf, Nikolaus Ludwig von (1700–60). In *Europe, 1450 to 1789: Encyclopedia of the early modern world* (pp. 256–257). New York: Charles Scribners & Sons. Online at www.encyclopedia.com/history/encyclopedias-alamanacs-transcripts-and-maps/zinzendorf-nikolaus-ludwig-von-1700-1760. Accesssed September 3, 2017.

Binswanger, Ludwig (1942). *Grundformen und Erkenntnis menschlichen Daseins.* Zürich: Niehans.

Binswanger, Ludwig (1957). *Sigmund Freud: Reminiscences of a friendship*. Norbert Guterman (Trans.). New York: Grune & Stratton.
Brabant, Eva, Falzeder, Ernst, and Giampieri-Deutsch, Patrizia (Eds.) (1993). *The correspondence of Sigmund Freud and Sándor Ferenczi, Vol. I, 1908–1914*. Cambridge, MA: Belknap/Harvard University Press.
Cooper-White, Pamela (2014). Why didn't Freud reject Pfister? *Pastoral Psychology, 63*: 91–95.
Falzeder, Ernst (1994). My grand-patient, my chief tormentor: A hitherto unnoticed case of Freud's and the consequences. *Psychoanalytic Quarterly, 63*: 297–331.
Freud, Ernst (Ed.) (1960). *Letters of Sigmund Freud*. T. and J. Stern (Trans.). New York: Basic Books.
Freud, Sigmund (1953). *The interpretation of dreams*. In J. Strachey (Ed.), *Standard edition of the complete works of Sigmund Freud*, Vol. 4–5 (entire). (Orig. publ. 1900.)
Freud, Sigmund (1955a). *Some reflections on schoolboy psychology*. In J. Strachey (Ed.), *Standard edition of the complete works of Sigmund Freud*, Vol. 13: 239–244. (Orig. publ. 1914.)
Freud, Sigmund (1955b). *Group psychology and the analysis of the ego*. In J. Strachey (Ed.), *Standard edition of the complete works of Sigmund Freud*, Vol. 18: 65–144. (Orig. publ. 1921.)
Freud, Sigmund (1958). *Recommendations to physicians practising psycho-analysis*. In J. Strachey (Ed.), *Standard edition of the complete works of Sigmund Freud*, Vol. 12: 109–120. (Orig. publ. 1912.)
Freud, Sigmund (1959a). *An autobiographical study*. In J. Strachey (Ed.), *Standard edition of the complete works of Sigmund Freud*, Vol. 20: 7–74. (Orig. publ. 1925.)
Freud, Sigmund (1959b). *The question of lay analysis*. In J. Strachey (Ed.), *Standard edition of the complete works of Sigmund Freud*, Vol. 20: 177–258. (Orig. publ. 1926.)
Freud, Sigmund (1961a). *The future of an illusion*. In J. Strachey (Ed.), *Standard edition of the complete works of Sigmund Freud*, Vol. 21: 1–56. (Orig. publ. 1927.)
Freud, Sigmund (1961b). *Civilization and its discontents*. In J. Strachey (Ed.), *Standard edition of the complete works of Sigmund Freud*, Vol. 21: 59–146. (Orig. publ. 1930.)
Gamwell, Lynn and Wells, Richard (Eds.) (1989). *Sigmund Freud and art: His personal collection of antiquities*. Binghamton, NY: SUNY Press and London: Freud Museum.
Gay, Peter (1987). *A godless Jew: Freud, atheism, and the making of psychoanalysis*. New Haven: Yale University Press.
Gay, Peter (1989). Introduction. In L. Gamwell and R. Wells (Eds.), *Sigmund Freud and art: His personal collection of antiquities*. Binghamton, NY: SUNY Press and London: Freud Museum.
Gay, Peter (2006). *Freud: A life for our time*. New York: W.W. Norton.
Gollnick, James (1992). *Love and the soul*. Waterloo: Wilfred Laurier University Press.
Hoffer, Wilhelm (1958). Obituary: "Oskar Pfister 1873–1956." *International Journal of Psycho-Analysis, 39* (January 1): 616. Online at http://search.proquest.com/docview/1298180261?pq-origsite=gscholar.
Holifield, E. Brooks (1983). *A history of pastoral care in America*. Nashville: Abingdon Press.
Jaspers, Karl (1947). *Von der Wahrheit*. Munich: Piper.
Jaspers, Karl (1971). *Philosophy of existence*. Richard F. Grabay (Ed. and Trans.). Philadelphia: University of Pennsylvania Press. (Orig. publ. 1935.)
Jaspers, Karl (1972). *General psychopathology*. Chicago: University of Chicago Press. (Orig. publ. 1913.)

Jones, E. (1955). *The life and work of Sigmund Freud*, Vol. 2. New York: Basic Books.

Jones, E. (1972). *The life and work of Sigmund Freud*, Vol. 1. New York: Basic Books.

Jonte-Pace, D. (2001). *Speaking the unspeakable: Religion, misogyny, and the uncanny mother in Freud's cultural texts.* Berkeley, CA: University of California Press.

Lee, David D. (2005). Pfister, Oskar Robert (1873–1956). *International Dictionary of Psychoanalysis.* Online at www.encyclopedia.com/psychology/dictionaries-thesauruses-pictures-and-press-releases/pfister-oskar-robert-1873-1956. Accessed December 21, 2016.

Masson, Jeffrey Moussaieff (Ed. and Trans.) (1985). *The complete letters of Sigmund Freud to Wilhelm Fliess 1887–1904.* Cambridge, MA: Belknap.

McGuire, Willam (Ed. and Trans.) (1974). *The Freud/Jung letters.* Cambridge, MA: Harvard University Press.

Meng, Heinrich and Freud, Ernst (Eds.) (1963). *Psychoanalysis and faith: The letters of Sigmund Freud and Oskar Pfister.* E. Mosbacher (Trans.). New York: Basic Books.

Moser, Alexander (2011). Zur historischen Entwicklung in der Deutschschweiz. Online at www.psychanalyse.ch/psychoanalyse/sites/default/files/publikationen/geschichte_der_sgpsa.pdf. Accessed August 18, 2016.

Nase, Eckart (1993). *Oskar Pfisters analytische Seelsorge: Theorie und Praxis des ersten Pastoralpsychologen, dargestellt an zwei Fallstuden.* Berlin: Walter de Gruyter.

Nase, Eckart (2000). The psychology of religion at the crossroads: Oskar Pfister's challenge to psychology of religion in the twenties. In Jakob Belzen (Ed.), *Aspects in contexts: Studies in the history of the psychology of religion* (pp. 45–90). Amsterdam: Editions Rodolphi.

Noth, Isabelle (2007). "Deine Ehrfurcht und meine Liebe": Oskar Pfister (1873–1956) und Albert Schweitzer (1875–1965). In Isabelle Noth and Christoph Morgenthaler (Eds.), *Seelsorge und Psychoanalyse (Praktische Theologie heute), 89*: 46–58. Stuttgart: Kohlhammer.

Noth, Isabelle (2010). *Freuds bleibende Aktualität: Psychoanalyserezeption in der Pastoral- und Religionspsychologie im deutschen Sprachraum und in den USA.* Stuttgart: Kohlhammer.

Noth, Isabelle (Ed.) (2014). *Sigmund Freud–Oskar Pfister Briefwechsel 1909–1939.* Zürich: Theologischer Verlag.

Noth, Isabelle and Morgenthaler, Christoph (2014). The friendship between Sigmund Freud and Oskar Pfister. *Pastoral Psychology, 63*: 81–90.

Pfister, Oskar (1898). *Die Genesis der Religionsphilosophie A.E. Biedermanns untersucht nach Seiten ihres psychologischen Ausbaus.* Unpublished PhD dissertation, University of Zürich.

Pfister, Oskar (1903). Die Unterlassungssünden der Theologie gegenüber der modernen Psychologie. *Protestantische Monatshefte, 7*: 125–140.

Pfister, Oskar (1904). *Die Willensfreiheit: Eine kritisch-systematische Untersuchung.* Berlin: Reimer.

Pfister, Oskar (1907). *Die soziale Entwicklung als Kampf um die Menschenwürde: Ein Mahnwort.* Zürich: Bopp.

Pfister, Oskar (1909a). Psychoanalytische Seelsorge und experimentelle Moralpädagogik. *Protestantische Monatshefte, 13* (1): 6–42.

Pfister, Oskar (1909b). Ein Fall von psychoanalytischer Seelsorge und Seelenheilung. *Evangelische Freiheit, 9* (3): 108–114, 139–149, 175–189.

Pfister, Oskar (1910). *Die Frömmigkeit des Grafen Ludwig von Zinzendorf.* Leipzig: Deuticke. Online at https://archive.org/details/diefrmmigkeitde00pfisgoog. Accessed March 12, 2017.

Pfister, Oskar (1911a). Hysterie und Mystik bei Margaretha Ebner 1291–1351. *Zentralblatt für Psychoanalyse, 1*: 468–485.

Pfister, Oskar (1911b). *Zinzendorfs Frömmigkeit im Lichte der Psychoanalyse.* Tübingen: J. C. B. Mohr.

Pfister, Oskar (1911–12). Zur Psychologie des hysterische Madonnenkultes. *Zentralblatt für Psychoanalyse, 1*: 30–37 and *5*: 263–271.

Pfister, Oskar (1912a). *Die psychologische Enrätselung der Glossolalie und der automatischen Kryptographie.* Leipzig: Deuticke.

Pfister, Oskar (1912b). Hat Zinzendorf die Frömmigkeit sexualisiert? *Zeitschrift für Religionspsychologie, 5*: 56–60.

Pfister, Oskar (1913). Kryptolalie, Kryptographie und unbewusstes Vexierbild bei Normalen. *Jahrbuch für Psychoanalytische und Psychopathologische Forschungen, 5*: 117–156.

Pfister, Oskar (1917). *The psychoanalytic method.* Charles Rockwell Payne (Trans.). (Orig. German publ. 1913; 1917; reprint edition: New York: Routledge, 2014).

Pfister, Oskar (1920a). Die Entwicklung des Apostels Paulus: Eine religionsgeschichtliche und psychologische Skizze. *Imago, 6*: 243–290.

Pfister, Oskar (1920b). *Zum Kampf um die Psychoanalyse.* Vienna: Internationaler Psychoanalytischer Verlag.

Pfister, Oskar (1921). Plato als Vorläufer der Psychoanalyse. *Internationale Zeitschrift für Psychoanalyse, 7*: 264.

Pfister, Oskar (1922). *Expressionism in art: Its psychological and biological basis.* Barbara Low and Maximilian Mügge (Trans.). London: Paul, Trench & Trubner. (Orig. publ. 1922.)

Pfister, Oskar (1923). Die alte und die neue Pädagogik. *Schweiz. Pädagog, 33*: 97–102, 129–138, 161–164, 193–197.

Pfister, Oskar (1924a). *Love in children and its aberrations: A book for teachers and parents.* Eden Paul and Cedar Paul (Trans.). New York: Dodd & Mead. (Orig. publ. 1922).

Pfister, Oskar (1924b). *Die psychoanalytische Methode. Eine erfahrungswissenschaftlich-systematische Darstellung,* 3rd ed. Leipzig: Klinkhardt.

Pfister, Oskar (1925). *Die Liebe von der Ehe und ihre Fehlentwicklungen: Eine Tiefenpsychologie Untersuchungen im Reiche des Eros.* Bern, Switzerland: E. Bircher.

Pfister, Oskar (1926). *Die Legende Sundar Singhs: Eine auf Enthüllungen protestantischer Augenzeugen in Indien gegründete religionspsychologische Untersuchung.* Bern: Haupt.

Pfister, Oskar (1927a). *Analytische Seelsorge: Einführung in die praktische Psychoanalyse für Pfarrer und Laien.* Göttingen: Vandenhoeck & Ruprecht.

Pfister, Oskar (1927b). [Autobiography]. In Erich Hahn *et al.* (Eds.), *Die Pädagogik der Gegenwart in Selbsdarstellungen,* Vol. 2 (pp. 161–207). Leipzig: Meiner.

Pfister, Oskar (1928). *Psychoanalyse und Weltanschauung.* Vienna: Internationaler Psychoanalytischer Verlag.

Pfister, Oskar (1931a). Aus der Analyse eines Buddhisten: Eine Studie zum psychologischen Verständnis des Buddhismus. *Pschoanalytische Bewegung, 4*: 307–328.

Pfister, Oskar (1931b). Der Innerste Richter und seine Seelsorgliche Behandlung. Leipzig: [Pfeiffer – unpubl. MS].

Pfister, Oskar (1931c). Psychoanalytische Äusserung über einen jugendliche, Gewohnheitsdieb, Morphinisten und Totschläger. *Zeitschrift für Psychoanalytische Pädagogik, 5*: 240–251.

Pfister, Oskar (1932). Instinktive Psychoanalyse unter den Navajo-Indianern. *Imago, 18*: 81–109.

Pfister, Oskar (1934). *Neutestamentliche Seelsorge und psychoanalytische Therapie.* Vienna: Internationaler Psychoanalytischer Verlag.

Pfister, Oskar (1935a). Die verschiedenen Arten des Unglaubens in psychoanalytischer Beleuchtung. *Zeitschrift für Religionspsychologie, 8*: 20–31.

Pfister, Oskar (1935b). Diskussion über den narzisstisch-triebhaften Charakter. *Zeitschrift für Psychoanalytische Pädagogik, 9*: 184–192.

Pfister, Oskar (1940). Lösung und Bindung von Angst und Zwang in der Israelitisch-christlichen Religionsgeschichte. *Internationale Zeitschrift für Artzliche Psychoanalyse, 25*: 206–213.

Pfister, Oskar (1943). *Religionshygiene: Die psychohygienische Aufgabe des theologischen Seelsorgers.* Basel: Schwabe.

Pfister, Oskar (1944). Bindung und Befreiung in der Israelitisch-christlichen Religionsgeschichte. *Schweiz. Reformierttes Volksblatt, 78*: 286–288.

Pfister, Oskar (1947). *Calvins Eingreifen in die Hexer- und Hexenprozesse von Peney 1545 nach seiner Bedeutung für Geschichte und Gegenwart: Ein kritischer Beitrag zur Charakteristik Calvins und zur gegewärtigen Calvin-Renaissance.* Zürich: Artemis.

Pfister, Oskar (1948a). Calvin im Lichte der Hexenprozesse von Peney: Ein Epilog. *Theologische Zeitschrift, 4*: 411–434.

Pfister, Oskar (1948b). *Christianity and fear.* London: Allen & Unwin. (Orig. publ. 1944.)

Pfister, Oskar (1949). Die ethischen Grundzüge der Psychoanalyse Sigmund Freuds. *Der Psychologe: Berater für gesunde und praktische Lebensgestaltung, 1*: 287–294.

Pfister, Oskar (1952). Karl Jaspers als Sigmund Freuds Widersacher: Eine kritische Apologie. *Psyche, 6*: 241–275.

Pfister, Oskar (1953). *Aus meinem Leben: Zur Feier seines 80. Geburstages am 2.2.1953 für seine Ehefrau aufgezeichnet.* Zürich-Witikon. Unpublished manuscript, Keller family.

Pfister, Oskar (1955). Gesundheit und Religion. *Geistige Hygiene: Forschung und Praxis, 12*: 533–548.

Pfister, Oskar (1993). The illusion of a future: A friendly disagreement with Prof. Sigmund Freud. Paul Roazen (Ed.), Susan Abrams and Tom Taylor (Trans.). *International Journal of Psycho-Analysis, 74*: 557–579. (Orig. publ. 1928.)

Reijzer, Hans (2011). Pfister and Freud, a friendship. In *A dangerous legacy: Judaism and the psychoanalytic movement* (pp. 51–65). London: Karnac.

Riklin, Franz (1915). *Wishfulfillment and fairy tales.* William A. White (Trans.). New York: Nervous and Mental Disease Publishing. (Orig. publ. 1908.) Online at https://archive.org/stream/wishfulfillments00rickrich/wishfulfillments00rickrich_djvu.txt. Accessed August 19, 2016.

Rizzuto, Ana-Maria (1979). *The birth of the living God: A psychoanalytic study.* Chicago: University of Chicago Press.

Rizzuto, Ana-Maria (1998). *Why did Freud reject God?* New Haven, CT: Yale University Press.

Salisbury, Stephan (1989). In Dr. Freud's collection, objects of desire. *New York Times,* September 3.

Scharfenberg, Joachim (1988). *Sigmund Freud and his critique of religion.* O. C. Dean (Trans.). Philadelphia: Fortress Press.

Schweitzer, Albert (2001). *The quest of the historical Jesus.* John Bowden (Ed.), W. Montgomery, J. R. Coates, Susan Cupitt, and John Bowden (Trans., 1910 ed.). Minneapolis: Fortress Press. (Orig. publ. 1906, 1910, 1950.)

Shamdasani, Sonu (2012). *Liber Novus*: The "Red Book" of C. G. Jung. In Introduction to C. G. Jung, *The Red Book: A reader's edition* (pp. 1–96). New York: W. W. Norton.

Sprengnether, Madelon (1992). *The spectral mother: Freud, feminism, and psychoanalysis.* Ithaca, NY: Cornell University Press.

St. Germain, Mark (2011). *Freud's last session.* New York: Dramatists' Play Service.

Thurneysen, Eduard (1988). Rechtfertigung und Seelsorge. In Friedrich Wintzer (Ed.), *Seelsorge: Texte zum gewandelten Verständnis und zur Praxis der Seelsorge in der Neuzeit* (pp. 73–94). Munich: Kaiser. (Orig. publ. 1928.)

Westerink, Herman (2009). Theology beyond psychoanalysis. In *Controversy and challenge: The reception of Sigmund Freud's psychoanalysis in German and Dutch-speaking theology and religious studies* (pp. 51–93). Vienna: Lit Verlag.

Yerushalmi, Yosef H. (2013). The purloined Kiddush cups: Reopening the case on Freud's Jewish identity. In David Myers and Alexander Kaye (Eds.), *The faith of fallen Jews: Yosef Hayim Yerushalmi and the writing of Jewish history* (pp. 333–342). Waltham, MA: Brandeis University Press. Online at https://muse/jhu.edu/chapter/1050250 (Essay orig. publ. 1991.) Accessed January 28, 2017.

Zulliger, Hans (1966). Oskar Pfister 1873–1956: Psychoanalysis and faith. In Franz Alexander, Samuel Eisenstein, and Martin Grotjahn (Eds.), *Psychoanalytic pioneers* (pp. 169–179). New York: Basic Books.

Chapter 4

"Enduring life without illusion"
Theodor Reik (1888–1969)

Theodor Reik is perhaps best known in psychoanalytic circles for his emphasis on self-analysis and the analyst's continual reflection on his or her own unconscious, which he termed "listening with the third ear."[1] Although he was deeply dedicated to Freud and always viewed his own work as beholden to Freud's genius, his contributions have recently been re-appropriated by relational psychoanalysis[2] with its emphasis on empathy, countertransference as a positive channel of understanding the patient, and a "two-person" psychology in which both analyst and patient may be "surprised" by the emergence of unconscious material that benefits the patient's insight.[3] Reik was a lifelong Freudian, but he had no patience for what he viewed as the rigid dogmatism and theoretical jargon of "classical" psychoanalysis, especially among the psychoanalytic establishment in America where he eventually emigrated to escape the Nazis. A "Leitmotiv"[4] (his word) running through his works was "the essential matter of psychoanalysis cannot be learned; it can only be lived."[5]

Steeped in literature and philosophy, especially the works of Nietzsche, Schopenhauer, and Kierkegaard, he had an existentialist bent. He wrote, "It is more useful for the student of psychology to read the great writers than the *Psychoanalytic Quarterly*."[6] While he retained the abstinent listening stance of a classical Freudian, and employed interpretation with careful timing ("*Takt*"[7]), he was opposed to the emphasis in ego psychology[8] on interpretation of resistance and defense. For him, psychoanalysis was more an art than a science,[9] and he saw applied psychoanalysis and cultural studies as ultimately a more important contribution to civilization than clinical treatment.[10] His correlation of psychoanalysis with philosophy and the humanities, drawing strength from Freud's personal encouragement, caused him to hold out for a psychoanalysis guided by the analyst's own unconscious intuition, or "hunches,"[11] honesty, and common human understanding: "[T]here is something of the worst in the best of us and something of the best in the worst of us."[12] His ethical compass revolved around "inner truthfulness." "If I were asked what quality I regard as most important for an analyst, I should reply: moral courage."[13]

Less is known about Reik's lifelong interest in the psychoanalytic study of religion, particularly Judaism. This began early for Reik, as part of the Wednesday

Night Society's investigations in applied psychoanalysis. Impressed by Freud's application of psychoanalysis to the primal roots of religion in *Totem and Taboo*,[14] Reik introduced himself to Freud with a draft of his thesis on a psychoanalytic reading of Flaubert's *Temptation of Saint Anthony*, influenced by Freud's *Interpretation of Dreams*.[15] He continued writing articles on religious themes for the journal *Imago* beginning in 1913, and numerous reviews of others' books on psychology and religion.[16] In 1918 at the 5th International Congress in Budapest, Freud designated two prizes of 1,000 Kronen each for "outstanding pieces of work, one each in the field of medical and of applied psycho-analysis," awarding Reik the latter prize for his essay in *Imago* on "Puberty Rites among Savages."[17] Freud further honored Reik by writing the foreword to Reik's first book, *Ritual*, a collection of essays on religion.[18]

Reik continued to write about religion until he emigrated from Nazi Europe in 1934, including a second book in 1923, *Der eigene und der fremde Gott* ("The Strange God and One's Own God"),[19] and a lengthy, laudatory review of Freud's *Future of an Illusion*[20]—first presented at a Wednesday night meeting in 1927.[21] After a long hiatus, Reik returned to the subject again, with a revised edition of *Ritual*,[22] and six more books published in the 1950s and 1960s, often revisiting questions he had raised in his earlier works: *Dogma and Compulsion*,[23] *Myth and Guilt*,[24] *Mystery on the Mountain: The Drama of the Sinai Revelation*,[25] *The Creation of Woman: A Psychoanalytic Inquiry into the Myth of Eve*,[26] *Jewish Wit*,[27] and his last book, *Pagan Rites in Judaism: From Sex Initiation, Magic, Mooncult, Tattooing, Mutilation, and Other Primitive Rituals to Family Loyalty and Solidarity*.[28]

Biography[29]

Reik was born on May 12, 1888, in Bohemia,[30] the sixth of seven children.[31] The family moved soon thereafter to Vienna, which he considered his *Heimat*—his beloved homeland. His childhood was weighed down by death. When he was still very small, an older sister died at the age of six, and their mother Caroline "fell into a pathological mourning," abandoning Theodor to a harsh Moravian nanny.[32] His mother eventually recovered from her grief and made Theodor her favorite child.[33] His father, Max, a lower-middle-class Jewish government clerk, died in 1906 when Reik was eighteen. Reik had run to the pharmacy to get a life-saving injection for his father, but returned too late, prompting a traumatic guilt complex. A resulting obsessional neurosis took the form of a compulsion to read all the works of Goethe—who became a literary father-figure. Reik's mother died just four years later.

Reik described the Jewish influences on his upbringing mainly in connection with his grandfather, a "businessman and Jewish scholar,"[34] who had lived most of his life in Mattersdorf, a "sort of ghetto" on the Austro-Hungarian border. This grandfather, after his wife's death, moved in with Theodor's family in Vienna and encouraged them to take part in the religious rites which we could only imperfectly follow, but by which we were deeply impressed ... [and] left their lasting marks on our minds. Very ancient synagogue choral music ... comes to my mind even now.[35]

Reik recounted how, upon the very day of his arrival, his grandfather took a hammer to the marble bust of a classical Greek god and struck off its nose:

My grandfather, who was fanatically devout, would on no account tolerate images in rooms inhabited by him, since those images were strictly forbidden by the Jewish commandments.... This act was the beginning of a bitter struggle, lasting for many years

between Reik's observant grandfather and his more humanist father.[36] Although "despotic" in his attempts to enforce strict Kosher observance in the household, which caused the children eventually to "detest" him, his deep piety, and his prayers and rituals at the moment of Reik's father's death, left a lasting impression of admiration.[37]

Reik met Freud shortly after his parents' deaths, and in many ways Freud became his father-figure for the rest of his life. Reik's family was of limited means, but had the same aspirations for him as did his Jewish contemporaries in the Vienna Society. After reading Reik's dissertation on Flaubert's *Saint Anthony* (a work Freud himself had long appreciated[38]), Freud invited him to visit. Freud was immersed at that time in his own work on the origins of religion and the Oedipus complex,[39] and hoped that Reik would continue to extend the reach of psychoanalysis into cultural studies.

Poor and without parental help, Reik hoped to improve his circumstances by pursuing a medical degree at the University of Vienna, but Freud persuaded him to study psychoanalysis instead, saying "he had other plans for him."[40] Reik took Freud's advice, and was the second[41] doctoral student (following Rank) to graduate with a psychoanalytic PhD dissertation, "The Temptation of Gustav Flaubert's Saint Anthony" in 1912.[42] Meanwhile in 1911, Freud invited Reik to join the Wednesday Night Society.[43] Reik's first paper presented to the Vienna Society was on death and sexuality,[44] showing a "fusion" of the concepts of sex and death throughout the history of religion and mythology. Reik's conclusion, as recorded in the minutes, was "thus the ring is closed, the ring that is formed by coming into being and perishing, by Eros and Thanatos"[45]—a theme that would be elaborated just two weeks later by Sabina Spielrein (see Chapter 6).[46] This paper earned him unanimous admission as a member of the Society.[47]

Reik remained a loyal member of the Society until 1933, long after his departure from Vienna. With Freud's encouragement, he wrote and published numerous essays on psychology and religion, along with other more standard clinical and theoretical subjects along the lines of infantile sexuality and the Oedipus complex. Reik was regarded by others as one of Freud's favorites during this time, together with Rank and Sachs with whom Reik had a close relationship.[48] Although Reik experenced Freud as somewhat distant in his manner, Freud was nonetheless generous and caring,[49] and supported Reik materially as well as intellectually. Freud referred patients to him and found him work with his publisher Hugo Heller.[50] When Reik expressed anxiety about the obsessional thoughts that had plagued him after the death of his father (notably, his Goethe obsession), Freud sent him off for two years (1913–14)—with funds—for analysis with Abraham in Berlin.[51] Reik later referred to this as his training analysis,[52] and specialized thereafter in the treatment of obsessional neuroses.[53]

The year 1914 was eventful. Reik married his first wife, Ella Oratsch, in August—his childhood "puppy love."[54] She was "half-Jewish," with "a pretentious and anti-Semitic father whom Reik hated and feared. For several years their relationship was painfully and sweetly covert."[55] Reik attributed his intense interest in Zionism to the period of hatred for his father-in-law, and identification with own father.[56] Ella gave birth to their only child, Arthur, just one year after the marriage. A great chunk of Reik's rambling, highly confessional autobiography, *Fragment of a great confession*,[57] is given to his psychoanalytic reflections on Goethe's abandoned love, Friederike,[58] a thinly veiled retelling of Reik's self-analysis surrounding his love for Ella since his youth, as well as numerous, guilt-ridden sexual infidelities.

It was in 1914, too, that Reik's essay on the ritual of "Couvade," published in *Imago* in 1914, began to gain him more notoriety as an anthropological and psychoanalytic writer. Finally, this was also the year Reik was recalled to Vienna for military duty in World War I. Drafted into the army cavalry,[59] Reik encountered many horrors, which he detailed to Freud for use in his 1919 essay "The Uncanny."[60] Reik later wrote his own account of these traumas in his book *The Compulsion to Confess*.[61]

Reik's war experiences included numerous instances of fearing for his life under artillery fire (he was decorated for bravery).[62] He further suffered what today would be considered "moral injury,"[63] being commanded to sentence an old Italian man and his son to death for owning a gun (prohibited by the Austrian occupying army), and failing in another instance to prevent the hanging of a man. These traumatic events had an indelible impact on Reik's character.[64] Reik's opposition to capital executions, his research interests in crime and punishment, guilt and masochism did not begin with his military experience, but were no doubt intensified by them.[65] Moreover, for many years after his discharge from the army, Reik was preoccupied with thoughts and images of death (not a new problem, but exacerbated by his war trauma).

His opportunity to attend the 5th International Congress in Budapest in September, 1918, must have been a welcome respite, and a chance to reflect on the impact of the war—which was not yet over. The theme of the entire conference was psychoanalytic treatment of war neuroses, and nearly all the participants arrived in uniform.[66] Freud himself was preoccupied with the psychological sequelae of war, organizing the inaugural volume of a new *Internationale*

Psychoanalytische Bibliothek around the subject.[67] Freud was also asked by the Austrian War Ministry to serve as an expert witness in a legal case against university professor Julius Wagner-Juaregg's[68] and other psychiatrists' use of electrical stimulation to treat war veterans.[69] Freud's description of the mental torment of war neurosis stands as an early recognition of post-traumatic stress in the history of modern psychiatry.[70]

Psychoanalysis persisted amid the poverty, hunger, and demoralization of the early post-war years, as well as its own internal tribulations. After Reik's military discharge he was again teaching psychoanalysis and seeing patients in Vienna, and also teaching in Berlin. Following Rank's resignation from the Vienna Society in 1924, Reik also became its secretary. Meanwhile Stekel, who had been ejected from the Society before the war (see Chapter 1), had been fulminating against non-medical analysts. In an apparent act of revenge against Reik as one of Freud's favorite insiders, Stekel alerted Wagner-Juaregg and the psychiatric establishment that there were lay analysts at work in Vienna, and directly accused Reik of "unauthorized pursuit of medical practice."[71] That November, a prominent physiologist Walter Dürig asked Freud to render an expert opinion on lay analysis. The following month, Wagner-Juaregg requested a list of all the Vienna clinics where psychoanalysis was practiced, in order to ferret out unauthorized therapists.[72] Reik was called to a hearing by city magistrates, and after a round of legal proceedings, was ordered to stop practicing analysis in February, 1925.[73]

With the aid of both Freud and an attorney, he appealed the decision and continued seeing patients. But then an American doctor, Newton Murphy, who had come to Vienna hoping for a treatment with Freud and was referred to Reik instead, sued Reik for malpractice.[74] The upshot of this was Freud's vigorous defense, *The Question of Lay Analysis*.[75] The Vienna Society itself was divided between medical and lay analysts,[76] and not all of the members shared his point of view, but Freud declared to Federn, "As long as I live, I shall balk at having psychoanalysis swallowed by medicine."[77] This was an echo of Freud's encouragement to Reik to pursue a PhD in psychoanalytic study rather than medicine, and also perhaps a compensatory gesture toward Reik whose career had been so impacted by that earlier decision.[78]

This was not the last time Reik encountered prejudice and exclusion from psychoanalytic circles because of his non-medical status. Murphy's lawsuit was dropped in May 1927, but in spite of Freud's defense, Reik's professional reputation in Vienna was irreparably damaged.[79] He moved to Berlin in 1928, where he taught and practiced successfully for six years. After Hitler's accession to power, Reik emigrated to The Hague, where in 1934 he continued both teaching and clinical practice. In spite of his refugee status and his wife's increasing health problems, he was successful there, and produced one of his better known works, again with significant autobiographical elements: *Masochism in Modern Man*.[80]

Reik's character was to be undeterred by hardship, writing during this time, "Suffering, consciously experienced and mastered, teaches us wisdom."[81] He sought a brief analysis with Freud to help him overcome a psychosomatic illness with "the most vivid sensations of dying"[82]—precipitated by guilt over his unfaithfulness to Ella, who had by now become an invalid. This "emergency" entailed all the issues that had preoccupied Reik's conscious and unconscious life—desire for sexual freedom, and corresponding guilt and self-punishment in the form of masochism and obsessional thoughts of death.[83] Reik later compared himself to the biblical figure of Job, who in Reik's interpretation did not suffer as much from his wounds and diseases as he did from the longing for a clear indictment for which he could finally stand before God and answer[84]—a theme also pursued in his book *The Compulsion to Confess*.[85]

Ella died in 1934 after an arduous trip to visit their son and his wife in Palestine and her parents in Vienna. She died minutes after arriving home in The Hague.[86] After Ella's death, Reik soon remarried, and his second wife, Marija Cubelic, gave birth to two daughters, Theodora (in The Hague) and Miriam (in the United States).[87] It was Ella, however, who remained his preoccupation all his life. It is perhaps telling that his autobiography contains many introspective and often guilty—as well as idealized—references to Ella, but virtually none (and none at all by name) to Marija.[88] This was autobiography as expiation as much as introspection.

In 1938, as Hitler advanced into Austria and other European territories, Reik moved again with his family, this time to New York (a move Freud viewed with disapproval),[89] where he lived until his death in 1969. Reik later compared the pain of this exile to the Jews' flight from Egypt in the Book of Exodus.[90] Freud's death in 1939 compounded the sense of loss and dislocation. Recalling his actual father's death, Reik wrote,

> I wanted to prove to him that I was capable of a great effort.... During the weeks after his death I had the bitter feeling that I had been too late.... I had a similar emotion when Freud died in 1939.[91]

Even though he had arrived bearing Freud's imprimatur, he was refused full membership by "the hateful New York Psychoanalytic Society,"[92] where only medical doctors were allowed to practice. The founder of the institute, A.A. Brill, was adamantly opposed to lay analysis. Unwilling to fly under the radar and practice only as a "research analyst," Reik began gathering his own followers, and in 1948 founded the National Psychological Association for Psychoanalysis (NPAP).[93]

Reik spent his remaining two decades in exile from orthodox psychoanalysis in the U.S., but as a prolific writer, admired teacher, and increasingly public interpreter of psychoanalysis for lay audiences. He wrote over twenty books and hundreds of papers on topics ranging from clinical treatment, psychopathology, and criminology, to cultural studies of literature and music, Jewish humor, and religious practices both ancient and modern. He died on New Year's Eve in 1969, after battling cardiac illness for over two years.[94]

Reik on religion

As previously noted, Reik's psychoanalytic writings on religion fell into two separate periods of productivity—the first during his years in Vienna and Berlin and the second during his latter years in America. Throughout both periods, Reik viewed his work on religion as a faithful application of Freud's method to "ethnopsychological material and the psychic tendencies of religious conceptions."[95] However, his works became more prolific and more adventurous in the second half of his life (after Freud's death). Like Freud, he identified strongly as a Jew by heritage, but not belief—he referred to himself in his autobiography as an "infidel Jew."[96]

Early period

While still living in Vienna, Reik focused his anthropological research on psychodynamic interpretations of religious rituals,[97] closely following Freud's analogy between religious ritual and obsessional neurosis, and on psychoanalytic biblical exegesis from the perspective of oedipal and drive theory.[98] Although he hewed closely to the speculative prehistoric origins of religion Freud set out in *Totem and Taboo*,[99] he delved into new topics with the verve of a nineteenth-century heroic explorer (not unlike Freud's own analogy between psychoanalysis and archaeology). Reik scholar Murray Sherman describes his writing style thus:

> One result of Reik's approach is that the reader is made to feel that he is on the very scene of discovery. Whereas Freud's books on primitive ritual read like brilliantly argued debate, Reik paints a colorful, intimate canvas upon which the reader may personally enter. Freud built abstract theories of mental structure; Reik supplies concrete details of daily living in times primeval.[100]

In his essay "The Mark of Cain,"[101] Reik worked through a chain of associations from blood sacrifice for guilt, to castration, to symbolic castration in the form of circumcision. This followed the same logic as his first major paper, "Couvade,"[102] in which he asserted that ritual wounds inflicted in couvade[103] symbolize castration—a compromise formation in which the father, who in "primitive" times regarded his child as a reincarnation of his rival father, now can identify with his father instead, and express tenderness toward his wife and child.

Reik's volume, *Ritual*,[104] was his first published book and, as such, established him as a pre-eminent practitioner of applied psychoanalysis. Freud contributed a laudatory preface. Deeply interested in the psychological underpinnings of the Jewish tradition, Reik distinguished himself by moving further and further into the exploration of the prehistoric origins of Judaism. In *Ritual*, he included his previously published essays "Couvade," "The Puberty

Rites of Savages," and two previously unpublished lectures given to the Vienna Psychoanalytic Society: "Kol Nidre" in 1918,[105] and "The Shofar (The Ram's Horn)" in 1919. The latter two essays closely follow Freud's speculative narrative of the prehistoric murder of the father by the primal horde of sons, their subsequent rituals of expiation, the re-establishing of worship of the father—now deified—and the establishment of brotherly law. Reik drew on multiple ancient tribal rituals worldwide to trace liturgical elements of Yom Kippur and Rosh Hashanah back to ritualized vestiges of the oedipal drama. Reik emphasized in each case the psychological impact of the dramatic action, and the performative imprint made by the rituals on their participants.[106]

Reik followed *Ritual* with another volume of collected essays in 1923, *Der eigene und der fremde Gott* ("The Strange God and One's Own God"), in which he attempted to "explain from a psychological and analytical point of view the appearance of religious enmity and intolerance and to research the root causes of religious differences."[107] The title essay, first delivered at the 6th International Congress in 1920, addressed the "uncanny impression" that could arise when encountering the gods of other people and religions. He ascribed this feeling to primitive tribesmen who, when encountering the gods of other clans, were actually re-encountering "a caricatured double" of their own gods. As civilization had advanced and tribes proliferated, alien gods had the quality of a return of the repressed as "the uncanniness represents the return of earlier phases of development."[108] Reik felt this could account for religious prejudice and hatred. The threatened irruption of instinctual forces stimulated by another god and

> the pre-existence of the guilty conscience toward one's own god is a determinant for religious persecution (Jewish pogroms, Armenian massacres). The strange god was once one's own god that was alienated from the masses through the pressure of development and advance of civilization, and which appears in its cruder and more primitive form now as uncanny.[109]

Other essays in the volume range across topics including collective forgetting, Jesus and Mary in the Talmud, "resurrected gods," God and the devil, instinctual equivalences between opposites, and the concept of differentiation. This was a courageous effort at uncovering and, thereby, neutralizing the roots of religious hatred, in consideration of the hopeful liberalism that was sweeping Vienna in the early 1920s, but also the rising tide of conservatism and antisemitism.

In 1927, Reik published a review of a book on pastoral care, "The Relationship of Psychoanalysis to Ethics, Religion, and Pastoral Care" by Carl Müller-Braun-schweig of Berlin (a Gentile analyst who later became implicated in the Nazis' "Aryanization" of psychoanalysis during World War II).[110] Reik's attitude during this time does represent a prime example of what Peter Gay characterized (see Chapter 1 above) as "[t]he attempts of some later psychoanalysts to reconcile psychoanalysis with religion would never have found the slightest sympathy in Freud and his colleagues."[111] While acknowledging Müller-Braunschweig's clarity about "the libido theory, the analytical processes, developmental history, and the functions of the superego and of conscience,"[112] Reik strenuously objected to the idea that psychoanalysis and religion exist on separate levels (the scientific and the sacred) and could be of mutual assistance based on their common aims toward the attainment of the good.[113]

This was not something about which he was to change his mind. In his auto-biography, *From Thirty Years with Freud*, he again wrote,

> I have hopes that the young psychoanalysts of religion, whom the official religious psychologists superciliously condemn, will come to even more revealing, and perhaps conclusive discoveries. We are still a long way from a thorough psychological understanding of the arcane ways of religion; but analytic research has come closer to piercing the mysteries than all previous religious science.[114]

In his review in *Imago* of Freud's *Future of an Illusion*, first presented to the Vienna Society in December, 1927, Reik pointed out that although many educated people would disavow any belief in God, there was often still a substratum of belief, or at least superstition, at the unconscious level.[115] God was an unconscious *revenant*, the return of a repressed idea: "Most educated people do not believe in God, but they fear him.... '*Ce sont les morts qu'il faut qu'on tu*' ['These are the dead who must be killed']."[116] Reik returned to this idea two years later in an article on the final stages of religious and obsessional beliefs, in which he compared the exculpatory practices of the obsessional neurotic to an insurance policy against divine damnation.[117] Thus, alluding to Freud's claim that psychoanalysis was the third intellectual revolution against the Church after Copernicus and Darwin,[118] Reik considered this revolution to be incomplete when it came to people's subliminal beliefs. More than minute vestiges of superstition remained even among educated people, just as people might seek out therapy but still cling to their neuroses and their irrational beliefs.

At a more sophisticated level, he pointed to those who would accept Freud's critique, but who still valued "the metaphysical value of religion" as having some "transcendent truth in symbolic form." Religion can be disguised intellectually in the language of "the Absolute."[119] Reik applauded Freud for persisting in putting the last nail in the coffin of religious belief. Acknowledging that some suffering was sure to come as a result of Freud's rejection of religion, he concluded, ironic-ally enough, with the quote "*Nulla crux, nulla corona*" ("No cross, no crown").[120]

In 1929 Reik pressed upon his colleagues at a technical seminar of the Vienna Society the importance of studying religion psychologically.[121] He anticipated a rough crowd, made up of clinicians uninterested in psychoanalytic studies of culture. In a reversal from the usual method of applied psychoanalysis (in which psychoanalytic theory and Freud's prehistory of the human race were the tools to interpret cultural phenomena), Reik argued that "the study of the genesis, devel-opment and mode of operation of religious (and moral) ideas is of extraordinary significance for the therapy—let it be noted, for the *therapy*—of the neuroses,"[122] particularly analysis of resistances, and obsessional problems of guilt and punishment. Who knew more about guilt, he argued, than could be found in "three thousand years of living religion"? Religion had "prepared the ground for science, and theology has been the precursor of scientific psychology."[123]

Reik veered quite closely toward Jung's idea of the collective unconscious—as well as Freud's Lamarckian views on evolutionary cultural inheritances—saying that the "cultural demands of the world," which conditioned a child's sense of guilt even more than parental prohibitions, were "collective formations (deposits of the demands of many generations...), ... psychic forces of peculiar and enduring efficacy."[124] The study of religion, therefore, would not only aid in therapeutic understanding of individuals, but would also advance Freud's aim of "collective therapy and prophylaxis, or if you like, psycho-social hygiene."[125] He cited Freud's claim that "he had the whole of mankind for his patient."[126] Reik showed considerable sympathy for the tragic dimension of the human condition:

> An animal living in freedom could not become neurotic, so long as it was spared the demands of culture. Just as little could a God do so ... since he is not subject to instinctual claims. Neurosis is surely reserved, is it not, for the laughable and pitiable animal that wishes to be a God but cannot?[127]

Later writings

Only in his later years in America, well after Freud's death, did Reik venture to expand the psychoanalytic study of religion beyond the parameters of Freud's own applied psychoanalysis. His first major departure from Freud, which is not on religion per se, but which perhaps paved the way for more independent thinking, was his work on the theme of love in 1944, *A Psychologist Looks at Love*, in which he asserted that love (Eros) was a separate motivating drive from the sexual instinct per se. While finding warrant for this in Freud's later works, the faithful son was beginning to loosen the reins after Freud's death: "Thus Eros is not identical with sex, even in Freud's later view. It dawned upon him later in his life, although he never recognized and clearly acknowledged it, that love is a psychical power in its own right."[128]

Two years later, returning to another lifelong theme, *Masochism in Modern Man*,[129] Reik devoted a chapter to "The Paradoxes of Christ," in which he portrayed Jesus not as the Christian theologians' "sweeten[ed] and soften[ed] ... character,"[130] but as a "great heretic," like "the old prophets, who attacked the most cherished institutions of his people."[131] While he saw a deep masochistic substrate in the "prototype of suffering"[132] glorified in later Christian theology, Reik portrayed Jesus himself as a prophet wielding paradox as a verbal weapon in the tradition of the Jews—setting the unjust world as it was on its head:

> The paradox was the apt way of expression for a thought which slapped all tradition in the face, even when it ordered one to turn the other cheek when

smitten on the right.... The paradoxical words of Christ were not meant to display a dying ember, but to kindle a new flame from the ashes. One may accept or refuse his moral claims—but nobody has the right to question their seriousness.[133]

Like Freud, Reik rejected religious faith as a delusion and a re-enactment of oedipal submission,[134] and viewed religious revelations as "distinctly of earthly origin and earthly motivation."[135] But in the historical figure of Jesus he saw a positive continuity with the Jewish prophetic tradition.

In 1951 in *Dogma and Compulsion*, Reik further departed—this time method-ologically—from Freud's strictly anthropological approach to the study of reli-gion, widening his interpretive lens from religious *practices* to matters of *belief*.[136] Turning his attention to the development of religious ideas from "primi-tive" times to Christianity, he made a detailed study of dogma as "the com-promise formation of repressed and repressing tendencies," considering both obsessional neuroses and oedipal interpretations of theological doctrines.[137] He argued that in the course of development from the rituals of animism and totem-ism to belief-based theistic religions, the evolution of dogma represented a further series of compromise formations in which theological thought itself served the purpose of allaying neurotic anxiety.[138] Religion, although most accessible through its ritual practices, was therefore "a system of thought," and dogmatics was "the theoretical exposition of this system."[139]

Unusually for Reik, this book was focused on Christianity—primarily Catholicism—as the dominant dogmatic religion of the times, but he also noted that "all the more highly evolved religions—Islam, Judaism, Confucianism, etc.—have doctrines" which entail intellectual elaborations on correct theology and practice.[140] Displaying an impressive study of early Christian history, Reik traced the origins of doctrine back to the need of the ancient church to suppress doubt and heresy. Gnosticism was a religion of the triumph of the son over the father, but this in turn demanded instinctual reparation to God the Father, result-ing in the compromise of the Trinity.[141] The highly abstract elaboration of dogma in "rational theology,"[142] as in the elaborate proofs of God's existence during the Scholastic era,[143] represented for Reik an example of collective obsessional thought.[144]

Systematic theology, according to Reik, simultaneously allowed the continua-tion of the religion's instinctual satisfactions through the perpetuation of its fan-tasies,[145] while purifying it from them: it "gives it a rational motivation" and "disguises its genesis from the animistic myths whose real content was the expression of aggressive and sexual instinctual impulses."[146] The heavily sym-bolic nature of religious ritual, and the scrupulosity involved in legalistic doc-trinal debates echoed neurotic compulsions,[147] as Freud had suggested many years earlier.[148] Reik also saw the cannibalistic origins of religion laid bare in the eating of Christ's body in the Eucharist[149]—a barely disguised totem meal.[150] "Miracle is the favorite child of faith," he thought, because it indulged instinctual fantasies with a supernatural rationalization.[151] By assigning dogma to divine revelation, primal taboos could be inscribed in the heavens, and enforced by fear of death and eternal damnation.[152]

Echoing Freud's description of the tragic but real necessity of repression and renunciation of the drives in the service of civilization,[153] Reik wrote, "The norm of faith thus protects the moral norm, the commandments imposed by the ancestors, which had to be set up against the elementary instinctual impulses of violence, of aggression, and of the sexual drives."[154] In this sense, religion could not be regarded in Reik's thesis as any more negative than the reality principle was for Freud—at its best, religion served as a form of sublimation. Participation in the Eucharist in Reik's view was "comparable to that of the onlooker at a performance of Oedipus Rex."[155] Like the functioning of ancient Greek *catharsis*, the long-repressed memories of primal sex and aggression would be reactivated and sublimated in ritual and intellectual theology.[156] Again adopting Freud's version of prehistory, Reik asserted,

> There lies buried the omnipotent chieftain of the primeval horde, who was once upon a time murdered by his united sons, and who afterwards became the Almighty God. Though the pinnacles of the cathedral may soar toward the heavens, its foundations reach down into those depths in which the strongest and most primitive instinctual impulses, the sexual and hostile impulses of humanity, have found their concealed satisfaction.[157]

Nevertheless, Reik thought the increasing rationalism of doctrinal formulation, culminating in the Reformation, also contained the seeds of religion's undoing. Citing Adolf von Harnack and other prominent theologians, he stated,

> [L]iberal Protestantism means the end of Christianity—it is really an atheism covered with a thin layer of belief in God.... Logically, if one wishes to be religious, one can only be orthodox, or one is no longer religious.... The Catholic Church has justly described dogma as *vinculum unitatis* ("unifying vine"). In Protestantism the intellect dances in the chains which it dragged out of prison after it.[158]

In his conclusion, Reik questioned the practicality of Freud's call for the substitution of rational science for religious dogma (alluding to Freud's *Future of an Illusion*):[159]

> With the decay of religion among the civilized peoples dogma must collapse, and with it rational theology, apologetics, and dogmatics.... In the place of religious dogma another dogma will appear—perhaps socialistic, perhaps scientific. Its external forms and psychical effects will not differ essentially from those of religious doctrine.... The capacity to doubt, and in particular the ability to endure doubt for a long time, is one of the rarest

things on this planet. As a matter of fact, man is a mammal who cannot well endure uncertainty. He cherishes a profound longing for firm convictions. The craving for immediate and impregnable security and certainty show how little man has evolved during the millennia.... Humanity is not capable of enduring life without illusion. The content of the illusion is not of crucial importance. *Plus que ça change, plus c'est la même chose.*[160]

Fellow émigré and founder of the "New Left" movement in America in the 1950s and 1960s, Herbert Marcuse, praised this work of Reik's, calling it "one of the ever-rarer attempts to keep alive the great philosophical insights of Freudian theory and to counteract the decline of psychoanalytic theory into the anxiously guarded domain of technical specialists."[161]

Mystery on the mountain

Several other books followed *Dogma and Compulsion*, including *Jewish Wit* in 1962,[162] in which Reik perceived a dark tragic perspective beneath the surface of Jewish humor—"the actual misery of a poor minority deprived of elementary civil rights."[163] Reik recognized "behind the comic façade not merely something serious, as in other witticisms, but something horrible ... the tragic countenance of the world is reflected along with its comic mask."[164] During the same period he also produced his "tetralogy"[165] of researches into the prehistoric Israel and the origins of modern Judaism—*Myth and Guilt* (1957),[166] *Mystery on the Mountain: The Drama of the Sinai Revelation* (1959),[167] *The Creation of Woman: A Psychoanalytic Inquiry into the Myth of Eve* (1960),[168] and *Pagan Rites in Judaism: From Sex Initiation, Magic, Moon-cult, Tattooing, Mutilation, and Other Primitive Rituals to Family Loyalty and Solidarity* (1964).[169] These writings in the last decade of Reik's life are a testimony to his attention to and preoccupation with the origins of Jewish rituals.

In all these books, Reik continued to pursue his well worn path of anthropological, theological, and historical research, integrated with his method of applied psychoanalysis, to investigate the psychological and social origins of Jewish beliefs and practices. He stressed the uniqueness and familial kinship of the Jews, going back—through extrapolation from biblical, anthropological, and historical scholarship—even to pre-Mosaic times. At his most speculative, for example, in *The Creation of Woman* he proposed that the second creation story in the Book of Genesis symbolized not so much the birth of woman, but the second birth of man from dependency on the mother. From personal anecdote to scholarly literature, he explored the roots of one practice after another, drawing a line from primitive myth and rite to modern Judaism as an "ancient living religion."[170]

Perhaps the most personally, as well as professionally, significant project of his later years following *Dogma and Compulsion*, was his work *Mystery on the Mountain*, published in 1959.[171] In the introduction to the book he described how he had conceived of the project decades earlier—the idea that there was a parallel between the revelation on Mt. Sinai and the puberty ritual of prehistoric peoples—only to return to it nearly twenty years after Freud's death. It is Reik's own *Moses and Monotheism*,[172] and shares at many points the speculative nature of Freud's work. But Reik had his own ideas about the figure of Moses and the revelation on Mt. Sinai, and endeavored to back them up with some of the best biblical scholarship of his day (e.g., works by W. F. Albright[173] and Martin Noth[174]). He also continued, as he had since the early days of applied psychoanalysis, to rely on the works of Hungarian analyst and anthropologist (and frequent contributor to *Imago*) Geza Roheim,[175] as well as American archaeologist James Henry Breasted,[176] and British anthropologist James Frazer.[177] Reik set this work in the context of a dialogue not only with Freud's *Moses and Monotheism*,[178] but also Martin Buber's *Moses* (Buber's critical reply to Freud).[179] Reik's anthropological bent hewed closer to Freud's; nevertheless, he presented Buber's view as complementary to psychoanalysis, "from the perspective of depth-psychology,"[180] not only religious faith.

Contradicting Freud outright at the beginning, Reik declared:

> I am compelled to disagree with my great master on two counts: (1) I am not persuaded that Moses was an Egyptian; he seems to me surely to have been a Hebrew. (2) To my mind, it seems at least questionable to ascribe the origins of historic monotheism to the Egyptians.[181]

Reik went on to describe Moses (following the biblical narrative) as the adopted Hebrew child of an Egyptian princess (a mythological version of Freud's "family romance")[182]—an assimilated Jew in a foreign land. Reik made the parallel between high-ranking Egyptian Jews (going back to Joseph) and the assimilated Jews of Germany and Austria at the turn of the twentieth century.[183] He compared those Jews who remained in Canaan to the close-knit Jews of the eastern European *shtetl*, and the Egyptian Jews with acculturated German Jews. Regime change in Egypt re-stigmatized the Jews there, just as Habsburg tolerance in the nineteenth century gave way to increasing discrimination and oppression of Jews in twentieth-century Europe. There is a Zionist theme in Reik's comments as well: the Egyptian Jews in their disillusionment and sense of betrayal by a new Egyptian dynasty had to learn to "depatternize" as they escaped Egypt and wandered in the wilderness before being able to rejoin their kinspeople in Palestine. Reik identified this process as a salutary "regression" to old folkways—just as contemporary Jews needed to repudiate their love of German culture and rejoin their more tradition-observing Jewish brethren in the post-Holocaust diaspora.

In his exploration of ritual, Reik maintained that the events of the Exodus and the giving of the Law at Mt. Sinai replicated the pattern of puberty rites in prehistoric cultures. He retained the language of "savage" and "primitive" religions from the early years of applied psychoanalysis, and the idea that religions proper—the worship of deities—evolved out of earlier totem rituals. The ancient rites in which pubescent boys were symbolically killed and brought back to life as men, Reik proposed, became the pattern for the death and resurrection of an entire people in the Exodus. The giving of the Law was the rite by which the leader Moses initiated them into a new-old Covenant—repudiating the multiple gods and mystery cults of Egypt and returning to the more austere practices and beliefs of the ancient Jews. Now the class and cultic hierarchies of Egypt were undone in favor of a democratic society of "chosen people" in which the whole society was a priesthood, oriented toward an ethical devotion to Law rather than a tangible, visible deity. Remnants of the primal totemic cult, such as elements of sacrifice, could be discerned in the Passover ritual.

Reik now declared that he was going beyond Freud's characterization of Jewish pride derived from the self-identity as God's chosen people.[184] For Reik, what was most significant was the internalization of the Law by an entire people as a "collective super-ego."[185] God no longer needed to be seen, because God's Word had been heard by the people. God had revealed God's name to everyone (no longer just the secret few of the mystery cults), and that name was linked with the commandments.[186] In this way, Reik asserted, "The regression to simpler forms of initiation, hidden behind the revelation tradition, led later to a rigid monotheism, but also to a progress in spiritualization of the idea of God."[187]

Christianity threw a wrench into this highly ascetic, ethical religion. The worship of Christ reintroduced a more explicit and more ritually sensual return to the pagan worship of the dying and rising God (who mythologically represented the passage from puberty to adult manhood, and whose death and resurrection symbolically incorporated them in this salvation). Moreover, in the figures of Jesus and Mary, the worship of the divine Son and the divine Mother were reintroduced into Judaism's exclusive worship of a Father-god. Reik asserted that Judaism and Christianity split over their separate interpretations of the Messiah (as well as Paul's rejection of certain practices of the Law in favor of the dissemination of Christianity to the Gentiles). Yet, citing the existentialist Lutheran theologian Paul Tillich, Reik also noted that Christianity could never "supersede the Synagogue … [T]he existence of Judaism is important because it is the 'corrective against the paganism that lives along with Christianity'."[188]

> In brief [Reik said], [t]he image-cult and magical use of names were reintroduced into Christianity according to the dynamic pattern of the "return of the repressed." The re-emergence of those banned concepts marks the end of this chapter of Israel's long journey. It does not, however, mean the end of the story.[189]

Reik concluded, in a section called "The Living Past: Retrospect and Prospect," that "Exodus-Sinai is for Judaism 'the interpretive center of redemptive history as Calvary is for the Christian'."[190] Jews did not seek salvation in an afterlife, but rather in personal identification with the liberation that had already occurred in the Exodus, and the subsequent making of a great and ethical nation.

This had profound resonance with the post-Holocaust experience of the Jews of Reik's generation. Horrors might occur again, just as themes reappear throughout history. Like the return of the repressed, "[h]istory does not simply repeat itself," he wrote, "it returns to certain collective experiences which reappear in various forms as the motifs of a symphony reoccur in later elaboration."[191] Nevertheless, the Sinai revelation stood, for Jews, as a sign of "the mystery of Jewish survival." Reik declared his belief that an

> analysis of the early history of the [Jews] and how much of its fate can be attributed to the vicissitudes of an early phase "when Israel was a child" ... might illuminate the present and future of religion in the Western world.[192]

Two decades after Freud's death, Reik still regarded this liberated thought experiment in *Mystery on the Mountain* as an act of "moral courage," which he had been unable to summon while still a pupil of Freud's.[193] His personal experience of fleeing the Holocaust, combined with his decades-long immersion in the allied disciplines of history, anthropology, and theology, were now deployed in his "tetralogy" as an ode to Jewish identity and spirituality—which had against all odds survived the onslaught of the Nazis and the centuries of antisemitism that had preceded it. Reik felt both the trauma and the triumph of that survival in his bones, and demonstrated an overdetermined compulsion to give repeated utterance to these experiences in only barely disguised scholarly form. The epilogue to *Mystery on the Mountain*, quoting Richard Beer-Hoffman's "Lullaby for Miriam," summed up his deep sense (not unlike Freud's own) of a connection between ancient, even prehistoric Judaism and twentieth-century Jewish identity and pride post-*Shoah*: "And deep within us an ancestor's seed,/Their pride and their pain, their vision, their deed,/Their past now returning to children and heirs./You are not alone, and your life is theirs."[194]

Conclusion

At two o'clock in the morning on June 19, 1940, Reik sat at his desk and listened to the radio for news of "the terms that Hitler and Mussolini will offer vanquished France."[195] Meditating on a framed etching of Freud that hung over his desk, he clung to the hope that, in the end, Freud's god *Logos* might prevail against the current darkness:

> The future of humanity will not be wrought by wars and conquests, but by the quiet work of the mind. The lamp that burns in the night over the scientist's desk gives more powerful light than artillery fire. Freud shall live long after Hitler and Mussolini are dust.[196]

The comprehensive testimony of Reik's writings, taken together, represent a hope-against-hope, even after experiencing the worst of collective human evil.

The psychoanalyst's unique insights, gained by "listening with the third ear" for what is unspoken and shrouded in history, allowed him to believe in the possibility of healing and *Tikkun O'lam* (from the Kabbalah)—the mending of the world.

Notes

1 Reik, 1948; see also Aragno, 2011; Arnold, 2006; Grotjahn, 1950, 1981–82; Kupersmidt, 2006; Lothane, 1987, 2006; Safran, 2011; Sherman, 1963, 1968. First developed as a paper in 1932 (Sherman, 1965: 29n1) and published the following year (Reik, 1933). *Listening with the Third Ear* has been influential in Jewish and Christian books on pastoral care and counseling (e.g., Kaufman *et al.*, 2005; Day-ringer, 2010: 80).

2 Safran (2011) reclaims Reik's emphasis on self-analysis as a forerunner of contemporary relational analysts and neo-Kleinians, with some distinctions. Aragno (2011) also reclaims Reik as an important psychoanalytic forebear, but argues from a classical viewpoint that Reik would not have approved of "the relationalists," whom she criticizes for non-analytic self-disclosure and "laxity of current practice" (p. 195).

3 Reik, 1948, 1958.

4 Literally, a "leading motif," most often associated with the composer Richard Wagner—a recurring musical theme representing a character or dramatic element.

5 Reik, 1940, citing his own *Surprise and the Psycho-Analyst* (1936).

6 Reik, 1948: 99.

7 Ibid., 317.

8 Term used to describe "classical" psychoanalysis, emphasizing Freud's (1961a/1923) structural model (ego, id, and superego), theory of anxiety and defense (1959b/1926), and Anna Freud's (1948) writings on ego defenses. This constituted an analytic orthodoxy dominant in the U.S. after World War II.

9 Alby, 1985: 62.

10 Reik, 1949a: 302.

11 Grotjahn, 1950: 57.

12 Reik, 1948: 58.

13 Ibid., 493.

14 Freud, 1955a/1913.

15 Reik, 1940: 25–26, 1949a; Alby, 1985: 17.

16 Cf. Reik, 1912a, 1912b.

17 Reik, 1915–16; Freud, 1955e/1919: 269; Reik, 1940: 27.

18 Freud, 1955f/1919.

19 Reik, 1923.

20 Freud, 1961c/1927.

21 Reik, 1928, 1940: 18–139.

22 Reik, 1946.

23 Reik, 1951.

24 Reik, 1957.

25 Reik, 1959a.

26 Reik, 1960.

27 Reik, 1962.

28 Reik, 1964.

29 Reik was a highly self-revelatory author, and the story of his life can be pieced together from his autobiographical works (1940, 1949a). One must read past his personal agendas, however—his passionate lifelong devotion to Freud, and his resentment toward the American psychoanalytic establishment—as well as minor factual

errors in his recollections. Alby's (1985) critical biography (in French) is thematic as well as chronological. (There is no critical biography in English.) Briefer summaries include Natterson (1966), Sherman (especially 1965, 1970–71, see also 1981–82), and Tréhel (2012).

30 Part of the Austro-Hungarian Empire, now in the Czech Republic.
31 Alby, 1985: 12.
32 Reik, 1949a: 477.
33 Ibid., 478.
34 Reik, 1940: 234.
35 Ibid., 235.
36 Ibid.
37 Ibid., 236–237.
38 Tréhel, 2012: 456n2.
39 Freud, 1955a/1913.
40 Freeman, 1971: 87; Reik, 1949a.
41 Alby, 1985; Reik, 1940. Reik reported that his dissertation was the first; documentary evidence shows that Rank's preceded him (on Lohengrin, in 1911).
42 Alby, 1985: 11, 139.
43 Reik, 1949a: 301. Reik erroneously dates this 1910. (Cf. Nunberg and Federn, 1974: 281, 320.)
44 Nunberg and Federn, 1974: 310–319. This may also reflect the influence of composer Gustav Mahler, with whom Reik developed a close, admiring relationship (Reik, 1949a: 8; Alby, 1985: 21–22).
45 Ibid., 312.
46 Ibid., 329–335.
47 Ibid., 1974: 310–319.
48 Tréhel, 2012: 457, citing reminiscences of Robert Jokl.
49 Reik, 1940: 4–5. Reik was experienced similarly by his own students in New York (Sherman, 1970–71: 543).
50 Bronner, 2008: 57.
51 Reik, 1949a: 301.
52 Tréhel, 2012: 456, citing Reik, 1953.
53 Ibid., citing a 1924 letter from Reik to Freud.
54 Reik, 1949a: 230.
55 Natterson, 1966: 253; Reik, 1949a: 230, *et passim*.
56 Reik, 1949a: 338–339.
57 Reik, 1949a.
58 Ibid., 31–211.
59 Tréhel, 2012: 457–458.
60 Freud, 1955d/1919.
61 Reik, 1959b/1929; see also Tréhel, 2012: 457.
62 Reik, 1949a.
63 E.g., Brock and Lettini, 2012.
64 Tréhel, 2012.
65 E.g., Reik, 1959b/1929, 1949b, 1957.
66 Tréhel, 2012: 458, citing Grosskurth, 1991.
67 Freud, 1955b/1919.
68 Freud 1955c/1920: 213. For full biography, including Wagner-Juaregg's turn to Nazism, see Witrow, 1993.
69 Freud, 1955c/1920.
70 Ibid., 212–213.
71 Gay, 2006: 490, citing unpublished letter, Reik to Abraham, 1925.

72 Tréhel, 2012.
73 Gay, 2006: 490.
74 Ibid., 490–492.
75 Freud, 1959c/1926.
76 Sherman, 1970–71: 536.
77 Gay, 2006: 491, citing an unpubl. letter, Freud to Federn, 1927.
78 Ibid.
79 Tréhel, 2012: 457.
80 Reik, 1949b.
81 Natterson, 1966: 257.
82 Reik, 1949a: 424.
83 See Ibid., 421–411; Reik, 1953, cited in Tréhel, 2012: 458, 463. Sherman, 1965: 22.
84 Reik, 1949a: 448–449.
85 Reik, 1959b.
86 Ibid., 458. See also Alby, 1985: 141; Natterson, 1966: 258.
87 Alby, 1985: 141–142.
88 Reik, 1949a.
89 Alby, 1985.
90 Sherman, 1970–71: 541.
91 Reik, 1949a: 14.
92 Ibid., 320.
93 National Psychological Association for Psychoanalysis, 2016.
94 Alby, 1985: 121, 142.
95 Reik, 1951: 11.
96 Reik, 1949a: 332.
97 Reik, 1951: 165–228.
98 Compiled in ibid., 229–276.
99 Freud, 1955a/1913.
100 Sherman, 1963: 4–5.
101 Reik, 1917.
102 Reik, 1914.
103 A practice known in many cultures in which a man undergoes a ritual form of labor, sometimes involving cutting or pain to the genitals, during or shortly after his wife gives birth. Sympathetic labor pains are known as "couvade syndrome."
104 Reik, 1919.
105 Falzeder et al., 1996: 283. Freud wrote to Ferenczi that Reik had presented a "splendid" lecture about Kol Nidre on May 15, 1918.
106 More detailed summary in Rose, 1998: 155–162.
107 Reik, 1923: Preface (translation PC-W).
108 Reik, 1920: 351.
109 Ibid.
110 On Müller-Braunschweig, see Lockot, 2005.
111 Gay, 2006: 533.
112 Reik, 1927: 550 (translation PC-W).
113 Ibid.
114 Reik, 1940: 156–157.
115 Reik, 1928.
116 Ibid., 185.
117 Reik, 1946/1930. Around the same time, Reik (1929a) was ruminating on Jewish humor as a defense—an oscillation between melancholy and mania (similar to Melanie Klein's later idea of a "manic defense").

118 Freud, 1961b/1925.
119 Reik, 1928.
120 Reik, 1940: 198.
121 Reik, 1929b.
122 Ibid., 297, emphasis original.
123 Ibid., 295.
124 Ibid., 293–294.
125 Ibid.
126 Ibid., 300.
127 Ibid., 293.
128 Reik, 1944: [4, 7–8].
129 Reik, 1949b.
130 Ibid., 344.
131 Ibid.
132 Ibid., 346.
133 Ibid.
134 E.g., his "Note on [Freud's] 'A Religious Experience'," in Reik, 1940: 140–157.
135 Ibid., 156.
136 Reik, 1951: 15–17.
137 Ibid., 48.
138 Ibid., 48ff.
139 Ibid., 91.
140 Ibid., 17.
141 Ibid., 24–47.
142 Ibid., 88.
143 Ibid., 96.
144 Ibid., 154.
145 Ibid., 97.
146 Ibid., 91.
147 Ibid., 98–101.
148 Freud, 1959a/1907.
149 Reik, 1951: 148.
150 Ibid., 136.
151 Ibid., 137.
152 Ibid., 119.
153 Freud, 1961d/1930.
154 Reik, 1951: 157.
155 Ibid.
156 Ibid.
157 Ibid., 137.
158 Ibid., 154–155.
159 Freud, 1961c/1927.
160 Reik, 1951: 160–161.
161 Marcuse, 2011/1957: 108.
162 Reik, 1962.
163 Ibid., 148.
164 Reik, 1940: 190, 196.
165 Reik, 1964: vii.
166 Reik, 1957.
167 Reik, 1959a.
168 Reik, 1960.
169 Reik, 1964.

170 Reik, 1960: 89.
171 Reik, 1959a.
172 Cf. Freud, 1964/1939.
173 Reik, 1959a: 13, 15, 19–20, *et passim.*
174 Ibid., 93, 138, 156.
175 Ibid., xiii, 150; cf. Roheim, 1955.
176 Ibid., 14, 27, 129, 144.
177 Ibid., xii, 39, 62, 102, 106, 113.
178 Freud, 1964/1939.
179 Buber, 1946/1939.
180 Reik, 1964: xii.
181 Reik, 1959a: 1.
182 Ibid., 16–17.
183 Ibid., 16, 26–27.
184 Ibid., 142.
185 Ibid., 169.
186 Ibid., 168.
187 Ibid., 176.
188 Ibid., cf. pp. 177, 204n7.
189 Ibid., 177.
190 Ibid., 181.
191 Ibid., 187.
192 Ibid.
193 Ibid., x.
194 Ibid., iv.
195 Reik, 1946/1930: vii.
196 Ibid., xi.

References

Alby, Jean-Marc (1985). *Theodor Reik: Le trajet d'un psychoanalyste de Vienne "fin de siècle" aux États-Unis.* Paris: Éditions Clancier-Gueand.

Aragno, Anna (2011). Listening with a third ear, a second heart, and a sixth sense: Standing on the shoulders of Theodor Reik. *Psychoanalytic Review, 98*: 183–204.

Arnold, Kyle (2006). Reik's theory of psychoanalytic listening. *Psychoanalytic Psychology, 23* (4): 754–765.

Brock, Rita Nakashima and Lettini, Gabriella (2012). *Soul repair: Recovering from moral injury after war.* Boston: Beacon.

Bronner, Andrea (Ed.) (2008). *Vienna Psychoanalytic Society: The first 100 years.* Vienna: Christian Brandstätter Verlag.

Buber, Martin (1946). *Moses.* Oxford, UK: East and West Library. (Orig. publ. 1939.)

Dayringer, Richard (2010). *The heart of pastoral counseling,* rev. ed. New York: Routledge.

Falzeder, Ernst, Brabant, Eva, and Giampieri-Deutsch, Patrizia (Eds.) (1996). *Correspondence of Sigmund Freud and Sandor Ferenczi,* Vol. 2, 1914–19. Cambridge, MA: Belknap/Harvard University Press.

Freeman, Erika (1971). *Insights: Conversations with Theodor Reik.* Englewood Cliffs, NJ: Prentice-Hall.

Freud, Anna (1948). *The ego and the mechanisms of defense.* New York: International Universities Press.

Freud, Sigmund (1955a). *Totem and taboo*. In J. Strachey (Ed.), *Standard edition of the complete works of Sigmund Freud*, Vol. 13: 1–162. (Orig. publ. 1913.)

Freud, Sigmund (1955b). *Introduction to psycho-analysis and the war neuroses*. In J. Strachey (Ed.), *Standard edition of the complete works of Sigmund Freud*, Vol. 17: 205–210. (Orig. publ. 1919.)

Freud, Sigmund (1955c). *Appendix: Memorandum on the electrical treatment of war neurotics*. In J. Strachey (Ed.), *Standard edition of the complete works of Sigmund Freud*, Vol. 17: 211–216. (Orig. publ. 1920.)

Freud, Sigmund (1955d). *The uncanny*. In J. Strachey (Ed.), *Standard edition of the complete works of Sigmund Freud*, Vol. 17: 217–252. (Orig. publ. 1919.)

Freud, Sigmund (1955e). *A note on psycho-analytic publications and prizes*. In J. Strachey (Ed.), *Standard edition of the complete works of Sigmund Freud*, Vol. 17: 267–270. (Orig. publ. 1919.)

Freud, Sigmund (1955f). *Preface to Reik's* Ritual: Psycho-analytic studies. In J. Strachey (Ed.), *Standard edition of the complete works of Sigmund Freud*, Vol. 18: 257–264. (Orig. publ. 1919.)

Freud, Sigmund (1959a). *Obsessive actions and religious practices*. In J. Strachey (Ed.), *Standard edition of the complete works of Sigmund Freud*, Vol. 9: 115–128. (Orig. publ. 1907.)

Freud, Sigmund (1959b). *Inhibitions, symptoms and anxiety*. In J. Strachey (Ed.), *Standard edition of the complete works of Sigmund Freud*, Vol. 20: 75–176. (Orig. publ. 1926.)

Freud, Sigmund (1959c). *The question of lay analysis*. In J. Strachey (Ed.), *Standard edition of the complete works of Sigmund Freud*, Vol. 20: 177–258. (Orig. publ. 1926.)

Freud, Sigmund (1961a). *The ego and the id*. In J. Strachey (Ed.), *Standard edition of the complete works of Sigmund Freud*, Vol. 19: 1–66. (Orig. publ. 1923.)

Freud, Sigmund (1961b). *The resistances to psycho-analysis*. In J. Strachey (Ed.), *Standard edition of the complete works of Sigmund Freud*, Vol. 19: 211–224. (Orig. publ. 1925.)

Freud, Sigmund (1961c). *The future of an illusion*. In J. Strachey (Ed.), *Standard edition of the complete works of Sigmund Freud*, Vol. 21: 1–56. (Orig. publ. 1927.)

Freud, Sigmund (1961d). *Civilisation and its discontents*. In J. Strachey (Ed.), *Standard edition of the complete works of Sigmund Freud*, Vol. 21: 59–146. (Orig. publ. 1930.)

Freud, Sigmund (1964). *Moses and monotheism*. In J. Strachey (Ed.), *Standard edition of the complete works of Sigmund Freud*, Vol. 23: 3–138. (Orig. publ. 1939.)

Gay, Peter (2006). *Freud: A life for our time*. New York: W. W. Norton.

Grosskurth, Phyllis (1991). *The secret ring: Freud's inner circle and the politics of psychoanalysis*. Reading, MA: Addison-Wesley.

Grotjahn, Martin (1950). About the "third ear" in psychoanalysis. *Psychoanalytic Review, 37*: 56–65.

Grotjahn, Martin (1981–82). Remembering Theodor Reik and the third ear. *Psychoanalytic Review, 68*: 473–476.

Kaufman, Gus, Jr., Lipshutz, Wendy, and Setel, Drorah (2005). Responding to domestic violence. In Dayle, Friedman (Ed.), *Jewish pastoral care*, 2nd ed. (pp. 275–302). Woodstock, VT: Jewish Lights.

Kupersmidt, Jane (2006). Review in retrospect: "Listening with the third ear" by Theodor Reik (1948). *Journal of the American Psychoanalytic Association, 54*: 1045–1051.

Lockot, Regine (2005). Müller-Braunschweig, Carl (1881–1958). *International Dictionary of Psychoanalysis*. Online at www.encyclopedia.com/psychology/dictionaries-thesauruses-pictures-and-press-releases/muller-braunschweig-carl-1881-1958. Accessed September 3, 2017.

Lothane, H. Zvi (1987). Listening with the third ear as an instrument in psychoanalysis. *Psychoanalytic Review, 68*: 487–503.

Lothane, H. Zvi (2006). Reciprocal free association: Listening with the third ear as an instrument in psychoanalysis. *Psychoanalytic Psychology, 23*: 711–727.

Marcuse, Herbert (2011). Theory and therapy in Freud. In Douglas Kellner and Clayton Pierce (Eds.), *Philosophy, psychoanalysis and emancipation: Collected papers [of Herbert Marcuse]*, Vol. 5. New York: Routledge. (Orig. publ. 1957.)

Natterson, Joseph M. (1966). Theodor Reik b. 1888: Masochism in modern man. In Franz Alexander, Samuel Eisenstein, and Martin Grotjahn (Eds.), *Psychoanalytic pioneers* (pp. 249–264). New York: Basic Books.

NPAP (National Psychological Association for Psychoanalysis) (2016). About us. Online at http://npap.org/about-us.

Nunberg, Herman and Federn, Ernst (Eds.) (1974). *Minutes of the Vienna Psychoanalytic Society*, Vol. 3. M. Nunberg (Trans.). New York: International Universities Press.

Reik, Theodor (1912a). Erstes Erlebnis. Vier Geschichten aus Kinder-land. *Imago, 1* (2): 209–211.

Reik, Theodor (1912b). Wie die Kinder Fabulieren. *Imago, 1* (3): 298–299.

Reik, Theodor (1914). Die "Couvade" und die Psychogenese der Vergeltungsfurcht. *Imago, 3*: 409–455.

Reik, Theodor (1915–16). Die Pubertätsriten der Wilden: Übereinstimmungen im Seelenleben der Wilden und der Neurotiker. *Imago, 4* (3): 125–144 and 189–222.

Reik, Theodor (1917). Das Kainszeichen: Ein psychoanalytischer Beitrag zur Bibelerklärung. *Imago, 5* (1): 31–42. (Presented to the Vienna Psychoanalytic Society, December, 1914.)

Reik, Theodor (1919). Psychoanalytische Studien zur Bibelexegese. I. Jaákobs Kampf. *Imago, 5* (5/6): 325–363. (Presented to the Vienna Psychoanalytic Society, February, 1918.)

Reik, Theodor (1920). The strange God and one's own God. *International Journal of Psycho-analysis, 1*: 350–351. (Proceedings of the 6th International Congress of the International Psycho-analytic Association, September, 1920.)

Reik, Theodor (1923). *Der eigene und der fremde Gott: Zur Psychoanalyse der religiösen Entwicklung.* Leipzig: Internationaler Psychoanalytischer Verlag.

Reik, Theodor (1927). Religionspsychologie. Veröffentlichungen des Wiener Religionspsychologischen Forschungsinstituten. Hg. Karl Bett. Heft 1, 2, 3, Braumüller, Wien u. Leipzig, 1926–27. ("Psychology of religion: Publications of the Vienna Institute for the Psychology of Religion") [book review]. *Imago, 13*: 550–551.

Reik, Theodor (1928). Bemerkungen zu Freuds "Zukunft einer Illusion." *Imago, 14* (2–3): 185–198. (Presented to the Vienna Psychoanalytic Society, December, 1927.)

Reik, Theodor (1929a). Anspielung und Entblößung. *Psychoanalytische Bewegung, 1* (2): 127–134.

Reik, Theodor (1929b). The therapy of the neuroses and religion. *International Journal of Psycho-analysis, 10*: 292–302. (Presented to a Technical Seminar of the Vienna Psycho-Analytical Society, May, 1928.)

Reik, Theodor (1933). New ways in psychoanalytic technique. *International Journal of Psycho-analysis, 14*: 321–344.

Reik, Theodor (1936). *Surprise and the psycho-analyst.* Margaret M. Green (Trans.). Abingdon, UK: Routledge, Trench, Trubner & Co. (Orig. publ. 1935.)

Reik, Theodor (1940). *From thirty years with Freud.* Richard Winston (Trans.). New York: Farrar & Rinehart.

Reik, Theodor (1944). *A psychologist looks at love:* New York: Farrar & Rinehart.

Reik, Theodor (1946). *The psychological problems of religion: I. Ritual, psychoanalytic studies.* D. Bryan (Trans.). New York: Farrar, Straus & Co. (Orig. publ. 1914–19; 1930.)

Reik, Theodor (1948). *Listening with the third ear: The inner experience of the psychoanalyst.* New York: Farrar, Straus.

Reik, Theodor (1949a). *Fragment of a great confession: A psychoanalytic autobiography.* New York: Farrar, Straus.

Reik, Theodor (1949b). *Masochism in modern man.* New York: Farrar, Straus.

Reik, Theodor (1951). *Dogma and compulsion: Psychoanalytic studies of religion and myths.* New York: International Universities Press.

Reik, Theodor (1953). *The haunting melody: Psychoanalytic experiences in life and music.* New York: Farrar, Straus.

Reik, Theodor (1957). *Myth and guilt: The crime and punishment of mankind.* New York, Braziller.

Reik, Theodor (1958). *The search within: The inner experiences of a psychoanalyst.* New York: Farrar, Straus & Cudahy.

Reik, Theodor (1959a). *Mystery on the mountain: The drama of the Sinai revelation.* New York: Harper.

Reik, Theodor (1959b). *The compulsion to confess: On the psychoanalysis of crime and punishment.* New York: Farrar, Straus & Cudahy. (Orig. publ. 1929.)

Reik, Theodor (1960). *The creation of woman: A psychoanalytic inquiry into the myth of Eve.* New York: Braziller.

Reik, Theodor (1962). *Jewish wit.* New York: Gamut Press.

Reik, Theodor (1964). *Pagan rites in Judaism: From sex initiation, magic, moon-cult, tattooing, mutilation, and other primitive rituals to family loyalty and solidarity.* New York: Farrar, Straus.

Roheim, Geza (1955). Some aspects of semitic monotheism. *Psychoanalysis and the Social Sciences, 4*: 194.

Rose, Louis (1998). *The Freudian calling: Early Viennese psychoanalysis and the pursuit of cultural science.* Detroit: Wayne State University Press.

Safran, Jeremy D. (2011). Theodor Reik's *Listening with the third ear* and the role of self-analysis in contemporary psychoanalytic thinking. *Psychoanalytic Review, 98*: 205–216.

Sherman, Murray H. (1960). [Review of] *Mystery on the mountain: The drama of the Sinai revelation,* by Theodor Reik. *Psychoanalytic Review, 47*: 120–121.

Sherman, Murray H. (1963). Introduction: In the tradition of Theodor Reik. *Psychoanalytic Review, 50*: 3–6.

Sherman, Murray H. (1965). Freud, Reik, and the problem of technique in psychoanalysis. *Psychoanalytic Review, 52*: 19–37.

Sherman, Murray H. (1968). Theodor Reik and individualism in psychoanalysis. *Psychoanalytic Review, 55*: 3–6.

Sherman, Murray H. (1970–71). Dr. Theodor Reik: A life devoted to Freud and psychoanalysis. *Psychoanalytic Review, 57*: 535–543.

Sherman, Murray H. (1981–82). The paradox of Theodor Reik. *Psychoanalytic Review, 68*: 467–472.

Tréhel, Gilles (2012). Theodor Reik (1888–1968): Sur l'effroi. *L'information Psychiatrique, 88* (6): 455–468. Online at www.cairn.info/revue-l-information-psychiatrique-2012-6-page-455.htm. Accessed January 27, 2017.

Witrow, Magda (1993). *Julius Wagner-Juaregg (1857–1940).* London: Smith-Gordon.

Chapter 5

Soul, will, and the search for immortality

Otto Rank (1884–1939)

Otto Rank is best known today for two works: *The Trauma of Birth*,[1] in which he first departed significantly from Freud's psychoanalytic theory, and *Art and Artist*,[2] a philosophical-psychological work from his mature independent period. Ernest Becker's Pulitzer prize-winning book, *The Denial of Death*,[3] in which Becker drew heavily on Rank's *Art and Artist*, brought fresh attention to Rank's existentialist legacy in the 1970s. Rank's synthesis of depth psychology (diverging considerably from Freud's) and existential thought (drawing heavily on Nietzsche) were the product of a lifetime of insatiable reading, complex writing, and relentless self-observation. A lay analyst like Reik, he was steeped in the humanities and philosophy, and investigated ancient myths as an extension of Freud's interests in applied psychoanalysis. Like Reik, he also benefited from Freud's father-like care and financial support. For many years, Rank was Freud's closest adopted son in spirit.

But unlike Reik, he rebelled during Freud's lifetime on matters of both theory and clinical practice, and took his place among other brilliant defectors who were expelled from the psychoanalytic establishment. The split between Rank and Freud, played out over several years with great ambivalence on both sides, was one of the most emotionally painful for Freud, and was a sharp but perhaps necessary loss for the mature Rank. In his later work he returned to the philosophical preoccupations of his youth, and pursued an idiosyncratic historical interpretation of the human longing for immortality, expressed through art and the will/soul. His late works, written at the very beginning of World War II, turned almost entirely to religious, existential, and societal matters of "ultimate concern."[4]

Biography[5]

Rank was born the third and youngest child of an artisan class Jewish family, the Rosenfelds. His parents were emigrés from eastern Hungary, living in the Leopoldstadt district of Vienna. His brother, Paul, was three years older; a previously born sister had died as an infant.[6] It was a troubled household: "Almost no word was spoken in the house, but if a voice ever became loud, it became very loud (i.e., it screamed). For every one of us had a deep rage inside, to which he tried to give vent."[7] His father would fly into alcoholic frenzies,[8] and Paul would engage with the father in shouting matches while Rank and his mother would retreat. Rank attributed his "iron industry" to surviving that period of his life.[9]

Rank's parents divorced, and in order to support his mother, Rank was sent to technical school to be a machinist, and then to work in a machine shop where he "suffered horribly."[10] Recurring bouts of rheumatic fever caused him to be transferred to his uncle's office, and he found this work boring and enervating.[11] A sensitive and literate young man, he recurringly felt trapped and stifled, and compensated by reading voraciously and writing in his journal. This journal contained not only personal reflections, but drafts of essays, poems, novels, and plays.[12] In an autobiography he wrote for his own reflection in 1903, he named Schopenhauer, Nietzsche, and Ibsen as his primary intellectual influences, as well as Darwin, Wagner, Wedekind, Stendhal, and Dostoevsky.[13] He wrote his own Ten Commandments, with clear inferences from both his reading (especially Nietzsche) and his personal travails:

1. Thou shalt have no God. 2. Thou shalt not suffer any other besides thyself. 3. Thou shalt not bear false witness against thyself. 4. Thou shalt create daily for thyself a day of joy (holy day). 5. Fathers and mothers: Honor your children and love them so that you do not beget them if you are not able to support and educate them. 6. Thou shalt not want to steal. 7. Thou shalt not contract marriage. 8. Thou shalt not give birth reluctantly. 9. Thou shalt not desire thy neighbor's wife, for there are plenty of others. 10. Thou shalt not venture to want to tell the truth.[14]

In May 1904, he wrote, "Today I bought a weapon to kill myself. Afterwards the keenest lust for life and the greatest courage toward death grew up in me."[15] He embarked on a psychological self-analysis thereafter, as a way to explore the mysteries of consciousness and the soul:

Before everything, I want to make progress in psychology. By that I understand not the professional definition and explanation of certain technical terms established by a few professors, but the comprehensive knowledge of mankind that explains the riddles of our thinking, acting, and speaking, and leads back to certain basic characteristics. For an approach to this idealistic goal, which only a few souls have tried to reach, self-observation is a prime essential and to that end I am making these notes. I am attempting in them to fix passing moods, impressions, and feelings, to preserve the stripped off layers that I have outgrown and in this way to keep a picture of my abandoned way of life, whereby if, in reading these notes later on I want to trace the inner connections and external incidents of my development, I shall have the material for it, namely, my overcome attitudes and viewpoints displayed in order before me.[16]

The product of this study was "The Artist,"[17] completed the following year at age twenty-one. Through this work he lived out his secret life as an intellectual and a creative personality, more in tune with the nineteenth-century romanticism in which he had immersed himself by night than the technologically booming twentieth century in which he labored by day.

In 1906, already having read Freud's *Interpretation of Dreams*, he was introduced to Freud by Adler (his family's physician), with whom he first broached his interest in psychoanalysis.[18] Rank presented Freud with a copy of "The Artist." Rank was enraptured with Freud's erudition and insights into the depths of the human psyche. Freud, in turn, was so taken with Rank's brilliance that he immediately took him under his wing—inviting him to join the Wednesday Night Society and employing him as its paid secretary. Sensing his promise as a leader of the next generation, Freud also prompted him to go back to school, this time to *Gymnasium* (academic high school), after which he subsidized Rank's matriculation at the University of Vienna to become a lay analyst. Rank produced the first psychoanalytic PhD dissertation, an interpretation of the Lohengrin myth, in 1911.

Having granted Rank the status of favorite son, Freud entrusted him not only with the post of secretary, but as a founding editor of both *Imago* and the *Internationale Zeitschrift für Psychoanalyse* in 1912 and 1913, respectively.[19] Rank also became one of the guarantors of psychoanalytic orthodoxy whom Freud admitted to his "secret Committee" in 1912 (after Adler's departure in 1911 and during the final heating up of the painful conflict with Jung).[20] Rank dined weekly with the Freuds and became a virtual member of the family.[21] Freud became the benevolent and inspiring father Rank had never had, and "little Rank" (as Freud referred to him)[22] became Freud's amanuensis—taking dictation for his letters, and even bringing him water and lighting his cigars.[23] Rank was not just a lackey, however. From the very beginning of his membership in the Society, he was a highly intelligent and productive writer and interlocutor.

Rank experienced his admission to Freud's inner circle as a rebirth, and an affirmation of all he had wanted to become. In one of his many acts of self-creation over the decades, three years into his membership in the Vienna Psychoanalytic Society, he changed his last name from Rosenfeld to "Rank" (an admired character in Ibsen's *Doll House*[24]), renouncing his Judaism in the process.[25]

Rank was called up for military training in the spring of 1914.[26] His wartime experience was considerably different from Reik's traumatic horrors. In January, 1916, he was posted to Cracow, a cosmopolitan city with a fine university library, museums, and cultural life. He was appointed editor of the German-speaking daily regional newspaper.[27] He had a relatively comfortable billet, and was able to attend concerts to write music reviews, and to pursue his interest in the arts. Rank continued productively to study psychology as well, although he struggled with what we would now diagnose as bipolar disorder, writing often to Freud of depression and mood swings between "*Rausch*" (rush/high) and

"*Katzenjammer*" (hangover/downswing).[28] Nevertheless, during this enforced separation from Freud and the psychoanalytic world, he grew up in many ways. He established himself as an independent thinker.

He also met "the woman who is created for me," Beata "Tola" Mincer, whom his first biographer Jessie Taft described as "a beautiful young wife, whose intellectual attainments rivaled her charm."[29] The couple married at the end of the war. Rank re-converted to Judaism in order to have a Jewish wedding.[30] In 1920 they had one daughter, Helene,[31] who was greeted like royalty by the Freud household.[32] Rank returned to Vienna a changed man—more confident, more physically fit, happily married, and mature. He was no longer Freud's scrawny obedient shadow, although their collaboration continued to be amicable for several more years.[33] As Jones described the transformation,

> I was very much astonished at the remarkable change the war years had wrought in Rank. I had last seen him a weedy youth, timid and deferential, much given to clicking of heels and bowing. Now in stalked a wiry, tough man with a masterful air whose first act was to deposit on the table a huge revolver. I asked him what he wanted with it, and he nonchalantly replied: "*Für alle Fälle*" ("for any eventuality").[34]

Rank resumed his place by Freud's side and on the Committee, and began seeing patients in psychoanalysis. After the Vienna Society outgrew Freud's waiting room, it was Rank and Sachs who walked him home to Berggasse 19 following their meetings.[35] In 1919, using the same bequest that funded Reik's prize for applied psychoanalysis, Freud was able to establish (on a shoestring, given the post-war economy) an official psychoanalytic publishing house, the *Internationaler Psychoanalytischer Verlag*, and appointed Rank as its managing editor. He handed his finances over to Rank, rankling Freud's son Martin,[36] who was also just back from the war.

Rank was the only member of the Committee living in Vienna at the time, and jealousies inevitably began to simmer.[37] He continued to enjoy all the privileges of a Freud family member, and was the first of the colleagues to be told the traumatic news of Freud's initial cancer diagnosis in 1923—even before Freud himself had been informed.[38] Freud survived his initial treatments and went on to live for another sixteen years, outliving both Abraham and Ferenczi, and preceding Rank in death by only a month. But in the immediate aftermath of his diagnosis and anticipated imminent loss, his inner circle reacted by enacting a guilt-ridden oedipal war of succession. Factions developed within the Committee, with Rank and Ferenczi on one side, and Abraham and Jones (who by that time was in deep personal conflict with Rank)[39] on the other. "[T]hey fell on Rank like dogs."[40] Freud, who now was gravely ill and in pain, was once more in the position of attempting to mediate among squabbling heirs.

While personalities were certainly involved, there were also serious theoretical and clinical differences. Rank published two books in close succession, which could be read as shots across the bow, signaling his increasing independence. The first was a book on psychoanalytic technique co-authored with Ferenczi,[41] *The Development of Psychoanalysis*, shown to Freud in manuscript form in 1922. In it, the two colleagues suggested that analysis could be briefer, with less emphasis on retrieval of memories from early childhood and a more "active" technique, focusing on the emotional experiences of the patient and the "here-and-now"[42] relationship between the analyst and the patient. They critiqued then-standard psychoanalytic technique as "an unnatural elimination of all human factors in analysis" and a "theorizing of experience."[43] Despite their departure from his approach, Freud initially encouraged them (Freud's own technique being notably less rigid than the "Freudians" had become, and less doctrinaire than his own writings on technique).[44] Freud wrote to Rank that September, "Your alliance with Ferenczi has as you know my complete sympathy. The fresh daredevil initiative of your joint draft is really gratifying." He had always been afraid, Freud added, that he might be keeping those closest to him from taking up independent positions; now he was "pleased to see proofs to the contrary."[45] But the opposition, headed up by Abraham, was appalled. Abraham and Jones entered into an exchange of letters with Freud in which they warned him with ever-increasing urgency that the new approach of Ferenczi and Rank was a danger to the entire edifice of psychoanalysis.

Rank's second book, *The Trauma of Birth*, was even more distressing to Freud's followers. Rank presented the manuscript to Freud as a birthday present in May, 1923.[46] It was printed by the *Verlag* in December, 1923, with a dedication to Freud, and released in January. In this work, Rank asserted his belief that it was the universal angst of being pushed through the birth canal into the external world that was the source of all anxiety (both personal and cultural), and at the root of all neurosis. He saw himself as expanding on an idea of Freud's about "the danger of suffocation in the act of birth" and "the act of birth as a source of anxiety," a remark Freud had made after Rank had presented a paper to the Society in 1908.[47] Freud had taken the idea seriously enough at the time that he also added it as a footnote when revising *The Interpretation of Dreams* the following year.[48]

Initially, Freud was willing to view Rank's *Trauma of Birth* positively, although he thought it was quite speculative. Writing to Ferenczi in late March, he stated rather hyperbolically, "I don't know whether 66 or 33 percent of it is true, but in any case it is the most important progress since the discovery of psychoanalysis."[49] But Abraham, Jones, and others saw in this project a direct threat to one of the core tenets of Freudian theory—the oedipal conflict. As early as 1919, Rank had de-emphasized the role of the father, so prominent in Freud's own thinking, and located the primary source of all pathology in the pre-oedipal relationship to the mother from the very moment of birth.[50]

Freud made every effort to keep his potentially wayward son in the fold. Shortly after the book's publication, he defended Rank to the others, stating that "'complete unanimity in all questions of scientific detail and on all newly broached themes' is not 'possible among half a dozen people of differing nature.' It [is] not even desirable."[51] But Abraham and Jones continued to mount charges of heresy. Ferenczi lined up with Rank against the accusers, and the war to expel Rank was on. By March, 1924, Rank realized in a conversation with Freud that the latter had not read his book completely or with understanding, just as Freud now told him he was formulating a rebuttal[52] (eventually incorporated into *Inhibitions, Symptoms, and Anxiety*[53]). Rank's resentment was rising. Freud, still wishing to stave off further controversy, proposed a meeting of the Committee to review the matter, but it was clear that he had begun to heed Abraham's and Jones' adamant objections.

Rank, tired of taking the heat and excited about invitations to speak, teach, and see patients in New York, sailed off to America toward the end of April, just after his fortieth birthday. His reception there was mixed. His ideas—which he presented as both Freudian and new—startled some of the more knowledgeable analysts,[54] and he was perceived as overbearing in his efforts to organize the New York Society.[55] Nevertheless, as a direct emissary from Freud in Vienna he gained much attention, and earned considerable money compared to what was possible in post-war Vienna.[56] Like the embattled Jung before him, he experienced the adulation of the Americans as a shot in the arm. Meanwhile, the conflict back home continued through correspondence. Freud began to worry that in America Rank was feeling his oats too much, and was misrepresenting psychoanalysis with his own most radical ideas. In Rank's absence from Vienna, and in light of Freud's terminal diagnosis, Freud appointed Federn as vice-president of the Vienna Society (i.e., his successor) in Rank's stead.[57]

Rank returned to Vienna that October to find his status much diminished within the Society. Determined to establish a practice in America for a portion of each year, he resigned his positions as editor of the *Zeitschrift* and of the *Verlag*. Freud publicly expressed gratitude for Rank's devoted service of many years, but privately wrote to Lou Andreas-Salomé that Rank

> felt his livelihood to be threatened by my illness and its dangers, looked round for a place of refuge, and hit upon the idea of making his appearance in America. It is really a case of the rat leaving the sinking ship.[58]

Jones recorded Freud saying

> an open break has been averted.... But all intimate relations with him are at an end.... Not only I ... found it very hard to regard him as honest.... I was throughout very fond of Rank, so that I too suffer an intense regret at the course fate has chosen.[59]

The drama was still not over. In reaction to the sea of disapproval all around him, Rank went into a spasm of guilt and self-doubt. He set sail once again for America late that fall, but after reaching Paris, he turned tail and went back to

Vienna. He sought an extremely brief analysis with Freud for depression. In an act of abject contrition, he then sent a *Rundbrief* (circular letter) to all the members of the Committee, in which he confessed that he had "come to recognize in Professor's life-threatening illness the trauma that precipitated the whole crisis, and, furthermore … the Oedipus and brother complex."[60] The colleagues (including his former friend Sachs) responded with a letter on Christmas Day, guardedly welcoming him back but warning him to toe the line.[61] His brief therapy and reconciliation with Freud enabled him to return to America in January, 1925, with a clearer conscience, but damage was done on both sides. Both men felt hurt and betrayed by each other. In 1926 Freud was diplomatic no longer, calling Rank a *gonif* (Yiddish for the Hebrew *ganav*, or thief).[62]

Rank embarked on a two-year period of restlessness, moving back and forth from New York to Vienna to Paris, nursing growing anger and resentment toward the European analytic establishment. Rank's last visit to Freud, just before Freud's seventieth birthday, was tense. He sent Freud a lavish leather-bound edition of Nietzsche's writing as a birthday present shortly thereafter. On the surface a wonderful gift, this was likely also a symbolic declaration of independence—a return to his early existential philosophical path—and a two-edged sword, in historian Paul Roazen's words, "as if Rank's gift were challenging Freud's priority of ideas, saying, 'You accuse me of taking from you, when look what you have taken from Nietzsche'."[63]

In Paris, he and Tola set up a joint analytic practice. It was a heady time in Paris, with many American intellectuals taking up residence, including Gertrude Stein, Ernest Hemingway, George Gershwin, and Sinclair Lewis.[64] The couple befriended—and treated—artists and writers including Anaïs Nin and Henry Miller.[65] Their relationships were multiply entangled both professionally and personally.[66] During this period, Rank began producing most of his later, more philosophical writings, and became excited about picking up the thread of his ideas about art and the artist.

After Freud

As Peter Gay observed, "Once the most orthodox of Freudians, he became a Rankian."[67] Rank had rebirthed himself again. After leaving Freud for good in 1926, Rank continued to travel back and forth to New York, where he was able to earn enough to finance the couple's lavish Parisian lifestyle.[68] However, in 1934 in reaction to the rise of National Socialism,[69] he settled permanently (without Tola) in New York.[70]

Rank wrote prolifically after his final departure from Vienna. Initially, working on his *Outlines of a Genetic Psychology*,[71] he was still thinking along the lines of psychoanalysis, greatly modified. The trauma of birth had completely replaced the oedipal complex by now in Rank's thinking, but he still located the roots of neurosis in the past—in the pre-oedipal mother-child relationship (anticipating, though very much in Rank's own way, Melanie Klein and the object relations school).

At the same time, Rank had come to believe firmly that therapy should be much briefer than a standard psychoanalytic treatment, and should focus more on the here-and-now relationship between the therapist and the patient, rather than on the past. For Rank, the emotional life of the patient was the royal road to the *will*. As Anaïs Nin reported in her diary, he had come to "believe analysis has become the worst enemy of the soul. It killed what it analyzed."[72] Rank, she said, "discovered that what restores life to science is art."[73]

This "here and now" approach to analysis became a hallmark of existential psychotherapy, but few if any psychoanalysts even today would jettison the analysis of childhood experience as Rank did. Although Rank's esteem in some circles was rising, A. A. Brill, then president of the American Psychoanalytic Association (APsA) and an opponent of lay analysis in general, publicly denounced Rank in 1930, and Rank, as well as his former trainees, were ejected from the APsA.[74]

Finally having thrown off the shackles of obedience to the psychoanalytic establishment—and having been disowned by them as well—Rank soon developed an entire system of thought that was as much philosophical as psychological. He began to utterly repudiate all his previous psychoanalytic ideas in favor of a new anti-rationalist, anti-psychoanalytic perspective.[75] Rank was returning after his break with Freud to the philosophical preoccupations of his youth. Rank's mature theories brought him full circle to his pre-Freudian philosophical and psychological speculations. In Menaker's words, "Like the nautilus which, having outgrown its old abode, builds new chambers to accommodate its growth, so Otto Rank structured his understanding of human problems through creatively overcoming the confines of his own emotional struggles."[76]

At the same time, his earlier ideas were now deepened by the psychoanalytic hermeneutic if not by its particular theoretical contents. Rank's book *Truth and Reality: A life history of the human will*[77] was his final declaration of independence. During this same period, he was simultaneously working on his statement of therapeutic practice, *Will Therapy.*[78] These two works, taken together, constitute a comprehensive statement of his mature psychological theory and corresponding clinical approach.

Beginning with the ego, Rank set out to revise or replace all the major constituent parts of Freud's structural model. The ego was no longer a passive mediator between the id and the super-ego.[79] In Rank's metapsychology, the ego was now the prime actor, which was imbued with the will of the individual person— parallel to a cosmic will that shaped the forward movement of the world. Rank rejected a purely sexual definition of the libido, much as Jung had done, and quite knowingly placed it in a spiritual realm as a cosmic force of creativity, which had its "temporal" manifestation in the will of the individual.

The ego was now the representative of this will, both within the psyche, and in relation to the outer world. Desire, therefore, shifted away from the id as the reservoir of infantile wishes, into the domain of the ego. The old instinctual wishes were no longer subject to unconscious repression, but could be put down by a strong enough ego in the service of the will. Creativity, therefore, was no longer to be viewed as sublimation of the drives, but as a manifestation of the will, and of the creativity of the cosmic will itself.[80] "Consciousness," Rank wrote, "originally is itself probably a will phenomenon,"[81] meaning that consciousness arose in the evolution of the human animal as a means for will to manifest itself. Nature becomes conscious of "herself" [sic] through the human person.[82]

Rank saw a problem arising, however, in the child's relationship to parental and social rules, giving the Oedipus complex some residual due.[83] The will formed a "counter-will" within the child, not out of fear of castration, but because the will would always resist any kind of constraint. However, this created a problem, because when the child did something against the parents' wishes and was punished, s/he would take it to mean not only that her *act* of will was bad, but that her will *itself* was bad.[84]

Internal rebellion was bound to follow, because now the will naturally resisted being suppressed by the counter-will. The ego was strengthened again in puberty through the maturing of individual identity, but confronted a "new, alien and more powerful counter-will"—in the form of sexual compulsion.[85] Rank went so far as to say that a person did not internalize the parents as an internal prohibition, but on the contrary, the ego took those same moralizing parents as *allies* in its efforts to put down the *counter-will* (which Rank now equated with the sex drive), in service of the greater creative aims of the *will*.[86] In the healthiest outcome, the will then would strive to get free of this parental crutch, and to form its own inner ethical ideals from external models of its own choosing (a parallel to Freud's "ego ideal," but independent of the parents). If the will were unable to triumph in any of these phases, non-creative social conformity, neurosis, or psychopathy would result.

Therapy in every case, then, rather than being geared toward helping the neurotic individual *adapt* to the constraints of "reality" in the form of societal norms (Rank's critique of psychoanalysis), had as its aim the "individualization" of the patient, via the acceptance of his or her own will.[87] With *Truth and Reality*, Rank completely departed from anything resembling a psychoanalytic or "depth psychological" point of view:

> Consciousness, as an instrument of knowledge turned toward the inside seeks truth, that is, inner actuality in contrast to the outer truth of the senses, the so-called "reality." Instinct lifted into the ego sphere by consciousness is the power of will, and at the same time a tamed, directed, controlled instinct, which manifests itself freely within the individual personality, that is, creatively.[88]

A new problem arose, however, with self-acceptance of the individual will: *guilt*. By its very nature, according to Rank, individualization is antisocial. It refuses to conform to outward norms and directives. With this problem in mind, he saw three potential solutions, corresponding with three types of personality. These three types were based on the strength of will each one has (presumably this is a matter of individual constitution): (1) The "average" person, whose will is weak, gives in to the pressures of family, society, and external reality, and cedes his or her personal authority to those in power. (2) The "neurotic" type, which at certain points Rank suggested would include most people, is one whose will is strong, but whose guilt paralyzes individualization and action contrary to external society. It is this type who needs therapy the most, in order to embrace his or her will and transform thought into creative self-expression.[89] The neurotic is the "artiste-manqué," who has the strength of will to create, but fails because s/he is inhibited by guilt. (3) The third type, the "creative" type, which Rank clearly regarded as superior, is the individual whose will is strong and who, in spite of the guilt engendered by his or her antisocial individuality, forges ahead and takes action—creating him/herself anew. (4) In *Art and Artist*,[90] Rank also described a fourth type—the antisocial, criminal, or psychopathic—who has a strong will but *no* guilt. S/he has the opposite problem from the neurotic—not inhibition, but a lack of impulse control.[91]

Freud's "methodological error," according to Rank, was recognizing the normal and the neurotic types, but not recognizing the "positive, creative affirmation of will, which the moralistic therapist wants to translate into normal [ego] adaption [to reality/culture.]"[92] Psychoanalysis was therefore internally conflicted, according to Rank, because it perpetuated a pessimistic moralistic split between good and bad institutions of the mind, over which the ego had little power.[93] Esther Menaker suggests that Rank had one of the first truly social understandings of guilt because "it is the inescapable hallmark of human relatedness,"[94] a recognition that will is narcissistic by definition, setting the individual against others; yet, because will is universal, we are united in this tragic will-guilt predicament, which only creativity true to oneself can begin to resolve. Rank's philosophical-psychological theory culminated in his masterpiece, *Art and Artist*[95] bringing to bear all of his new psychological formulations on the quest for transcendence through the free expression of the will and liberated self-creation.

An ethical critique of this entire system is that Rank's "will" has no content per se. In spite of his critique of psychoanalysis' emphasis on individualism, his valorization of the will seems subjective, without external criteria. It is vaguely identified with creativity, a manifestation of the cosmic will, but creativity in what ethical sense?[96] Rank wrote, in a strangely bias-laden passage in *Truth and Reality*,

> The will itself is not as "evil" as the Jew-hating Schopenhauer believes along with the Old Testament, nor as "good" as the sick Nietzsche would like to see it in his glorification. It exists as a psychological fact and is the real problem of psychology, first as to its origin, how it has evolved in man, and second why we must condemn it as "bad" or justify it as "good," instead

of recognizing and affirming it as necessary.... [W]e must guard against bringing in moralistic evaluations before we have recognized their psychological source.[97]

Perhaps Rank assumed that his readers would be able to differentiate intuitively between the artist-hero and the antisocial personality, but in his rejection of social and cultural norms as the source of the ethical ideal,[98] he left the definition of "ideal" up to the will of each individual:

> there is no criterion for what is good or bad, as there is no absolute criterion for true or false, since it is one thing at one time, and another at another.... At all events, we can expect to find the answer only in the individual himself and not in the race or its history.[99]

One clue to Rank's sense of ethics is, perhaps paradoxically, his definition of guilt as the recognition of the narcissistic self-directedness of the individual's will. He offered no foundation of why the ego should feel this realization as guilt—it simply does. It enters "inevitably into the functioning of the psychic mechanism like the friction in the operation of a machine."[100]

Rank did consider that the artist would not rise from the "artiste-manqué" even after producing a great work from his or her will, if it was not recognized and affirmed by others in society. Perhaps from his negative valuation of the antisocial personality, and his valuation of relatedness in his definitions of guilt and artistic success, we can extrapolate an ethical, social sensibility. But in his eagerness to distance himself from what he viewed as the moralism of psychoanalysis and its goal of "adaptation," these themes remain inchoate and implicit. Nietzsche's ideal of the *Übermensch* ("over-man" or "superman"),[101] which Rank absorbed eagerly in his youth, remained a strong influence in his ideal of the artist-hero. Rank wrote that

> Nietzsche, who experienced thoroughly the whole tragedy of the creative man and admitted in his *amor fati* (love of fate) the willingness to pay for it, is in my opinion the first and has been up to now the only psychologist.[102]

Yet as history proved in the ideology of National Socialism, which drew (idiosyncratically to be sure) on Nietzsche, such freedom to create oneself (or one's race) could have catastrophic social consequences. Erich Fromm, in fact, critiqued Rank harshly for "kinship with the elements of Fascist philosophy."[103]

In the end, one of the difficulties in pinning down a "Rankian" theory is that Rank himself did not believe in a final, once-and-for-all theory of human consciousness, because for Rank, will itself was inherently a force of transformation. Rank was in a very real sense a kind of process philosopher; he was familiar with the works of Alfred North Whitehead.[104] For Rank, however, the relationship between the cosmic and the individual will was not causal, merely parallel.[105] There could be no final theory because the cosmic will is always in a state of flux:

> Theory formation of every kind is then only an attempt to oppose to the manifold spontaneous attempts at interpretation by will and consciousness a single interpretation as constant, lasting, true. This, however, ... is exactly anti-psychological, since the essence of psychic processes consists in change and in the variability of the possibilities of interpretation.[106]

Death, guilt, and atonement

In the last years of his professional life, Rank taught and had a significant influence on the University of Pennsylvania's School for Social Work in Philadelphia, mainly in collaboration with his former patient (and first biographer), the social worker Jessie Taft.[107] Taft was a tireless supporter of Rank's ideas, first inviting him to teach at the school in the fall of 1927,[108] and translating Rank's *Truth and Reality* and *Will Therapy* in 1936.[109] They created a "functional" approach to social work using short-term analytic treatment focused on the here-and-now relationship between the social worker and the client.[110]

In his personal life, tensions had been growing. Tola, who had never severed ties with Freud or the Vienna Society, was "hit very hard" by the split between her husband and Freud.[111] After five years of separation, Rank filed for divorce in Nevada in 1939 in order to marry his Swiss-American secretary and companion Estelle "Sandra" Buel on July 31.[112] Less than three months after the wedding, Rank tragically died at the age of fifty-five on October 31, 1939, of complications from a post-surgical throat infection.

This was also just a month after Freud's death (September 23).[113] Perhaps the emotional impact of Freud's death—albeit at great distance—may have contributed to his illness, and even on some subliminal level, a wish to die. This is certainly speculative, and Rank's death was by no means a suicide—he had much to live for with a new marriage and a successful career. He wrote ebulliently to Jessie Taft that he was "starting a new life at 55½!"[114] And in the manuscript version of the preface to his last book, *Beyond Psychology*, he declared, "My life work is completed too—*not because I have no more time to live but I have no more time for work.*"[115] But Rank had hinted earlier in his own writings that

> [f]or with men even the biological factors are placed in large measure under the control of will and thus certainly are also exposed to the danger of manifesting themselves destructively because of the guilt problem. We know just from psychoanalytic experiences that men can sicken and die when they will it, that however, just as often in a miraculous fashion they can escape death—if they will it. It is just this conflict of the individual will with the biological compulsive forces that constitutes the essentially human problem, in its creative as in its destructive manifestations.[116]

Rank still had much to feel guilty about with regard to Freud—just as in his theories the creative man must still bear the burden of guilt for his rebellion against all authorities, internal and external. Rank had lost his first father early in life, and at the end of his life he had returned to the literary and philosophical sources that in some sense had fathered him intellectually and carried him to Freud's door. Now the spiritual father of his young adulthood, who had fostered his creative genius, was gone, and World War II was about to draw the United States into its violent morass. Borrowing from the language of family systems theory, a cut-off can be one of the strongest psychic bonds. Freud never stopped referring to Rank in his own writings—even obliquely in his very last work, *Moses and Monotheism*.[117] The adamant tone of Rank's denial of psychoanalysis in his later years may have been his paradoxical affirmation of its deep importance in his life.

Rank on religion, mythology, and the soul

Early writings

Menaker points out that in "The Artist," his work before Freud,

> Rank speaks of religion as mankind's creative attempt to deal with the universal problem of human suffering and conflict. Unlike Freud, for whom religion was an infantile, regressive escape from the "realities" of life, Rank views it positively as a spontaneous mass therapeutic phenomenon which derives inevitably from the nature of man's being in the world. It is the inevitability of human suffering that is important here, for this emphasis on the very nature of life itself, rather than on pathology, permeates all of Rank's later work, and has a profound influence on his view of the therapeutic task.[118]

In 1908, Rank presented his paper, "The Myth and Birth of the Hero," to the Vienna Society.[119] In this work, published the following year, he endeavored to apply Freud's method of dream interpretation—demonstrating common elements in heroic birth narratives from ancient Mesopotamian, Egyptian, and Greek mythology, European folk tales, and the Bible (especially Moses and Jesus). Rank interpreted along oedipal lines—but also retained much of what he had internalized from Nietzsche regarding the "will to power" and the hero's self-determination.[120] In response, Freud, far from insisting on a strict adherence to his oedipal theory, speculated that in these myths, "the conflict with the father has its origin not in sexual rivalry for the mother, but in the father's concealment of the facts about the sexual processes concerned with birth."[121] It was to these ideas about the relationship of the infant to the mother that Rank would return in the 1920s. Intriguingly, his handwritten dedication in Freud's copy read: "To the father of this book in gratitude from" (not the son but) "the Mother."[122]

In 1914 Rank presented a paper on the *Doppelgänger* ("Double") as an early narcissistic stage of development, interpreting it as a "primitive belief in a bodily soul as an expression of a deep-rooted belief in immortality."[123] This work, subsequently published in *Imago*,[124] was expanded and published as a book by the *Verlag* in 1925.[125] Rank's concern with immortality foreshadowed his later rejection of the oedipal theory as the primary dynamic source either of individuals' psychic life, or of culture, in favor of a theory based on the fear and denial of death, and "will to immortality."

Self-creation and rebirth: "truth and reality"

In the 1920s, as noted above, Rank's ideas about religion began to diverge from Freud's, just as his psychology and clinical practice theories were also departing from Freudian psychoanalysis. He was still no more favorably inclined toward organized religion than he ever had been—he saw the religions of the world as evolutionary stages in the development of human consciousness, progressing toward atheism in modernity. Yet in his development of the idea of the will as simultaneously personal and cosmic,[126] he was moving into a quasi-theological mode of philosophy along the same borderline as Schleiermacher's idea of a universal religious *Gefühl* (an innate human feeling of absolute dependence and absolute freedom).[127]

Rank opened his book *Truth and Reality* with a paradoxical epigraph: "Jesus: *I am come to bear witness unto the truth*. Pilate: What is truth?"[128] "Truth," for Rank, was now the truth of the soul, or innermost self,[129] and "reality" was its dialectical opposite—the external factor in life, the "no," the limits imposed by living among others in the world (not unlike Freud's reality principle). Rank viewed religion as a "priestly deception,"[130] by which the guilty human could project forgiveness and redemption upon God. He reinterpreted the myth of the Fall in Genesis as the conflict between will and self-consciousness—by eating the fruit of the tree of knowledge, Adam "loses his naïve unity with the unconscious, with nature ... with the wholesome, the good."[131] He became subject to consciousness, which brought both awareness of fate, and guilt. The difference between Adam and the ancient Greek hero was that the Greek hero was subject to fate and could not predict his own downfall, whereas the Adam of biblical myth had a moral system of good and evil, and of sin. Will became associated with the sin of pride.[132] "Knowing is sin, knowledge creates guilt."[133] In Rank's formulation, then, the will–guilt conflict was played out in the world's religious and mythological systems, where knowledge would promote guilt (associated with Schopenhauer's philosophy of will),[134] whereas godlike creative heroic action (associated with Nietzsche's optimism about the will)[135] would result in death.

Rank accused psychoanalysis of moralism because it reinforced the notion that the will, as id and instinct, was evil in terms of its voracious self-interest and refusal to adapt to civilization.[136] By blaming "bad thoughts" on the id and the repressed unconscious, psychoanalysis denied the reality of the will and perpetuated its suppression.[137] Thus, traditional psychoanalysis (unwittingly) suppressed the creative will of the individual and reinstalled a conventional "Jewish–Christian morality."[138]

In *Truth and Reality*, Rank also proposed an historical evolution of religions that paralleled his three personality types (the "normal" or conformist, the neurotic, and the creative): Three "different attempts to solve the will–guilt problem, the real, the ideal, and the spiritual,"[139] were represented by three corresponding historical eras in the evolution of religion: Judaism, Greek mythology, and Christianity.[140] Judaism, he wrote, began with a "warlike nation of herdsmen who needed and created a strong willed, confident god of battle as an ego ideal." As the people evolved and flourished, they replaced the warlike god with a creative God, who became the justification for their earlier "horrors and conquests of war," and to whom they willingly submitted.[141] This God, who became more protective and less destructive, "bore the maternal character, as for example, the Egyptian and even Athena in the Homeric world picture,"[142] while the destructive God, "a manifestation of the evil counter-will," was transmuted over time into the Judaeo-Christian devil.[143]

The Greeks replaced submission to one god with a complex relation among humans and multiple gods with their "passions" and "strong wills." The "self-ruling creative hero" took the place of the creative God. However, guilt was ushered in through the self-consciousness of the Greek tragedies in which the hero "makes himself fully responsible for himself and pays, atones, with death."[144]

> [Christianity,] as an immediate reaction to Roman tyranny, representing paternal authority, presents in the symbolism of the rebellious son, the passive hero, who conquers, not by means of will assertion but by means of will submission, conquers spiritually even though corporeally, physically, he fails.[145]

Rank saw this progression in history as a progression from the "moralistic" (group conformity), to the "ethical" (self-responsibility), to the "spiritual,"[146] in which the self-sacrificing God of Christianity embodies the mother principle of love over against patriarchal domination, and divinizes the son, the creaturely human. "[I]n Christianity, God represents guilt and the individual subjects his will to the God conquered and overcome by himself."[147]

From this creaturely, self-giving God, Rank thought, it was a short step to withdrawing idealized projections from the spiritual realm, and "taking the Gods from heaven and to the humanizing of the omnipotent creative will."[148] The post-religious creative man or woman might then seek salvation (that is, relief from the will–guilt problem) in romantic love, but this, too, was bound to fail, because after the initial bliss of romance and the reduction of guilt through care for the other, the harmony of a couple would again be "shattered" on the rocks of their separate wills.[149] This "love solution" might produce a child as its creative product, but Rank clearly esteemed cultural creation above procreation.[150] (All of this had a sadly autobiographical subtext in relation to his own failed marriage with Tola.[151])

Ultimately, Rank asserted, "individual salvation for which the modern type strives, is to be found only in individual happiness."[152] "For the neurotic who cannot master guilt, this may mean suicide"[153]—as Rank himself had considered in his youth. However,

> if the will is affirmed and not negated or denied, there results the life instinct, and happiness, like salvation, is found in life and experience, in the creation and acceptance of both without having to ask how, whither, what and why.... For happiness can only be found in reality, not in truth, and redemption never in reality and from reality, but only in itself and from itself.[154]

Psychology and the soul

One year after completing *Truth and Reality* and *Will Therapy*, while still ferrying between Paris and New York, Rank wrote *Psychology and the Soul*,[155] his most comprehensive work on an explicitly religious subject. By this time, for Rank, it was the fear of death and the denial of mortality—as well as the will, the life-force—that was the central motivating principle for all religious and psychological phenomena. Like his other works, this, too, had autobiographical roots:

> Death, the mysterious phenomenon that many thinking people have attempted to explain, became a problem to me above all. I still remember that I did not sleep for many nights and thought only about dying with terror and chattering teeth.[156]

The denial of death and the quest for immortality had always been in Rank's mind throughout his life. He linked his work on *Psychology and the Soul* to his early work on the *Doppelgänger* as his first essay on "primitive" peoples' first attempt to theorize an immortal soul.[157]

In this work, Rank reinterpreted the Oedipus myth in light of the pursuit of immortality by means of the wish to be reborn through the mother, rather than sexual conquest and patricide.[158] Dreaming itself, Rank asserted, was not an expression of wish fulfillment as Freud thought, but proof of immortality in the face of the deathlike nature of sleep.[159] For Rank, it was no longer the drives of sex and aggression that were the primary motivators of human behavior, but rather the will—to live, and to resist death.

Rank's view of the interpretation of religion had departed entirely from the anthropological search for oedipal origins by his Viennese compatriots a decade earlier: "Psychology deals only with interpretations of soul phenomena—whether these are already concretized, or are subjective phenomena within the self and involving the ego. But interpretation itself is nothing but an intellectualized will-phenomenon."[160] For Rank, the "spiritual" realm belonged to the realm of will and the human "ideal,"[161] not to "psychological truth" which he now viewed as destructive. To understand the human person, one had to turn to this ineffable, individually expressed realm, not any longer to intellectual or scientific analysis. As Rank concluded the book, he insisted that the scientific objectivity claimed by psychology was merely one more interpretation, one more self-deceptive creed. In the end, like every other ideology, the true "psychological creed of mankind is immortality."[162]

In *Psychology and the Soul*, Rank revised his evolutionary stages of human history in light of this human quest for an immortal soul. The first stage, derived from his early work, *Der Doppelgänger*, was the "narcissistic stage," in which early humans imagined an earthly double who would live on beyond them. They also came to fear the *revenant* of one whom they had killed—leading to the first taboo, that of murder.[163] They could not understand the sleeplike phenomenon of natural death, and so blamed such deaths on ghosts or demons. A second stage, totemism, was a kind of proto-religion, in which clans banded together to ensure collective immortality: "the *creative* side of belief in immortality."[164] "*[R]eligio*," he stated, "means joining or reuniting. Various immortality beliefs were unified in a religious system, but more important, in this soul-system individuals were united in social groups."[165] This was later preserved, Rank thought, in Judaism through its communal and familial ties.[166] The mechanics of procreation were not yet understood, Rank believed, and children were "ensouled" by a totem animal—a bird or crawling creature or spiritual symbol thereof—which invaded women at the time of conception. Rank attributed the myth of Jesus' conception by the Holy Ghost (the dove) to this "old soul-bird."[167] Further, in Christianity, "children conceived normally are born with original sin and ensouled through baptism, which symbolizes fertilization by the spirit; without baptism they forfeit the soul's immortality."[168]

A third "humanized" stage evolved with a better understanding of the sexual process of procreation. Rank believed this to be a matriarchal period of human evolution. Women were revered (*Mutterrecht*—"matriarchy" or "mother-law") as the soul-bearers. It was they who passed the soul along to the child.[169] Primogeniture was not yet a concern: "The first problem for early humans was not that of their descent but of their future, not the mystery of beginning but that of perishing."[170] As the father's role in procreation became clearer, there was a power shift from matriarchy to patriarchy, reflected in ancient Hebrew and Roman cultures. A "sexual era" ensued, in which the father's soul was thought to be transmitted to the child through procreation—and possibly lost by him in the process. "[T]his implies a sexual danger, a threat to immortality when a man's soul enters his child."[171] Rank therefore theorized that men feared sexual intercourse, leading to rituals of abstinence.[172]

Rank drew on his study of hero sagas here, proposing that "the hero plays the fool to deny soul-threatening knowledge of sex."[173] The hero

> is only the late form of primeval soul-belief, in which the powerful, strong-willed superman, in place of totem and god, has the right and duty to impregnate women with his soul-stuff. Originally a sacred custom, this right later became frivolous abuse,[174]

as in the "Don Juan type." In later Christian legends, "bad, forbidden sex" came to be personified by the devil[175] and women were denigrated as a "symbol of sex-without-soul."[176]

In Rank's view, Christianity retained the collective nature of totemism, transmitted via Judaism. In Christianity, however, immortality was spiritualized through belief in individual survival of the soul *after* death, mediated by the resurrection of Christ. In Judaism, immortality was earthly, a "familial sexual immortality" that was "codified as a religious idea."[177] Further, Rank proposed, once Christianity was adopted by "princes of nations," the immortality of the soul was linked with the perpetuation of the state.[178] Christianity ushered in the "era of the child," or son. Now the son had become "the soul-bearer as well as the perpetuator of his father's life on earth."[179] The Trinity incorporated this divine son with two earlier soul beliefs—the matriarchal period's ensoulment of the child by an outside spiritual being (the Holy Spirit), and the father's role in creation (as God the father/creator).[180]

Rank observed that as the power of the Church and individual religious belief waned, romanticism evolved as the next "orientation to and expression of the soul problem."[181] Absent belief in a supernatural creator or soul-bearer, woman once again became the soul-bearer in man's quest for romantic love. This was no solution, however. As Rank already theorized in *Truth and Reality*, "in romantic love we reach a valuable compromise between individual and collective claims on the soul: a community of two," but "witness its collapse in a new reaction of individualism against spiritual absorption in another person. One is not willing to be used as the soul of another."[182] Romanticism quickly led, then, to psychology—an individual soul quest hearkening back to Greek philosophy.[183]

More than halfway through *Psychology and the Soul*, Rank made a strong connection between his concept of will and humans' belief in a soul. Will, he argued, is the positive wish for immortality, and essentially *creates* the belief in the soul as eternal: "Soul-belief stems from the idea of death and from death fear, but there is another, more positive side of the soul construct that was understood by the primitives as life-force, vital energy (i.e., *mana*)."[184] In this book, Rank completed his equation of will with *mana* or a cosmic creative force. "This force essentially comprises the human will as I see it in the creative personality: a force beyond natural causality which can freely choose to change it."[185] "Mana," he wrote, "is not associated with the idea of any supreme being; it is a concept neither god- or soul- but energy-related."[186] It came to be associated historically with both belief in God and belief in the immortal soul, but at its origin and in its continuation in post-religious life, it was simply a force, of creativity:

> Unlike belief in immortality, which comes from death-fear, the concept of God—a higher, supernatural being—develops from the life-wish, and mana expresses the energy and power of this wish. God personifies the willing self that feels immortal when it has mana. The soul corresponds to collective immortality, which the mortal self must be assured of. In this light, the soul would be everyone's collective mana—the folk-mana, so to speak—received when mana-bearing personalities yield it to all as a community through religion.[187]

He added an ethical note, that "[p]rimitives expect bearers of mana to use their power communally (for the tribe), not selfishly."[188] In later religious developments, people used this collective "will-God" to justify their individual willing.[189] As Rank noted previously in *Truth and Reality*, submission to a deity reinterpreted the individual's will as evil, associating it with sex, sin, and guilt. And, as in the ancient cultures, "personal will to immortality, or hubris—whether for oneself or the community—is 'punished' by death."[190] So, death itself, because equated with damnation, came to be viewed as evil.[191] Rank went on to equate the God who punishes as well as rewards with the monotheistic father-god of Judaism, and Eve became "the death goddess of the underworld" as well as "the mother of all living things."[192] A moral-religious system of good and evil developed from humans' projection of their (now evil) will onto God, a transcendent version of the patriarchal mana-bearer of the tribe in earlier times.[193]

Finally, Rank identified one more era of humanity, the modern "era of psychology."[194] The way had been paved by philosophers such as Schopenhauer and Nietzsche, who viewed the will as a force existing apart from any supernatural divinity. In a final chapter, Rank edged toward postmodernism, proposing that the discoveries of this new era had overturned the psychoanalytic and scientific emphasis on order and causality in favor of a recognition of the randomness in the universe (citing quantum physics).[195] This was "a new phase of spiritual development, one that affects both physics and psychology."[196] Rank cited the impact of the observer on the observed, as in the Heisenberg principle,[197] as a refutation of any possibility of objective interpretation.[198]

Further, he perceived a "pulling force of the future," as well as a pushing or causal force from the past, which relativized the classical psychoanalytic emphasis on a patient's early childhood. Rank's view had become teleological rather than deterministic. A person must allow the will to be pulled forward by a future s/he cannot yet see, just as an atom is pulled by an invisible goal.[199] This may seem supernatural because "one sees its effects without knowing their cause," but from this new perspective, the "causal principle" is simply another intellectual manifestation of willing, and a justification for the will's propulsion.[200] The ancients had it right, he thought, when they saw the link between rain and rain magic as a matter of fate rather than causality.[201] This was lost in the turn to religion, when God as "first cause" replaced fate.

The turn to science in the nineteenth century jettisoned the deity, Rank observed, but retained causality as its world view.[202] Yet the new physics was challenging Newtonian laws of cause-and-effect—and by implication, psychoanalysis, too, with what Rank saw as its purely biological determinism—in favor of a cosmic indeterminacy:

> This dethrones psychology as self-knowledge and reestablishes ethics [by which he meant following the dictates of the will] and epistemology [examining and questioning the foundations of all previous "knowledge"] in its place. Psychology can no more replace knowledge gained through [rational] thought than it can replace religion and morality.[203]

Psychology, with its dual etymology of *psyche* (both soul and mind), had become the modern place to seek the soul, but Rank believed it had lost the soul (free will) by attempting to limit it to scientific biologism and materialism:

> I have characterized psychology itself as a creative expression of free will in the spiritual sense: I have shown how psychology, which sprang from soul-belief, still tries, like its source, to preserve the ideology of immortality. Yet psychology no longer believes in that to which it owes its existence, the soul.[204]

This leaves us, Rank stated, in a paradoxical dilemma, hearkening back to the conclusion reached by Freud in *The Future of an Illusion*[205]—psychology cannot replace religious belief; it can only shatter its illusions.[206] Rank rejected psychology as a negative, destructive ideology—an ideology of resentment in Nietzsche's sense. It destroys illusions and ideologies that cannot resist advancing consciousness, and it cannot stop until it reaches and destroys itself as the last ideology.[207]

Rank did not end in despair at this realization. Rather, he turned again to the importance of creativity and action in response to the inner promptings of the will:

> We live primarily as moral, not biological, beings, and this contradiction sheds light on all human problems. Will is manifest in the biological sphere as action, and in the moral sphere as reaction; the task of all education and therapy is to transform these reactions into actions again, in other words, to transpose will-compulsion into free will.[208]

Foreshadowing the constructivist[209] and relational turn in psychoanalysis in recent decades, he asserted that "in psychology, too—perhaps more than elsewhere—the crucial thing is not to proclaim the current favorite as the interpretation, and certainly not as the reality underlying every interpretation. In the psychic real, the only reality is the Now."[210]

He concluded *Psychology and the Soul* with a play on Buber's title *I and Thou*: "The I and the Now."[211] Again citing physics, he declared, "The now-point [is] the border between past and present without recourse to psychic [i.e., causal] factors."[212] For Rank, the concept Now was intimately connected with the concept of "self." Psychology, in the final analysis, then was "a science of relationships—a way of observing relationships and relativities."[213] Sounding much like Gadamer and other philosophers of hermeneutics, Rank saw no Archimedean point from which to observe, no pure objectivity, and certainly no religiously grounded eternal truth—only will, and its manifestation in individual persons as "soul." In his final statement in the book, he pointed to a relational path forward, but with a caveat about the ever-recurring illusory wish for immortality:

> Psychology is not even an interpretation of facts (like physics and biology) but an interpretation of attitudes of the self, which in so-called objective psychology we project onto others. Psychology is self-interpretation through others, just as physics is self-interpretation through nature. In this way psychology as knowledge of others is self-affirmation, self-assertion. Psychology as self-knowledge is self-deception, that is, belief: the psychological creed of mankind is immortality.[214]

Beyond psychology

Rank was finishing his last work, *Beyond Psychology*, at the time of his death in 1939.[215] It was his only book written first in English, published posthumously in 1941. In this final compendium of his ideas Rank reiterated much that he had already expressed in *Truth and Reality* and *Psychology and the Soul*, particularly his view of epochs of evolution in religious thought, his idea of the *Doppelgänger* as the first emergence of the idea of immortality, and his essentialist views on "feminine psychology and masculine ideology" throughout human history.[216] There is a curious essentialist form of feminism in Rank's writings, in which he aligned masculinity with sadism and what he viewed as a distorted version of femininity with masochism, while advocating for some kind of equality within complementary "natural" roles. Rank also cited Schopenhauer, Nietzsche, and Weininger in drawing "a definite parallel between the psychology of the Jew and the woman" seeing both depicted as "enslaved, inferior, castrated," and suffering a similar fate, "namely, suppression, slavery, confinement, and subsequent persecution."[217] Foreshadowing a very recent argument by Sander Gilman,[218] he accused Freud of attempting to "save the crumbling ideology of the strong Old Testament father-ideal" via a "projection of those feminine characteristics of the Jew upon the woman, thereby achieving a kind of therapeutic self-healing for the Jewish race."[219]

Writing perhaps autobiographically, his main characters,

> the hero, the artist, the neurotic appear once more upon the stage, not only
> as participants in the eternal drama of life but after the curtain has gone
> down, unmasked, undressed, unpretentious, not as punctured illusions, but
> as human beings who require no interpreter.[220]

He asserted, "My own life work is completed."[221]

Rank stated the aim of his project as developing a truly social psychology
beyond the underlying bourgeois assumptions of individual psychology (whether
Freud's, Adler's, or Jung's).[222] In the Preface to the book, he wrote: "Man [*sic*]
is born beyond psychology and he dies beyond it but he can live beyond it only
through vital experience of his own—in religious terms, through revelation, conversion or re-birth."[223] As Menaker interprets,

> This statement is not a call for a specific religious or mystical experience.
> Rather, it is an elaboration of the spiritual capacity of the creative will to
> deal with the bitter reality of its own end by identifying with the continuity
> of life itself. According to Rank it is the will to live rather than the fear of
> death which spurs the creative impulse to reach for immortality.[224]

Rank repudiated the ideal of human equality as a romantic fiction, arguing that all
revolutions begin in a fight against evil and end up with a bureaucracy of "virtue."[225]
The self, Rank insisted, is naturally irrational. Neither appeals to the supernatural,
nor to rationalism, can undo the force of irrationality and "the willful assertion of
difference, economically, politically, and racially."[226] Surveying the psychologies of
Freud, Jung, and Adler, he claimed that his final arrival-point was "beyond these
differences in psychologies to a psychology of difference."[227] All psychologies
reflected the prevailing ideologies of their contexts. His program of finding a way
toward social psychology and social change digressed for most of the book into a
recapitulation of matters that had preoccupied him throughout his intellectual life,
including "the double as immortal self," "the emergence of the social self" in the
form of totemism as the first form of religion and the first expression of collective
immortality, "the creation of personality" and the "inspirational" type, a tour of
world religions in relation to *Eros* and *Agape* as the "two kinds of love," "the creation of the sexual self" as a pursuit of immortality through the Other, and "feminine psychology and masculine ideology." Yet, his over-arching theme was the
human longing for self-transcendence. Ultimately, he thought, neurosis was not
determined by either nature or nurture per se, but rather "as the result of an excessive control on the part of the individual's will over his own nature."[228] He wrote,

> [T]he individual is not just striving for survival but is reaching for some
> kind of "beyond," be it in terms of another person, a group, a cause, a faith
> to which he can submit, because he thereby expands his Self.[229]

Delving directly into his view of the history of religions once more, he contrasted the survival of a racial, tribal Judaism with the development of a Christian universal ideology.[230] Thus, he thought the problem of Jewish statelessness would be solved "by replacing biological and social fatherhood by spiritual fatherhood," and exchanging righteousness for love[231]—accessible to all through the love of God, and expressed as mother-love in the veneration of Mary. Rank attributed the "creation of personality" to Christianity, in which a "new type of man" was characterized by the shift from outward observance of the law to an inner experience of faith, love, and salvation through a universal divine savior. By basing the messiah's prophesied succession not only on biological, tribal descent (from King David) but on adoption by God, Christianity moved beyond the supernatural magical beliefs of primal tribes, beyond the intellectual succession of the Greeks through philosophy, and beyond the Roman succession based on legal biological inheritance, toward a cosmic inheritance through Christ.

Rank spent considerable time discussing the role of the apostle Paul in bringing Christianity to dominance in the western world, and an accompanying "democratic ideology" that made salvation possible for all. In Christ, Rank argued, the heroic personality type (from his previous writings) was elevated, "became flesh in Paul and through the Apostle in mankind." The "average man" found his elevation in identification with such priestly figures, and with Christ through baptism. The sublime potential of such an elevation was doomed, according to Rank, because mass psychology continually undermined it with the desire to equate goodness with conformity. The struggle with harsh reality would continually reawaken theologies of human sinfulness in a duality between good and evil, even within the self. In a shift from *Truth and Reality*, however, Rank was now embracing Christianity's "spiritual solution" of the will–guilt problem rather than seeking to overcome it through artistic self-creation. Christianity, Rank now asserted, was more hopeful, in that sin could be redeemed, rather than merely accepted as the cost of consciousness, as in Judaism. In the modern romantic era, as he had asserted in earlier writings, *Eros* became a substitute for the more difficult *Agape* (unconditional, non-antagonistic love of others).[232]

In this vein, Rank made (for a Jew, even if a non-confessing one) an astonishing claim:

> Herein is epitomized the fundamental difference between the Jewish and Christian philosophy of life. The one is based on self-hatred [citing Theodor Lessing], leading to persecution not through their faith but through their own self-depreciation; the other is based on self-love, in the meaning of an acceptance of the self as fundamentally good, which leads to an optimistic philosophy of life grounded in the experience of grace and resulting in a forgiving attitude towards others.[233]

Rank characterized the Jewish culture as parasitic on other cultures, beginning with their enslavement in Egypt.[234]

Surviving the two kinds of love historically represented by *Eros* of antiquity and *Agape* of Christianity, the Jew lived on his religion of difference and hatred, which has been revived at present in Nazi tribal fanaticism representing as much a religion of racial separatism as Communism is the religion of the early Christian brotherhood in terms of economic equality.[235]

He reinterpreted antisemitism "not so much a racial hatred as it is a resentment of a certain type" who, by surviving persecution in one adopted land after another, achieve "real immortality."[236] It is impossible not to read such statements as a form of blaming the Jews for their own persecution, and elevating Christianity above Judaism as a higher form of evolution in human consciousness.[237]

To what degree this conformed with transformations in Rank's own biography (his closest relationships toward the end of his life were with non-Jewish women—his wife Estelle, and close colleague Jessie Taft), or with his prior writings, is debatable. As a Jew himself, he appeared to be expressing the very *Selbsthass* he had cited from Lessing and critiqued as a mass Jewish neurosis. The self-hatred and self-depreciation of which he wrote evokes the specter once again, as in the Wednesday Night Society, of internalized antisemitism. At the same time, it is not clear how much of a hand Estelle Rank had in shaping this last work after Rank's death. The preface, written by Rank himself shortly before their marriage, suggests that the bulk of the work was completed and the ideas were his own. Rank biographer James Lieberman notes, however, that the phrase "in religious terms, through revelation, conversion, or rebirth" appears only in the edited publication but not in Rank's manuscript.[238] In any case, the Christian notion of *Agape* as non-possessive love, seems to have captivated Rank in his later years. Henri Ellenberger in his history of the idea of the unconscious wrote that Rank "was moving toward a kind of religious psychotherapy"[239] and Rollo May cited Rank numerous times in his lectures to Methodist students on pastoral counseling.[240]

Late in his life, Rank became devoted to the idea that it was necessary for psychology to transcend its focus on the individual psyche, giving greater attention to the social sphere, just as in individual life the self would find its fullest creative potential in relationships with others. In *Beyond Psychology* he fused the ideals of democracy with a humanistic Christianity—although the danger of both was a collapse of individual creativity under the virtue of equality. For the average person, conforming to the Christ ideal would too easily be co-opted into the prevailing morality of the day.[241] However, he found in both Christ and Paul "highly creative personalities who, by destroying outworn values, liberated new life forces."[242] Times of political crisis gave rise, he thought, to more communal longings for immortality.[243] Citing the Catholic activist-philosopher Jacques Maritain, he stated, "No revival of a new Christendom is possible without a real fulfilment of democracy, which so far has been only symbol and image."[244] However, he continued, "It is only in a new Christendom, in the future, that the ethical and affective value of the word democracy, which corresponds to what may be called a popular civic consciousness, will be really achieved."[245]

Rank proposed that modern democracies contained a seed of

the Christian philosophy of life to counteract the anti-Christian ideologies of modern secular religion. Whether we can evoke a new Christian type of man or have to find another positive antidote will depend at large upon our ability for any kind of really deep experience, religious or otherwise.[246]

He did not see this happening within Christianity until Christianity could devote itself more fully to the cause of "political and economic freedom."[247] And equality, whether between the sexes or in other political spheres, lay in embracing difference: "There is no other equality possible than the equal right of every individual to become and to be himself, which actually means to accept his own difference and to have it accepted by others."[248]

He saw totalitarianism as a striving for immortality and a revolutionary assertion of will by a people whose individuation had been suppressed for too long, resulting in a domino effect of one revolution after another unless there could be some equilibrium between freedom and equality (which in itself tended toward conformity and sameness).[249] His final and most radical critique of psychoanalysis, foreshadowing the criticisms of such later figures as Erich Fromm, Frantz Fanon, Thomas Szasz, and Félix Guattari, was that it was a "utility tool" enforcing individuals' adaptation to the dominant culture, masculine power structures, and political ideologies.[250]

In the end, Rank turned from will to love in relationship—not romantic love, much less the primal longing for a Double, but

the ego needs the Thou in order to become a Self, be it on the individual plane of human relationship or on the social plane of a foreign group-ideology, or on the broadest basis of one civilization needing another for its development and maintenance.[251]

"The psychology of the Self is to be found in the Other, be that Other the individual Thou, or the inspirational ideology of the leader, or the symbiotic diffusion of another civilization."[252] He viewed complementarity as necessary for development, although its irrationality and tendency toward conflict infused this very human need with an element of tragedy: "The tragic element in this process is that the ego needs a Thou to build up an assertive self *with and against* this Thou" (emphasis added).[253] Conflict, even violent revolution, was inevitable in personal, social, and political relations because of the drive of "two opposing personalities or ideologies or civilizations" to "assert their difference."[254] This was too often "condemned as neurotic by the rational self."[255]

Nevertheless, Rank concluded, such irrationality was fundamental in human nature and must be accepted, not pathologized. In Dan Merkur's words, "Where Freud placed his faith in a rational universe, to which all irrationality was to be reconciled, Rank envisioned a paradoxical universe whose irrationality was to be negotiated but never resolved."[256] In the final sentence of this last published book, Rank wagered in favor of irrationality as still holding the potential for a more humane future:

> Granted an acceptance of the fundamental irrationality of the human being and life in general with allowance for its dynamic functioning in human behavior, we have the basis for the emergence of everything of which mankind is capable in personal and social capacity for betterment.[257]

Conclusion

Throughout his life, Rank was both a psychologist and a philosopher of life, death, and the longing for immortality. A lifelong atheist like Freud, Rank nevertheless viewed religion as an evolutionary phase of humankind, directed by the will/life force as a path to eternal life and, on the temporal plane, a compromise for the sake of civilization in the form of moral systems. Shorn of causality, Rank's psycho-philosophical system had no specific precepts of its own other than the "ethical" imperative of the creative person—the artist—to give his or her will free expression for the betterment of others and the community. But Europe was going up in flames again while Rank lay dying, and in his final work he seemed to have arrived at a place of faith—not a theistic belief, but a form of existential hope that sprang from the fusion of democratic principles with the *agape* love he had found in Christian thought.

Both Freud and Rank died on dates with religious significance—a coincidence that might have had more unconscious or symbolic meaning to themselves than to modern interpreters. Freud died in 1939 on the Jewish Day of Atonement—a fact Rank apparently noted aloud on his own deathbed as "*komisch*" (in German, meaning not merely comical but odd and ironic).[258] Rank himself died on the Christian festival of "All Hallows Eve," the night before the dead are remembered in solemn ritual on All Saints Day. This was also the pre-Christian European festival Samhain, when people lit bonfires and made sacrifices to keep the dead away from the living. However one may prefer to interpret these coincidences, it is clear that to the very end of Rank's life, Freud was both an ancestor to be revered, and a ghost to be kept at bay.

Notes

1 Rank, 2014/1924.
2 Rank, 1989b/1932.
3 Becker, 1973.
4 Term from Tillich (e.g., 1959: 22). There is a chance (although no known documentary evidence) that Rank met Tillich. Rank died two years before the start of the eclectic New York Psychology Group that Tillich attended (Cooper, 2006: 147–194). Tillich's apartment at Union Theological Seminary was a haven for intellectual

emigrés, including many psychologists, and Rank may have found his way there (Cooper, personal communication, September 14, 2016). Cf. Cooper-White, 2016.

5 Several sources on Rank's life and works informed this chapter. In English: Taft (1958), Menaker (1982), and Lieberman (1985); in German: Zottl (1982). Briefer summaries include Eisenstein (1966), Gay (2006: 470–489), Roazen (1975: 392–418), J. Jones (1968), and Kramer (n.d.). E. Jones (1957: 48–74) focuses on the conflict with Freud, and is not objective. On Rank's legacy, cf. Rudnytsky (1984, 1991, 2002).
6 Taft, 1958: 10.
7 Ibid., 14.
8 Ibid., 16.
9 Ibid., 14.
10 Ibid., 24; cf. Nin, Vol. 1 (1966): 278.
11 Lieberman, 1985: 3.
12 Excerpted in Taft, 1958: 3–58.
13 Ibid., 7; cf. Lieberman, 1985: 8–13, 30–34; Rudnytsky, 1984: 327.
14 Taft, 1958: 5–6; Kramer, n.d.
15 Taft, 1958: 29.
16 Ibid., 4; Menaker, 1982: 14.
17 Rank, 1907.
18 Lieberman, 1985: 41.
19 Gay, 2006: 471.
20 Roazen, 1975: 323; Gay, 2006: 229–230.
21 Nin, Vol. 1 (1966): 267–336. Cf. Sachs, 1944: 14–15.
22 Unpublished letter, Freud to Abraham, 1911, in Gay, 2006: 179.
23 Roazen, 1975: 395.
24 Ibid., 393; Rudnytsky, 1984: 325–326.
25 Lieberman, 1985: 4; Lieberman and Kramer, 2012: 89.
26 Taft, 1958: 67.
27 Lieberman and Kramer, 2012: 62; Taft, 1958: 67. Freud's son, Oliver, was also posted there in 1916; Rank helped him settle in.
28 Lieberman and Kramer, 2012: 62.
29 Taft, 1958: 70.
30 Lieberman and Kramer, 2012: 89.
31 Taft, 1958: 263.
32 Roazen, 1975: 396.
33 Taft, 1958: 70.
34 E. Jones, 1957: 13.
35 Sachs, 1944: 62; Taft, 1958: 63.
36 Roazen, 1975: 395.
37 Rudnytsky, 1984: 331.
38 Ibid., 334.
39 E. Jones, 1957: 48–51.
40 Roazen, 1975: 401.
41 Rank and Ferenczi, 1925/1924.
42 Rank, 1978b/1929: 38–45.
43 Rank and Ferenczi, 1925/1924: 40–41.
44 E.g., Freud, 1958/1912: 115.
45 Unpublished letter, Freud to Rank, July 8, 1922, in Gay, 2006: 472.
46 Roazen, 1975: 398.
47 Nunberg and Federn, 1967, II: 71–72.
48 Freud, 1953/1900: 400–401n, cited in Gay, 2006: 475.

49 Cited in Roazen, 1975: 398; Rudnytsky, 1984: 335–336.
50 E. Jones, 1957: 31; Roazen, 1975: 397.
51 Gay, 2006: 474. Archival letter from Freud to "Dear Friends," January, 1924.
52 Letter from Rank to Ferenczi, cited in Gay, 2006: 474.
53 Freud, 1959b, 1926.
54 Gay, 2006: 477n.
55 Roazen, 1975: 405.
56 Gay, 2006: 477. Freud's best post-war income also came from American analysands paying dollars (p. 389).
57 For more on the Freud–Rank split, see Lieberman, 1985: 227–260.
58 Roazen, 1975: 406.
59 E. Jones, 1957: 75; Roazen, 1975: 407.
60 Lieberman, 1985: 249; Taft, 1958: 110–111; Roazen, 1975: 407.
61 Gay, 2006: 479.
62 Roazen, 2001: 213, quoted in Merkur, 2013: 45.
63 Roazen, 1975: 412; on Freud's aversion to granting priority of ideas to Nietzsche or Schopenhauer, see ibid., 199.
64 Lieberman, 1985: 271.
65 Ibid., 328.
66 Nin, Vols. 1–3, 1966–71; Lieberman, 1985. Rank treated Miller briefly (p. 328).
67 Gay, 2006: 471.
68 Roazen, 1975: 408.
69 Menaker, 1982: xvi; Taft, 1958: 196–197.
70 Taft, 1958: 197–199.
71 Rank, 1927–28, 1928.
72 Nin, Vol. 1 (1966): 277; Lieberman, 1985: 334; Roazen, 1975: 413.
73 Nin, Vol. 1 (1966): 277; Lieberman, 1985: 334.
74 Lieberman, 1985: xxii.
75 Rudnytsky, 1984.
76 Menaker, 1982: 38.
77 Rank, 1978a/1929.
78 Rank, 1978b/1929
79 Freud, 1961a/1923.
80 Rank, 1978b/1929: 5.
81 Ibid., 9.
82 Ibid., 11.
83 Ibid., 22.
84 Ibid., 32.
85 Ibid., 50.
86 Ibid., 53.
87 Parallels Jung's "individuation" although Rank does not cite him (1978b/1929: 23). Cf. Rank's critiques of Jung in *Beyond Psychology* (2001/1941: 29–39, 276).
88 Rank, 1978a/1929: 24.
89 Ibid., 27.
90 Rank, 1989b/1932.
91 Ibid., 41.
92 Ibid., 45.
93 Ibid., 31.
94 Menaker, 1982: 55.
95 Rank, 1989b/1932.
96 Cf. J. Jones, 1968: 9.
97 Rank, 1978a/1929: 19.

98 Ibid., 48–61.
99 Rank, 1978b/1929: 29.
100 Ibid., 25.
101 Nietzsche, 2006/1883.
102 Rank, 1978b/1929: 18.
103 Lieberman, 1985: 185–187.
104 E.g., Whitehead, 1929; see Lieberman, 1985: 381.
105 Rank, 1978b/1929: 2, 4.
106 Ibid., 9–10.
107 Taft, 1958; Lieberman, 1985: 366–399.
108 Lieberman, 1985: 273.
109 Rank, 1978a/1929, 1978b/1929.
110 A division within social work between Rank's "functional school" and a larger, Freudian-based "diagnostic," or "psychosocial" school (Lloyd, 2008).
111 Roazen, 1975: 410. Tola had become an experienced analyst in her own right; at Helene Deutsch's invitation, she practiced and supervised a children's clinic in Boston after Rank's death.
112 Taft, 1958: 262; Lieberman, 1985: 361, 387–388.
113 Lieberman, 1985: 389.
114 Ibid., 388.
115 Ibid., 387. Italicized portion excised by Jessie Taft for publication.
116 Rank, 1978b/1929: 97.
117 Rudnytsky, 1984: 339–340.
118 Menaker, 1982: 16.
119 Rank, 2004/1909.
120 Freud, 1959a/1909.
121 Nunberg and Federn, 1962, Vol. I: 72; published in Rank, 2004/1909: 124.
122 Lieberman and Kramer, 2012: 8.
123 Rank, 1998/1930: 11; cf. Nunberg and Federn, 1962, Vol. IV: 252.
124 Rank, 1914.
125 Rank, 1989a/1925.
126 Rank, 1978b/1929: 2.
127 Schleiermacher, 2016/1830–31: 22–24.
128 Rank, 1978a/1929: ix.
129 Translation is tricky here. In this period of Rank's work, the spiritual and the psychological are as ambiguous as the German words themselves.
130 Rank, 1978a/1929: 15.
131 Ibid., 27–28.
132 Ibid., 28–29.
133 Ibid., 32.
134 Ibid., 31.
135 Ibid.
136 Ibid., 15.
137 Ibid., 26.
138 Ibid., 22.
139 Ibid., 71. These three religious eras do not correspond precisely to the philosophical worldviews he proposes in *Truth and Reality*: The Apollonian ("know thyself"), the Dionysian ("be thyself … not only anti-social but also unethical"—inducing madness), and the Critique of Reason ("determine thyself from thyself") (pp. 60–61).
140 From Swiss anthropologist Bachofen (ibid., 76n1), who proposed a prehistoric matriarchy. Rank knew Bachofen's work (e.g., 2014/1924) (Dan Burston, personal communication, January, 2017).

141 Rank 1978a/1929: 71.
142 Ibid., 75.
143 Ibid.
144 Ibid., 72.
145 Ibid.
146 Ibid., 73.
147 Ibid.
148 Ibid., 80.
149 Ibid., 94.
150 Cf. Rank, 1907.
151 Taft, 1958: 263.
152 Rank 1978a/1929: 96.
153 Ibid., 96–97.
154 Ibid., 97.
155 Rank, 1998/1930.
156 Taft, 1958: 11.
157 Rank, 1998/1930: 11. Cf. Rank's own description of *Psychology and the Soul* in *Art and Artist* (1989b/1932: xxvi).
158 Ibid., 82.
159 Ibid., 81–82, 92–93.
160 Ibid., 125.
161 Rank, 1989b/1932: 103.
162 Ibid., 128.
163 Rank, 1998/1930: 11–13.
164 Ibid., 14 (emphasis in original).
165 Ibid., 51.
166 Ibid., 53.
167 Ibid., 21.
168 Ibid.
169 Ibid., 18.
170 Ibid., 20.
171 Ibid., 27. Rank attended Spielrein's (1995/1912) talk on "Destruction as a Cause of Coming into Being," and his reasoning bears traces of her argument. (See Chapter 6.)
172 Rank, 1998/1930: 34.
173 Ibid., 35.
174 Ibid., 38.
175 Ibid., 39.
176 Ibid., 48.
177 Ibid., 58.
178 Ibid.
179 Ibid., 55.
180 Ibid.
181 Ibid., 57.
182 Ibid., 55, 62–63.
183 Ibid., 58.
184 Ibid., 95–96.
185 Ibid., 97.
186 Ibid., 98.
187 Ibid., 98–99.
188 Ibid.
189 Ibid., 100.

190 Ibid., 101.
191 Ibid., 102.
192 Ibid., 102–103.
193 Ibid., 107.
194 Ibid., 109.
195 Ibid., 111.
196 Ibid., 111, 113.
197 Ibid., 113–114.
198 Ibid., 113.
199 Ibid., 117.
200 Ibid., 118.
201 Ibid., 119.
202 Ibid., 120.
203 Ibid., 123.
204 Ibid., 124.
205 Freud, 1961b/1927.
206 Rank, 1998/1930: 125.
207 Ibid., 126.
208 Ibid., 126.
209 E.g., Hoffman, 1998.
210 Rank, 1998/1930: 127.
211 Ibid.
212 Ibid.
213 Ibid.
214 Ibid., 128.
215 Rank, 2001/1941.
216 Ibid.
217 Ibid., 288. Cf. Gilman, 1993.
218 Gilman, 1993: 36–48. See Chapters 7–8.
219 Rank, 2001/1941: 288.
220 Ibid., 16.
221 Ibid.
222 Ibid., 28–38.
223 Ibid., 16.
224 Menaker, 1982: 81.
225 E.g., ibid., 42–43.
226 Rank, 2001/1941: 61.
227 Ibid., 29.
228 Ibid., 48.
229 Ibid., 195.
230 Ibid., 141.
231 Ibid., 149.
232 Ibid., 189–190.
233 Ibid., 191–192.
234 Ibid., 281. Rank saw little hope for a literal promised land (Zionism), for the convo-
     luted reason that the lack of persecution would remove the "better chance for sur-
     vival which the under-privileged seem to enjoy … notwithstanding Darwin…"
     (ibid., 284–285).
235 Ibid., 192.
236 Ibid., 285.
237 Cf. Lieberman, 1985: 396.
238 Ibid., 396.

239 Ellenberger, 1970: 860.
240 May, 1939; cf. Lieberman, 1985: 397.
241 Rank, 2001/1941: 163.
242 Ibid., 167.
243 Ibid., 169.
244 Ibid., 193.
245 Ibid., 193–194.
246 Ibid., 192.
247 Ibid.
248 Ibid., 267.
249 Rank 2001/1941: 40–43, 55–56; cf. J. Jones, 1968: 8.
250 Rank 2001/1941: 28–31, 37.
251 Ibid., 290.
252 Ibid.
253 Ibid.
254 Ibid.
255 Ibid.
256 Merkur, 2010: 60.
257 Rank, 2001/1941: 290–291.
258 Lieberman, 1985: 389.

References

Becker, Ernest (1973). *The denial of death*. New York: Free Press.

Cooper, Terry (2006). *Paul Tillich and psychology*. Macon, GA: Mercer University Press.

Cooper-White, Pamela (2016). Paul Tillich's legacy, psychology and pastoral psycho-therapy. *Bulletin of the North American Paul Tillich Society, 42* (2): 28–34.

Eisenstein, Samuel (1966). Otto Rank: The myth and birth of the hero. In Franz Alexander, Samuel Eisenstein, and Martin Grotjahn (Eds.), *Psychoanalytic pioneers* (pp. 36–50.) New York: Basic Books.

Ellenberger, Henri (1970). *The discovery of the unconscious*. New York: Basic Books.

Freud, Sigmund (1953). *The interpretation of dreams*. In J. Strachey (Ed.), *Standard edition of the complete works of Sigmund Freud*, Vol. 4–5 (entire). (Orig. publ. 1900.)

Freud, Sigmund (1955). *Group psychology and the analysis of the ego*. In J. Strachey (Ed.), *Standard edition of the complete works of Sigmund Freud*, Vol. 21: 65–144. (Orig. German publ. 1921.)

Freud, Sigmund (1958). *Recommendations to physicians practicing psycho-analysis*. In J. Strachey (Ed.), *Standard edition of the complete works of Sigmund Freud*, Vol. 12: 109–120. (Orig. publ. 1912.)

Freud, Sigmund (1959a). *Family romances*. In J. Strachey (Ed.), *Standard edition of the complete works of Sigmund Freud*, Vol. 9: 235–242. (Orig. publ. 1909.)

Freud, Sigmund (1959b). *Inhibitions, symptoms, and anxiety*. In J. Strachey (Ed.), *Standard edition of the complete works of Sigmund Freud*, Vol. 20: 75–176. (Orig. publ. 1926.)

Freud, Sigmund (1961a). *The ego and the id*. In J. Strachey (Ed.), *Standard edition of the complete works of Sigmund Freud*, Vol. 19: 1–66. (Orig. publ. 1923.)

Freud, Sigmund (1961b). *The future of an illusion*. In J. Strachey (Ed.), *Standard edition of the complete works of Sigmund Freud*, Vol. 21: 5–56. (Orig. publ. 1927.)

Gay, Peter (2006). *Freud: A life for our time.* New York: W. W. Norton.

Gilman, Sander L. (1993). *Freud, race, and gender.* Princeton, NJ: Princeton University Press.

Hoffman, Irwin (1998). *Ritual and spontaneity in the psychoanalytic process: A dialectical-constructivist view.* Hillsdale, NJ: Analytic Press.

Jones, Ernest (1957). *The life and work of Sigmund Freud, Vol. 3: The last phase 1919–1939.* New York: Basic Books.

Jones, Jack (1968). Rank, Otto. *International Encyclopedia of the Social Sciences.* Online at www.encyclopedia.com/topic/Otto_Rank.aspx. Accessed August 15, 2016.

Kramer, Robert (n.d.). Otto Rank 1884, Vienna–1939, New York. Online at www.ottorank.com/about_otto_rank_120167.htm. Accessed August 12, 2016.

Lieberman, E. James (1985). *Acts of will: The life and work of Otto Rank.* New York: Free Press.

Lieberman, E. James (1998). Translator's introduction. In O. Rank, *Psychology and the soul: A study of the origin, conceptual evolution, and nature of the soul.* G. C. Richter and E. J. Lieberman (Trans.) (pp. xi–xxvi). Baltimore: Johns Hopkins Press.

Lieberman, E. James and Kramer, Robert (Eds.) (2012). *The letters of Sigmund Freud and Otto Rank.* Baltimore: Johns Hopkins University Press.

Lloyd, Mark Frazier (2008). The functional school of social work. Excerpt from 100 years: A centennial history of the University of Pennsylvania's School of Social Policy and Practice (pp. 54–59). Philadelphia: University of Pennsylvania Press. Excerpt online at https://socialwelfare.library.vcu.edu/social-work/the-functional-school-of-social-work. Accessed August 14, 2016.

May, Rollo (1939). *The art of counselling.* Nashville: Abingdon Press.

Menaker, Esther (1982). *Otto Rank: A rediscovered legacy.* New York: Columbia University Press.

Merkur, Dan (2010). Otto Rank's will therapy. In *Explorations of the psychoanalytic mystics* (pp. 53–70). Amsterdam: Rodolpi.

Merkur, Dan (2013). *Relating to God: Clinical psychoanalysis, spirituality, and theism.* Lanham, MD: Jason Aronson.

Nietzsche, Friedrich (2006). *Thus spoke Zarathustra.* Adrian Del Caro and Robert Pippin (Eds.), Adrian Del Caro (Trans.). Cambridge, UK: Cambridge University Press. (Orig. publ. 1883–92.)

Nin, Anaïs (1966–80). *The diary of Anaïs Nin* (7 vols.). Gunther Stuhlmann (Ed.). New York: Swallow Press. (Orig. unpublished writings 1931–74.)

Nunberg, Herman and Federn, Ernst (Eds.) (1962–75). *Minutes of the Vienna Psychoanalytic Society*, Vols. I–IV. M. Nunberg (Trans.). New York: International Universities Press.

Rank, Otto (1907). *Der Künstler: Ansätze zu einer Sexual-Psychologie.* Vienna: Hugo Heller. (2nd ed. 1918/1925, Vienna: Hugo Heller; 3rd ed. 1925, Leipzig: Internationaler Verlag.)

Rank, Otto (1914). Der Doppelgänger. *Imago, 3* (2): 97–164.

Rank, Otto (1927–28). *Grundzüge einer genetischen Psychologie auf Grund der Psychoanalyse der Ichstruktur, Bd. 1–2.* Leipzig: F. Deuticke.

Rank, Otto (1928). *Outlines of a genetic psychology.* Philadelphia: Pennsylvania School of Social Work.

Rank, Otto (1978a). *Truth and reality: A life history of the human will.* Jessie Taft (Trans.). New York: Alfred A. Knopf. (Reprint of Taft 1936 translation. Orig. publ. 1929.)

Rank, Otto (1978b). *Will therapy.* Jessie Taft (Trans.). New York: W. W. Norton. (Reprint of Taft 1936 translation. Orig. publ. 1929.)

Rank, Otto (1989a). *The Double: A psychoanalytic study.* Harry Tucker (Ed. and Trans.). Chapel Hill, NC: University of North Carolina Press. (Orig. publ. 1925.)

Rank, Otto (1989b). *Art and artist: Creative urge and personality development.* Charles Francis Atkinson (Trans. 1932). New York: W. W. Norton. (Orig. 1932 manuscript *Kunst und Künstler* remained unpublished until 2000: Psychosozial Verlag. www.psychosozial-verlag.de/1023.)

Rank, Otto (1998). *Psychology and the soul: A study of the origin, conceptual evolution, and nature of the soul.* G. C. Richter and E. James Lieberman (Trans.). Baltimore: Johns Hopkins Press. (Orig. publ. 1930.)

Rank, Otto (2001). *Beyond psychology.* New York: Dover. (Reprint of orig. private publ. Philadelphia: E. Hauser, 1941.)

Rank, Otto (2004). *The myth and birth of the hero: A psychological exploration of myth with an introductory essay by Robert A. Segal,* 2nd ed. G. C. Richter and E. James Lieberman (Trans.). Baltimore: Johns Hopkins Press. (Orig. publ. 1909; 2nd ed. 1922.)

Rank, Otto (2014). *The trauma of birth.* London: Routledge. (Orig. publ. 1924.)

Rank, Otto and Ferenczi, Sándor (1925). *The development of psychoanalysis.* Caroline Newton (Trans.). New York: Nervous and Mental Disease Publishing Company. (Orig. publ. 1924.)

Roazen, Paul (1975). *Freud and his followers.* New York: Alfred A. Knopf.

Roazen, Paul (2001). *The historiography of psychoanalysis.* New Brunswick, NJ: Transaction.

Rudnytsky, Peter (1984). Rank: Beyond Freud? *American Imago, 41*: 325–341.

Rudnytsky, Peter (1985). Nietzsche's Oedipus. *American Imago, 42*: 413–439.

Rudnytsky, Peter (1991). *The psychoanalytic vocation: The legacy of Otto Rank and Donald Winnicott.* New Haven: Yale University Press.

Rudnytsky, Peter (2002). *Reading psychoanalysis: Freud, Rank, Ferenczi, Groddeck.* Ithaca, NY: Cornell University Press.

Sachs, Hanns (1944). *Freud, master and friend.* Cambridge, MA: Harvard University Press.

Schleiermacher, Friedrich (2016). *The Christian faith,* Vol. 1. Catherine Kelsey and Terrence Tice (Eds.), Terrence Tice, Catherine Kelsey, and Edwina Lawler (Trans.). Louisville: Westminster John Knox Press. (Orig. publ. 1830–31.)

Spielrein, Sabina (1995). Destruction as a cause of becoming. S. K. Witt (Trans.). *Psychoanalysis and Contemporary Thought, 18*: 85–118. (Orig. publ. 1912.) Online at www.pepweb.org/document.php?id=pct.018.0085a&type=hitlist&num=3&query=zone 1%2Cparagraphs%7Czone2%2Cparagraphs%7Cauthor%2CSpielrein%7Cviewperiod %2Cweek%7Csort%2Cauthor%2Ca#hit1. Accessed September 22, 2015.

Taft, Julia Jessie (1958). *Otto Rank: A biographical study based on notebooks, letters, collected writings, therapeutic achievements and personal associations.* New York: Julian Press.

Tillich, Paul (1959). The theology of pastoral care. *Pastoral Psychology, 10* (7): 21–26.

Whitehead, Alfred North (1929). *Process and reality: An essay in cosmology. Gifford Lectures Delivered in the University of Edinburgh during the Session 1927–1928.* New York: Macmillan and Cambridge, UK: Cambridge University Press.

Zottl, Anton (1982). *Otto Rank: Das Lebenswerk eines Dissidenten der Psychoanalyse.* München: Kindler Verlag.

Chapter 6

Death and resurrection

Sabina Spielrein (1885–1942)

The most creative approach to religion among the Viennese analysts is perhaps to be found in the early writings of Sabina Spielrein. Popularly best known as a psychiatric patient caught up in an erotic relationship with C.G. Jung, Spielrein has sadly been an object of sexual curiosity and speculation. Once buried in a forgotten archive, that story of Spielrein's young adult years came to light as a scandal at the heart of early psychoanalysis[1]—further sensationalized in the recent movie "A Dangerous Method"[2] with its celebrity cast and fabricated scenes of sado-masochistic spankings.[3] Yet her serious contributions to psycho-analysis were many, often anticipating the work of better known analytic theo-rists across several decades. In the words of two early biographers, she was

> … a woman of restless intellectual and emotional energy, with a capacity which never abated for intense relationships, and for being alive to the right things at the right time. A passionate idealist, a woman of immense strength of character and resilience, Spielrein was the first woman psychoanalyst of significance, and she was until very recently almost entirely forgotten.[4]

Feminist psychoanalytic scholars have resisted the sensationalized depiction of Spielrein, and have begun to publish essays and monographs exploring the full range of her contributions,[5] as well as English translations of selected papers.[6] Thanks to John Launer,[7] we also now have a well-documented history of Spiel-rein's entire life in English.[8] Her many publications are still being translated into English.[9] As Adrienne Harris has written,

> Far from being an obscure sexual object on the fringes of psychoanalysis in the early twentieth century, Spielrein has now emerged as a subject in her own right, with numerous publications spanning twenty years. Many of her ideas either anticipated more famous men's theoretical writings, or captured ideas in the Zeitgeist before others were able to distill them. Her influence extends not only to Jung and Freud, but also in later years to Piaget, Vygot-sky, and Luria.[10]

From obscurity to "a dangerous method": the recovery of Spielrein's story

Spielrein's contributions had already been signaled by a few footnotes. Freud granted her priority (in her ideas about a "death instinct") in *Beyond the Pleasure Principle*[11] and cited her in the "Schreber" case.[12] Jung cited her sixteen times in *Symbols of Transformation*.[13] Others at the time were aware of the originality and influence of her ideas on Freud and others.[14] Footnotes in others' writings are only the tip of the iceberg, and represent the work of a significant figure in the development of psychoanalysis whose history has deserved excavation. If psychoanalysis teaches anything, of course, it is that important people, events, and desires are never merely "forgotten," but repressed. When Spielrein's diaries and letters were discovered in the Palais Wilson in Geneva in 1977,[15] they revealed a complex and dramatic story of emotional entanglements, exploitation, misogyny, and feminine protest in which Spielrein was variously cast as a victim, a muse, a serious scholar, and a witch—and most notably an object of contention between Jung and Freud. With John Kerr's account of Spielrein as Jung's patient-turned-lover and her appeal to Freud for help, she was quickly mythologized as a pawn caught up in the battle between two famous men.[16] But until very recently, her whole story—and indeed, her significant contributions to psychoanalytic theory and practice over four decades—continued to be ignored.[17]

As Swiss analyst Sabine Richebächer has observed,

> The question of repression can also be applied to the history of psychoanalysis itself. We could say: first Sabina Spielrein was forgotten. There were reasons enough for that. Her person, her name, undoubtedly recalled the break between Freud and Jung in 1913 which was so traumatic for the psychoanalytic movement. Spielrein was moreover an independent person and someone with a will of her own who would not allow herself to be slotted into the interests of the psychoanalytic movement as a mere apparatchik. In the patriarchal structures of psychoanalysis she caused offence again and again; Ernest Jones, the one time President of the International Psychoanalytic Association, could not stand her.... Thus we are faced with the strange finding that, of all disciplines, psychoanalysis, which is founded on a belief in the healing power of memory, stubbornly resists its own history. And the handing down of a false diagnosis—which Sabina Spielrein was given retrospectively—ensures that nothing changes.[18]

A further repressed trauma at the heart of psychoanalysis, the Holocaust, also appears in Spielrein's story. Unlike the majority of psychoanalyst colleagues who were able to flee Germany and Austria and continue their careers in safety, Spielrein was murdered by the Nazis in her Russian hometown of Rostov-on-Don. Yet, this horror is most often mentioned as a kind of footnote to a perpetually tragic and (purportedly)[19] masochistically-tinged life.

Spielrein was born in 1885 in the cosmopolitan Russian port city Rostov-on-Don to Jewish parents, Nikolai and Eva, who by all accounts were wealthy, neurotic, and brutal. Like many Jewish girls of her time and place, Spielrein was a diligent and talented student who yearned for more exposure to the European culture in which they were all being schooled. She was top in her graduating class, skilled in music, humanities, and science, and knew French, English, German, biblical Hebrew, Greek, and Latin.[20] Her parents literally beat proper behavior and educational achievement into her—pressure for which her father apologized late in his life.[21] But it is notable that, as a girl, Spielrein was given as formal and rigorous a *Gymnasium* education as her two brothers, and was further encouraged to pursue medical studies abroad—in fact, Zürich was home to an entire colony of aspiring Russian students, the majority of whom were young women who could not pursue medical training at home.[22]

Remarkably, Spielrein was able to achieve much of this academic and artistic success while beset with physical illnesses—many of them psychosomatic, or symptomatic of "hysteria." Today, we would almost certainly understand her symptoms in terms of post-traumatic stress disorder as a result of the beatings she endured at the hands of both her father and mother from an early age (as well as witnessing beatings of her siblings). Some of her father's punishments were bizarrely cruel.[23] A cumulative picture of her symptoms from her own diaries and letters, clinical notes, and Jung's case studies, shows a teenage girl tormented by the sexual exposure and arousal from her father's beatings (often in front of her brothers). Her father manipulated the family with threats of suicide and "tyrannized" the household.[24] She was unconsciously attempting to deal with the feelings through alternating bouts of self-stimulation and repressive "conversion" symptoms of grimaces, physical pains, disgust, horror, self-loathing, and violent rages. Her symptoms became florid after the death from typhoid at age six of her beloved younger sister Emilia, when Spielrein was just finishing high school.[25]

Following a pattern that was not uncommon among the Spielreins' social circle in Rostov, her parents shipped her off to a sanitarium in Interlaken, Switzerland, where she was subjected to the common treatments of the day: blasting water showers and electrical stimulation. Spielrein depicted her treatment there in a drawing with the Russian captions "electrocute" and "devil" (or "hell"—"*chort*").[26] When that treatment (unsurprisingly) failed, they took her to the Russian neurologist Monakov's clinic at the University of Zürich, but he would not take her, considering her too agitated.[27] Finally, she was escorted by an uncle and a medical police officer to the famous Burghölzli psychiatric hospital in Zürich (August 18, 1904). Her intake was assigned to Jung, and her diagnosis was "hysteria."[28] While this psychiatric crisis is often depicted as evidence of Spielrein's mental instability and a central theme in her life's drama, it was also her ticket out. It took her precisely where she wanted to be—out of the provinces, and into the cutting edge of European cultural and scientific intellectual life for which she longed.

The Burghölzli psychiatric clinic, directed at that time by Bleuler, was well established by the time of her admission in 1904 as a beacon of modern, humane psychiatric practice. Beginning with Bleuler's predecessor, Auguste Forel, doctors, students, and patients all lived on campus and ate their meals together.[29] Bleuler further extended respect toward his patients, who, as part of their cure, were often enlisted not only as research subjects but also as research assistants.[30] Spielrein herself was recruited to assist in the "association experiments,"[31] and together with Jung's wife Emma helped him prepare his *Habilitationsschrift* (professorial dissertation).[32] It was milieu therapy at a time when mental illness in most of Europe meant incarceration in dark, grim structures like the *Narren-turm* ("fools' tower") next to the office where Freud spent his residency at the Vienna General Hospital. Often such confinement was for life, as mental illness was considered an incurable hereditary "degeneracy." At the Burghölzli, Forel had already eliminated solitary confinement, electrical stimulation, and cold baths in favor of hypnotherapy.[33] Bleuler implemented more humane treatments including all of the latest non-physiological treatments—including Breuer's "talking cure"[34] and Freud's psychoanalysis (just becoming known in Switzerland).

Spielrein's wildest behavior at the Burghölzli, including suicidal gestures and attempts to run away, suggests a pattern of disordered attachment as part of her overall post-traumatic symptomatology. She was desperately enacting the longing for a safe and stable father figure, while fleeing the brutality of her actual father in Russia. Jung fit the bill perfectly. Relatively young himself, handsome, energetic, and full of self-confidence, Jung's attention toward Spielrein quickly captured her love and admiration.

Spielrein's symptoms were mitigated in fairly short order, although there were some lingering effects including lifelong regressions to depression,[35] and even, for a few years, suicidality.[36] Both Jung and Spielrein attributed her "cure" to Jung's treatment, using some combination of his association experiments and what he knew of Freud's methods. It is more likely that the entire team of psychiatrists were involved at some level, under Bleuler's supervision,[37] and Spielrein had a significant attachment to both Bleuler and Jung—but it was to Jung she gave her full devotion.

Initially put off by her chaotic and erotic transference, Jung eventually came to recognize Spielrein's talent and intelligence. Once she was discharged and began her medical training upon Bleuler's recommendation, Jung began to reciprocate her "friendship," which she ecstatically embraced. Launer characterizes this period as one of hero worship on her part, not a longing for an actual sexual relationship.[38] Her diary entries and letters from this period bear this out. Still a virgin, she expressed passionate love and idealization, but mostly in the manner of an inexperienced adolescent crush.

What followed after her discharge was a seduction, which Spielrein repeatedly described as having been initiated by Jung, not herself.[39] The full extent of their sexual involvement is not known. Jung's accounts greatly minimized his involvement (and framed it eventually as his having been victimized by an erotic transference he was unprepared to handle).[40] Spielrein always cloaked her own descriptions of their intimacy under the single word "poetry."[41] The two shared a fantasy of being mother and son, strongly reinforced by their mutual love of Wagner and the story of the hero Siegfried's (incestuous) birth.[42] At times, Spielrein saw Jung as her "Siegfried"—both as savior and as "little son";[43] at other times, she fantasized that her writing was the son "Siegfried" that she would give to Jung.[44]

Jung's psychological power, and the transferential father dynamic, increased all the more during the years Spielrein pursued her medical studies. He persuaded her to allow him to analyze her—or, perhaps more accurately based on the record, to engage in some informal mode of mutual analysis.[45] As was not uncommon among all the early analysts, their therapeutic conversations blended seamlessly together with discussions about psychoanalytic theory. They exchanged ideas about the libido as a transformational life force, and mythological and religious symbols in the psyche. As their ideas grew more entwined, Spielrein turned to Jung for supervision of her dissertation. Her official *Doktorvater* was Bleuler,[46] the other transferential father figure from her hospital treatment. Bleuler was becoming increasingly disenchanted with both Freud and Jung, however, and seemed only too pleased to hand her off, at least informally, although he remained her advisor of record.[47]

For all these reasons, Jung's power over Spielrein was profound, and partially clandestine—he was her *un*-official analyst, her *un*-official dissertation supervisor, a rising star in the profession she had chosen for herself, senior in age as well as status, and a charismatic man of high intellect and cultural knowledge. Moreover, in a time of widespread antisemitism and devaluation of Jews, he was a Gentile—even the son of a minister—and must have represented to Spielrein many of the same Germanic cultural ideals and dreams of assimilation that had so attracted Freud himself to Jung. Spielrein had considerable inner strength, however. Whatever did or did not occur between them, based on certain cryptic statements by both of them, Spielrein was savvy and strong enough to not put herself in danger of becoming pregnant, thus ruining her chances at a career, marriage, and children. She had her own dreams and ambitions, and a strong spiritual sense of vocation.

Much of the self-analysis conducted in her diary reveals strong, idiosyncratically spiritual and religious themes, long pre-dating her years with Jung. Spielrein's fantasies, mystical and idealistic since childhood, were no doubt amplified by Jung's own metaphysical and occult leanings. From the early age of seven or eight she communed in German with a fantasized *Schutzgeist*[48] or "guardian spirit."[49] Until she lost her faith in God around age twelve and began to pursue medical science as a career, she prayed vociferously, influenced by her mother's Hasidic legends of angels and demons.[50] In spite of her atheism, she held on to her belief in her guardian angel well into adulthood.[51] In grandiose fashion, she recorded in her diary that "my Guardian Spirit tells me I can do anything I want to,"[52] and when she felt most conflicted over her love for Jung and the see-sawing closeness and distance of their tumultuous relationship, this "genius within me" exhorted her to be strong and not to be a "damp poodle."[53]

She believed that she had a "higher calling," which in part was inherited by her grandfather and great-grandfather, both revered rabbis "and therefore— God's elect."[54] As a Jew passionately involved with her "Aryan" hero, she began to write about a messianic sense of call to unite the Jewish and Aryan races through their relationship, by synthesizing Jung's and Freud's increasingly diverging theories. This was not the only time Spielrein considered Jewish-Christian differences, or desired friendships with both Jewish and Christian medical student colleagues. As part of her self-analysis, she also wrote about the many Jewish-Christian marriages in her family's history.[55]

In September, 1910, while her involvement with Jung was lurching between passion and academic friendship, and Emma Jung was about to give birth to a third daughter, Spielrein was writing in her diary about the turbulent love lives of four "pairs" of Jewish and Gentile friends.[56] Alternately enraged and depressed, she fantasized committing suicide by taking poison in Jung's presence.[57] Yet in the same entry, the idea of a "great destiny" to unite the Aryan and Jewish races also occurred to her in a triumphant rush of words. With rose-colored glasses, she inter-preted Jung's desire for her not as a racist, romanticizing tendency within antisemitism to idealize the exotic Jewess, but a noble calling like her own. Com-paring Jung and Freud in terms of Gentile and Jew, she wrote,

> The Christian in [the pair]—my friend, he is a doctor, married. Other ele-ments, such as the strong religious sense and the sense of calling, are things of which he possesses more than enough, for his father was a minister! ... He told me that he loved Jewish women, that he wanted to love a dark Jewish girl. So in him, too, the urge to remain faithful to his religion and culture, as well as the drive to explore other possibilities through a new race, the drive to liberate himself from paternal edicts through an unbelieving Jewess. His friend is Prof. Freud—a Jew, old *pater familias*.... Here, too, the Christian is the "son" of the Jew. The latter is older and more inde-pendent. But at the same time my friend is my little son, so that *volens-nolens* we are married to Prof. Freud. I do not love Freud, because he robbed me of my most beautiful possession, namely my friend. Now my friend will perhaps fall in love with Freud's daughter. Why should I go on torturing myself? What must be will be.... But I intend to cling to my belief that a great destiny awaits me. And now, what shape will matters take? ... There is so much fire and so much love in me. *I feel the unshakeable conviction: Siegfried lives, lives, lives!* No one can rob me of that certainty [*Glauben*—faith/belief] except my own death.[58]

Days later Spielrein wrote, obviously agitated at "almost 3 in the morning," "the two of us love each other as much as it is possible to love," but acknowledging that he was not "free," she wrote "let me record my firm decision: I want to be free of him!"[59] She vowed to her Guardian Spirit that she was determined to escape from "these emotional storms" to achieve her own destiny, and set her intention "to "gather my forces to begin my new study, 'On the Death Instinct!'."[60] Nevertheless, more "poetry" occurred shortly thereafter, distracting her from studying for her exams and beginning her independent work. Still determined in her own mind to end the relationship, she wrote on December 8, "Fate, may something good come out of this, and let me love him nobly. A long, ecstatic kiss in farewell, my beloved little son!"[61]

Their last meeting was shortly before Christmas when Jung again "fell into the 'Don Juan' role" that was "so repulsive" to her.[62] She expressed offense that Jung only wanted her as a mistress, and did not respect her either as a potential wife or a professional colleague. She completed her medical examinations in January, and noted tersely in her diary, "He is gone, and 'tis good thus."[63] She departed immediately for Montreux and then Munich, to begin a new life. She did not feel the need to confide in her diary for almost a year thereafter. While their correspondence would continue—and was a necessary part of her pursuing publication while Jung was still at the helm of the *Jahrbuch*—the "poetry" was finally at an end.

The relationship, such as it was, had been bound to crash on the rocks either of Jung's ego or of his sexual restlessness. Spielrein was not content merely to be a mirror for Jung's theorizing. Her mind was scholarly and active, and they began to debate in increasingly acrimonious terms. Perhaps Jung had tired of arguing, or perhaps his "polygamous tendencies"[64] were beginning to set in again. In his role as academic advisor, he did not withhold critique, sometimes severe, which though crushing emotionally did not deter her from continuing to seek knowledge both from him and through her own independent research and medical studies. In Munich, Spielrein began recovering from the dramatic highs and lows of their relationship, and began reclaiming her own independent spiritual streak. She wrote in her diary on February 11,

> Now, Fate! And this is my final word. I remain defiant, disregarding the dreadful anxiety that robs me of sleep and appetite and drives me crazily from one place to the other.... I remain defiant, because I have something noble and great to create and am not made for everyday routine. This is the life-or-death struggle. If there is a God-Father, may he hear me now: no pain is unbearable to me, no sacrifice too great, if only I can fulfill my sacred calling! ... Calm superiority reigns in me, I am free of "tension" in the depths of my soul, an indication of the capacity for powerful deeds. Just as before my final examination, I cry: "Help me, Fate, for my mind is fixed on the good, and my will—is the divine will!" ... [A]s the descendant of several generations of religious men I believe in the prophetic powers of my unconscious. One can actually get close to this "God" that one can speak with Him and learn what He wishes, that is, what is the most useful outlet

for the total energy of countless generations, which one calls individuals. So what do you wish, God? Or, stated more correctly what have you decided in your councils, ye Gods? Reveal to me your final purpose, and may it be done! ... I cannot understand why I am so terribly depressed, as if there were no hope of salvation for me. Could it be because the gods are contending against one another deep within me? Is it a premonition of my end, or is this pain a sacrifice of the sort every great work requires? Will the time come for me, too, when I am undividedly happy? I cannot be condemned to eternal torture?! Now I want to think and speculate as little as possible. I shall attempt to leave myself entirely in the hands of divine might to see whether I do not receive some message.[65]

No grand message came, however, and by the end of the month she resigned herself to believing she had not had a prophetic dream after all.[66] After her travels in Montreux and Munich, and a warm visit with family in Rostov, she traveled to Vienna where she was "so lonely," but determined to devote herself single-mindedly to her work.[67] Still addressing Spielrein in his letters as "meine Liebe!," Jung advised,

Freud will certainly welcome you. He has spoken many times of your dissertation—the best evidence that you have made an impression on him. You don't need my recommendation. Approach him like a great master and rabbi, then everything will go well.[68]

Jung's sarcasm and thinly veiled antisemitism toward Freud can hardly be mistaken.

On October 11, 1911, Spielrein somehow made her way to the "special session" of the Vienna Society held in the Café Arkaden, and stumbled into the midst of the planned expulsion of "the whole Adler gang."[69] (See Chapter 1.) Still a party to the triangle among himself, Spielrein, and Jung, Freud commented briefly to Jung just two days later that "Dr. Spielrein ... turned up unexpectedly. She said I didn't look malicious, as she imagined I would."[70] The evening was, in Freud's words, "not exactly a glorious one."[71] The only other woman analyst, Margarethe Hilferding, had stormed out with Adler's group. Freud wrote to Spielrein after two more meetings in which she had not spoken, perhaps in response to her reflections on the conflict she observed,[72] thanking her for her sensitivity and conciliatory presence as a woman "to remove our frowns and wrinkles with a soft hand," and encouraging her to "feel quite at home in our circle."[73] About a month later, on November 8, Spielrein eventually spoke up, contributing a number of remarks on infantile sexuality, phylogeny, and— foreshadowing a later interest in time and space—the timelessness of the unconscious.[74] Rank recorded that she "preface[d] her comments by saying that she can consider these matters only from the standpoint of her school [Jung]."[75] Freud noted in a letter to Jung a few days later that she "spoke up for the first time; she was very intelligent and methodical."[76] By the following meeting, she was more confidently referring to ideas of her own, asserting her thesis that "thoughts about death are contained in the sexual instinct itself."[77]

Jung published Spielrein's dissertation "On the Psychological Content of a Case of Dementia Praecox" in the *Jahrbuch* in 1911,[78] alongside a veritable "who's who" of psychoanalysis at that time, including both Freud and Jung. After her initial reluctance, Spielrein also spoke regularly at the Wednesday night meetings—often alluding, as in her later published works, to matters of women's sexuality and child development.[79] It is clear that Freud took her seriously, subjecting her to the same unsparing critiques of her work theoretically, but at the same time encouraging her professionally, and even personally at times behaving toward her in a protective, fatherly manner. He kept up a warm correspondence with her for years after she left Vienna. Perhaps Spielrein's longing for a benevolent father—combined with some remorse on Freud's own part for not having defended her early enough when she had turned to him for help concerning Jung[80]—had invoked Freud's countertransference as well.

"Destruction as a cause of coming into being"

Spielrein's 1911 paper "Destruction as a Cause of Coming into Being"[81] represents some of Spielrein's most innovative contributions to psychoanalysis at a time of particular creativity and ferment in the still newly forming field. It represents a crucial turning point in Spielrein's claiming of her own authority as an analyst and a theorist drawing from a wide range of ideas that had interested her for many years, including biological, psychological, mythological, and religious sources. Although she began writing the paper in earnest after her graduation from medical school, her ideas for the paper were already percolating perhaps even as early as 1907–08, as revealed in diary entries and correspondence drafts.[82] The paper also stands at the crossroads of her journey both intellectually and literally from Jung to Freud.

A death instinct within the libido

Rank recorded the title of Spielrein's paper in the Society's minutes as "On Transformation." He wrote:

> Taking as her point of departure the question of whether a normal death instinct exists in man, Dr. Spielrein endeavors to prove that the component of death is contained in the sexual instinct itself: inherent in that instinct is at the same time a destructive component which is indispensable to the process of coming into existence.[83]

To summarize from the published version of the paper,[84] Spielrein was raising a seemingly straightforward psychoanalytic question to tackle the question of a relationship between sex and death/destruction: Why does this most powerful drive, the reproductive instinct, harbor negative feelings in addition to the inherently anticipated positive feelings? Her paper began in a frankly Freudian vein, referencing Freud and the neurotogenic effects of repressive, moralistic child-rearing. She then quoted Jung, still on the first two pages—this was the Jung who was still under the sway of Freudian ideas about the centrality of sexuality, but also the Jung who was moving toward a dialecticism of his own in which every important phenomenon also bears its own opposite: "Passionate longing," she wrote, citing Jung's *Transformations and Symbols of the Libido* (Part 1),[85]

> ... i.e., *the libido, has two aspects: it is the power that beautifies everything and, in certain cases, destroys everything.* Often, one cannot recognize the source of this creative power's destructive quality. A woman who, in today's society, abandons herself to passion soon leads herself to ruin. One need only contemplate the current bourgeois state of affairs to understand how a feeling of unbounded insecurity occurs in those who unconditionally surrender to Fate.... Fate usually contains hidden dangers. The wish not to wrestle in the dangerous struggle of life explains the continual hesitation of neurotics to take risks. Whoever relinquishes experiencing a risky undertaking must stifle an erotic wish, committing a form of self-murder. This explains the death fantasies that often accompany the renunciation of the erotic wish [emphasis added].[86]

It is clear in this first quotation that Spielrein's research was also markedly autobiographical. The dialectic of passion and destruction certainly characterized much of what she experienced in her own passionate love for Jung. The quote may also describe Jung's own ambivalence as well—one either gives in to the passionate libido in a heroic surrender to Fate (as he did with Spielrein), or one neurotically cowers under the repression of bourgeois propriety (as he did only briefly, once after the birth of his first son and again after Spielrein's departure, before taking up a lifelong sexual relationship with another young patient, Toni Wolff).[87] There is perhaps even a sense in which Spielrein, with her newly minted doctorate, was throwing Jung's ideas back at him, showing him his hypocrisy in the form of a scientific paper that would be her ticket to Freud's inner circle.

Following the introduction, Spielrein continued by recruiting facts and sources as evidence for her thesis. She did not clearly state this thesis at the outset, but it is helpful to note that her aim, as expressed at the very end of the paper, was:

> to establish the destructive component of sexuality in individual psychological or mythological forms ... that, corresponding to the biological facts, the reproductive drive also consists psychologically of two antagonistic components, a destructive drive as well as a drive for coming into being.[88]

As summarized in this final sentence, she investigated three areas to support her argument: (1) "Biological Facts," (2) "Individual Psychological Observations," and (3) "Life and Death in Mythology."

The biological section: invasion, destruction, and reconstruction

The first section of the paper is quite brief, likely shortened for publication based on Freud's critique that the paper was too biologically reductionistic.[89] She noted that many species such as the mayfly forfeit their lives during procreation. In order for fertilization to occur, she wrote, "an alteration comes over the whole organism; destruction and reconstruction, which under usual circumstances always accompany each other, occur rapidly." She asserted that sexual pleasure is mixed with anxiety and disgust because the sexual partners can sense "the destructive component of the sexual instinct." Referring in particular to women's experience, she described this as a process of invasion: the ovum by the sperm and the female by the male.[90]

Individual psychological observations: "when word becomes deed"

In the second section of her paper Spielrein moved on to psychological observations, reasserting Freud's premise that nothing is affectively charged in the present without a re-experiencing of "feeling-toned contents that now lie hidden in the unconscious."[91] She gave several examples, such as a girl's fantasy of being a witch as a displacement of identification with her mother, but then moved more toward Jung's concept of the collective unconscious, by describing how in dream images the sea represents not only the individual mother, but the archetypal "Great Mother (the unconscious)" and "the undifferentiated mother [earth]." Coming-into-being is therefore much more than a biological birth and maturation, or merely individual ego development. Echoing Jung's idea of individuation as transformation by tapping into both the personal and the collective unconscious, she stated that *Weltschmerz* (deep weariness with the world's material struggles and benefits) results "when each seed of our being longs to re-transform in its source so that a new coming into being may emerge."[92]

Ascribing multiple motives for "the whole of psychic life," she went on to assert (anticipating both Freud's structural model with its dynamic conflict among ego, id, and superego, as well as Jung's concept of complexes): "The psyche is composed of many individual parts. It is Jung who speaks of autonomous complexes. According to him, we do not possess an undivided ego, but rather various complexes that struggle with each other for priority."[93]

Drawing on several case examples, she declared (foreshadowing contemporary multiple-self theory),

> I have come to the conclusion that the chief characteristic of an individual is that he is "dividual." The closer we approach our conscious thoughts, the

more differentiated our images; the deeper we penetrate the unconscious, the more universal and typical the images. The depth of our psyche knows no "I", but only its summation, the "We". It considers the ego to be an object observed and subordinated to other similar objects.[94]

How she brought this back to the theme of destruction as an intrinsic aspect of creativity is a bit tortured. Her argument traveled through this contest between the individual ego-organized psyche and the collective psyche. The ego seeks self-preservation, while the collective psyche desires dissolution of the individual into "new, more richly adorned images."[95] The artist walks this tightrope, she asserted, in which the [arche-]typical is projected into a work of art that taps the collective unconscious. Thus, the new creation—whether artistic, or procreative—results in the death of the old "ego-particle"[96] alongside the birth of "perhaps a more beautiful form of the content, originating at [its] expense."[97] Such creative dissolution and "working through" (borrowing from Freud) is required for relationship, she stated, because "the purely personal can never be understood by others."[98]

Taking yet another turn, she asserted that love itself is dangerous and destructive. Rather than allowing for sublimation of the "[arche-]typical" in the expression of images, in the actual consummation of love, the lover, unconsciously seeking a "parental resemblance," collapses the spiritual into the material.

> [W]ord becomes deed, the corresponding cluster of images fades, producing a pleasurable feeling of released tension. At this moment, one is psychically wholly unproductive. Every image attains its peak in life as it intensely awaits transition into reality; with realization, it immediately is destroyed.[99]

However, love is only one among many avenues by which the unconscious may emerge. For example, as Eros it may be sublimated in art, or as the destructive instinct it may be "deranged" in war.[100] The highest symbols of "primal experience," which bear elevated mythological or religious status—such as the Sun, Nature, or Christ—"remain in the psyche as an intense longing for a return to the source [of life], specifically a merging with the parents."[101] This explains, she said, "why religion as the highest is so readily symbolized by the lowest, i.e., sexual activity."[102]

Using the Christian imagery of Christ's resurrection, she argued for the close association among symbols of death, birth, and rebirth.[103] Similarly, in mythology, the symbol of the snake is simultaneously a "life- and death-bringing god."[104] Invoking Nietzsche's *Also Sprach Zarathustra*, she romanticized,

> Love and knowledge consist of sucking both the sun and the sea's depths into himself. Accordingly, knowledge for Nietzsche is nothing other than a desire for love, for creation. The glowing sun suckles at the sea like a loved one. The wildly moving sea reaches toward the sun with a thousand breasts

seeking parched kisses like a love-starved woman.... If the Mother represents his inner depths, union with the Mother also can be understood as an autoerotic union with one's self.[105]

Quoting Nietzsche, she again intertwined love and death: "Loving and dying have gone together from eternity. The Will to Love: that is to be willing to die!"[106]

Spielrein then took an idiosyncratic excursus, describing how one loves and is loved as both subject and object, and how the woman, because of her more passive role in sexuality, comes more readily to identify with the man's view of her as beloved, transforming this into a "wish-personality" with which she may auto-erotically engage. She ended this section with the argument that the destructive component of the sexual instinct may thereby lead to sadistic or masochistic identifications and, further, that "the boundary is not so sharply drawn because every human is bisexual."[107] From there she returned to her primary thesis by stating, "These [masochistic acts] are merely different forms and degrees of self-destruction. The procreative act per se leads to self-destruction."[108] Echoing Jung's fascination with the archetype of Phanes, the orphic child-god (e.g., in the *Red Book*,[109] and later carvings at Bollingen), she invoked a Nietzschean/Jungian liturgical tone: "You must know how to overcome (destroy) yourself. Otherwise, how could you create the highest, the child?"[110]

Thus, in this central portion of the paper, Spielrein outlined a death instinct, but one very different from what either Freud or Jung would eventually propose.[111] Rather than setting libido and aggression/death as opposing internal forces (as Freud did) or relegating the death instinct to a problematic dimension of mental life such as "introversion" (as Jung did),[112] she placed destruction *within* libido, as inextricably interwoven with a cosmic demand that, for life to come into being, life-as-it-is must die. Both physiologically and in the psyche, the transformation that leads to newness of life—whether literal birth or psychic birth/individuation—requires the death of the old and the relinquishment of the self-preserving status quo, or the ego, to the primal, untamed force of Life itself.[113]

Life and death in mythology: "the savior pattern"

In the final section of the paper, Spielrein sought to illustrate this assertion with imagery drawn from religion and mythology. In a kind of stream of consciousness conflating numerous sources—similar to other writings of the time such as Frazer's *Golden Bough*[114] and many of Jung's later writings on myth and symbolism—she attemped to show how life and death are frequently merged in symbolic images. She cited the Tree of Life, in both the Bible and other ancient cultic sources, as bearing both death (for sexual activity) but also resurrection to new life. This is echoed in Christ's crucifixion on the tree of the cross, resulting in redemption and new life for humankind, the legend of Adam being revived by his son Seth by planting three apple seeds in Adam's mouth (Spielrein notes here "Freudian displacement above"), and the twig as a phallic symbol of life and sexual potency.[115]

"What role does Christ, God's son, play in this?" Spielrein continued.[116] She leaped to the myth of the Nibelungen, from which Wagner derived his Ring Cycle. "Brünhilde (earth)," she wrote,

> whom we find in winter's sleep, is saved by Siegfried's victorious light (sun) when he pierces her suit of armour (ice-crust) with his sword. In this way she is fertilized. Here the process is not called fecundation as in the earth-sun tales; instead, the sword's thrust represents the actual act of fertilization and a kiss emphasizes its erotic connotation. It is critical that Siegfried, in Brünhilde, impregnates his mother. Indeed, Siegfried's mother is Sieglinde; however, Brünhilde, [Sieglinde's] sister, loves whomever Sieglinde loves, that is, Siegmund.... In this respect, Sieglinde is Brünhilde's "wish"—or sexual personality. Since Brünhilde redeems Siegfried, she redeems her own wish, her child.[117]

This would seem to be wildly off the rails of Spielrein's argument if it were not for the association she revealed in her letters and diaries between her relationship with Jung and the relationship between Brünhilde and Siegfried, with Jung as her "beloved little son,"[118] as noted above. Upon submitting the manuscript, she wrote to Jung, "Receive now the product of our love, the project which is your little son Siegfried."[119] In her fantasy, Siegfried not only represented a child to bind Jung to her permanently, but a deed of cosmic significance—to "give birth to 'a great Aryan-Semitic hero' who would unite these different and warring races forever."[120] Nearly seven years later, Spielrein would write to Jung of her "profound and shattering" realization that "he is alive after all, her Siegfried!" and that it was (still) her "high religious vocation" to "create a great Aryan-Semitic hero."[121]

"Like Eve," Spielrein continued in her paper,

> Brünhilde acts against her father's commandment, and, as Eve is banished from Paradise, Brünhilde is banished from the Gods' kingdom. Trespassing against the commandment brings Brünhilde to the death-like sleep from which she is awakened by the spring's son, Siegfried.[122]

Echoing her passion for Jung, she stated,

> In Wagner, longing for death is often desire for dying in love. Brünhilde, joined with her steed, dies in the fire (love's fire) and, in dying, calls out.... "In the glowing fire,/There lies thy heart/Siegfried, my blessed Hero./... Siegfried, Siegfried!/I salute and bless thee!" In this case [she interprets], death is a victorious song to love! Brünhilde, as it were, merges

into Siegfried: Siegfried is fire, the redeeming sun's incandescence. In this primal procreator, Brünhilde dissolves, becoming fire. For Wagner, death is often nothing other than the destroying components of the instinct coming into being.[123]

This, she stated, was "the savior pattern," also seen in Wagner's opera *The Flying Dutchman*. Wagnerian lovers

> ... sacrifice themselves to their love and die.... Christ also is a savior proto-type who sacrifices himself for mankind. Siegfried is the sun god and his beloved—Mother Earth; Christ is also a sun God. Christ dies on the Tree of Life; he is nailed to it and hangs there as though he were its fruit. As with fruit, Christ perishes and is placed in Mother Earth as a seed. This fructifica-tion leads to the formation of new life, to the resurrection of the dead. Through Christ's death and resurrection, Adam's guilt is atoned.[124]

Spielrein went on to discuss sacrifice for sin in both Christian and Jewish sources, as well as ancient Persian and Greek mythology. Thus, she concluded, "I believe that my examples sufficiently show that, corresponding to the biologi-cal facts, the reproductive drive also consists psychologically of two antagonistic components, a destructive drive as well as a drive for coming into being."[125]

In the last section of the paper, Spielrein also sounded a note of caution regarding the symbolism of life, death, and eternal life. Eternal life, she asserted, is dangerous, while death is paradoxically "a salutary blessing since it leads into a coming into being."[126] Eternal life is sterile, a life of the walking dead, like the Flying Dutchman who is condemned to endless voyaging from place to place, "yearn[ing], in vain, for an object." The Dutchman can only be saved from his eternal curse of wandering the earth by the true love of a (mortal) woman (named Senta in the legend). Spielrein interpreted that

> the Flying Dutchman shows us that the desired death is erotic, leading to a new coming into being: Senta and the Dutchman rise from the waves embracing [like the return of the ring of the Nibelungen to the earth].... The world can be saved only when life returns to its primal source.[127]

With this final argument, Spielrein was perhaps simultaneously chiding Jung for fleeing from the erotic embrace of sacrificial passion, *and* having her revenge by asserting her allegiance once again to Freud's theory of the centrality of sexuality.

Death and resurrection

"Destruction as the Cause of Coming into Being" is best known, when it is refer-enced at all, as perhaps the earliest published theory of the death instinct. But as we have seen, this is a quite different articulation of a death instinct than Freud's. Freud adopted aggression and the death instinct as two versions of a drive placed in direct opposition to the libido, continuing his approach to the mind as a hydraulic system of opposing forces, or a battle between the instinctual life and the accommodation of the ego to civilization. Spielrein, on the other hand, made no such concession to civilization. She located generativity primarily in the wildness of the collective, primal life force, which must overrun the socially tamed ego in order that new life can emerge, both biologically and in the psyche. While Freud's logic eventually brought him to the assertion that "where id was, there ego shall be"[128]—a triumph of the rational—Spielrein argued in her paper for the necessity of allowing ego to dissolve in the primal forces of life, even sacrificially, in the service of growth and transformation. In Spielrein's own pithy formulation, "Where love reigns, the ego, the ominous despot dies."[129]

For Spielrein, death and destruction were not opposed to life, but were inherent in both sexual pleasure and (although she continually nodded to Freud's primacy of the sexual drive) in all psychic growth and development. It was not in the rational individual's self-mastery or in the neurotic's ambivalent resistance as discussed by Freud, but in Spielrein's female psychotic patients' dissolution of the ego that she found compelling evidence of a deeper layer of vitality that, through sublimation—*not* hyper-rationality—could be made available to everyone. Spielrein's clinical examples and frequent references to women's experience also suggest a counter-narrative to the largely male-dominated world of early psychoanalysis. Although we might disagree at many points—perhaps especially with her romanticizing of masochism—she was claiming feminine modes of experience— as she herself defined them—as authoritative sources for argumentation, including passivity, masochism, and sacred sacrifice, but also auto-eroticism and bisexuality.

It is striking that Spielrein, a Jew, returned again and again to the symbolism of Christ's sacrifice. This is most likely explained both by her absorption of Jung's own exploration of Christ as an archetypal figure and by her sense of a heroic calling to create a rapprochement between Aryans and Jews. After his break with Jung, Freud warned against this idealism as naïve and dangerous, writing to her in the summer of 1913,

> I am, as you know, cured of the last shred of my predilection for the Aryan cause, and would like to take it that if [your] child turns out to be a boy he will develop into a stalwart Zionist.... We are and remain Jews. The others will only exploit us and will never understand or appreciate us.[130]

That Spielrein herself identified with the hero as well as with the "eternal feminine"—and perhaps even with Christ's sacrifice—is revealed in a letter to Jung written later, in 1918:

> According to Freud, the Siegfried fantasy is merely wish fulfillment. I have always objected to this merely. I told myself I was slated for something

great, I had to perform a heroic deed: if analysis now reveals that my love for X was not perfectly platonic; as I was convinced it was and wanted it to be—why should I resist and not view it as my heroic deed to sacrifice myself after all for this sacred love and create a hero?[131]

Her ease in exploring mythological, archetypal themes of course certainly reflected Jung's influence. She delved deeply into the Wagnerian/mythological themes of love and sacrifice that had provided romantic and mystical fodder for both herself and Jung.[132] Ironically, even as Spielrein and Jung had played out a mother-son fantasy of mythical proportions, Freud and Jung were enacting an increasingly toxic oedipal struggle of father vs. son and king vs. rebellious crown prince. Spielrein ended up presenting her paper in self-imposed exile from Jung's Zürich circle. Perhaps she held out some hope that, like Brünhilde in her deathlike sleep on the mountaintop, she might still be revived by her own Siegfried—Jung. In the meantime, however, Jung was actually busy killing the Siegfried hero within himself and getting closer and closer to his own creative madness, leading to the visions that would become the kernel of *The Red Book*.[133]

Spielrein's ideas were shifting, too. Her focus on libido, neurosis borne of repression, and countervailing forces of death and destruction show her growing allegiance—and, as well, a growing erotic/oedipal transference—toward Freud (which she confessed in a self-analysis in her diary in 1912: "Now Prof. Freud is the one who causes me to glow; … Dr. J.['s] … love would leave one cold").[134] And as Launer has suggested,[135] her interest in biology and the role of evolutionary adaptation, following Darwin, represented yet a third, fairly independent strand of thought derived from her medical training.

Kerr observed that the "Destruction" paper, whose circulation coincided with the widening and increasingly public break between Freud and Jung, "reads like nothing so much as an attempt to mediate between the two theoretical worlds of Zürich and Vienna."[136] This effort was doomed to fail, however, as the rift between Freud and Jung was widening. Jung was editing Spielrein's paper for the *Jahrbuch* even while bringing to a conclusion Part 2 of his own *Symbols and Transformations of the Libido.*[137] This was the work Jung foresaw would cost him his friendship with Freud once and for all.[138]

Other writings on religion and symbolism

No other works of Spielrein's rose to the level of religious preoccupation seen in her "Destruction" paper. In her dissertation, a case of "dementia praecox" (schizophrenia),[139] Spielrein was again intrigued by the psychological dynamics of religious difference, only this time between Protestant and Catholic faith traditions. She recounted working with a Protestant woman who struggled with her Catholic husband.[140] Some of Spielrein's ideas in the "Destruction" paper also appeared in her dissertation. The patient was upset about her husband's infidelities, and was overcome with thoughts of guilt and inadequacy, punishment and death. Spielrein, unlike most of her psychiatric colleagues at the time, believed that psychotic symbolism revealed a deeper hidden truth about her patient's inner reality. Like Jung, she saw these symbols and dreams as a way to understand both the individual psyche and the collective unconscious, as psychotic dreams and symbols often corresponded with universal mythological images. In a similar vein, in her paper "Contributions to an Understanding of the Child's Mind," she reflected on the symbolism in Mozart's Masonic opera "The Magic Flute" and other mythological themes to illuminate a case of anxiety in a young boy.[141]

In her later works, Spielrein focused mainly on child development, and no longer displayed the interest in mythological and religious symbols so prominent in her early writings. Her life continued to be characterized by work that influenced many others without adequate recognition, personal emotional struggles of attachment and separation, and ultimately tragedy as she and her family were caught up in the political storms of Stalinist Russia and the Nazi Holocaust. While her writing ceased to reflect religious themes, her life as a Jew in the increasingly dangerous antisemitic climate of Europe bears witness to pervasive dynamics of horror and denial. The abuses of Stalin and Hitler replicated at a massive political level her own lifetime of trauma at the hands of fathers, both real and projected.

Later life and Jewish identity: from coming into being to destruction

After her time in Vienna, which lasted only about six months, Spielrein said goodbye to Freud at Berggasse 19 and returned precipitously to Rostov to marry an observant Jewish doctor, Pavel (Paul) Sheftel.[142] Her brother Isaac was pursuing Jewish studies around the same time.[143] Launer surmises that Spielrein's parents, who had contracted with a traditional marriage broker previously, also had arranged this match.[144] Freud approved of the marriage, but worried that Spielrein was only "half cured" of her "neurotic dependence on Jung," and stated,

> My wish is for you to be cured completely. I must confess, after the event, that your fantasy about the birth of the Saviour to a mixed union [Mischvereinigung] did not appeal to me at all. The Lord [Herrgott], in that anti-Semitic period, had him born from the superior Jewish race. But I know these are my prejudices.[145]

Earlier that summer, Freud had alluded to the possibility of her returning to Vienna for an analysis "to break" her "dependence on Jung."[146] Now he demurred, saying that her positive view of her new husband might be

> badly prejudiced by treatment so soon after your marriage. Let him first try to see how far he can tie you to himself and make you forget the old dreams. Only what remnant he fails to clear up belongs properly to psychoanalysis.[147]

Freud revealed some concerns that the match might only be a temporary or *faute-de-mieux* union, adding,

> Meanwhile, it might happen that someone else will turn up who will have more rights than both the old and the new man put together. At this stage it is best for analysis to take a back seat. I shall always take the keenest interest in your life and your plans.[148]

Spielrein convinced Sheftel to move with her to Berlin, where Freud had encouraged her to work with Abraham.[149] There she produced ten more papers, focusing on children's fantasies, relationships with mothers and fathers, and in one case, again, the parallel between fantasies and mythological symbols.[150] She also gave birth to her first child, Renate (whose name means "reborn").[151] Jung and Freud exchanged their final acrimonious letters in January, 1913, and both wrote to Spielrein about it. Freud continued to insist that she...

> ... cast aside as so much trash your infantile dreams of the Germanic champion and hero, but rather to ... warm your life's intentions with your inner fire instead of burning yourself up with it. Nothing is stronger than controlled and sublimated passion. You can achieve nothing while you are at loggerheads with yourself. There will be a warm welcome for you if you stay with us here, but then you will have to recognize the enemy over there.[152]

Nevertheless, for some time thereafter Spielrein continued to dream of a reconciliation between her two father figures as the fulfillment of her vision of a Jewish-Aryan union.[153] When World War I broke out, she returned to Zürich with a reluctant Sheftel. Soon after, Sheftel was called up for military duty in Russia, and Spielrein moved with Renate to Lausanne.[154] Sheftel was vacillating about asking for a divorce, and in any case had returned to Russia for good. Spielrein's family had high hopes for the Bolshevik Revolution. During the war years, Spielrein battled illness and financial strain.[155] In 1918 she began corresponding again with Jung about Siegfried, although it was no longer clear to either of them what form this took in her mind. Meanwhile, their correspondence reflected a new, more formal status as their salutations shifted from intimate to professional forms of address.[156] In early January, Jung admonished her for trying to "drag the Siegfried symbol back into reality."[157]

In the course of her continued correspondence with Jung, she found herself needing to defend the Jewish people against some of his comments, which she found prejudicial. Jung wrote that her prophetic vocation was not out of the question:

> The Jews also had prophets. There is a part of the Jewish soul which you are not yet living, because you still have your eye too much on the outside. That is—"unfortunately"—the curse of the Jew: the aspect of his psychology

which belongs to him most deeply he calls "infantile wish-fulfilment," he is the murderer of his own prophets, even of his Messiah.[158]

Spielrein replied, "It is not only the Jewish people who murdered their prophet; indeed, it seems to be the fate of prophets that they are never recognized in their own country during their lifetime."[159] She continued, "I must counter that there is scarcely any other people as prone to seeing mystical and prophetic import everywhere as the Jewish people,"[160] and she praised Freud's "grandeur."[161] In her next letter she confessed that the confusion between Siegfried as a symbol versus a real child was played out psychosomatically in her very nearly losing her pregnancy:

> The struggle was very difficult for me, and the guilt resulting from missing my life goal so great that Siegfried almost took my baby daughter's life. *What contradiction exists between Siegfried and my little Renate that the two components found themselves locked in such a bitter struggle within me when little Renate was to be born?*[162]

She continued to debate whether her dream of creating a "great Aryan-Semitic hero" was a true destiny, or "a pathological attempt at self-aggrandizement ... megalomania."[163] Yet, she quickly rejected this interpretation:

> Even if I intellectually accepted this ... explanation, my whole being resists it, for reality would be much too barren for me without belief in Siegfried. Could it really be merely "wish fulfillment," my former dream that my grandfather or father blessed me by laying on his hands and pronouncing, "A great fate awaits you, my child"? Siegfried for me = Christ, and yet it is not exactly the same.

Pointedly referring to Jung, she added, "He arose from the life I shared for years with a German [Aryan]."[164] Although Jung did not respond for over a month, his next letter warned that she had a "murderous tendency,"[165] and her thoughts were suspect on account of "the fickleness of the female spirit."[166] He perhaps believed that her fantasies of "killing Siegfried" might bring real harm to Renate, but hoped that she would make use of her dreams to recognize Siegfried as an expression of the divine instead:

> Your little daughter is quite safe when you do not want to kill the "strange being" whom you call Siegfried. For this produces a harmful effect only when it is not accepted as a divine being but just as "phantasy." ... Your influence will be good and rich in blessing if you accept this being and worship it inwardly. *I wish your child everything that is good.* I wish too that you would learn to accept "Siegfried" for what he is. This is important as much for your child's sake as for your own. How you must accept

Siegfried I cannot tell you. That is a secret. Your dreams can help. Dreams are compensatory to the conscious attitude. Reality and the unconscious are primary. They're two forces that work simultaneously but are different. The hero unites them in a symbolic figure. He is the centre and the resolution. The dream contributes to life, as does reality. The human being stands between two worlds. Freud's view is a sinful violation of the sacred. It spreads darkness, not light; that has to happen, for only out of the deepest night will the new light be born. One of its sparks is Siegfried. This spark can and will never be extinguished. If you betray this, then you are cursed.

Jung went on (somewhat callously?) to address a matter not spelled out in extant documentation but which must have been upsetting to Spielrein—the execution of Karl Liebknecht, her Marxist brother-in-law, by a right-wing militia just a week or two earlier.[167]

What has Liebknecht to do with you? Like Freud and Lenin, he disseminates rationalistic darkness which will yet extinguish the little lamps of understanding. I kindled a new light in you which you must protect against the time of darkness. That must not be betrayed externally and for the sake of external arguments. Surround this inner light with devotion, then it will never turn into danger for your little daughter. But whoever betrays this light for the sake of power or in order to be clever will be a figure of shame and will have a bad influence. With best wishes, yours sincerely, Dr. Jung.[168]

That spring, following one more technical letter from Jung (expounding on his theory of personality types), their correspondence ended for good.

Spielrein continued vigorously to pursue her career as an analyst, teacher, and writer. Moving to Geneva in the early 1920s, she had a second period of scientific creativity. Little Renate became a research subject for her, as she concentrated mainly on child development. She briefly analyzed Jean Piaget at the new Rousseau Institute—an analysis she terminated because "she felt it wasn't worth wasting an hour a day on a man who wouldn't accept the [Freudian] theory."[169] After some initial collaboration based on shared interest in early childhood development, they parted ways, disagreeing about Piaget's focus on cognition as the only important area of study.[170]

Idealism, romanticism, and denial—the final destruction

In 1923, following the death of her mother, Spielrein returned to Russia and built a successful career in Moscow, lecturing, teaching, and conducting research. The following year, Spielrein reunited with her husband and gave birth to a second daughter, Eva, in 1926.[171] Psychoanalysis was flourishing under Trotsky in the early 1920s.[172] As a senior psychoanalyst with the imprimatur of Vienna upon her, Spielrein influenced the thinking of the Soviet developmental psychologists Lev Vygotsky and Alexander Luria.[173]

The political winds were shifting, however, and by the 1930s her life devolved into a series of losses and deaths. With Stalin's rise to power, psycho-analysis, and eventually also the study of child development, were suppressed. Her entire family, as educated, upper-class scientists, were under suspicion. Her job was terminated along with her entire profession. Her father was tortured and all his property taken from him. Isaac was sentenced to hard labor and eventu-ally was shot in 1937.[174] Sheftel died of a heart attack in 1937. Her remaining two brothers were shot within the first six months of 1938, and their father, Nikolai, died of shock in August. According to the later recollections of family members, Spielrein lived in a converted stable, impoverished, "old before her time," and "a broken woman."[175] Only her work, which she courageously con-tinued under the title of school psychologist, and her daughters' musical accom-plishments sustained her.[176]

In a tragic paradox, Spielrein's insights into the "shadow side" of sexuality, and her assertion that destruction was inherent in the life force, love, and creativ-ity, did not help her to see the approaching Nazi threat with life-saving clarity. Even as the news from Europe became more dire, her niece Menicha recalled that Spielrein "could not believe that the Germans could do such terrible things."[177] Pogroms against Jews had been common in Russia from the late eighteenth century, when Russian territorial expansion led to the concentration of Jewish populations[178] within a "Pale of Settlement" or ghetto.[179] But Rostov had been considered a safe haven. A pogrom had taken place there in October, 1905, while Spielrein was beginning medical school in Zürich,[180] but there were few thereafter until the Germans invaded Russia in 1941. By the time the Nazis occupied Rostov, Freud's books had been burned in Germany,[181] Hitler was in Vienna, and the Freud household had fled to London. Friends and remaining family members urged Spielrein to take her daughters and leave. Whether or not escape might have been possible for her, Spielrein remained in Rostov.

The same romantic idealism that was a source of creative explorations into the realms of love, heroism, and the deep truths available in myth and symbol perhaps also served in the end to blind her to her own peril.[182] She could not view Siegfried—whose legend served now as symbol of the Aryan Übermensch in the twisted ideology of Nazism—as evil, when he bore such tender and heroic personal meaning in her own life. She loved Wagner and German culture, and German was the chosen language of most of her scholarship. Margarita Khatyat-uryan, a classmate and friend of Sabina's younger daughter Eva, said in an inter-view, "People said they should leave the city. But Sabina Nikolajewna told me: 'I studied in Germany. I know the Germans very well. They are not able to act like that. They would never kill us'."[183]

In spite of their sometimes less-than-friendly motives, perhaps both Freud and Jung perceived something cautionary in their assessments of Spielrein, which they shared both with her and with one another. Freud's description of her as "abnormally ambivalent" may have been picking up on some splitting that no doubt did contribute to her ability to idealize external (male) heroes while sinking into self-blame and depression. Her history of physical punishment at the hands of her father may have instilled her tendency—noted in contemporary accounts of her dress and behavior—to ward off humiliation by assuming a posture of humility. As Coline Covington describes,

> During this period of her life, Spielrein was described by relatives as a solitary figure, intense, serious, working long hours and puritanical in dress, wearing old clothes, some of them torn, so as not to spend money on herself. Her idealisation of self-sacrifice seems to have resulted in self-deprivation.[184]

As Jung had warned her, regarding "always trying to drag the Siegfried symbol back into reality"

> … in fact it is the bridge to your individual development. Human beings do not stand in one world only but between two worlds and must distinguish themselves from their functions in both worlds. That is individuation. You are rejecting dreams and seeking action. Then the dreams come and thwart your actions. The dreams are a world, and the real is a world. You have to stand between them and regulate the traffic in both worlds, just as Siegfried stands between the gods and men.[185]

Perhaps the tragedy is that while Spielrein could identify the link between destruction and coming-into-being, she was never able to give up her longing for the Siegfried hero to manifest concretely in her life. And when the Nazi devil came in the disguise of her beloved hero, she could not recognize him. On July 27, 1942, eyewitnesses observed Spielrein and her daughters being marched to the Zmeyevsky gully on the outskirts of Rostov, where they were shot and killed along with 10,000 other civilians.

In her 1911 paper, Spielrein had written, "Self-destruction can be replaced by sacrificial destruction…. From the Christian point of view, self-destruction generates an image of burial, a re-implantation in Mother Earth. Resurrection is rebirth."[186] It is painful to contrast this idealized vision of death and resurrection with the image of Spielrein and her daughters tumbling into a mass grave in a ravine. In the following chapter, the impact of antisemitism and its culmination in the Holocaust will be discussed in relation to all those analysts who, like Spielrein, clung to the myth of German civility, to their peril.

Notes

1 Carotenuto, 1982; Kerr, 1994.
2 Cronenberg, 2011.

3   The film otherwise hews fairly strictly to Kerr's (1994) account.
4   Appignanesi and Forrester, 1992: 205.
5   E.g., Richebächer, 2008; Covington and Wharton, 2015; Harris, 2015; Cooper-White, 2014, 2015a, 2015b, 2015c; Cooper-White and Kelcourse, 2017; Kelcourse, 2014; Noth, 2015.
6   Carotenuto, 1982; Lothane, 2015; Covington and Wharton, 2015; Cooper-White and Kelcourse, 2017. Two English translations of the "Destruction" paper appeared one year apart: Spielrein, 1994/1912 and 1995/1912.
7   Launer, 2015.
8   Cf., in German, Höfer, 2000; Richebächer, 2008.
9   E.g., Cooper-White and Kelcourse, 2018. Translations of the dissertation and other early works, and a projected critical edition in English are also under discussion (Peter Rudnytsky and Ruth Cape, personal communications).
10 Harris, 2015: 730.
11 Freud, 1955b/1920: 55n. Jones (1957: 296, 296n3) also credited Spielrein for the idea of "the independent existence of an aggressive instinct," noting Freud's initial resistance to it and eventual "confession" in *Civilization and Its Discontents* (Freud, 1961/1930: 118–122). Cf. Strachey's Introduction, ibid., 61–63.
12 Freud, 1958a/1911: 80.
13 Jung, 1967/1912.
14 Rudnytsky, 2002: 151.
15 Carotenuto, 1980, 1982.
16 Kerr, 1994.
17 The main exception until Launer (2015) was Márton's (2006b) docu-drama. Primary sources include Carotenuto, 1982, 1986; Covington and Wharton, 2015; Spielrein's original works in *Imago, Jahrbuch, Zentralblatt*, etc.; Hensch, 2006; and the critical German edition (Spielrein, 2002).
18 Richebächer, 2003: 246–247.
19 Launer, 2015: 6; Harris, 2015: 754. Launer and Harris dispute Spielrein's masochism as lifelong.
20 Launer, 2015: 20.
21 Ibid., 125.
22 Ibid., 54–55.
23 E.g., encouraging one son to poke the other's eyes out with a fork (ibid., 20).
24 Wharton, 2015b: 61–62, recorded in an intake interview by Jung. Cf. Launer, 2015: 17.
25 Launer, 2015: 23.
26 Wharton, 2015b: 59, 65; cf. Launer, 2015: 43.
27 Launer, 2015: 25.
28 Wharton, 2015b: 57. Graf-Nold (2015) reports it was one of the first times this diagnosis was used at the Burghölzli, and was of great interest to both Bleuler and Jung (p. 97). Richebächer (2003) notes that later descriptions of her case, including such diagnostic labels as psychosis, hysteria with schizoid characteristics, and borderline personality disorder, appear to be exaggerated (p. 247).
29 Graf-Nold, 2015: 85.
30 Ibid., 87–88.
31 Word association experiments designed to ferret out repressed information, similar to Freud's method of free association but with stricter empirical controls. Jung's early reputation was built on this research (Jung, 1973; cf. Bair, 2003: 64, *et passim*).
32 Appignanesi and Forrester, 1992: 207.
33 Launer, 2015: 26.

34 Breuer, 1955/1893.
35 Carotenuto, 1982: 49. E.g., diary entry *c*.1912.
36 Launer, 2015: 21, 32, 40, 122, 124, 150; Carotenuto, 1982: 32.
37 Launer, 2015: 5, 30–35, 47–51, 60, asserts that it was Bleuler, not Jung, who actu-
    ally treated Spielrein at the Burghölzli (Launer, 2015: 51; Graf-Nold, 2015: 109),
    and that once she was discharged, Jung pressured Spielrein to let him analyze her as
    a part of their friendship, but never officially as her therapist (p. 98). Contra Kerr
    (1994). Cf. Graf-Nold, 2015; Wharton, 2015b: 71–78. Neither Kerr (1994) nor
    Launer (2015, e.g., pp. 126–127) fully represent the sexual turn in Spielrein's and
    Jung's relationship as professional misconduct or sexual exploitation.
38 Launer, 2015: 56.
39 In a letter to Freud, she writes, "My love for him transcended our affinity until he
    could stand it no longer and wanted 'poetry.' For many reasons I could not and did
    not want to resist" (Carotenuto, 1982: 96–97).
40 Letter, Jung to Freud, June 21, 1909, in McGuire, 1974: 236.
41 There is no consensus whether by "poetry" Spielrein is indicating sexual intercourse
    or a passionate intimacy that stopped short of that for both practical (pregnancy) and
    romantically idealistic reasons. Lothane has vigorously refuted the idea of inter-
    course, at least while Spielrein was a patient, and characterizes the relationship
    generally as "erotic-sensual" (Lothane, 2015: 131, 139–153, cf. Lothane, 2007,
    2013, 2016). Spielrein's own accounts in letters and diary entries (e.g., Carotenuto,
    1982: 8–13, 33) suggest that it mostly consisted of passionate kissing and mutual
    expressions of longing. The sensationalistic, sado-masochistic scenes in "A Danger-
    ous Method" (Cronenberg, 2011) are nowhere supported by the documentary
    evidence.
42 In the Nibelung legend that is the basis for Wagner's Ring Cycle, Siegfried himself
    is the child of the incestuous union of the twins Siegmund and Sieglinde, and it is
    Brunhilde's charge from her father, Wotan, to protect Siegmund. The tables are
    turned when Siegfried becomes her savior.
43 Carotenuto, 1982: 3. Diary entry, December 8, 1910.
44 Covington and Wharton, 2015: 5.
45 Lothane, 2015: 131–139. Launer (2015) finds evidence for Jung pressing unwanted
    analysis on Spielrein (pp. 71–72, 75–76, 98–99).
46 Launer, 2015: 110–111.
47 Launer (2015) notes, "the exchanges of the months that followed Spielrein's lecture
    in Vienna can be seen as a four-way struggle with Bleuler as a protagonist, too,"
    with Bleuler representing empirical science (p. 148). Cf. Balsam, 2003: 324.
48 E.g., Carotenuto, 1986: 73.
49 Launer, 2015: 19.
50 Ibid.
51 Wharton, 2015b: 63. In his clinical notes, Jung wrote that Spielrein had realized that
    God had sent her this angelic voice "because she was an extraordinary person." Cf.
    Graf-Nold, 2015: 97; Launer, 2015: 41.
52 Carotenuto, 1982: 12–13.
53 Ibid., 15.
54 Ibid., 21–22.
55 Launer, 2015: 97, 122. Cf. Carotenuto, 1982: 22–23 for Spielrein's account of her
    mother's attraction to a Christian man.
56 Ibid., 113–114. For the full text, see Carotenuto, 1982: 27–30.
57 Carotenuto, 1982: 21, 32; cf. Launer, 2015: 122. Diary entries, October 19, 1910.
58 Carotenuto, 1982: 30; Carotenuto, 1986: 70–73. Diary entry, October 19, 1910.
59 Carotenuto, 1982: 33. Diary entry, October 24, 1910.

60 Ibid.
61 Ibid., 37. Diary entry, December 8, 1910.
62 Ibid., 38. Diary entry, December 21, 1910.
63 Ibid.
64 Letters of Jung to Spielrein, August 12, 1908 and December 4, 1908, in Wharton, 2015a: 32, 34; Spielrein to Freud, June 11, 1909, cf. Launer, 2015: 99. McLynn, 1996: 161, catalogues numerous affairs.
65 Carotenuto, 1982: 39. Diary entry, February 1911. Cf. Carotenuto, 1986: 80–81.
66 Carotenuto, 1982: 40. Diary entry, February 28, 1911.
67 Ibid., 40–41. Diary entry, January 7, 1912.
68 Carotenuto, 1986: 202, translation by this author; Launer, 2015: 134.
69 McGuire, 1974: 447. (See Chapter 1.)
70 Ibid.
71 Carotenuto, 1982: 115. Letter of Freud to Spielrein, October 27, 1911.
72 Launer, 2015: 136.
73 Carotenuto, 1982: 115; also cited in Launer, 2015: 136. Letter of Freud to Spielrein, October 27, 1911.
74 Nunberg and Federn, 1974: 302–303.
75 Ibid., 302.
76 McGuire, 1974: 458; also cited in Launer, 2015: 136.
77 Nunberg and Federn, 1974: 316.
78 Spielrein, 1911.
79 Nunberg and Federn, 1974.
80 Freud confessed this to Spielrein in a letter of June 24, 1909 (Carotenuto, 1982: 114–115).
81 Spielrein, 1912, 1994/1912.
82 Launer, 2015: 74, citing an undated letter draft from Spielrein to Jung in Hensch, 2006: 131; cf. Carotenuto, 1982: 20, 29; Kerr, 1994: 319.
83 Nunberg and Federn, 1974: 329.
84 Summary adapted, in part, from Cooper-White (2015c), used by permission, Springer. A separate version will also appear in Cooper-White and Kelcourse (2018), used by permission, Routledge.
85 Jung, 1967/1912.
86 Ibid., 155–156.
87 Bair, 2003: 248–249; Healy, 2017.
88 Spielrein, 1994/1912: 184.
89 Letter, Freud to Jung, November 30, 1911, in McGuire, 1974: 469.
90 Spielrein, 1994/1912: 157.
91 Ibid.
92 Ibid., 158.
93 Ibid., 160.
94 Ibid.
95 Ibid., 163.
96 Ibid.
97 Ibid.
98 Ibid., 164.
99 Ibid.
100 Ibid., 165.
101 Ibid.
102 Ibid.
103 Ibid., 166.
104 Ibid., 167.

105 Ibid., 167–168.
106 Ibid., 168. Parallel to visions Jung had in December, 1913, after the publication of this paper, subsequently painted in his *Red Book* (e.g., Jung, 2009, image 119). For Jung, the imagery of the mother was becoming increasingly ambivalent—not only the romantic, life-giving "eternal feminine," but also terrible and destructive (Kerr, 1994: 331). For Spielrein, however, destruction remains transformational only through surrender to love and passion. Kerr asserts, "Behind the image of the 'destructive mother' of Jung's reverie … stands the unabashed authoress of 'Destruction as a Cause of Coming into Being'" (Kerr, 1994: 333).
107 Speilrein, 1994/1912: 169.
108 Ibid., 170.
109 Jung, 2009, image 113.
110 Spielrein, 1994/1912: 170.
111 On similarities and differences, see Chambrier, 2006.
112 E.g., Jung, 1967/1912; cf. Kerr, 1994: 327–328.
113 A theme Jung would also develop in his *Red Book* (2009).
114 Frazer, 2012/1911–15. Freud also consulted Frazer's *Totemism and Exogamy*, in his own *Totem and Taboo* (Freud, 1955a: 3n1, 2, *et passim*).
115 Spielrein, 1994/1912: 175–176.
116 Ibid., 176.
117 Ibid., 176–177.
118 Carotenuto, 1982: 37. Diary entry, December 8, 1910.
119 Letter, Spielrein to Jung, early August, 1911, in Carotenuto, 1982: 48. (For correct dating, cf. Carotenuto, 1986: 138.)
120 Covington and Wharton, 2015: 5.
121 Carotenuto, 1982: 88; Covington and Wharton, 2015: 6.
122 Spielrein, 1994/1912: 177.
123 Ibid., 177–178.
124 Ibid., 178.
125 Ibid., 184.
126 Ibid., 183.
127 Ibid., 183–184.
128 Freud, 1964/1933: 80.
129 Spielrein, 1994/1912: 174.
130 Carotenuto, 1982: 120–121; Kerr, 1994: 458–459.
131 Carotenuto, 1982: 80, cited in Covington and Wharton, 2015: 5.
132 Lothane (2016) describes the Siegfried identification in detail.
133 Jung, 2009: 241–242; cf. Jung, 1989/1963: 180–181.
134 Carotenuto, 1982: 43.
135 Launer, 2015: 73, 144, *et passim*.
136 Kerr, 1994: 396.
137 Later renamed *Symbols of Transformation*. Jung, 1967/1912.
138 Kerr, 1994: 399.
139 Spielrein, 1911; Spielrein, 2002: 11–97.
140 Ibid. Launer provides a summary (2015: 131–133).
141 Spielrein, 1913.
142 Richebächer, 2003; Launer, 2015: 153–157.
143 Launer, 2015: 158.
144 Ibid., 156.
145 Letter, Freud to Spielrein, August 20, 1912, in Carotenuto, 1982: 116–117; Carotenuto, 1986: 120.
146 Carotenuto, 1982: 116.

147 Ibid., 117.
148 Ibid.
149 Carotenuto, 1982: 117. Letter, Freud to Spielrein, October 13, 1912.
150 Described in Launer, 2015: 161–162, 287–288.
151 Carotenuto, 1982: 87. Letter, Spielrein to Jung, January 27–28, 1918. Spielrein chose the name as instructed in a dream.
152 Ibid., 122–123. Letter, Freud to Spielrein, June 12, 1914.
153 Ibid., 112. Letter, Spielrein to Freud, 1914.
154 Launer, 2015: 168, 170.
155 Ibid., 170–171.
156 Wharton, 2015a: 33; Carotenuto, 1986: 187–226, 139–141.
157 Wharton, 2015a: 49. Cf. Carotenuto, 1986: 219.
158 Wharton, 2015a: 49–50. Cf. Carotenuto, 1986: 219; Launer, 2015: 183. Letter, Jung to Spielrein, January, 1918.
159 Carotenuto, 1982: 82. This may have been an oblique reference to the execution on January 15, 1919 of her brother-in-law Karl Liebknecht who had co-founded the Marxist Spartacus League with Rosa Luxemburg (Wharton, 2015a: 56; Launer, 2015: 130, 184). She may also have had in mind Freud's lack of acclaim in his "own country" of Vienna.
160 Ibid., 83.
161 Ibid., 85.
162 Carotenuto, 1982: 87, emphasis original.
163 Ibid., 89.
164 Ibid., 88–89.
165 Wharton, 2015a: 50.
166 Ibid., 51.
167 See note 159 above.
168 Wharton, 2015a: 51. Cf. Carotenuto, 1986: 221; Launer, 2015.
169 Interview with Jean Piaget, 1977, quoted in Launer, 2015: 201.
170 For details of their relationship, see Noth, 2015; Launer, 2015: 201–207.
171 While separated, Sheftel had a relationship with Olga Snitkova in Rostov (Lothane, 2013: 11). Their daughter Nina was part of the family. Sheftel also fathered a baby with another woman, whom he visited until his death (Launer, 2015: 233).
172 Etkind, 1997.
173 Harris, 2015.
174 Isaac's wife and daughter survived in central Asia. Emil's family also survived, and Evald settled in Moscow after the war. His son Vladimir Shpilrain lives in New York (Lothane, 2013: 12).
175 Etkind, 1997: 176; Launer, 2015: 233.
176 Launer, 2015: 233.
177 Maehler, 2006: 9. Cf. Lothane, 2013: 12.
178 The first Russian "pogrom" (Russian for "wreak havoc") was in Odessa in 1821 (U.S. Holocaust Museum, n.d.).
179 Klier, 2010.
180 Launer, 2015: 61.
181 Richebächer, 2008: 245; cf., Launer, 2015: 239–243.
182 This portion of this chapter adapted from Cooper-White (2015c), used by permission, Springer, 2017.
183 Márton, 2006a: 11.
184 Covington and Wharton, 2015: 13.
185 Wharton, 2015a: 49.
186 Spielrein, 1994/1912: 182.

References

Appignanesi, Lisa and Forrester, John (1992). *Freud's women*. New York: Basic Books.
Bair, Deirdre (2003). *Jung: A biography*. Boston: Little, Brown.
Balsam, Rosemary (2003). Women of the Wednesday Society: The presentations of Drs. Hilferding, Spielrein, and Hug-Hellmuth. *American Imago, 60* (3): 303–342.
Breuer, Josef (1955). Fräulein Anna O., case histories from studies on hysteria. In J. Strachey (Ed.), *The standard edition of the complete psychological works of Sigmund Freud*, Vol. 2: 19–47. (Orig. publ. 1893.)
Carotenuto, Aldo (1980). *Diario di una segreta simmetria: Sabina Spielrein tra Jung e Freud*. Rome: Astrolabio.
Carotenuto, Aldo (1982). *A secret symmetry: Sabina Spielrein between Freud and Jung*. Arno Pomerans, John Shepley, and Krishna Winston (Trans.). New York: Pantheon.
Carotenuto, Aldo (1986). *Tagebuch einer heimlichen Symmetrie: Sabina Spielrein zwischen Jung und Freud*. Freiburg: Kore.
Chambrier, J. (2006). Sabina Spielrein (1912): Die Destruktion als Ursache des Werdens. In A. Karger and C. Weismüller (Eds.), *Ich hieß Sabina Spielrein: Von einer, die auszog, Heilung zu suchen* (pp. 85–98). Göttingen: Vandenhoeck & Ruprecht.
Cooper-White, Pamela (2014). Beyond "a dangerous method": Sabina Spielrein and the "death instinct." Fulbright lecture presented at the Sigmund Freud Museum, Vienna, January 17.
Cooper-White, Pamela (2015a). A comparative timeline: Spielrein, Freud, and Jung. *Pastoral Psychology, 64* (2), 235–240.
Cooper-White, Pamela (2015b). Introduction to special symposium: Beyond "a dangerous method": Reclaiming Sabina Spielrein's voice in the field of psychology and religion. *Pastoral Psychology, 64* (2), 231–233.
Cooper-White, Pamela (2015c). "The power that beautifies and destroys": Sabina Spielrein and "Destruction as a cause of coming into being." *Pastoral Psychology, 64* (2), 259–278.
Cooper-White, Pamela and Kelcourse, Felicity (Eds.) (2018, in press). *Sabina Spielrein and the beginnings of psychoanalysis*. New York: Routledge.
Covington, Coline and Wharton, Barbara (Eds.) (2015). *Sabina Spielrein: Forgotten pioneer of psychoanalysis*, 2nd ed. New York: Brunner-Routledge.
Cronenberg, David (Director) (2011). A dangerous method (film). Los Angeles: Sony Pictures Classics.
Etkind, Aleksandr Markovič (1997). *Eros of the impossible: The history of psychoanalysis in Russia*. Noah Rubins (Trans.). Boulder, CO: Westview Press.
Frazer, James (2012). *The golden bough*, 3rd ed. (12 vols.). Cambridge, UK: Cambridge University Press. (Orig. publ. 1911–15; 1st ed. 1890.)
Freud, Sigmund (1955a). *Totem and taboo*. In J. Strachey (Ed.), *Standard edition of the complete works of Sigmund Freud*, Vol. 8: vii–162. (Orig. German publ. 1913.)
Freud, Sigmund (1955b). *Beyond the pleasure principle*. In J. Strachey (Ed.), *Standard edition of the complete works of Sigmund Freud*, Vol. 18: 1–64. (Orig. German publ. 1920.)
Freud, Sigmund (1957). Lecture 1, in *Five lectures on psycho-analysis*. In J. Strachey (Ed.), *Standard edition of the complete works of Sigmund Freud*, Vol. 11: 9–20. (Orig. German publ. 1910.)
Freud, Sigmund (1958a) *Psycho-analytic notes on an autobiographical account of a case of paranoia (dementia paranoides) ["The Schreber Case"]*. In J. Strachey (Ed.),

Standard edition of the complete works of Sigmund Freud, Vol. 12: 1–82. (Orig. German publ. 1911.)

Freud, Sigmund (1958b). *The theme of the three caskets.* In J. Strachey (Ed.), *Standard edition of the complete works of Sigmund Freud*, Vol. 12: 303–310. (Orig. German publ. 1913.)

Freud, Sigmund (1961). *Civilization and its discontents.* In J. Strachey (Ed.), *Standard edition of the complete works of Sigmund Freud*, Vol. 21: 57–146. (Orig. German publ. 1930.)

Freud, Sigmund (1964). *New introductory lectures on psycho-analysis.* In J. Strachey (Ed.), *Standard edition of the complete works of Sigmund Freud*, Vol. 22: 1–182. (Orig. German publ. 1933.)

Graf-Nold, Angela (2015). The Zürich school of psychiatry in theory and practice: Sabina Spielrein's treatment at the Burghölzli Clinic in Zürich. Barbara Wharton (Trans.). In Coline Covington and Barbara Wharton (Eds.), *Sabina Spielrein: Forgotten pioneer of psychoanalysis* (pp. 83–113), 2nd ed. New York: Brunner-Routledge.

Harris, Adrienne (2015). "Language is there to bewilder itself and others": Theoretical and clinical contributions of Sabina Spielrein. *Journal of the American Psychoanalytic Association, 63*: 727–767.

Healy, Nan Savage (2017). *Toni Wolff and C.G. Jung: A collaboration.* Los Angeles: Tiberius.

Hensch, Traute (Ed.) (2006). *Sabina Spielrein: Nimm meine Seele—Tagebücher und Schriften* ("Take my Soul: Diaries and Writings"). Freiburg: Freitag.

Höfer, Renate (2000). *Die Psychoanalytikerin Sabina Spielrein.* Rüsselheim am Main: Göttert.

Jones, Ernest (1957). *The life and work of Sigmund Freud, Vol. 3: The last phase 1919–1939.* New York: Basic Books.

Jung, C. G. (1967). *Symbols of transformation, Parts I and II.* In *The collected works of C. G. Jung*, vol. 5. R. F. C. Hull (Trans.), Bollingen Series 20. Princeton, NJ: Princeton University Press. (Orig. publ. 1912, 2nd ed. 1952.)

Jung, C. G. (1973). Studies in word association, in *Experimental researches.* In *The collected works of C. G. Jung*, vol. 5. R. F. C. Hull (Trans.), Bollingen Series 20 (pp. 3–482). Princeton, NJ: Princeton University Press. (Orig. publ. 1906–09.)

Jung, C. G. (1989). *Memories, dreams, reflections.* Aniela Jaffe (Ed.), Clara and Robert Winston (Trans.). New York: Vintage. (Orig. publ. 1963.)

Jung, C. G. (2009). *The red book.* S. Shamdasani (Ed. and Trans.). New York: W. W. Norton.

Kelcourse, F. (2014). Spielrein, Sabina. In D. Leeming (Ed.), *Encyclopedia of psychology and religion* (pp. 1706–1710). New York: Springer.

Kerr, John (1994). *A most dangerous method: The story of Jung, Freud, and Sabina Spielrein.* New York: Vintage.

Klier, John (2010). Pale of settlement. *YIVO Encyclopedia of Jews in Eastern Europe.* Online at www.yivoencyclopedia.org/article.aspx/Pale_of_Settlement. Accessed April 20, 2017.

Launer, John (2015). *Sex versus survival: The life and ideas of Sabina Spielrein.* New York: Overlook.

Lothane, H. Zvi (2007). The snares of seduction in life and therapy, or what do young girls (Spielrein) seek in their Aryan heroes (Jung) and vice versa? *International Forum of Psychoanalysis, 16* (1): 12–27 and *16* (2): 81–94.

Lothane, H. Zvi (2013). The real story of Sabina Spielrein: Or fantasies vs. facts of a life. Online at www.scribd.com/doc/159946712/Henry-Zvi-Lothane-MD-The-real-story-of-Sabina-Spielrein-or-fantasies-vs-facts-of-a-life. Accessed September 19, 2015.

Lothane, H. Zvi (2015). Tender love and transference: Unpublished letters of C. G. Jung and Sabina Spielrein (with an addendum/discussion). In Coline Covington and Barbara Wharton (Eds.), *Sabina Spielrein: Forgotten pioneer of Psychoanalysis* (pp. 126–157), 2nd ed. New York: Brunner-Routledge.

Lothane, H. Zvi (2016). Sabina Spielrein's Siegfried and other myths: Facts versus fictions. *International Forum of Psychoanalysis, 25*: 40–49.

Maehler, Signe (2006). Sabina Spielrein. In cine-notes to Elisabeth Márton, *My name was Sabina Spielrein* (DVD), pp. 7–9.

Márton, Elisabeth (Director) (2006a) Interviews with Sabina Spielrein's family and friends. In Cine-Notes to Elisabeth Márton, *My name was Sabina Spielrein* (DVD), pp. 10–11.

Márton, Elisabeth (Director) (2006b). *My name was Sabina Spielrein* (DVD). Chicago: Facets Video. (Orig. released as *Ich hieß Sabina Spielrein*, produced by Helgi Felix/Idé Film Felixson AB, 2002.) With brief interviews with Sabina Spielrein's family and friends, in Cine-Notes to *My name was Sabina Spielrein* (DVD) (pp. 10–11). Chicago: Facets Video.

McGuire, William (Ed. and Trans.) (1974). *The Freud/Jung letters: The correspondence between Sigmund Freud and C. G. Jung*. Cambridge, MA: Harvard University Press.

McLynn, Frank (1996). *Carl Gustav Jung*. New York: St. Martin's.

Noth, Isabelle (2015). "Beyond Freud and Jung": Sabina Spielrein's contribution to child psychoanalysis and developmental psychology. *Pastoral Psychology, 64* (2): 279–286.

Nunberg, Herbert and Federn, Ernst (Eds.) (1974). *Minutes of the Vienna Psychoanalytic Society, 1906–1938*, Vol. 3. M. Nunberg (Trans.). New York: International Universities Press.

Richebächer, Sabine (2003). "In league with the devil, and yet you fear fire?" Sabina Spielrein and C. G. Jung: A suppressed scandal from the early days of psychoanalysis. B. Wharton (Trans.). In C. Covington and B. Wharton (Eds.), *Sabina Spielrein: Forgotten pioneer of psychoanalysis* (pp. 227–249). New York: Brunner-Routledge.

Richebächer, Sabine (2008). *Eine fast grausame Liebe zur Wissenschaft*. Munich: BTB.

Rudnytsky, Peter (2002). *Reading psychoanalysis: Freud, Rank, Ferenczi, Groddeck*. Ithaca, NY: Cornell University Press.

Spielrein, Sabina (1911). Über den psychologischen Inhalt eines Falles von Schizophrenie (Dementia Praecox) ("On the psychological content of a case of schizophrenia"). *Jahrbuch für Psychoanalytische und Psychopathologische Forschungen, 3*: 329–400.

Spielrein, Sabina (1912). Die Destruktion als Ursache des Werdens. *Jahrbuch für Psychoanalytische und Psychopathologische Forschungen, 4*: 465–503.

Spielrein, Sabina (1913). Beiträge zur Kenntnis der kindlichen Seele ("Contributions to an understanding of the child's mind"). *Zentralblatt für Psychoanalyse, 3*: 57–72.

Spielrein, Sabina (1994). Destruction as the cause of coming into being. K. McCormick, (Trans.). *Journal of Analytical Psychology, 39*: 155–186. (Orig. German publ. 1912.) Full text online at www.arizonapsychoanalyticsociety.com/downloads/sabrina.pdf. Accessed February 12, 2014.

Spielrein, Sabina (1995). Destruction as a cause of becoming. S. K. Witt (Trans.). *Psychoanalysis and Contemporary Thought, 18*: 85–118. (Orig. German publ. 1912.) Online at www.pep-web.org/document.php?id=pct.018.0085a&type=hitlist&num=3&query=z

one1%2Cparagraphs%7Czone2%2Cparagraphs%7Cauthor%2CSpielrein%7Cviewperi
od%2Cweek%7Csort%2Cauthor%2Ca#hit1. Accessed September 22, 2015.

Spielrein, Sabina (2002). *Sabina Spielrein: Sämtliche Schriften*, 2nd ed. Foreword by
L. Lütkehaus. T. Hensch (Ed.). Gießen: Psychosozial-Verlag/Edition Kore. (Orig. publ.
1987.)

U.S. Holocaust Museum (n.d.). Pogroms. *Holocaust Encyclopedia*. Online at www.
ushmm.org/wlc/en/article.php?ModuleId=10005183. Accessed April 20, 2017.

Westerink, Hans (2014). Response to Pamela Cooper-White, Beyond A Dangerous
Method: Sabina Spielrein and the "death instinct," Fulbright lecture presented at the
Sigmund Freud Museum, Vienna, January 17.

Wharton, Barbara (Trans.) (2015a). The letters of C. G. Jung to Sabina Spielrein. In
Coline Covington and Barbara Wharton (Eds.), *Sabina Spielrein: Forgotten pioneer of
Psychoanalysis* (pp. 30–56), 2nd ed. New York: Brunner-Routledge.

Wharton, Barbara (Trans.) (2015b). Burghölzli Hospital Records of Sabina Spielrein. In
Coline Covington and Barbara Wharton (Eds.), *Sabina Spielrein: Forgotten pioneer of
Psychoanalysis* (pp. 57–82), 2nd ed. New York: Brunner-Routledge.

Part III

The shadow of antisemitism

Chapter 7

"Father, don't you see I'm burning?"

Antisemitism as total context

A father lies sleeping, weighed down by grief. After a sickbed vigil lasting many days, his beloved young son has died, and his body is laid out in the next room. Having hired an older man to watch over the boy, the father has allowed himself to lie down and rest, leaving the door ajar. He has fallen asleep, and dreams an uncanny dream: his boy is alive, and is tugging him by the arm. The boy whispers urgently, desolately, "Father, don't you see I'm burning?" The father startles awake to see a bright light flickering in the doorway. He runs to the adjacent room to find that one of the candles set up next to his son's body has fallen, burning one of the arms. The old watchman has fallen asleep.

This poignant story of a bereaved father's dream introduces Chapter 7 of Freud's *Interpretation of Dreams*, entitled "The Psychology of the Dream-Processes."[1] The telling of this dream is peculiar in a number of aspects. We know nothing of the child's illness, or whether the child's reproach in the dream represents an element of guilt in the father's grief. We know nothing of the mother, who seems entirely absent. The dream has clear religious overtones, but these are ignored except as bare facts of the story. The dream is not told by the dreamer himself, but by "a woman patient who had heard it in a lecture," and then, strangely enough, "proceeded to 're-dream' it … so that she might express agreement with it on one particular point." (That point is never elucidated in Freud's re-telling.) So the dream appears as a fourth-hand dream, having traveled from original dreamer, to lecturer, to patient, and on again to Freud. The fact that Freud lifts up this particular dream for a public readership, via the process of writing (mirroring the prior lecturer's use of it), gives it a heightened significance and perhaps invites an even wider social interpretation. I will return to this point at the end of this chapter.

Freud agrees with his patient, who agreed with the lecturer, that the father was awakened by the brightness of the light through the open door,[2] and that perhaps he had already been alert even while asleep due to a suspicion that the watchman was not fully competent. Freud adds the likelihood that the words the boy spoke in the dream must also have been spoken while he was still alive— perhaps he had said he was burning with fever; perhaps the rebuke "Father, don't you see?" had been spoken another time during "some other highly emotional situation of which we are in ignorance."[3] Going deeper, then, Freud finally asks why the father did not awaken even sooner, "when the most rapid possible awakening was called for." Here, Freud finds further proof of his thesis in the *Interpretation of Dreams*, that at a deeper unconscious level, dreams represent a wish fulfillment. The longer the father remains asleep, even for an additional moment, the longer he is able to believe his son is still alive. Freud sums up this desire in words that seem to join in the felt reality of the dream itself: "If the father had woken up first and then made the inference that led him to go into the next room, he would, as it were, have shortened his child's life by that moment of time."[4]

Freud uses the dream to describe how there is an entirely different psychical reality in dreams from that of waking consciousness. There is no "what if" or "if only," as in a waking wish or daydream—only a continual here and now. And what would be expressed as a thought in conscious life, is now expressed as a sensory experience. So the father does not *wonder* if the child's body is burning in the adjacent room—the child *is* burning, and he experiences this as a physical tug on his arm and a whisper in his ear. It is through this description of the alternate dream reality that Freud introduces his "topographical model" of conscious (waking thought), preconscious (that which is thinkable but not yet thought), and unconscious (that which is not yet verbally formulated, or even accessible to cognitive reflection—a different kind of "knowledge" that is expressed in imagery and sensory impressions).[5] So dreams become the "royal road to the unconscious,"[6] because in dreams, we are in that imagistic realm of immediate sensory experience—driven by repressed desires, and disguised in layers of symbolism (in order to preserve sleep undisturbed). Further, there is always a level of depth beyond which no further interpretation can be made. In one of his most enigmatic statements, Freud writes, "There is at least one spot in every dream at which it is unplumbable—a navel, as it were, that is its point of contact with the unknown."[7]

The mysterious figure of the watchman is perhaps a clue to further layers of meaning in this dream specimen. The watchman is hired, not a member of the family. He sits "beside the body murmuring prayers."[8] The scene suggests that the family is Jewish, and the older man is performing the required role of the *Shomer* (a guard, usually not a family member) who accompanies the body from death until burial, and recites psalms continually during the vigil. This is usually arranged by a *chevra kadisha* (burial society—literally, a "holy group") who according to Jewish law purify and shroud the body, and protect it from any form of desecration (intentional or accidental) until the burial. This scene is a good example of how, in analyst Jill Salberg's words, many of Freud's vignettes transparently involved Jewish customs and speech—"hidden in plain sight"—half-repressed, half disguised, just enough that Gentile readers would not be aware of their context.[9]

The dream of the burning child is "uncanny," in Freud's own sense of the word[10]—the return of the repressed, a chilling awareness of something—an affect-laden half-memory or intuition of a long-ago experience or desire once hidden away in the unconscious as intolerable, yet still able to rise up unbidden and haunt one's dreams and unguarded moments of twilight consciousness. This nightmarish "uncanny" is the horror we have always, already known but banished from our minds. *What is being repressed here?* The death of one child? Memories of conflictual aspects of a particular father–son relationship? Is the burning child only one grieving man's spiritual devastation, or could it also be a cultural *revenant*—a premonitory image of violence and desecration beneath the surface of Vienna's glittering balls and salons?

The uncanny was everywhere and nowhere in fin-de-siècle Vienna. Young girls dressed in virginal white made their society debuts at the vertiginous January waltzes while Schnitzler's *süsse Mädeln*[11] survived by entertaining the same girls' fathers in back-street apartments. Government positions and aristocratic titles were bestowed in back-room deals. Sex and power, exploitation and violence, were denied and hidden, like the nude bodies Gustav Klimt painted and then covered with ornate geometric designs. The repressed in Vienna was an open secret. And beneath the mannered *Gemütlichkeit* that made everyone appear to be an aristocrat, Jews became the repository for Gentile Austrians' projections of their own envy, greed, and sexual hunger. Vienna was burning from the inside with the fever of its own hysterical contradictions.

Antisemitism

The theme of antisemitism emerged in my research not just as one theme among many, but as the *over-arching context and reality*—even when not spoken about at all—without which none of the early analysts' writings about religion can be fully understood or evaluated. As noted in Chapter 2, the theme of antisemitism itself only rarely appears in the Society's discussions, and only in reference to neurotic patients.[12] Given the wide range of other topics there is no evidence that Rank bowdlerized the minutes of these in-group conversations. Yet antisemitism does present itself more subliminally and more pervasively in the surrounding history and culture than a surface reading of the documents reveals.

The term *antisemitism* itself requires some unpacking. It is fundamentally understood as "a form of prejudice based on hatred towards, contempt for and irrational beliefs about Jews and Jewish influence."[13] Its historical roots go back to the division between Christianity and Judaism, and even earlier.[14] But prejudice, or even subjective hatred, does not account for the complexity of political, cultural, religious, and ethnic hostilities that have simmered in the Christianized nations of the west for two millennia, nor the ways in which their overt expression has waxed and waned over decades and centuries, and across different geographical landscapes.

Three common approaches to defining antisemitism, as Beller points out,[15] are Sander Gilman's "discursive methodology"[16] by which antisemitism is examined as a dominant discourse; the pathological metaphors for antisemitism as "madness," a "virus," or "disease"[17]; and Zygmunt Bauman's opposite approach of viewing antisemitism (at least in light of the Holocaust) as a product of Enlightenment rationalism, an extreme version of an instrumental "science" that expedited the shift from cultural hatred to the invention of racialized hierarchies, and from sporadic violence to a highly technologized genocide on an unprecedented scale.[18] In my view, a combination of Gilman's and Bauman's analyses is most compelling in relation to Freud's Vienna and the radical surge of antisemitism from 1897 on. This surge entailed a confluence of ethnic animosities fueled by ancient religious schisms and superstitious hysterias; displacement of transgressive sexual desires; economic upheavals in the wake of industrialization and toxic envy as wealth changed hands; and in the midst of war, disease, poverty, the consolidation of right-wing nationalist power using an old familiar scapegoat.

In addition, what makes Bauman's view so compelling is his recognition of the ways in which hatred of the Jews was so normalized, rationalized, technologized, and institutionalized—echoing Hannah Arendt's description of the bureaucracy of the Nazi murder machine as the "banality of evil."[19] Bauman writes:

> The unspoken terror permeating our collective memory of the Holocaust (and more than contingently related to the overwhelming desire not to look the memory in its face) is the gnawing suspicion that the Holocaust could be more than an aberration, more than a deviation from an otherwise straight path of progress, more than a cancerous growth on the otherwise healthy body of the civilized society; that, in short, the Holocaust was not an antithesis of modern civilization and everything (or so we like to think) it stands for. We suspect (even if we refuse to admit it) that the Holocaust could merely have uncovered another face of the same modern society whose other, more familiar face we so admire. And that the two faces are perfectly comfortably attached to the same body. What we perhaps fear most, is that each of the two faces can no more exist without the other than can the two sides of a coin.[20]

All of these interpretations of antisemitism, of course, beg the question regarding the *object* of this hatred: *who is a Jew?*[21] While antisemitism and anti-Judaism have been recorded from ancient Hellenistic and biblical periods,[22] it is Christian antisemitism, with its roots in the division between Christians and Jews, that characterized the Austrians' hostility. This division began to occur in the first centuries BCE, but as Daniel Boyarin has written,

> For at least the first three centuries of their common lives, Judaism in all of its forms and Christianity in all of its forms were part of one complex religious family, twins in a womb, contending with each other for identity and precedence, but sharing with each other the same spiritual food.[23]

The original followers of Jesus were, like Jesus himself, Jews, and as Boyarin argues, there were many Jewish sects, with a blurring of boundaries and identities for much longer than the traditional narrative in each religion has surmised. By the fourth century, however, imperial enforcement of Christianity as the established religion pushed both groups toward greater division and mutual suspicion.[24] By the fifth century, in response to the Christian Church's doctrine of "the universal brotherhood of Jesus Christ, the Rabbis established genealogy (as opposed to belief or practice) as the primary definition of Jewishness."[25] Jews at this time came to identify themselves by descent as well as belief and custom, just as Christians were rejecting descent and custom as defining characteristics in favor of doctrine and sacramental practices.

Although perhaps a fine line by some definitions, the ensuing religious, ethnic, and cultural hatred of Jews that followed this division for centuries did not entirely constitute racism per se, because the very notion of *racial* taxonomy was not introduced until the nineteenth century as a systematic "scientific" anthropology. Categories remained somewhat fluid through the mid-nineteenth century. Even the antisemitic Mayor Lueger could declare for reasons of political expediency, "*Wer ein Jud' ist, bestimme ich*" ("I decide who is a Jew").[26] But by the turn of the twentieth century in central Europe, pseudoscientific racial hierarchies were accepted as universal truths,[27] and antisemitism had shifted from a (sometimes deadly) ethnic, cultural, and religious hatred, toward a full-blown and eventually genocidal racism.

Eliza Slavet has argued against the post-Holocaust inclination to shun racial interpretations of Jewishness and antisemitism, making the case that the ways in which antisemitism operated by the twentieth century was (and is) indeed racism, and that the social construction of racial identity tends to reproduce what it indoctrinates.[28] She writes, "Rather than repressing the racial elements of Jewish definition, Freud suggests that a vigilant scrutiny of these elements is crucial if there is to be any hope of controlling these 'peculiar' forces rather than being controlled by them."[29] Following Boyarin,[30] Geller,[31] Gilman,[32] and others, she points out that Jewishness, along with misogyny and homophobia as they were intertwined at the turn of the twentieth century, generated a racial representation of Jewishness and Judaism that could give rise "to *both* ethnic pride and racial hatred."[33] "[R]ather than focusing on only the racial, genealogical, and bodily elements of Jewish identity or on the intellectual and abstract concepts of Judaism, Freud's work compels us to explore the relationship between the two."[34] In 1930, Freud himself declared in the preface to the Hebrew translation of *Totem and Taboo* that if a secular Jew were asked "what is left to you that is Jewish? he would reply, 'A very great deal, and probably its very essence (*Hauptsache*)'."[35]

While this view has strong historical warrant in the unfolding of events in the twentieth century, and even in some of the more late nineteenth-century racialized aspects of Freud's thinking and that of his Viennese followers, there is a danger in conflating the notion of race entirely with ethnic heritage or genealogy. The self-definition of Jews in Freud's time—while bending toward essentialism—nevertheless embraced a complexity of cultural and ethnic inheritances, founded in ancient times as a tribe with distinctive religious beliefs and practices, but also, since modernity, separable as a secular but genealogical identity. Freud and his followers used the various vocabularies of race, ethnicity, and cultural history ambiguously—seemingly interchangeably, but with considerable slippage among the various concepts.

In keeping with this ambiguity—because of its inherent complexity—I will follow Beller's interpretation of "who was a Jew in Vienna at the turn of the century?"[36] Beller carefully parses the competing merits of identifying Jewishness by descent (even after conversion), by subjective identity, by inherited religious and cultural traditions, or by having a worldview influenced by the status of being assimilated.[37] Beller argues that being a "product of the process of the historical event of the assimilation" in itself constituted a worldview distinct from Gentiles who did not need to assimilate in order to participate in the dominant culture. Beller concludes that a good approach to the history of the Jews in Austria, without relying on narrow and problematic pseudo-biological forms of racial identification, must be both complex and contextual: "a dynamic historical process," seen in terms of "a network of family resemblances, association by common historical origin rather than by being part of some impossible metaphysical construction."[38]

This is not to say that antisemitism did not—or does not now—*function* in the world as racism does—because race, even as a social construct, creates and perpetuates real and deadly social effects. At the same time, the construct of race itself must be continually interrogated as an always potentially genocidal fabrication—not founded in real science (although disguised as such), but in structures of social and political power and dominance. While oppressions cannot be conflated, and there are many differences between contemporary American racism and antisemitism, it is notable that skin color prejudice was also implicated in twentieth-century German and Austrian antisemitism. Jews were called "*Schwarzen*" and "*Kaffers*" ("Blacks" and "N–gers"), and numerous descriptions in both popular and scientific literature referred to Jewish skin as dark, swarthy, diseased, "filthy," "stinking," perverted, and ugly.[39]

This leads to one more aspect of antisemitism as prejudice and hatred. As ingrained as these are in western culture—internalized by both Jews and non-Jews as all racist and ethnic stereotypes are—prejudice and hatred are not enough in and of themselves to perpetuate systematic institutional discrimination, much less industrialized genocide. The wisdom of the American Civil Rights movement, that racism = prejudice + power, helps make the cognitive leap from personal and cultural loathing (as bad as that can be) to the systematic dispossession, expulsion, and finally annihilation that constituted Hitler's "final solution" to the euphemistic "Jewish problem." The Vienna analysts, nearly all of whom were Jewish, had first experienced antisemitism as prejudice per se, which could perhaps be dismissed as ignorance, or denied psychologically as a case of mistaken identity—confusing them with the insular *Ostjuden* from whose religious and cultural orthodoxy they had distanced themselves. But as liberal reforms were rolled back and prejudice became increasingly alloyed with military and political power with the rise of the Christian Socialists in Austria, antisemitism increasingly generated the violence that characterizes all racism.

These more dramatic incidents of violence (both physical and economic) were harder to ignore—or forgive—and they impacted the educated classes as much as the Yiddish-speaking new immigrants. Klein documents how as Jewish immigrants' numbers increased in *Gymnasien* and in the university, racially motivated slurs and physical attacks grew in intensity, and professional and economic doors closed.[40] Edmund Engelman, who photographed Berggasse 19 for posterity before the Freud family's flight to England, wrote,

> During my years as a student, 1926–31, [the *Technische Hochschule*] was a center of intense, often violent, conservative "pan-German" political activities. Jews and other "aliens" walked carefully on campus, pitifully intent on not "causing trouble"—yet Jewish students were regularly beaten up by gangs from the nationalistic fraternities. The police, meanwhile, stood off-campus, scrupulously avoiding interference with the traditional "academic freedom" that allowed the university to pretend to be a state unto itself.[41]

In his memoirs Stekel also recorded several confrontations with antisemitism during his university days.[42] Freud's son Martin reported being wounded by a knife in an antisemitic brawl. That evening at dinner, Freud "threw me a sympathetic glance," and Pfister, who happened to be a guest that same evening,

> got up and approached me to shake hands warmly, congratulating me on being wounded in so just and noble a cause. This sympathy and kindliness from a dignified leader of the Christian Church heartened me considerably, making me feel less like a battered ruffian.[43]

In a letter to Romain Rolland, Freud recalled his disillusionment with "love extended to all mankind," following his "sobering experiences as a Jew in Vienna."[44] Peter Gay observed, "Vienna, never in reality the city of operettas and flirtations, was, even in Freud's time, a city of ugly rehearsals; it made Freud the Jew suffer even more because he was a Jew than because he was Freud."[45] As Gay trenchantly described,

> In Vienna, anti-Semitism was more than the confused broodings of psychopaths; it pervaded and poisoned student organizations, university politics, social relationships, medical opinions. To be the destroyer of human illusions, as Freud was by intention and by results, was to make oneself into a special target of the anti-Semite.[46]

Yet within the upwardly mobile Jewish bourgeoisie—not to mention the very wealthy, whose palaces and grand ornate houses lined the *Ringstrasse*—the future seemed for a time not only (relatively) safe but bright.[47] Denial of catastrophe abounded. The liberal newspaper most widely read by affluent Jews, the *Neue Freie Presse*, "tended not to comment on anti-Semitic outrages, despite (or perhaps, because of) having Jewish editors."[48] Citing Arendt, Michael Billig points out that most Jews at the time continued in denial and "self-deception,"[49] partly due to their precarious position in society, but also imagining that the current wave of antisemitism would pass over—as it had in the past. Martin Freud recalled no discussions of antisemitism in the Freud home, nor any overt experiences of discrimination as a young child.[50]

Martin recalled how the family judged Freud's sister Adolphine ("Dolfi") to be "somewhat unusual and subjective to impressions, or forebodings, of coming disasters which we thought ridiculous or even a little silly."[51] He recalled one day when Dolfi believed she heard a man on the street call her "a dirty stinking Jewess and said it was time we were all killed."[52] Decades later, Martin observed,

> It seems strange that while none of us—professors, lawyers, and people of education had any idea of the tragedy which would destroy the children of the Jewish race, a lovable but rather silly old maid foresaw, or appeared to foresee, that future. Dolfi herself died of starvation in the Jewish ghetto in Theresienstadt.[53]

Martin also recalled the family's frequent visits to his grandmother until her death in 1930, describing Amalie Freud—despite her intellectual, rabbinic heritage—as having all the embarrassing traits of the Galician Jews, "a peculiar race" who "had little grace and no manners; and their women were certainly not what we should call ladies."[54] Similarly, his maternal grandmother Emmeline's orthodox Jewish observances and "melodious" sung prayers when visiting them on the Sabbath "seemed alien to us children who had been brought up without any instruction in Jewish ritual."[55]

Within the mostly Jewish professional circles in which they traveled, Freud and his followers could thus believe that the Austrian Nazi Party was simply a fringe group of uneducated extremists, and not a danger to them personally. "From the perspective of those times, too clear a gaze at the public irrationality could itself seem irrational."[56] In the recovery from World War I, successful Jews were the leaders in business and finance, art and culture. Yet their very success was fueling resentment among the Gentiles, whose financial ruin after World War I had left them in poverty and humiliation, and eager for a scapegoat. Even at the height of the Jewish professionals' success between the world wars, antisemitism was everywhere in the air that all Austrians breathed. Antisemitism had been a miasma covering Vienna for its entire history, and it permeated the German culture that many Viennese—both Christian and Jewish—emulated and aspired to join.

A brief history of Jews in Vienna

Vienna had long been a place of immigration and (ambiguous) refuge for Jews going back to the early middle ages when Austria was a part of Bavaria under the Holy Roman Empire. From earliest times, Jews were associated with finance, trade, and urban life, and were simultaneously the object of both envy and derision by Gentiles and the peasant class. The first recorded mention of Jews in Austria was an ordinance restraining Jewish commerce under the Carolingian king Louis the Child (r. 899–911). Although forbidden to work in many occupations, Jews, because of Christian usury laws, were recruited as tax collectors and money lenders—a dubious privilege that perpetuated hostility against them throughout medieval Europe.

The next documented mention of a Jew, with the traditional name of "Shlom" or "Shlomo" (Freud's own middle name), appears almost three centuries later in connection with his appointment as the *super officium monetae* under the Babenberg Duke of Austria, Leopold V. The Jewish community in Vienna, with Shlom's financial help,[57] built its first synagogue in 1204. The Babenberg rulers promoted tolerance toward the Jews, with official decrees against killing, assaulting, or forcing Jews to convert to Christianity.[58] Many Jews settled in Vienna as a place of relative safety and opportunity.

The thirteenth century was not one of good fortune for long, however. There were numerous antisemitic protests, and Pope Innocent III decreed that every adult Jew wear a distinctive yellow badge—the same as one worn by prostitutes.[59] When Emperor Rudolf I, the first Habsburg ruler and a member of the Ecclesiastical Christian Synod, annexed Austria to Germany in 1267, he outdid the Pope in humiliating Jews by ordering them to wear a *pileum cornutum*—a pointed hat as a sign of shame.[60] Rabbi Earl Grollman writes,

> As a consequence of the Vienna Church synod in 1267, masses of people were encouraged by the Emperor to incite bloodshed and massacres. The Jew was pelted and stoned, spat upon and cursed. Many of the synagogue laments which are preserved in the liturgy commemorate the elegy of this period.[61]

Throughout the period of the Renaissance, Jews were grudgingly tolerated for their expertise in banking and commerce. "Court Jews" were employed by the aristocracy to handle their finances, and taxed excessively for the privilege. In an unusual gesture of benevolence, in 1570, Rudolf II conferred the first title of nobility on Jacob Bassevi, the Official Receiver of Taxes, and protected the Jews from mercenaries during the Thirty Years' War.[62] However, Rudolf subsequently turned against the Jews, ejecting them from Austria with the support of the Church.[63]

In the religious arena, the official Catholic position remained resolutely antisemitic. The Reformation introduced the possibility of greater tolerance, as

Luther early on chided the Church for treating the Jews "like dogs."[64] However, even before Protestantism became established among the German princes, he turned against the Jews, aligning himself with a theological position that because of their "persistence to remain in their guilty ways [i.e., in denial of Christ], their head is shattered; they no longer have a kingdom, a government, a priesthood."[65] The common epithet of Jews as "Christ killers," who deserved eternal punishment, was endemic throughout Europe from the middle ages forward into the twentieth century. God's alleged wrath against the Jews was preached from both Catholic and Protestant pulpits.

The growth in importance of synagogues as gathering places for worship and study, and of a separate way of life as God's chosen people, was in large measure a response of the Jewish community in Vienna and elsewhere to persecution and forced ghettoization. Jews, including Freud himself, maintained a self-understanding of inherited difference (genealogical as well as religious) and even superiority, in their dedication to study and faithfulness to God under oppression. In Vienna a system of rabbinical ordination began in the sixteenth century, along with the publication in 1555 of a widely observed book on Jewish Law, the *Schulchan Aruch*.[66] But the study of Torah was considered the highest vocation for all men, not only the rabbis.

On a much more mundane level, Jewish humor was also a refuge from the grim realities of perpetual persecution[67] and an outlet for otherwise forbidden aggression—as both Freud[68] and Reik[69] found serious enough to analyze at length. Centuries later, humor is still used as both barb and psychic defense: In the words of the poet and literary critic Robert Schindel (whose life spanned most of the twentieth century in Vienna), "Death is omnipresent in Vienna, it is the intoxicated father of Viennese laughter.... You tell a joke and the past comes back."[70]

By the Baroque era, central Europe was caught up in the devastations of the Thirty Years' War (1618–48). Initially a conflict between the Protestant princes of northern Germany and the Holy Roman Emperor Ferdinand II, who upon his accession to the throne attempted to impose Catholicism throughout Europe, the war eventually drew in all the major powers of Europe. The 1648 Peace of Westphalia severely limited Habsburg power, and the war left millions dead (as many as half the men in many areas). The resulting poverty exacerbated the spread of plague. Warfare among Christian sects rose among Catholics, Lutherans, and Calvinists along artificially drawn territorial lines.[71] Internecine paranoia devolved into a resurgence of (literal) witch hunting and antisemitism.

In the midst of these turbulent decades, the Jewish community of Vienna under the leadership of Rabbi Yom-Tov Lipmann Heller chose separatism as a positive strategy rather than a condition of repression, and petitioned Ferdinand II in 1624 for a district where they could live together in peace. This *Unterer Werd* ("lower field" or "lower island"), situated between the Danube Canal and the Danube River, was carved out between two Catholic monasteries and an imperial hunting ground (partially preserved since 1766 as the famous park, the *Prater*, where 150 years later Freud enjoyed taking a stroll).[72]

The peace of the district was short-lived. Emperor Leopold I, under pressure from his magistrates and his Spanish Catholic queen,[73] expelled the Jews from Vienna in a series of decrees from 1669 to 1671, beginning by "cleansing" the city of the poorest among them, then the more wealthy, until finally all were banned throughout Lower Austria.[74] He renamed the district "Leopoldstadt," destroyed the main synagogue, and had an ornate church built on the same site in 1670 in his name ("Leopoldskirche").[75] Jewish homes and land in the area were confiscated and converted into a parsonage and Catholic cemetery, both consecrated in 1671. Institutional and governmental discrimination continued unabated throughout the eighteenth century. The empress Maria Theresa agitated to expel the Jews from Prague in 1744.[76] The Catholic Church for its part beatified a Tyrolean boy, Andreas of Rinn, the supposed victim of a fabricated Jewish ritual murder.[77]

Finally, in 1781, Emperor Josef II issued the Edict of Toleration ushering in a new era of relative peace for Jews in Austria. He abolished disproportionate taxation, the yellow badge, and former restrictions on choice of domicile and schools. But he also decreed that as equal citizens, all Austrians must learn German as the language of the realm. Devoted to Enlightenment-era reason and "philosophical morality"[78] more than religious faith, Josef offered a vision of liberation that held both promise and peril to the Jews of Austria: assimilate and earn worldly success in the metropolitan world of Vienna with its high education and culture—but at the price of renouncing Jewish separatism and a community and familial life centered around religious and cultural traditions. Although some urban Jews had already begun the road to assimilation as early as the 1670s,[79] this historical moment was the statutory beginning of the divide between those who aspired to German cultural status versus those who by birth or immigration from the eastern provinces remained more isolated in their Yiddish language, culture, and Orthodox faith.

Leopoldstadt retained the emperor's name[80] but did not forget its Jewish history, and again became a magnet for Jewish immigration in the nineteenth century (nicknamed the *Mazzesinsel*—"Matzoh Island").[81] As such, it was home to the largest concentration of Orthodox and Chassidic Jews, who brought their religious practices with them from the ghettoes in Russia and the eastern regions of the Habsburg realm. Leopoldstadt was the first home to the parents of Freud and many of the first generation of psychoanalysts (see Chapter 1). Earl Grollman, in his comprehensive book on Judaism in Freud's world, notes that the fathers of both Freud and Breuer were from Chassidic families.[82] David Bakan argues that Chassidism was foundational for Freud's theorizing.[83] The largest synagogue in Vienna, an imposing structure with ornate Baroque columns and windows, was built there over the years 1854–58.[84]

In the early nineteenth century, the situation began to improve again for the Jewish communities of Vienna, in spite of the reactionary attitude of Leopold's successor Franz II, crowned in 1792.[85] The Congress of Vienna in 1815 celebrated Vienna's modern outlook. Franz's son, the Emperor Ferdinand I (r. 1835–48) extended liberal reforms. Modernity sounded a siren call to many Jews, for whom education was already a central value, and hundreds sent their sons and daughters across the Canal to build free bourgeois Jewish enclaves in such neighborhoods as the 9th district, home to Freud and the majority of his Viennese patients. A few elite Jewish families established great banking houses; the Rothschilds were made barons, forming a "second nobility" just below the Habsburg aristocracy.[86] For a brief period, united by an anti-French nationalist sentiment, members of the high court and the upper Jewish bourgeoisie mingled in society and cultivated the arts; Fanny Arnstein's salon was the toast of Vienna.[87]

The threat of persecution, however, was always present—represented most visibly in the person of Prince Klemens von Metternich,[88] the Austrian foreign minister from 1809 to 1821 under Franz II, and Chancellor from 1821 to 1848 under both Franz and Ferdinand. As the final act of the Congress of Vienna in 1815, a "Holy Alliance" was signed by Austria, Prussia, and Russia.[89] This act was intended to enhance stability and to reassert the divine right of monarchs (an anti-revolutionary move) and, most relevant for Jewish life, to enforce Christianity as the established religion among the nations of the treaty. But stability was not achieved. The industrial revolution gained ground in Prussia and turned Prussian loyalties away from the less industrialized Austria, toward Germany. Ottoman wars to the east, and ethnic-nationalist movements for independence in eastern and central Europe, threatened Austria on multiple borders. A nationalist movement for Czech independence was fueling antisemitic hatred in the regions of Moravia and Bohemia.[90] The year 1848 saw both the Italian independence movement and the Hungarian revolt against Habsburg rule. The first wave of nineteenth-century pogroms began[91]—especially in eastern Europe. This often drove Jews to seek refuge in Vienna and other more hospitable cities to the west. In the years 1846 to 1850 alone, the Jewish population of Vienna grew from 3,739 to 14,000.[92]

A coalition of poor workers, liberals, and radical student movements in Vienna arose in reaction to the Metternich era throughout the 1820s and 1830s, culminating in Austria's own Revolution of 1848. Jews and Christians fought together for social reform, and drove Metternich out of Austria. A newly formed government granted more liberal rights to the Jews. Attracted by new freedoms and the promise of a "German" university education, the Jewish population of Vienna swelled from less than 2 percent in 1857 to 12 percent in 1890.[93] Jews gravitated toward districts where other Jews had preceded them, concentrating in the fairly close 1st (the old *innere Stadt*), 2nd (Leopoldstadt), and 9th (*Alsergrund*, the neighborhood of Freud, the Adlers, the Bauers, and Theodor Herzl).[94]

The liberal reforms of 1848 were extremely short-lived. The seat of constitutional government, Vienna, was liberal at the mid-century point, but most of the surrounding country was not. Frightened by the popular push for democracy, Ferdinand stirred up antisemitic sentiment by blaming the Revolution on the Jews. His successor Franz Josef I, to whom Ferdinand abdicated following the Revolution, continued this strategy. He put down the insurrection decisively in

1849 with the help of the Russian Czar, and in 1851 rescinded any rights granted the Jews during the period of liberalization.[95] Austria reasserted its sovereignty and independence from Germany, and a Concordat was passed in 1855 reinstating the close relationship between the Habsburg Empire and the Pope. Jews once again found their lives severely restricted. Some freedoms of movement and commerce could not be rolled back, however, because the economy had become dependent on Jewish bankers and industrialists.[96]

Finally, in 1861, recognizing that revolution and ethnic-nationalist rebellion were in the air throughout Europe, a new constitution was adopted under the reign of Emperor Franz Josef I, known as the "February Patent." A bicameral Parliament was formed, but its members were not elected democratically. The choice of Pallas Athena—a Greek goddess—as the gilded statue gracing the new Parliament building subtly represented the continuing reign of a quasi-democratic institution under a divinely appointed benevolent despot—rather than a true democracy, as might have been symbolized by one of the great orators of the Roman forum or even a statue of Liberty.[97] Nevertheless, this decree signaled the beginning of another period of relative liberalism, strengthened by a new constitution in 1867 that restored religious freedom and equal rights to education, property, and livelihood to all Austrians. By 1869 the Jewish population of Vienna had swelled to over 40,000,[98] and Viennese Jews entered into a "golden age" of creativity, commerce, and culture.[99]

Envisioning what in his mind would be a modern city to rival the great capitals of Europe, Franz Josef had the medieval *Bastei* (ramparts) torn down to make way for his signature building project, the *Ringstrasse*, encircling the old city. Built in the thirteenth century and fortified in the sixteenth and seventeenth centuries against Turkish sieges, ramparts were no longer needed by the nineteenth century, and had become an impediment to expansion into the unused *glacis* (moat-like meadowlands) surrounding the old city. Construction began on numerous massive buildings for government and culture in the *historische Stil*: some neo-Gothic (the *Rathaus*, city hall, representing the medieval city-state); some Baroque (the *Statsoper* and *Burgtheater*, representing empire and culture); and some Neo-classical (Parliament). All were ornate, encrusted with gold, and topped with winged statuary representing the unity of the enlightened city with its Greco-Roman gods. In Beller's words,

> The history of the Ringstrasse symbolized the fate of German liberalism's Vienna. It had started as a symbol of liberation and modernization. Vienna was freed from the medieval straitjacket of her city walls, just as the architects were freed from the uniformity imposed by the authorities. The resulting menagerie of historicist styles was seen as progressive ... well on the way to outshining Paris.[100]

It would, however, turn out to be the last grand gesture of Habsburg power, as the buildings of the Ring came to be recognized by some, like the architect Adolf

Loos, as a Potemkin Village.[101] The stock market crash of May 1873 set in motion a renewed spate of anti-Jewish scapegoating among the Gentile middle and working classes, who blamed the Jews for the economic crisis and turned away from liberalism in large numbers.

But the Ring's grandeur was irresistible. Although the construction lasted for five decades, filling the air with choking dust, it represented the fortress city's opening to the modern world, and thereby held out hope for a lasting era of emancipation "from the medieval walls of the ghetto."[102] Rich Jews (e.g., Todesco, Epstein, and the Ephrussi family described in Edmund de Waal's bestselling memoir *The Hare with Amber Eyes*[103]) built their *palais* on the Ring alongside those of the lesser Habsburg nobility, and threw them-selves into the glittering cultural life of the salon, the opera house, and the famous Viennese *Ballsaison*. At the turn of the century in 1899, the Jewish population was at its peak of almost 100,000 persons (12 percent of the Vien-nese population).[104]

At the same time,

> [i]n contrast to the splendor of the Ringstrasse façades, social problems and increasing political radicalization emerged as a concomitant to the massive economic and social changes in Vienna in the late nineteenth century. The lower middle classes were the classic losers in this modernization process and were thus highly receptive to politically incited antisemitism, which did not stop at exploiting stereotypes such as the "poor ragged Ostjude," the "socialist Jewish firebrand," or the "capitalist Jewish banker."[105]

The Jewish bourgeoisie of the 9th district and the *Ringstrasse*—"this society of the capitalist middle class," in Beller's words—"was a largely Jewish phenom-enon, isolated and without native support of any substance, existing in a society hostile to its values."[106] Surrounded by Catholic officialdom, many Jews con-verted to Christianity (often choosing Protestantism over the dominant Catholic church)[107]—some to meet a requirement for professional jobs in government and education, and others in the hope of gaining greater acceptance among the Vien-nese middle class who (unlike in Paris and other European capitals) modeled their taste and behavior after the aristocracy.[108] Conversion did not guarantee social acceptance, however.[109] And the great majority of Jews did not convert.[110] A large proportion of assimilated Jews, regardless of formal religious affiliation, privately regarded themselves as secular, following Enlightenment principles of equality and individual freedom rather than religious laws and doctrine. As Dennis Klein notes, for Jews prior to 1880, this alignment with an ideal of the brotherhood of humanity transcended their own political and social self-interest:

> [T]he Jewish wish for integration is not reducible specifically to social needs. It was not even exclusively Jewish. Integration or universality was a moral ideology that exerted a powerful influence on nineteenth century

historical beliefs generally. The meaning of Jewish integration must be understood in both of the ways assimilated Jews of this period understood it: as a reconciliation of hostile social differences that would directly benefit Jews, and a unifying, universal, moral ideal that would benefit all humanity.[111]

Within Judaism itself, the Reform and Conservative movements sprang up as rationalist and historic denominations, separating themselves from Orthodoxy. Tensions among groups often arose within the same family, as in Freud's own—his father was a scholar of the Bible, but led a liberal household; his mother was raised an Orthodox Jew and spoke Yiddish all her life.[112] His wife Martha's grandfather, Isaac Bernays, fought for Orthodox Judaism in Hamburg, Germany, and banned the Reform prayer book.[113] Tension between fragile hopes for assimilation and constant awareness of historic persecution (however much repressed) characterized the prevailing Jewish attitude toward Judaism at the end of the nineteenth century.

The emancipation of the Jews further engendered antisemitic backlash. The old hate needed a modern "rational" iteration: "The racialized/scientific form [of antisemitism] made Jews a social and national group with unchanging characteristics that could delegitimize them and undermine their attempt at equality."[114] Dramatist Arthur Schnitzler recalled in his autobiography,

It was impossible, especially for a Jew in the public eye, to ignore the fact that he was a Jew, for the others did not, the Christians did not, and the Jews even less. One had the choice of being regarded as insensitive, pushy and arrogant, or hypersensitive, shy and paranoid. And even when one could control one's internal and external behavior to the point that one avoided appearing as either of these, it was quite impossible not to be affected. It was like asking someone to remain indifferent when he had received a local anesthetic but had to watch with his own eyes dirty knives scraping, cutting into his skin, until the blood ran.[115]

Jews thus carried the weight of being the dominant culture's "Other," including all the usual sexualization, exoticism, envy, fear, and hatred that the "Other" invokes in homogenous cultural groups. Daniel Boyarin noted that the stereotype of the " 'Yeshiva-Bokhur,' a young unmarried man devoting himself to the study of Torah and Talmud,"[116] represented a "counter type to 'manliness' " and "an assertive historical product of Jewish culture"[117] that remained an ideal within many Jewish communities in the twentieth century; however, it also lent itself to an intersectionality of misogyny, homophobia, and antisemitism. Grollman wrote, "The Jew in Austria was the symbolic representation of such antithetical concepts as love and hate, dominance and submission, over-sexuality and impotency, communism and capitalism."[118] Jews, as both beneficiaries and agitators for social reform, were the natural enemy of the conservative Catholic elite. The more Jews succeeded in their strategy of assimilation, the more antisemitism festered among those who feared a threat to the "traditional" Austrian way of life, which was a somewhat incongruous amalgam of pan-German aristocracy and rural peasant *Volkskultur*.

By the end of the nineteenth century, cultural "otherness" was reframed in terms of racial differences, with a clearly articulated hierarchy of "European" over "Jew." A French count, Joseph Arthur de Gobineau, coined the terms "Aryan" and "Semitic" in his *Essay on the Inequality of the Human Races*.[119] Gobineau's aim was to offer (supposedly) scientific proof of the superiority of the Aryan race. He validated antisemitism as a reflection of the natural order. In 1872, an echo of Gobineau's argument appeared in an Austrian weekly paper *Ausland* ("foreign lands") as follows:

> The Jews are not merely a different religious community but—and this is to us the most important factor—ethnically an altogether different race. The European feels instinctively that the Jew is a stranger who immigrated from Asia. The so-called prejudice is a natural sentiment. Civilization will over-come the antipathy against the Israelite who merely professes another reli-gion, but never against the racially different Jew. The Jew is cosmopolitan, and possesses a certain astuteness which makes him the master of the honest Aryan. In Eastern Europe, the Jew is the cancer slowly eating into the flesh of the other nations. Exploitation of the people is his only aim. Selfishness and lack of personal courage are his chief characteristics; self-sacrifice and patriotism are altogether foreign to him.[120]

Public antisemitic rhetoric continued to rise in the late nineteenth century. The first use of the term "antisemitic" was in the name for a new anti-Jewish organ-ization, "The Antisemitic League" (*die Antisemitenliga*) founded in 1879 by a zealous Jewish convert to Christianity, Wilhelm Marr,[121] and promoted in his pamphlet "The Conquest of the Jews over the Germans."[122] By the 1870s, anti-Jewish student groups were forming in the *Gymnasien* and the university. In 1880, Georg Ritter von Schönerer[123] introduced an explicitly antisemitic move-ment, which was also anti-Habsburg, into Austrian politics.[124] Its leading dema-gogue, Karl Lueger (Hitler's model for leadership), founded the Christian Socialist Party with the support of another member of the aristocracy, Prince Liechtenstein. Schönerer coined the popular rhyme, "*Ohne Juda, Habsburg, Rome, bauen wir den deutschen Dom*" ("Without the Jews, Habsburg or Rome, we are building the German home.")[125] One year later, Eugen Dühring published *Die Judenfrage als Racen-, Sitten- und Culturfrage*,[126] articulating the German racial rationale for antisemitism. As Beller writes,

> It was a death blow to the Jewish involvement in German Nationalism. During the early 1880s all those Jews such as Adler, Friedjung, Herzl and Freud who had once been members of German National organizations either resigned or were kicked out.... The admirers of the German *Volk* had been

excluded by the very group who should have been their closest ally, the German national intelligentsia.[127]

At the same time pogroms erupted again across Russia and eastern Europe, prompting tens of thousands of Jews to emigrate to America and Palestine before the turn of the century (commemorated in a sanitized but touching portrayal in the popular musical *Fiddler on the Roof*). Hysterical accusations of ritual murder brought Jews to stand trial across central and eastern Europe from the 1880s to the early 1900s.[128] Freud actually testified on the psychology of a witness at one such trial.[129] This was no longer the religious or cultural antisemitism of nineteenth-century Austria, but a full-blown racial hatred. At the same time, as Beller notes, the Austrians did not need to subscribe to "racial anti-Semitism in its pure form" because "Vienna's own brand of antisemitism, that of the Christian Socials, was tremendously successful."[130] Schönerer, Lueger, and their compatriots were adept at exploiting the already festering economic resentments of the Austrian population and channeling it directly against the Jews.

After refusing four times to ratify Lueger's election as mayor, the Emperor finally capitulated to Viennese voters and the Pope, confirming the election in 1897. Lueger was particularly adept as mayor at using antisemitism as a means to power by sometimes granting favors to certain Jews, while perpetuating a rhetoric of hatred among his closest followers.[131] The statement "I decide who is a Jew" gave him considerable room to maneuver in Vienna's cynical back-room politics. Paradoxically, the Catholic Habsburg emperor Franz Josef became a hero for many Jews because of his opposition to Lueger and his adherence to Enlightenment values,[132] well after antisemitism took hold in the government and popular politics of Vienna in the late nineteenth century.[133]

In reaction to this antisemitic government, together with the widespread eastern pogroms and the reinstatement of arbitrary, draconian laws restricting the free movement and employment of Jews across central and eastern Europe, the first stirrings of Zionism arose.[134] Daniel Boyarin attributes Zionism at least in part to a remasculinization of the Jewish male image, influenced by a general rise in misogyny and homophobia in Vienna at the turn of the century. As Jill Salberg asserts, "In Freud's rejection of the passive, feminized, unheroic Jewish male we can see his move towards embracing what Max Nordau decried [in 1903] as a 'Jewry of Muscle,' i.e., Jews who do not step aside but fight back."[135]

A Russian Jewish doctor, Leo Pinsker, argued for voluntary resettlement in Palestine, and Jewish agricultural settlements were funded by Baron Edmond de Rothschild in Paris resulting in a tripling of the Jewish population there (from 12,000 in 1850 to 35,000 in 1882).[136] Defiant Jewish pride was resurgent. New synagogues were financed and built as a reaction against discrimination and as a locus of solidarity.[137] Jewish student groups formed in reaction to the expulsion from German nationalist societies—a movement which Freud and other early analysts joined while still students. In his *Autobiographical Study*, Freud asserted,

I found that I was expected to feel myself inferior and an alien because I was a Jew. I refused absolutely to do the first of these things. I have never been able to see why I should feel ashamed of my descent or, as people were beginning to say, of my race.[138]

Herzl's 1896 book *Der Judenstadt*[139] inaugurated the Zionist movement proper, greatly increasing the numbers of Jews who envisioned and worked for a new Jewish homeland in Palestine. In 1894, the French officer Alfred Dreyfus had been falsely accused of treason in France, and exiled to a penal colony until his exoneration in 1896. The real spy was a member of the royal house of Ester-hazy, but the damage was done among the public. The "Dreyfus affair" kindled further antisemitic demonstrations, fueling Lueger's popularity. As the Paris correspondent for Vienna's liberal *Neue Freie Presse*, Herzl covered the Dreyfus affair and was witness to violent antisemitic rallies. Herzl's family had emigrated to Vienna from Pest, Hungary,[140] when he was twelve years old, settling in the 9th district (Freud's neighborhood). A secular Jew and atheist, he had been an ardent admirer of German culture, following the usual bourgeois path of a university education and entrance into professional life. After Paris, however, and Lueger's rise to power in Vienna, he became disillusioned with assimilation as a strategy. He came to recognize antisemitism as ubiquitous, and to believe that the only emancipation possible would be by establishing a Jewish state.

The first Zionist Congress was convened in Basel in 1897 and gained many adherents from all walks of Jewish life. Freud himself had sympathy with Zionism, although he considered himself largely apolitical and did not officially join or endorse the movement. In a letter to Spielrein he wrote,

I am, as you know, cured of the last shred of my predilection for the Aryan cause, and would like to take it that if [your] child turns out to be a boy he will develop into a stalwart Zionist.[141]

At the turn of the twentieth century, the infamous *Protocols of the Elders of Zion* was published in Russia and disseminated widely across Europe in multiple translations. This counterfeit text aimed to "prove" that the Jews were plotting a world takeover.[142] (Hitler eventually used it as a primary source in *Mein Kampf*.) Pogroms continued, and often the Church was directly implicated. Ecclesiastical officials gave public consent and even encouragement to riots and looting, in collusion with the police (e.g., in Kishinev, Russia[143] in 1903—a massacre that gained international notoriety and pleas for aid.[144])

In spite of—or in defiance against—this growing discrimination, World War I saw many Jews enlisting in the united armies of Germany and Austria-Hungary. For many, especially assimilated Jews like Freud himself, there was a feeling of patriotism and the hope that by proving their loyalty to the realm, they would help to raise the esteem of Jews in the eyes of the Gentile population. Freud's sons served in the Austrian army, and initially, Freud expressed pride in them and in the German-Austrian cause—although he was greatly worried for them as well as the many younger analysts who enlisted (e.g., Reik, Ferenczi). As the years dragged on, however, and Austria was plunged into poverty and hunger,[145] Freud became embittered over the devastation of war, with its senseless displays of human brutality.

Pride versus assimilation

As noted in Chapter 2, there was great complexity in the early analysts' unconscious dynamics of Jewish identity versus the desire for assimilation into a culture that bore an indelible mark of Christianity—both as individuals and as a group. As the conspicuousness of antisemitism waxed and waned with various regime changes within the Habsburg monarchy and the Austrian state, the desire for assimilation or a distinctive identity also fluctuated. There was no single Jewish attitude or perspective. As Klein writes with regard to histories that tend to characterize "the Jews as a single, homogeneous whole, with characteristically Jewish experiences," much complexity is lost in such generalizations.[146]

> The Jews can become an abstraction which conceals and obscures the crucial differences among them, such as the diverse reactions to antisemitism that led some Jews anxiously to hasten their assimilationist efforts, and led others (fewer) to dissimilate and redefine their Jewishness.[147]

Freud's and the early analysts' attitudes toward assimilation also changed over time. Their eventual assumption of a more isolationist stance, combined with a sense of intellectual and political superiority, was simultaneously a point of pride, a compromise formation between denial of the full extent of their oppression, and a posture of conscious defiance. As Klein,[148] Oxaal,[149] and Gilman[150] have pointed out, historians have tended to fall into two camps regarding the influence of Judaism on the development of psychoanalysis. On one side of the divide, which Oxaal calls "ethnic minimalism,"[151] there are those who see Judaism as a fact of life for the Freudians, but otherwise peripheral to their theorizing in contrast to their German intellectual identity—for example, Peter Gay, who wrote,

> The claim for the Jewishness of psychoanalysis based on its materials or its intellectual inheritance have proved to be without foundation. The claim for an elusive Jewish quality that somehow, mysteriously, informed Freud's work, a claim he seems to have endorsed, is too insubstantial to carry the weight some of his biographers have put on it.... [I]t remains an impassioned, wishful guess, *nothing more* [emphasis added].[152]

Frank Sulloway, in *Freud, Biologist of the Mind*,[153] was explicit about demythologizing Freud in order to reach a "mythless history,"[154] and went to considerable lengths to debunk what he labeled as the prevailing "myth" of antisemitism in Freud's Vienna.[155]

On the other side, "ethnic maximalism," are those who emphasize the influence (direct or indirect) of Jewish intellectual thought, religious heritage, and social situation on Freud's ideas,[156] including a hermeneutical disposition reflecting Talmudic scholarship and learned argumentation,[157] vestiges of kabbalistic mysticism,[158] identification with Moses as the heroic herald of a promised land of freedom wedded to Enlightenment rationalism and cultural assimilation,[159] and, as well, Freud's tremendous professional ambition in frank rebellion against continual antisemitic obstacles.[160] Ostow points to ways in which Judaism and psychoanalysis share mutually reinforcing elements: a belief in the power of knowledge, a position of dual marginality (social marginality as Jews and academic marginality as psychoanalysts), a place to struggle with internal conflicts at the interface with a non-Jewish world, and finally psychoanalysis as a deepening approach to the understanding of Jewish religion.[161] More recently, Philip Cushman has again likened psychoanalysis to the Jewish method of midrash.[162] Lewis Aron and Libby Henik go so far toward the realm of Jewish spirituality as to state, "[f]or psychoanalysts, the human being, created in the image of God, is like a holy text, subject to ongoing and interminable analysis and interpretation."[163]

David Meghnagi views psychoanalysis as a product of and "event within" fin-de-siècle Judaism, contemporaneous with and influenced by the conflicts in vision between Zionists and the Jewish socialist reformers.[164] Over against Kafka, who viewed psychoanalysis as relevant only for Jews caught in the political struggles of the early twentieth century, Meghnagi views psychoanalysis as a "third answer" between Zionism and socialism, a depth understanding of the dynamics, structures, and motivations that create injustice in the human condition.

John Murray Cuddihy, who died in 2011, viewed psychoanalysis as an outgrowth of the failed social assimilation of Jews within Gentile culture in fin-de-siècle Vienna.[165] Cuddihy proposed that Freud's notion of the "importunate id" and, as well, the Oedipus complex, had their origins in the shame of the assimilated Jewish bourgeoisie toward the *Ostjude* (the "importunate Yid")[166]—and, more personally, Freud's shame and anger at his father's seeming cowardice over the incident with the antisemite in the street.[167] By transforming the moral opprobrium of social deviance, offensive behavior, and "*kvetches*" into a science of mental illness, Cuddihy claimed that Freud's theory, by pathologizing Jewish cultural differences, was an attempt to distance the cultured professional Jew from his eastern European counterpart—and his own pan-German identity from that of his Galician, Chasidic parentage.[168]

Beller points out that scholars do not even agree on the degree of exposure to Jewish religious traditions Freud received in his childhood home.[169] Freud himself later regretted not being trained to read Hebrew fluently as his father had been, and the household seems to have been run mainly along secular Jewish lines.[170] However, Freud's well documented fascination with and lifelong reference to Jewish figures in his writings and correspondence, as well as Rizzuto's detailed discussion of his relationship to his father, his father's Talmudic scholarship, and the family Bible (see Chapter 3), justify the idea that Freud's thinking was influenced by his Jewish heritage and identity.[171]

At minimum, as Beller affirms, the two major traditions of *education* and *ethics* that evolved from the earliest times within Judaism, and became life-sustaining in eastern European ghetto life, were central among Freud's lifelong values.[172] Already in the late eighteenth century the rabbi Moses Mendelssohn had created a rationalist Enlightenment movement within Judaism, called *Haskalah*, in which the study of science was encouraged as complementary rather than antithetical to religious belief.[173] Beller elaborates on the centrality of ethics in Judaism, and in particular the democracy and social justice that characterized European ghetto life, as a deep-rooted set of communal values that inspired Jewish involvement—and leadership—in the movements for social justice and in Marxism in Vienna in the twentieth century. Enlightenment values of rationality and equality further strengthened this commitment to social justice among Jews in Europe after the seventeenth century.[174] The commitment to a comprehensive humanistic education set a distinctive stamp on all the analysts, and informed the deeply held Socratic assumption that the unexamined life is not worth living.

Klein further frames the question of the importance of Judaism and Jewishness to the early analysts in terms of a tension between the particular and the universal.[175] As much as assimilation was an important social aim, there was also a countervailing impulse toward maintaining Jewish distinctiveness and establishing a Jewish intellectual subculture that was neither *Ostjude* nor German. Klein proposes that the Jews' position between full emancipation in the eighteenth century and the horrors of the twentieth century functioned as a liminal space, in which their particular situation simultaneously created both an impetus and a constraint to creativity. Psychoanalysis was a response to the particular situation of these socially ostracized but economically well-established Jewish intellectuals. It offered new insights for living their lives in a subculture of intellectual excitement and social reform, within the larger culture of antisemitism. These insights were fortifying for the members of their subculture—but also, generalizable to others: Klein writes,

> The meaning of Jewish integration must be understood in both of the ways assimilated Jews of this period understood it: as a reconciliation of hostile social differences that would directly benefit Jews, and as a *unifying, universal, moral ideal that would benefit all humanity* [emphasis added].[176]

The picture is more complex, of course, than either a dismissal or an elevation of the Jewishness implicit in psychoanalysis as a theory or a movement. As much as assimilation was an important social aim for most educated Jewish professionals, there was also a countervailing impulse toward maintaining their distinctiveness and establishing a superior Jewish intellectual subculture.[177] Through *Bildung* ("character-building education"), they aspired to be German in their cultural ascent—not Austrian or Viennese. All bourgeois children, Jewish and Gentile, received a humanistic *Gymnasium* education and visited the museums, concert halls, and other great cultural landmarks along the *Ring-strasse*. But for the Jews this was a matter of serious interest, not merely a social formality.[178]

By 1902, the year the Wednesday Night Society was founded, Freud's inner circle had become more disillusioned about grand Enlightenment ideals, and more willing to join together under two interlocking bonds of distinctiveness: psychoanalysts against the psychiatric mainstream, and Jewish intellectuals against the hegemony of Catholicism and antisemitism. As suggested in Chapter 2, the fact that they were an oppressed minority contributed to a feeling of intel-lectual freedom—they had less to lose in terms of power and prestige in the society at large, but also more to gain from the intellectual freedom which they had appropriated for themselves. On the other hand, the internecine conflicts among the Jewish members of the group before World War I were all the more intense because so much was at stake—other avenues to success had been relin-quished by becoming a card-carrying member of Freud's inner circle. Freud tried to dislodge this enclave mentality among the Viennese during the early years of his infatuation with Jung, prompted by his own ambition to expand psycho-analysis beyond its Viennese Jewish borders. For the Viennese analysts, however (as well as Karl Abraham in Berlin), the threat of being taken over by a Swiss Gentile and suspected antisemite was a bridge too far. The longstanding history of Austrian antisemitism, with its shifting tides and often sudden betrayals, sheds further light on the fierce resistance of the Viennese analysts—and eventually Freud himself—toward Jung, which only increased during the years between Jung's first visit to Vienna and the onset of World War I.

A growing threat

Upon their surrender at the end of World War I in 1918, Germany, Austria, and much of the eastern Austro-Hungarian Empire saw a severe reduction in land holdings and economic stability. The Treaty of Versailles, negotiated by the Allied Powers without representation from Germany, Austria, or Hungary, redrew the boundaries of European nations along ethnic lines. Britain and France demanded reparations. France wanted its border with Germany secured. The American president, Woodrow Wilson, hoping for peace, negotiated the creation of the League of Nations. The Allies hoped that by crushing their enemies politi-cally as well as militarily, they were eliminating any further threat of imperial aggression and that World War I would truly be the "war to end all wars." But the multi-national, ethnic, and regional resentments that had lit the fuse of World War I were further stoked in Germany, Austria, Hungary, and central Europe by the ensuing chaos, poverty, and political humiliation. Austria-Hungary had lost 1,200,000 soldiers, and Germany two million.

The Germans, who in 1914 had imperial ambitions of conquering all of Europe, now viewed themselves as victims of American and western European aggression. Only after bitter negotiations, and the threat of renewed war, did the German National Assembly finally vote to sign the treaty. A new government, the Weimar Republic, set about the herculean task of reconstruction. The treaty offered few concessions, and forced Germany to grant independence to Czecho-slovakia and Poland, as well as numerous other territories, along with colonies in Africa (which were turned over to Allied nations). The German army was reduced in size, and Allied troops occupied areas east of the Rhine.

Even as France and Britain were digging out from the rubble, the people of the former German and Austro-Hungarian nations were suffering under terrible conditions of poverty, disease, and starvation. Weakened by hunger and trauma, all of Europe was hit hard by Spanish flu in 1918 (the cause of death of Freud's own beloved daughter, Sophie). In subsequent years, inflation further destroyed the German and Austrian economics. Many Germans believed they had been betrayed by the Weimar Republic, and this popular *Dolchstosslegende* ("stabbed in the back" legend) undermined the democratic leadership, even as those leaders remained isolated from potential allies in the west. The far right-wing National Socialist ("Nazi") Party, initially considered extreme by a majority of citizens, gained momentum throughout the 1920s with its rhetoric of nationalist and racist "Aryan" pride. Many Germans blamed the Weimar Republic for giving in too easily to the Allied Powers, and Jews, communists, and socialists were suspected of collaborating with the enemy. The National Socialists capitalized on the same anthropological enthusiasm that had captivated both Freud and Jung and their followers—seeking the origins of separate ethnic groups' racial identities in ancient myths and legends. But the Nazis did so with a view toward asserting racial superiority and, eventually, the extermination of all others.[179]

In the 1920s in Austria, the government was mostly locked in a bipartisan impasse between the more liberal, Jewish-led[180] Social Democrats (the "Reds") and the conservative Christian Socialists (the "Blacks") who represented the former members of the Catholic–Habsburg alliance. Before the Nazi Party gained a majority, the Christian Socialists were already churning out antisemitic rhetoric—albeit mainly on political and economic grounds rather than a racial-ized view.[181] The party leader, Ignaz Seipel—a Catholic cardinal who served twice as Chancellor during the 1920s—promoted the idea that Jews and social-ists were trampling Austrian culture and tradition underfoot. He built up an alli-ance of wealthy Catholic industrialists and a paramilitary *Heimwehr*, which in July, 1926, fired into a crowd of workers with impunity, and brutally put down an ensuing three-day workers' strike. Although the socialists also had a small militia, the *Schutzbund* ("protective army"), they were no match for the *Heimwehr* and the Austrian police. Otto Bauer, the idealistic leader of the Social Democrats from the end of World War I,[182] was ineffective in his attempts to broker peace. This "Bloody Friday" was a watershed moment for the conservatives. The coalition of social reformers, which included the cream of Jewish intellectuals, was increasingly under threat.

Psychoanalysis and social reform

The psychoanalytic community in Vienna was hardly isolated from these events. Even after Adler's departure from the Society, many of the analysts considered themselves to be socialists, or shared the liberal ideals of "Red Vienna" for social reform, justice, and education for the poor.[183] Although Freud regarded himself as apolitical, there were numerous ties between Vienna's socialists and the Psychoanalytic Society. For example, Otto Bauer's sister Ida was in fact Freud's famous patient "Dora," whose case Freud himself viewed as botched (although mostly for the wrong reasons).[184] The Bauers' father had amassed considerable wealth in Bohemia as an industrialist. They emigrated to Vienna, where they lived on the same street as the Freud family and were part of the same circle of Jewish professionals.

Ida married Ernst Adler, an aspiring musician who eventually went into business with her father. She continued to suffer from what today would probably be diagnosed as post-traumatic stress disorder—although the common portrayal of "Dora" as a lifelong invalid has been revised by Decker in a feminist reappraisal of the biographical evidence and her considerable strength in later fleeing the Nazis.[185] Freud describes a dream of "Dora's" in which, shortly after Christmas, she stood for a full two hours gazing at Raphael's Madonna—a religious moment that Freud attributed to a fantasy of motherhood without the guilt of sexuality.[186] Blum suggests that the representation of the Madonna also represented to the young woman a replacement of a "denigrated Jewish mother and her own denigrated Jewish self-representation" with a vision of a loving mother hearkening back to her school days in a convent.[187]

Billig, moreover, notes that while Freud and "Dora" debated sexual interpretations, "both doctor and patient managed to avoid painful Jewish issues."[188] In spite of the consolidation of power by the Christian Socials between 1895 and 1902, boycotts of Jewish merchants by Viennese Gentiles, and the rise of accusations of ritual murder—including a notorious case in Ida's mother's home village in Bohemia just two years before Ida began treatment. Yet there was no apparent discussion of Jewishness or of antisemitism in her analysis.[189] Billig reinterprets "Dora's" dream of the Madonna to represent not only a denigrated Jewish mother and female self, as in Blum, but also, as a Jewish girl, staring for two hours at the image of Madonna and Jesus,

> identifying with the mother of Jesus with the Christians, who, in the context of Lueger and his Christian Socials, were oppressing in the name of Christianity both doctor and patient, and practically everyone they both knew. The logic of Dora's alleged identification with the Madonna, which is contained

in that two hour stare, is that she dreams of being a Christian mother—as, indeed, she was to become in the year following the publication of [Freud's] "Fragment". Thus, Dora, like Freud ... was edging towards admitting an identification with the oppressor.[190]

In addition to self-deception, Billig also observes—albeit in a footnote—that fear motivated denial as well, especially in public and in print. There was a self-protective desire to stay under the radar, and to blend in:

Freud himself may not have wished to make matters worse by drawing attention to faults which could be publicly labelled by anti-semites as "Jewish faults." One might speculate about Freud's reluctance to confront sexual misconduct, like that of Herr K, in the families of his patients. Freud's abandonment of the "seduction theory," in favour of the theory of infantile fantasy, took place between 1895 and 1897, at precisely the point when Lueger was advancing toward being mayor of Vienna. Freud would be aware that anti-semites would welcome a theory (or admission), proposed by a Jewish doctor, based upon analyses of predominantly Jewish patients, that fathers (Jewish fathers) regularly seduced their daughters.[191]

Although Ida Bauer's marriage had taken place in a Reform synagogue in Vienna, she chose to be baptized together with her newborn son in 1905. Such conversions, of course, ultimately saved no one. Ida Bauer was eventually forced to flee the Nazis both because of her Jewish heritage and her brother's longstanding Marxist activism. Barely escaping before the borders were closed, the Adlers emigrated to New York where Ida died in 1945.[192]

Breuer's famous patient "Anna O" (Bertha Pappenheim) was also Jewish, but followed a very different course. The daughter of a co-founder of the Schiffschul Synagogue in Vienna, she became a vocal Jewish activist, especially on behalf of Jewish women victims of sexual slavery. She founded the Federation of Jewish Women in 1904, and in 1909 a shelter for unwed mothers in Frankfurt, as well as helping at the Henry Street Settlement in New York. As Blum points out, "approximately the same time that Freud was lecturing at Clark University, citing the case of Anna O., Bertha Pappenheim was lecturing in America on problems of prostitution."[193] Her book *The Jewish Woman* was a manifesto for women's rights and education.[194] The younger generation of analysts who joined the Vienna Society in the 1920s shared a rebel cast of mind against the cultural inertia and moral hypocrisy of the Habsburg–Catholic hegemony, and after the World War I, a brief but heady sense (echoed by the idealistic politics of "Red Vienna") that social reform was truly possible.[195]

This post-war vision did not erupt without antecedents. As noted in Chapter 2, the *enragés* at the turn of the century had already laid the ground for social revolution (with even earlier predecessors—including their own parents and grandparents—in the Revolution of 1848). In a screed against the *Taufjude* (baptized Jews) in 1904, Wittels saw in psychoanalysis at its earliest stages a mission to "change the surface of the earth," and a catalyst for renewal, equality, and peace for both Aryans and Jews.[196] In 1905, in his essay *Das Wesen des Judentums* ("The Essence of Judaism"), Rank expressed a similar heroic mission for psychoanalysis—to be carried out specifically by the Jews because of their unique struggle against oppression and their resulting creativity.[197]

After the war, Anna Freud recalled in an interview,

> Back then in Vienna we were all so excited—full of energy: it was as if a whole new continent was being explored, and we were the explorers, and we now had a chance to change things—to come back from that continent, you could say, with what we had learned, and offer it to the world, to people who hadn't been there. What could be the result? ... Well, we didn't know exactly, but we certainly hoped that there would be some changes—some important changes. Even in the darkest years, the 1930s, some of that antici-pation and hope could be found—amid the doubts and skepticism.[198]

Their efforts in the 1920s resulted in the creation of a publishing house, a train-ing institute, liberal kindergartens, public housing (e.g., the Karl Marx Hof built in 1923), and an outpatient clinic (the Ambulatorium, a clinic for free psycho-analytic treatment of lower-class Viennese opened in 1922).[199] One housing block for workers was even named for Freud.[200] Analysts promoted free therapy, as well as offering vouchers to needy patients for free medical care.[201] As early as 1918, at the end of World War I, Freud exhorted his colleagues at the Fifth International Congress in Budapest to open free outpatient clinics, saying, "The poor man should have just as much right to assistance for his mind as he now has to the life-saving help offered by surgery."[202] In the absence of governmental assistance, he argued, private efforts should be initiated.[203] Historian Elizabeth Danto writes,

> Whereas his theory aimed to be ahistorical, a de facto science, Freud's clini-cal practice conformed to the social-democratic political ideology that pre-vailed in post-World War I Vienna.... In these years of nascent modernism, Freud's expressions of social conscience inspired the creation of at least twelve other cooperative mental health clinics from Zahgreb to London.... At least one fifth of the work of the first and second generation of psycho-analysts went to indigent urban residents.[204]

Caught up in these efforts, it is not clear that the analysts fully appreciated the advancing peril of Nazism, or took seriously enough the advancing conservatism of the rest of Austria around them. By 1931 the membership of the Vienna Society had increased to fifty-eight (thirty-nine men and nineteen women).[205] The training institute in particular fostered close relationships built on excite-ment about research, amplified by a hothouse atmosphere of relative isolation from non-analysts. Many marriages came about within the group,[206] and it was not uncommon for trainees in analysis to socialize with senior members of the training institute and the Society.[207] Dora Hartmann recalls,

> You were part of an enthusiastic group of young rebels if you belonged to the psychoanalytic movement at this time. And by this fact, already, all these people were very close, felt very close together. They all believed in something that was quite different, that was quite revolutionary, for which one got ostracized from the real academic circles, from which one knew one did not get prestige and could not make a lot of money.... Nevertheless, it was so important for this group at that time to gather around Freud and to feel that there was something completely new and completely different, and that they were part of it, ha[d] started something new.... There was nothing but talk about the new discoveries.[208]

The gathering storm

After Hitler's rise to power in Germany in January, 1933, a chill settled on the Vienna Psychoanalytic Society as their German colleagues began to make plans to flee. The Berlin Psychoanalytic Society was "Aryanized" by decree in April, Jewish analysts were driven out, and the Berlin polyclinic was transformed into a "triage center" where Nazi "psychoanalysts" condemned patients to death.[209] There was widespread foreboding about Hitler's aspirations to expand his borders. Nevertheless, Freud remained hopeful that the Allies would never permit Hitler to annex Austria, and that "Austria is not given to German brutality. In such ways we buoy ourselves up in relative security. I am in any event determined not to move from the spot."[210] The same year he replied to Ferenczi, who strongly urged him to leave Austria, "There is, I suppose, no personal danger." He compared the current "suppression of us Jews as extremely unpleasant" to the discomfort of becoming a refugee. In my opinion, flight would only be justified by direct danger to life; besides, if they were to slay, one is simply one kind of death like another."[211] As Gay reported, "Freud's reluctance to leave Vienna became a refrain in his letters."[212]

Within the next five years the situation in Austria did become deadly.[213] In 1934, protocols drafted in Rome created an alliance among Italy, Austria, and Hungary, and a fascist-Christian state was established. The relatively more liberal "clerico-fascist"[214] Austrian Chancellor Engelberg Dolfuss was assassinated in 1934 by Nazis in Vienna, to be replaced by Kurt von Schuschnigg. Schuschnigg promised security to a meeting of Jewish business leaders, and Freud believed him to be "decent, courageous, and a man of character."[215] Schuschnigg took a last desperate stand, calling for a plebiscite on Austrian independence in March, 1938, but was forced by Hitler to withdraw it and to resign. Freud wrote in his diary on March 11, "*Finis Austriae*."[216] Hitler's troops crossed the border triumphantly the next day to be met by throngs of cheering Austrians. As Wistrich describes,

Hitler's invasion of his former homeland in March 1938 turned the deeply rooted indigenous Austrian antisemitism into a veritable stampede. Huge crowds gathered in Vienna to cheer Hitler, and swastikas appeared everywhere—in the words of Carl Zuckmayer, "hell itself was let loose." Pillaging of Jewish property, arrests of Jews and attacks upon them by previously illegal Austrian SA and SS, as well as by Austrian civilians became routine.[217]

Quoting a contemporaneous news report, Wistrich continues,

[There] were the familiar scenes of Jews scrubbing pavements, with their bare hands, usually accompanied by a jeering mob of Viennese citizens. In many cases, acid was poured on the hands of the Jews ... a roar of delight from the crowds would announce ... "Work for the Jews at last, work for the Jews!"[218]

The Vienna Psychoanalytic Society disbanded in 1938 as the Nazis took over the clinic, the training institute, and the publishing house (and their funds). At least eleven of the Society's members, present and past, were murdered in the Holocaust.[219] Those fortunate enough to survive went into exile as part of a general Jewish diaspora after 1938.[220] Freud's terse diary comments record the main events in the following days:

Mar. 13: Annexation to Germany. Mar. 14: Hitler in Vienna. Mar. 15: Control over publishing house and home. Mar. 16: Jones. Mar. 17: Princess. Mar. 22: Anna at the Gestapo. Mar. 28: Admission to England secured. Ernst in Paris. Emigration appears possible.[221]

Freud had certainly continued in some degree of denial, in spite of the pleas of friends and colleagues—long after many other prominent Jews, including a large number of Viennese analysts, had seen the writing on the wall and escaped.[222] Many Jews never left, thinking that uprooting their lives was an overreaction. As the historian of the Holocaust Lucy Davidowicz writes, "Sensible people were sure that Hitler could not last long, that decency, rationality, and political order would—must—reassert themselves."[223] It is well known that Freud resisted leaving Vienna, considering himself either too famous internationally or too old and sick by the time of the *Anschluss* to be taken by the Nazis. But when Anna was detained for a day by the Gestapo, suicide pill in hand,[224] he was finally convinced to emigrate.[225]

Freud's immediate household was able to escape thanks largely to the intervention of the French princess Marie Bonaparte, Ernest Jones in London, and the American ambassador in France, William Bullitt.[226] (See Chapter 8.) Freud's four sisters living in Vienna were not allowed to join them, and were all subsequently murdered in concentration camps.[227] Berggasse 19 was converted into a

Sammelwohnung—an intermediary "collective housing apartment" where the Nazis gathered together Jews they had displaced from their original homes, before deporting them to the death camps.[228]

Father, don't you see I'm burning?

As noted at the beginning of this chapter, the dream of the burning child is uncanny not only in its content, but in its ever-widening circles of transmission—from the original dreamer to a lecturer to Freud's patient (re-dreaming it for unnamed psychic reasons of her own), to Freud, and finally to public dissemination in his multiply revised master work. From a private scene of anguish, the dream was cast abroad, and now stands as a vivid collective memory. To be sure, any further social interpretation of the dream must be purely speculative, so far removed it is in both time and perspective from the original dreamer. Yet, following Freud's own excursions into realms of cultural speculation, I will venture to ask the historicist question: What might this image of the burning child have to say about Freud, his Viennese circle, Vienna more generally, and the rising antisemitism that enveloped them all—including the dreamers of this very dream?[229]

The mother is absent. Was this merely another instance of Freud's habitual blind spot regarding the impact of his own mother on his unconscious life and his over-valuation of the role of the father, resulting in a redaction of the dream story that excluded the mother of the burning child? Was there some sense in which Freud identified not with the father in the story, but with the burning child—left unprotected by either father or mother or by a religious tradition that offered him no credible intellectual or emotional solace against the harsh demands of *Ananke* ("necessity")—the reality principle?

To what extent as the Nazi threat drew closer and closer was Freud unable to offer timely and authoritative security to his own children—both his personal family and his many adopted sons and daughters of the Vienna Psychoanalytic Society—underestimating the threat and refusing to leave Vienna before the moment of absolute crisis? Was Freud, desperately ill and in pain, and preoccupied with anxiety about the continuation of psychoanalysis into the future, unable to assume the role of protective father/group leader, much less the Moses of prophetic vision, at a time when events conspired to endanger the whole Jewish population of Europe?

The *Shomer*, whose sacred duty was to keep watch—to keep his eyes open— was old and weary, and fell asleep at his post. Perhaps symbolizing a certain neglect of the old traditions, the watchman neglected the seriousness of his vigil, and closed his eyes—unable or unwilling to take seriously the prospect of actual harm.[230] The dream father may have had a preconscious sense of foreboding, but nevertheless fell asleep, grieving and exhausted, and awoke too late to prevent the fire from starting when, in Freud's words, "the most rapid awakening was called for."[231] The longer the father remained asleep, even for an additional moment, the longer he could believe that destruction was not imminent. The father longed for the beloved child to be alive, yet was unable to see the advancing peril.

So the child's body *was* desecrated—precisely the catastrophe the *Shomer* was there to prevent in accordance with Jewish law. The boy was no longer accompanied by the ancient prayers of the Jewish heritage, in a dark room lit by holy flickering candles, but surrounded by the sound and smell of burning cloth and flesh, and the harsh glare of consuming flames. Just so, the longer that Freud, the father, could remain asleep in his denial even for an additional moment, the longer he could believe that his beloved child, psychoanalysis, would survive the advancing Nazi threat—even "when the most rapid awakening was called for." And although many of the original analysts survived, their whole world—including many people whom they loved—did not. The protective circle of Jewish heritage, ritual, and community was disfigured in an immolation whose lethality Freud and his Viennese followers could hardly foresee, and were unable to prevent.

Notes

1 Freud, 1953a/1900: 509–622.
2 Cf. ibid., 33.
3 Ibid., 510.
4 Ibid.
5 Ibid., 537.
6 Ibid., 608.
7 Ibid., 111n1.
8 Ibid., 509.
9 Salberg, 2007. Thanks to Jewish Theological Seminary students Lauren Henderson, Amanda Schwartz, and Rami Schwartzer for details of traditional Jewish mourning rituals.
10 Freud, 1955c/1919.
11 Literally, "sweet maiden," a term most often associated with the plays of Arthur Schnitzler, to refer to young women who provided wealthy urban men with sexual entertainment in exchange for economic support. This arrangement was tacitly tolerated in fin-de-siècle Vienna.
12 For example, Nunberg and Federn, 1962, cases by Adler, I: 139–140; Sadger, I: 141; Wittels, II: 73–74; Brill, II: 78.
13 Michael Salberg, definition drafted by the Anti-Defamation League, personal communication, March 31, 2017. See also Anti-Defamation League, 2017.
14 E.g., Nirenberg, 2013: 13–47; Wistrich, 2010: 14, 80–83.
15 Beller, 2015: 4.
16 Gilman, 1986.
17 Beller, 2015: 4.
18 Bauman, 2000.
19 Arendt, 1963.
20 Bauman, 2000: 7.
21 Beller, 1989: 11.
22 Most comprehensively described in Nirenberg, 2013: 13–47. E.g., the Book of Esther, and the Sophist Apion (c.20–30 BCE—45–48 CE). See also Reijzer, 2011: 19–20; Wistrich, 1991: 3–13, 2010: 14, 81; Nirenberg, 2013: 40–47. As Wistrich

(1991) observes, "Pagan anti-Jewishness … provided fertile soil for its Christian heirs…" (pp. xviii–xix).

23 Boyarin, 1999: 6.
24 Ibid., 1–21.
25 Slavet, 2009: 25; Boyarin, 2004: 22.
26 Beller, 1989: 195.
27 Gilman, 1993.
28 Slavet, 2009.
29 Ibid., 191; see also Slavet, 2010; Aron and Starr, 2013: 236–244.
30 Boyarin, 1997.
31 Geller, 2006, 2007.
32 Gilman, for example, 1991, 1993.
33 Slavet, 2009: 15.
34 Ibid.
35 Freud, 1955a/1934: xv.
36 Beller, 1989: 11.
37 Ibid., 11–13. See also Reijzer, 2011: 19–21.
38 Beller, 1989: 83.
39 Gilman, 1993: 19–21, 33, 42, 45, 103.
40 Klein, 1985: 48–55.
41 Engelman, 1976: 132.
42 Stekel, 1950: 53, 63, 70–71.
43 M. Freud, 1957: 166.
44 Letter, March 4, 1923, in E. Freud, 1960: 346; Klein, 1985: 55.
45 Gay, 1976: 46.
46 Ibid.
47 E.g., see McCagg, 1989: 140–145.
48 Billig, 1999: 236.
49 Ibid., 251.
50 M. Freud, 1957: 16, 101, cited in Billig, 1999: 251.
51 M. Freud, 1957: 16, cited in Billig, 1999: 252.
52 Ibid.
53 M. Freud, 1957: 16.
54 Ibid., 9. For more on Galician Jews and the wide differences among Jewish communities throughout the Habsburg Empire, see McCagg, 1989; Rozenblitt, 2001.
55 Ibid., 12.
56 Billig, 1999: 252.
57 Lohrmann, 2004: 17.
58 Grollman, 1965: 5.
59 Ibid., 6.
60 Ibid.
61 Ibid.
62 Ibid., 9.
63 Ibid.
64 Schramm and Stjerna, 2012: 10.
65 Ibid.
66 *Schulchan Aruch* (Code of Jewish Law), by Joseph Caro, cited in Grollman, 1965: 17.
67 Grollman, 1965: 14–15.
68 Freud, 1960/1905.
69 Reik, 1962.
70 Schindel, 2004: 11, 16.

71 Gay, 1995: 347–348.
72 The district has a history of settlement dating back to 1300, having passed through Turkish and Hungarian rule, and serving in the seventeenth century as a Carmelite cloister and hospital. The *Karmelitermarkt*, where the cloister originally stood, operates as an open-air market today. The other main remnant of the imperial hunting grounds, the *Augarten*, is today the home of the Vienna Boys' Choir, but also has a darker history: Due to the concentration of Jews in Leopoldstadt at the time of the Nazi occupation, Hitler built two impenetrable concrete bunkers there in defense against any local uprising or international intervention, becoming a target of Allied bombing. Many historic buildings in the neighborhood were destroyed and later replaced by austere Soviet-style buildings, when Leopoldstadt came under Soviet occupation during the Partition. The City of Vienna has never removed them, citing potential damage to surroundings. The monstrous structures loom above families playing in the park, and serve incongruously today as the site of a festively lit Christmas market/pub.
73 Jews had been banned from Spain since their violent expulsion in 1492.
74 McCagg, 1989: 1.
75 Wien Geschichte, 2014.
76 McCagg (1989) notes that although she "did not care for the Jews," late in her reign she initiated some of the relaxing of restrictions that would be completed by her son Emperor Josef II after her death in 1780, especially in Vienna (pp. 19–20).
77 Beller, 2015: 15.
78 Grollman, 1965: 24.
79 McCagg, 1989: 11–15, 28–30.
80 "Leopoldstadt," 2016. Vienna's 2nd district as of 1850, it still retains the name.
81 Ibid.
82 Grollman, 1965.
83 Bakan, 1990/1958.
84 Synagogue Memorial, 2017: Der Leopoldstädter Tempel. Destroyed by fire on *Kristallnacht*, the site on Tempelgasse is marked today by four imposing columns from the original building. A smaller synagogue occupies the site of the former north wing.
85 McCagg (1989) notes that Franz II instituted a series of harassing bureaucratic restrictions against Jews in Vienna, "making 'toleration' for Jews in Vienna a matter of exception, not of rule" (p. 51).
86 Ibid., 56.
87 Ibid., 60–63.
88 "Prince" was an honorary title. Metternich was German, not Habsburg.
89 Eventually other nations also signed on to the treaty, except the United Kingdom, the Vatican, and the Turkish Ottoman Empire. Britain did join in a subsequent political Quadruple Alliance in 1815 with the three leading nations of the Holy Alliance, and this expanded to the Quintuple Alliance when France joined in 1818. European unity was already being eroded, however, by nationalist movements and regional wars. By World War I, it had broken into two major alliances: Britain, France, and Russia (the Triple Entente) and Germany, Austria-Hungary, and Italy (the Triple Alliance).
90 The western and eastern regions, respectively, of today's Czech Republic; parts of the Habsburg Empire until its independent incorporation as Czechoslovakia at the end of World War I in 1918. (In 1993, Czechoslovakia split, becoming the Czech Republic and Slovakia.)
91 See Chapter 6.
92 Grollman, 1965: 56.

93 Beller, 1989: 166.
94 Rozenblitt (2010: 27) notes,

> Jews were 9 percent of the total population of the city, but they formed about 19 percent of the population of the first district…, 36 percent of the second…, and 18 percent of the ninth.… Within these [adjacent] districts … Jews also concentrated in certain areas, so that some parts of the city were—or at least seemed—almost wholly Jewish.

Cf. Rozenblitt, 1983; Beller, 1989.
95 Klein, 1985: 2.
96 Wistrich, 1990.
97 Schorske, 1981: 43. Part of original design, erected three decades later in 1902.
98 Beller, 1989: 44. Still only 6.6 percent of the population of Vienna.
99 Wistrich, 1990.
100 Beller, 1989: 172, citing Schorske, 1982: 24–111.
101 Beller, 1989: 172.
102 Klein, 1985: 3.
103 De Waal, 2010.
104 Beller, 1989: 44.
105 Jüdisches Museum Wien, 2015. See also McCagg, 1989: 156–158.
106 Beller, 1989: 173.
107 Billig, 1999: 235.
108 Schorske, 1981; Beller, 1989: 178, 189.
109 Billig, 1999: 235.
110 Beller, 1989: 190.
111 Klein, 1985: xvi.
112 Salberg, 2007: 207.
113 Grollman, 1965: 33.
114 Michael and Jill Salberg, personal communication, March 13, 2017.
115 Quoted in Beller, 1989: 205–206.
116 Salberg, 2007: 202.
117 Boyarin, 1997: 3.
118 Grollman, 1965: 35.
119 Gobineau, 2015/1853.
120 Quoted in Grollman, 1965: 62.
121 Grollman, 1965: 66.
122 Blum, 2010: 79.
123 "Ritter" is a title of nobility, equivalent to British "Sir."
124 Grollman, 1965: 67.
125 Klein, 1985: 10.
126 Dühring, 1881.
127 Beller, 1989: 191–192.
128 Grollman, 1965: 72.
129 At Tisza-Eszlár, Hungary, in 1882 (ibid., p. 74).
130 Beller, 1989: 193.
131 Ibid., 195.
132 Ibid., 203.
133 Rozenblitt argues for a "tripartite identity": "politically Austrian, culturally German, and ethnically Jewish" (Rozenblitt, 2010: 30; cf. Rozenblitt, 1983, 2001).
134 Boyarin, 1997: 78.
135 Salberg, 2007: 205, also citing ibid.
136 Grollman, 1965: 73.

137 Beller, 1989: 202.
138 Freud, 1959: 9.
139 Herzl, 2012/1925.
140 Eastern side of Budapest, formerly a separate city.
141 See Chapter 6.
142 For a detailed history, see Bronner, 2003.
143 Now Chişinău in Moldova.
144 *New York Times*, 1903.
145 See Chapter 1.
146 Klein, 1985: xv.
147 Ibid.
148 Klein, 1985.
149 Oxaal, 1988.
150 Gilman, 1993.
151 Oxaal, 1988.
152 Gay, 1987: 147.
153 Sulloway, 1992.
154 Contra Klein, 1985: xvi; Gilman, 1993: 5–6.
155 Sulloway, 1992: 6, 463–465, 491; cf. Ellenberger, 1970: 418–464.
156 E.g., Aron and Henik, 2010; Brickman, 2010; Cushman, 2007; Geller, 2007; Gilman, 1993; Klein, 1985; Reijzer, 2011; Robert, 1976; Said, 2003; Yerushalmi, 1991; and an exceptionally thoughtful discussion of Freud and Judaism as a racial construct, including a new reading of Freud's *Moses and Monotheism*, in Slavet, 2009.
157 E.g., Bloom, 1987; Frosh, 2005; Ostow, 1982; Yerushalmi, 1991. This began even in Freud's lifetime (e.g., Roback, 1929).
158 Bakan, 1990/1958; Ostow, 1982; Eigen, 1998, 2012; Merkur, 2014. For a contemporary correlation of Jewish mysticism and relational psychoanalysis, see also Aron and Starr, 2010; Starr, 2008.
159 Robert, 1976; Bergmann, 1982.
160 Frosh, 2005, 2010; Robert, 1976.
161 Ostow, 1982: Introduction, 1–44. Michelle Friedman also notes, "This comparison is reinforced throughout modern psychoanalysis with [Freud's] *Standard Edition* taking on similar status as the Torah as the foundational text—the written law, so to speak, on which the oral tradition is founded" (personal communication, February 13, 2017).
162 Cushman, 2007. See also Aron, 2005.
163 Aron and Henik, 2010, Preface, p. 17.
164 Meghnagi, 1993.
165 Cuddihy, 1974.
166 Ibid., 18.
167 Freud, 1953a/1900: 197 (see Chapter 2). Aron (2007), in a brilliant bit of exegesis links this incident of being knocked off the road to Freud's heroic discovery of "his own 'royal road'" (dreams as the *via regia* to the unconscious), in contrast to Jewish humiliation on the Edomite king's highway where Israelites were forbidden to walk (Numbers 20:17), and the crossroads where Oedipus killed the stranger who pushed him off the road—who would turn out to be his father, King Laius.
168 Cuddihy, 1974: 7–8, 19, *et passim*. See also Gilman, 1993.
169 Beller, 1989: 86.
170 Rizzuto, 1998: 30, quoting Freud's letter to Roback, February 20, 1930. Gay (1987: 132) writes,

> It may interest you to hear that my father did come from an Chassidic background.... My education was so un-Jewish that today I cannot even read your

inscription, which is evidently written in Hebrew. In later life, I often regretted this lack in my education.

171 Rizzuto, 1998.
172 Beller, 1989: 86–87.
173 Ibid., 91–92; Salberg, 2010: 7. For more on *Haskalah* and its influence on German *Bildung* (character-building education), and the intellectual Jewish Salons of the nineteenth–twentieth centuries, see Beller, 1989: 88–105.
174 Beller, 1989: 104–143.
175 Klein, 1985.
176 Ibid., xvi.
177 Ibid., xv.
178 Beller, 1989: 187. Beller draws a distinction (contra Schorske, 1981: 141, 149) between Jewish and "native" Austrian bourgeoisies. The Jewish upper middle class embraced the values of education, high culture, and social justice (now secularized but not abandoned), while the Austrians prized the trappings of social strivings but still preferred the *Heuriger* (local pub) to the literary coffee house (p. 183), and sought careers in bureaucracy rather than the professions of medicine, law, or banking.
179 Innumerable books have been written on World War I and its aftermath. The broad outlines recounted here are well known, but historians continue to debate the complexities and motivations of the various parties before, during, and after the war. See, for example, Blom, 2008; Clark, 2012.
180 Wistrich, 1991: 89.
181 Ibid. A smaller anti-immigrant pan-German *Grossdeutsche Volkspartei* also agitated for the expulsion of *Ostjuden* in the 1920s (ibid.).
182 Secretary of the Social Democratic Party in Austria before the war under Viktor Adler's leadership, and a leading leftist theorist. Bauer died shortly after the *Anschluss* at age fifty-six, of heart failure.
183 On "Red Vienna," see Gruber, 1991; Zaretsky, 2004: 220–225.
184 Freud, 1953b/1905. See Chapter 7.
185 Decker, 1991.
186 Freud, 1953b/1905: 95–101. Cf. Nunberg and Federn, 1974: 136.
187 Blum, 2010: 84.
188 Billig, 1999: 217.
189 Decker, 1991: 126; Billig, 1999: 236.
190 Billig, 1999: 243.
191 Ibid., 252n161, citing Wolff, 1988.
192 Their son Kurt Herbert Adler was an opera conductor and later director of the San Francisco Opera.
193 Blum, 2010: 81.
194 Ibid.
195 For example, Coles, 1993: 129–154; Rose, 1998: 1–66; Danto, 2007.
196 Klein, 1985: 139.
197 Ibid., 141.
198 Coles, 1993: 9.
199 Danto, 2007; see also Gruber, 1991.
200 Zaretsky, 2004: 220, citing Gruber, 1991.
201 Danto, 2007.
202 Freud, 1955b/1919: 167.
203 Danto, 2007: 1–2.
204 Ibid.
205 Mühlleitner and Reichmayr, 1997: 78.

206 Ibid.
207 Grinker, 1975: 219.
208 Cited in Mühlleitner and Reichmayr, 1997: 79.
209 Danto, 2007: 259. Cf. Gay, 2006: 180–183.
210 Jones, 1957: 194.
211 Grollman, 1965: 134. See also Gay, 2006: 595.
212 Gay, 2006: 595.
213 For a succinct account of the Holocaust in Austria, see Botz, 1992.
214 Wistrich, 1991: 89.
215 Unpublished letter, Freud to Ernst Freud, February 22, 1938, in Gay, 2006: 618.
216 Freud, 1996. Also quoted in Gay, 2006: 618.
217 Wistrich, 1991: 89–90.
218 Ibid., 90.
219 See Chapter 8.
220 Mühlleitner and Reichmayr, 1997: 79ff.
221 Freud, 1996, this author's translation.
222 Mühlleitner and Reichmayr, 1997: 79ff.
223 Davidowicz, 1976: 65, quoted in Jacoby, 1983: 76.
224 See Chapter 1.
225 Gay, 2006: 625–626.
226 Sigmund Freud Museum Wien, n.d.
227 More details on Freud's family members during the Holocaust will be given in Chapter 8.
228 Hübel *et al.*, 2003.
229 "Dora" (Ida Bauer) also dreamed of fire. Blum (2010: 84) interprets:

> The burning house in the first dream described is also the burning house of Jewish factories set afire in the periodic rioting since 1897 in Bohemia where her father's factories were located. (Bauer, Breuer, and Freud had roots in Bohemia.) … Dora's fleeing a burning house in the dream was over-determined. She was in flight from the burning homes and factories of the Jews that pre-figured the burning of books, synagogues, and Jews in the Holocaust.

Cf. Blum 1994.

230 Earlier in *The Interpretation of Dreams*, Freud himself referred to the metaphor of "closing the eyes" as one of denial (albeit of oedipal wishes) (1953a/1900: 263). Following his father's death, Freud dreamed of a sign on which was printed "You are requested to close the eyes" (Freud letter to Fliess, November 2, 1896, in Masson, 1985: 202) or "You are requested to close an eye" (in *Interpretation of Dreams*, 1953a/1900: 317). Freud interpreted this as a double meaning, referring to the duty of a (Jewish) son to close the eyes of his dead father, or—if winking (closing just one eye)—feeling guilt for having failed to take his duty seriously. This closing of the eyes has been interpreted by later analytic writers as Freud's obeying an inner wish/command to close his *own* eyes to his father's molestation of his siblings (noted by Freud to Fliess just three months later—Masson, 1985: 231–232). Krüll (1986) argues that Freud did indeed close his eyes at this time to his father's "perversion," and in so doing, turned away from the seduction theory (i.e., hysteria was caused by actual sexual abuse), reversing the logic in his oedipal theory so that it was now the child who desired his parent. Freud was long preoccupied with the symbolism of eyes. He associated eye symbolism with oedipal fantasies, and Oedipus' blindness as a symbol of castration (punishment for sex with his mother) (1953a/1900: 398n1). Freud may have closed his own eyes in denial, but the word "eyes" appears in *Interpretation of Dreams* at least ninety-three times. The theme of

fear of losing one's eyes as a disguised fear of castration appears again in "The Uncanny," in the grisly story of the Sand-Man from E. T. A. Hoffman's *Tales of Hoffmann* (Freud 1955c/1919: 227–233).
231 Freud, 1953a/1900: 510.

References

Anti-Defamation League (2017). Anti-semitism. Online at www.adl.org/anti-semitism. Accessed March 19, 2017.

Arendt, Hannah (1963). *Eichmann in Jerusalem: A study in the banality of evil*. New York: Viking.

Aron, Lewis (2004). The tree of knowledge: Good and evil conflicting interpretations. *Psychoanalytic Dialogues, 15* (5): 681–707.

Aron, Lewis (2007). Freud's ironically Jewish science: Commentary on paper by Jill Salberg. *Psychoanalytic Dialogues, 17* (2): 219–231.

Aron, Lewis and Henik, Libby (Eds.) (2010). *Answering a question with a question: Contemporary psychoanalysis and Jewish thought*. Brighton, MA: Academic Studies Press.

Aron, Lewis and Starr, Karen (2010). "Going out to meet you, I found you coming toward me": Transformation in Jewish mysticism and contemporary psychoanalysis. In Lewis Aron and Libby Henik (Eds.), *Answering a question with a question: Contemporary psychoanalysis and Jewish thought* (pp. 327–344). Brighton, MA: Academic Studies Press.

Aron, Lewis and Starr, Karen (2013). *A psychotherapy for the people: Toward a progressive psychoanalysis*. New York: Routledge.

Bakan, David (1990). *Sigmund Freud and the Jewish mystical tradition*, rev. ed. London: Free Association Books. (Orig. publ. 1958.)

Bauman, Zygmunt (2000). *Modernity and the Holocaust*, 2nd ed. Ithaca, NY: Cornell University Press.

Beller, Steven (1989). *Vienna and the Jews 1867–1938: A cultural history*. Cambridge, UK: Cambridge University Press.

Beller, Steven (2015). *Antisemitism: A very short introduction*, 2nd ed. Oxford, UK: Oxford University Press.

Bergmann, Martin S. (1982). Moses and the evolution of Freud's Jewish identity. In Mortimer Ostow (Ed.), *Judaism and psychoanalysis* (pp. 111–142). New York: KTAV.

Billig, Michael (1999). *Freudian repression: Conversations creating the unconscious*. Cambridge, UK: Cambridge University Press.

Blom, Philipp (2008). *The vertigo years: Europe, 1900–1914*. New York: Basic Books.

Bloom, Harold (1987). Freud and beyond. In *Ruin the sacred truths: Poetry and belief from the Bible to the present* (pp. 143–204). Cambridge, MA: Harvard University Press.

Blum, Harold P. (1994). Dora's conversion syndrome: A contribution to the prehistory of the Holocaust. *Psychoanalytic Quarterly, 63*: 518–525.

Blum, Harold P. (2010). Antisemitism in the Freud case histories. In Arnold D. Richards (Ed.), *The Jewish world of Sigmund Freud* (pp. 78–95). Jefferson, NC and London: McFarland.

Botz, Gerhard (1992). The dynamics of persecution in Austria, 1938–45. In Robert Wistrich (Ed.), *Austrians and Jews in the twentieth century* (pp. 199–219). New York: St. Martin's Press.

Boyarin, Daniel (1997). *Unheroic conduct: The rise of heterosexuality and the invention of the Jewish man.* Berkeley: University of California Press.

Boyarin, Daniel (1999). *Dying for God: Martyrdom and the making of Christianity and Judaism.* Stanford, CA: Stanford University Press.

Boyarin, Daniel (2004). The Christian invention of Judaism: The Theodosian empire and the rabbinic refusal of religion. *Representations, 85*: 21–57.

Brickman, Celia (2010). Psychoanalysis and Judaism in context. In Lewis Aron and Libby Henik (Eds.), *Answering a question with a question: Contemporary psycho-analysis and Jewish thought* (pp. 25–54). Brighton, MA: Academic Studies Press.

Bronner, Stephen Eric (2003). *A rumor about the Jews: Reflections on antisemitism and the "Protocols of the Elders of Zion."* Oxford, UK: Oxford University Press.

Clark, Christopher (2012). *The sleepwalkers: How Europe went to war in 1914.* New York: Harper Collins.

Coles, R. (1993). *Anna Freud: The dream of psychoanalysis.* New York: Da Capo Press.

Cuddihy, John Murray (1974). *The ordeal of civility: Freud, Marx, Levi-Strauss and the Jewish struggle with modernity.* New York: Basic Books.

Cushman, Philip (2007). A burning world, an absent God: Midrash, heremeneutics, and relational psychoanalysis. *Contemporary Psychoanalysis, 43* (1): 47–86.

Danto, Elizabeth Ann (2007). *Freud's free clinics: Psychoanalysis and social justice, 1918–1938.* New York: Columbia University Press.

Davidowicz, Lucy (1976). *The war against the Jews: 1933–1945.* New York: Bantam.

Decker, Hannah S. (1991). *Freud, Dora, and Vienna 1900.* New York: Free Press.

de Waal, Edmund (2010). *The hare with amber eyes: A hidden inheritance.* New York: Random House.

Dühring, Eugen (1881). *Die Judenfrage: Racen-, Sitten-, und Culturfrage.* Karlsruhe and Leipzig: H. Reuther. Online at https://archive.org/stream/Duehring-Die-Judenfrage-2/DuehringEugen-DieJudenfrageAlsRacen-Sitten-UndCulturfrage1881167S.Scan#page/n0/mode/2up. Accessed October 10, 2016.

Eigen, Michael (1998). *The psychoanalytic mystic.* London: Free Association Books.

Eigen, Michael (2012). *Kabbalah and psychoanalysis.* London: Karnac.

Ellenberger, Henri F. (1970). *The discovery of the unconscious: The history and evolution of dynamic psychiatry.* New York: Basic Books.

Engelman, Edmund (1976). *Berggasse 19: Sigmund Freud's home and offices, Vienna 1938—The photographs of Edmund Engelman.* New York: Basic Books.

Freud, Ernst (Ed.) (1960). *Letters of Sigmund Freud, 1873–1939.* Tania and James Stern (Trans.). New York: Basic Books.

Freud, Martin (1957). *Glory reflected: Sigmund Freud—man and father.* London: Angus & Robertson.

Freud, Sigmund (1953a). *The interpretation of dreams.* In J. Strachey (Ed.), *Standard edition of the complete works of Sigmund Freud*, Vol. 4–5 (entire). (Orig. publ. 1900.)

Freud, Sigmund (1953b). *Fragment of an analysis of a case of hysteria ["Dora"].* In J. Strachey (Ed.), *Standard edition of the complete works of Sigmund Freud*, Vol. 7: 3–124. (Orig. publ. 1905.)

Freud, Sigmund (1955a). *Preface to the Hebrew translation of* Totem and taboo. In J. Strachey (Ed.), *Standard edition of the complete works of Sigmund Freud*, Vol. 13: xv. (Orig. publ. 1934.)

Freud, Sigmund (1955b). *Lines of advance in psycho-analytic therapy*. In J. Strachey (Ed.), *Standard edition of the complete works of Sigmund Freud*, Vol. 17: 157–168. (Orig. German publ. 1919.)

Freud, Sigmund (1955c). *The uncanny*. In J. Strachey (Ed.), *Standard edition of the complete works of Sigmund Freud*, Vol. 17: 217–256. (Orig. publ. 1919.)

Freud, Sigmund (1959). *An autobiographical study*. In J. Strachey (Ed.), *Standard edition of the complete works of Sigmund Freud*, Vol. 20: 1–74. (Orig. publ. 1925.)

Freud, Sigmund (1960). *Jokes and their relation to the unconscious*. In J. Strachey (Ed.), *Standard edition of the complete works of Sigmund Freud*, Vol. 8 (entire). (Orig. German publ. 1905.)

Freud, Sigmund (1996). *Kürzste Chronik*. Michael Molnar (Ed.). Basel: Stroemfeld/Roter Stern. (Orig. unpubl. MS 1938, at the Freud Museum, London.) Excerpts online at www.wpv.at/geschichte/emigration-sigmund-freud/kuerzeste-chronik. Accessed January 14, 2017.

Frosh, Stephen (2005). *Hate and the "Jewish science."* New York: Palgrave Macmillan.

Frosh, Stephen (2010). "Foreignness is the quality which the Jews and one's own instincts have in common": Anti-Semitism, identity and the other. In Lewis Aron and Libby Henik (Eds.), *Answering a question with a question: Contemporary psychoanalysis and Jewish thought* (pp. 345–368). Brighton, MA: Academic Studies Press.

Gay, Peter (1976). Introduction. In Edmund Engelman, *Berggasse 19: Sigmund Freud's home and offices, Vienna 1938—The photographs of Edmund Engelman* (pp. 1–47). New York: Basic Books.

Gay, Peter (1978). *Freud, Jews and other Germans: Masters and victims in modernist culture*. Oxford, UK: Oxford University Press.

Gay, Peter (1987). *A godless Jew: Freud, atheism, and the making of psychoanalysis*. New Haven: Yale University Press.

Gay, Peter (1995). *The Enlightenment: An interpretation—the rise of modern paganism*. New York: W. W. Norton.

Gay, Peter (2006). *Freud: A life for our time*. New York: W.W. Norton.

Geller, Jay (2006). *Atheist* Jew or Atheist *Jew*: Freud's Jewish question and ours. *Modern Judaism, 26* (1): 1–14.

Geller, Jay (2007). *On Freud's Jewish body: Mitigating circumcisions*. New York: Fordham University Press.

Gilman, Sander (1986). *Jewish self-hatred: Anti-semitism in times of crisis*. New York: New York University Press.

Gilman, Sander (1991). *The Jew's body*. New York: Routledge.

Gilman, Sander (1993). *Freud, race, and gender*. Princeton, NJ: Princeton University Press.

Gobineau, Arthur (2015). *The inequality of human races*. Adrian Collins (Trans.). Andesite Press. (Orig. publ. 1853.)

Grinker, Roy, Sr. (1975). Reminiscences of Dr. Roy Grinker. *Journal of the American Academy of Psychoanalysis, 3*: 211–221.

Grollman, Earl A. (1965). *Judaism in Sigmund Freud's world*. New York: Appleton-Century/Bloch.

Gruber, Helmut (1991). *Red Vienna: Experiment in working-class culture, 1919–1934*. New York: Oxford University Press.

Herzl, Theodor (2012). *The Jews' state: A critical translation*. Hank Overberg (Trans.). Lanham, MD: Rowman & Littlefield. (Orig. publ. 1896.)

Hübel, T., Johler, B., and Marinelli, L. (2003). Freud's lost neighbors. C. Barber (Trans.). Unpublished text for special exhibit, March 26–September 28, 2003. Vienna: Sigmund Freud Museum.

Jacoby, Russell (1983). *The repression of psychoanalysis: Otto Fenichel and the political Freudians*. New York: Basic Books.

Jones, E. (1957). *The life and work of Sigmund Freud, Vol. 3: The last phase: 1919–1939*. New York: Basic Books.

Jüdisches Museum Wien (2015). Ringstrasse: A Jewish boulevard. Exhibition March 25 to October 18, 2015. Description online at www.jmw.at/en/exhibitions/ringstrasse-jewish-boulevard. Accessed September 8, 2016.

Klein, Dennis B. (1985). *Jewish origins of the psychoanalytic movement*. Chicago: University of Chicago Press.

Krüll, Marianne (1986). *Freud and his father*. New York: W. W. Norton.

"Leopoldstadt" (2016). Online at https://de.wikipedia.org/wiki/Leopoldstadt.

Lohrmann, Klaus (2004). A brief history of the Viennese Jews. In Michaela Feuerstein-Prasser and Gerhard Milchram (Eds.), Nick Somers (Trans.), *Jewish Vienna*, 3rd ed. (pp. 17–30). Vienna: Mandelbaum.

Masson, Jeffrey Moussaief (Ed. and Trans.) (1985). *The complete letters of Sigmund Freud to Wilhelm Fliess 1887–1904*. Cambridge, MA: Belknap/Harvard University Press.

McCagg, William O., Jr. (1989). *A history of Habsburg Jews, 1670–1918*. Bloomington: Indiana University Press.

Meghnagi, David (1993). A cultural event within Judaism. In *Freud and Judaism* (pp. 57–71). London: Karnac.

Merkur, Dan (2014). *Relating to God: Clinical psychoanalysis, spirituality, and theism*. Lanham, MD: Jason Aronson.

Mühlleitner, Elke and Reichmayr, Johannes (1997). Following Freud in Vienna. *International Forum for Psychoanalysis, 6*: 73–102.

New York Times (1903). Jewish massacre denounced. East Side mass meeting plans to helps victims of Russians in Kishinev. *New York Times*, April 28, p. 6, col. 2. Archived online at http://timesmachine.nytimes.com/timesmachine/1903/04/28/101992584.html?pageNumber=6. Accessed September 3, 2016.

Nirenberg, David (2013). *Anti-Judaism: The western tradition*. New York: W. W. Norton.

Nunberg, Herbert and Federn, Ernst (Eds.) (1962). *Minutes of the Vienna Psychoanalytic Society, 1906–1938*, Vol. 1. M. Nunberg (Trans.). New York: International Universities Press.

Nunberg, Herbert and Federn, Ernst (Eds.) (1974). *Minutes of the Vienna Psychoanalytic Society, 1906–1938*, Vol. 3. M. Nunberg (Trans.). New York: International Universities Press.

Ostow, Mortimer (Ed.) (1982). *Psychoanalysis and Judaism*. London: Karnac.

Oxaal, Ivan (1988). The Jewish origins of psychoanalysis reconsidered. In Edward Timms and Naomi Segal (Eds.), *Freud in exile: Psychoanalysis and its vicissitudes* (pp. 37–53). New Haven, CT: Yale University Press.

Reijzer, Hans (2011). *A dangerous legacy: Judaism and the psychoanalytic movement*. Jeannette Ringold (Trans.). London: Karnac.

Reik, Theodor (1962). *Jewish wit*. New York: Gamut Press.

Rizzuto, Ana-Maria (1998). *Why did Freud reject God? A psychodynamic interpretation*. New Haven, CT: Yale University Press.

Roback, A.A. (1929). *Jewish influence in modern thought*. Cambridge, MA: Sci-Art.

Robert, Marthe (1976). *From Oedipus to Moses: Freud's Jewish identity*. Ralph Mannheim (Trans.). New York: Anchor Books.

Rose, Louis (1998). *The Freudian calling: Early Viennese psychoanalysis and the pursuit of cultural science*. Detroit: Wayne State University Press.

Rozenblitt, Marsha (1983). *The Jews of Vienna, 1867–1918: Assimilation and identity*. Albany, NY: SUNY Press.

Rozenblitt, Marsha (2001). *Reconstructing a national identity: The Jews of Habsburg Austria during World War I*. New York: Oxford University Press.

Rozenblitt, Marsha (2010). Assimilation and affirmation: The Jews of Freud's Vienna. In Arnold D. Richards (Ed.), *The Jewish world of Sigmund Freud* (pp. 22–34). Jefferson, NC and London: McFarland.

Said, Edward (2003). *Freud and the non-European*. London: Verso/Freud Museum London.

Salberg, Jill (2007). Hidden in plain sight: Freud's Jewish identity revisited. *Psychoanalytic Dialogues, 17* (2): 197–217. [Reprinted in Arnold Richards (Ed.) (2010). *The Jewish world of Sigmund Freud: Essays on cultural roots and the problem of religious identity* (pp. 5–21). Jefferson, NC: McFarland.]

Schindel, Robert (2004). My Vienna. In Michaela Feuerstein-Prasser and Gerhard Milchram (Eds.), Nick Somers (Trans.), *Jewish Vienna*, 3rd ed. (pp. 9–16). Vienna: Mandelbaum.

Schorske, Carl (1981). *Fin-de-siècle Vienna: Politics and culture*. New York: Vintage.

Schramm, Brooks and Stjerna, Kirsi (Eds.) (2012). *Martin Luther, the Bible, and the Jewish people: A reader*. Minneapolis: Fortress Press.

Sigmund Freud Museum Wien (n.d.). *Vita Sigmund Freud*. Online at www.freud-museum. at/en/sigmund-and-anna-freud/vita-sigmund-freud.html. Accessed September 29, 2015.

Slavet, Eliza (2009). *Racial fever: Freud and the Jewish question*. New York: Fordham University Press.

Slavet, Eliza (2010). Freud's theory of Jewishness: For better and for worse. In Arnold D. Richards (Ed.), *The Jewish world of Sigmund Freud* (pp. 96–111). Jefferson, NC and London: McFarland.

Starr, Karen (2008). *Repair of the soul: Metaphors of transformation in Jewish mysticism and psychoanalysis*. New York: Routledge.

Stekel, Wilhelm (1950). *The autobiography of Wilhelm Stekel: The life story of a pioneer psychoanalyst*. E. A. Gutheil (Ed.). New York: Liveright.

Sulloway, Frank (1992). *Freud, biologist of the mind: Beyond the psychoanalytic legend*, 2nd ed. Cambridge, MA: Harvard University Press.

Synagogue Memorial Beit Ashkenaz (2017). Austrian synagogues. Online at www.austrian synagogues.com/index.php/archive. Accessed January 14, 2017.

Wien Geschichte (2014). Leopoldskirche. Online at www.wien.gv.at/wiki/index.php/ Leopoldskirche_(2,_Alexander-Poch-Platz). Accessed September 3, 2016.

Wistrich, Robert S. (1990). *The Jews of Vienna in the age of Franz Josef*. Oxford, UK: Oxford University Press.

Wistrich, Robert S. (1991). *Antisemitism: The longest hatred*. New York: Pantheon.

Wistrich, Robert S. (2010). *A lethal obsession: Anti-semitism from antiquity to the global Jihad*. New York: Random House.

Wolff, Larry (1988). *Postcards from the end of the world: An investigation into the mind of fin-de-siècle Vienna*. London: Collins.

Yerushalmi, Yosef Hayim (1991). *Freud's Moses: Judaism terminable and interminable*. New Haven: Yale University Press.

Zaretsky, Eli (2004). *Secrets of the soul: A social and cultural history of psychoanalysis*. New York: Alfred Knopf.

Chapter 8

"In the presence of the burning children"

Psychoanalysis, religion, and society—
then and now

> The Holocaust confronts us with unanswerable questions. But let us agree to one
> principle: no statement, theological or otherwise, should be made that would not
> be credible in the presence of the burning children.
>
> (Irving Greenberg)[1]

In the Introduction to this book, I described two theses—the one I went in
looking for (complexity in the early Viennese analysts' thoughts about religion)—
and the one that in a sense "found" me (the total context of antisemitism that
shaped and permeated those same thoughts). My research process involved a
shift from examining conscious attitudes and beliefs, to experiencing and bearing
witness[2] to the reality of antisemitism. This was a "return of the repressed," I
believe—a re-emergence of a centuries-old complex trauma that was both subliminal yet always present as an ominous background noise. This "uncanny"[3]
knowledge has been returning not only within my own subjectivity, but also as
part of a collective, in both the field of psychoanalysis and the psychology of
religion.[4] What are the implications of this uncanny return for the history of
psychoanalysis and religion? And what might be the implications for a wider
psycho-social analysis of the current situation in America and Europe—where
uncanny forms of fear and violence still operate in the global psyche?

In the presence of the burning children:
psychoanalysis, antisemitism, and the Holocaust

The Holocaust was a shattering of history, and has been investigated in every
generation since, with ever-deepening insights about the multi-generational
impact of trauma.[5] Only recently have psychoanalysts begun to unpack the
effects of the Holocaust on the analysts who escaped, on the institutes that
received them, and even on the shaping (or mis-shaping) of post-war psychoanalytic theory.[6] My project is slightly different, though related. The impact of
the Holocaust should never be underestimated, but it is my contention that
because it was, in Bettelheim's words, such an "extreme situation,"[7] the long
prior history of antisemitism in itself may become subsumed in its glare. I want to

argue that in addition to the Holocaust itself, the decades—as well as centuries—of antisemitism that led up to it are not incidental but are central to the development of psychoanalysis.

Freud's Jewishness has already been well examined as a dynamic factor in the development of psychoanalysis (see Chapter 2). Yet Jewishness in itself is not identical with antisemitism. The very long shadow of antisemitism *itself* must also be located as a catalyst at the *fons et origo* of psychoanalytic theory and practice—both in terms of what the first analysts saw (that no one else was seeing), and what they failed to see. This is not to say, of course, that antisemitism was the *only* factor in the development of psychoanalysis. The emergence of a science and a hermeneutic of the unconscious was overdetermined like everything else. Psychoanalysis incorporates a rich, complicated tapestry of sources and influences. Yet the core realization of psychoanalytic thought—that there is always more beneath the surface appearances of reality, and that this "more" is among other things affective, memory-laden, and psychological—cannot fail to have had something to do with the experiences of the first Jewish analysts in their position of marginality and oppression.

The influence of antisemitism

Antisemitism, as a belief system saturating the dominant culture of western Europe, perforce delineated the Jew as "Other," setting the Jewish community not literally but metaphorically "beyond the Pale."[8] As discussed in the previous chapter, Jews in different contexts at various times embraced this outsider position as a safe enclave, or sought to escape it through assimilation. But their view was always one from the margins, a view that Gentiles did not share or even perceive. As postcolonial theory has taught us,[9] the view from the margins is often more acute and penetrating than from the mountaintop of privilege.[10] Comparing Freud to other "great revolutionaries" of thought, Isaac Deutscher declared to the World Jewish Congress in 1968,

> as Jews they dwelt on the borderlines of various civilizations, religions, and national cultures. Their minds matured where the most diverse cultural influences crossed and fertilized each other. They lived on the margins or in the nooks and crannies of their respective nations. Each of them was in society and yet not in it, of it and yet not of it. It was this that enabled them to rise in thought above their societies, above their nations, above their times and generations, and to strike out mentally into wide new horizons and far into the future.[11]

As Dutch psychoanalyst Hans Reijzer has observed, "When people live between two cultures, they think dialectically and see society dynamically."[12] The Jews of Austria could speak and understand the language and culture of both oppressed and oppressor, and they also could not but view and judge themselves through the lens of the dominant culture. In his culture shock during his first visit to the Wednesday Night Society, Jung may have viewed the Viennese analysts as "cynical,"[13] but in their own context that was simply what came of being awake to the societal dynamics into which they were born. It was part and parcel of surviving in a hostile climate.

Yearning for acceptance and assimilation was one psychic force, which sometimes engendered both denial and hope. Realism and the knowledge of danger was a countervailing force. The former—the assimilationist story that psychoanalysis is a western science—is the narrative told most often. The latter—the subversive knowledge of oppression—is the uncanny truth of trauma, which returns again and again in disguised form, but can never remain entirely repressed.[14] The total context of antisemitism, and the first analysts' efforts to resist its penetrating logic of denigration, could not have failed to inform and shape their ethical sensibilities and their vision of social justice. Moreover, this experience infused them with a psychic need to analyze what dark secrets lay beneath the human psyche—of which sex and aggression were perhaps the most powerful in nineteenth- and twentieth-century Vienna. Thus antisemitism had an indelible impact, not only on their personal and professional lives and aspirations, but on the very formation of psychoanalytic theory.

The Holocaust

Of course the impact of the Holocaust itself on psychoanalysis should not be minimized. According to an exhaustive study of the biographies of all members of Freud's Vienna circle from 1902 to 1938, "[o]nly 18 of the 124 past or present members of the Viennese Psychoanalytical Society alive in 1938 were not [directly] affected by the persecutions, due to their descent, religion or place of residence."[15] Only five remained in Austria (Joachim, Pötzl, Aichhorn, Winterstein, and Nepallek).[16] Most emigrated in the years 1933 to 1938 to the United States, Palestine, South America, or other parts of Europe and Scandinavia.[17]

At least eleven psychoanalysts who had been members of the Vienna Society at some point between 1902 and its dissolution in 1938 were murdered in the Holocaust. The following analysts died in concentration camps or ghettoes: Alfred Bass was removed to the Łódź Ghetto in 1941 and presumed to have died there or in one of the transports to the death camps.[18] Sabina Spielrein was murdered by a Nazi firing squad in Rostov, Russia, in 1941 (see Chapter 6).[19] Margarete Hilferding, the first woman admitted to the Vienna Psychoanalytic Society was deported to Theresienstadt/Terezín in 1942 and died in the Treblinka extermination camp.[20] Isidor Sadger died in Treblinka, also in 1942.[21] Bukowina Czernowitz, Adolf Deutsch, Alfred Meisl, and David Ernst Oppenheim were all deported to Theresienstadt/Terezín in 1943 and presumed to have died there or in one of the transports to the death camps.[22] Karl Landauer emigrated several times after 1932, but in 1944 was deported from Amsterdam to Bergen-Belsen.[23] Nicola Sugar was deported to Theresienstadt/Terezín in 1944 and died there the following year.[24] Salomea Kempner was deported from Berlin to the Warsaw Ghetto and is presumed to have died in the early 1940s.[25]

More members of the Vienna Psychoanalytic Society may have died in the Holocaust, but complete biographical data is still unavailable.[26] Guido Brecher was exiled from St. Johann im Pongau near Salzburg; the details of his death are undocumented.[27] Frida Teller's death is unknown.[28] Others died during or soon after the war due to the toll on their general health. Stefanie ("Steff") Bornstein-Windholzova survived the Nazi attack on Czechoslovakia and was the last chairperson of the Prague Psychoanalytic Association, but died in Prague in 1939 of a heart attack while awaiting papers to emigrate to the United States.[29] Josef Reinhold survived internment in the Polish concentration camp in Drahobycze, secretly providing emergency medical care to the few prisoners who remained after the mass exterminations in 1942. He lived to witness the liberation of the camp by the Red Army in 1944, but died in 1947 of a heart attack.[30] Martin Pappenheim escaped Vienna, but died in Tel Aviv in 1943 at age sixty-two.[31]

Many other psychoanalysts from Germany, Czechoslovakia, and other parts of eastern Europe died, while others barely survived the Nazi camps. Ernst Federn, co-editor of the Minutes of the Vienna Psychoanalytic Society, was himself a survivor of Dachau and Buchenwald.[32] Many analytic patients in Vienna were also victims.[33] The Jewish population of Freud's 9th district was decimated. Four of Freud's own sisters, Rosa Graf, Marie ("Mitzi") Freud, Adolfine ("Dolfi") Freud, and Pauline Winternitz, perished.[34] Following *Kristallnacht*—the infamous night in November, 1938, when riots and looting broke out against Jewish homes and businesses—Freud recorded tersely in his diary, "Pogroms in Germany."[35] Safely settled in London, Freud was deeply worried about his sisters. Vienna's streets were scenes of nightmarish violence even exceeding those in Germany.[36] In the tense and difficult negotiations involved in gaining permission for Freud himself to leave, he had requested visas for them as well, but passage was only granted to his immediate household. In spite of further efforts by Marie Bonaparte to obtain visas to France or Greece, the four sisters did end up being deported. According to records compiled by Yad Vashem, Marie, Dolfi, and Pauli were among 1,005 Jews, most over age sixty, on Transport 29 from Vienna to Theresienstadt/Terezín in Czechoslovakia in June, 1942. Sleeping on one of countless thin boards stacked from floor to ceiling and forced to do physical labor, Dolfi died there at age eighty. On September 23, Marie (age eighty-one) and Pauli (age seventy-eight) were taken on another train, Transport "Bq," which carried 1,980 Jews to the death camp in Treblinka, Poland.[37]

Samuel Rajzman, a Treblinka survivor, said in his testimony before the Nuremberg International Military Tribunal in 1946 that he had witnessed their arrival in the camp. He described one of the sisters—it was not clear which—approaching the commander of the camp, showing him an identifying document, saying she was the sister of Sigmund Freud and asking to be given light office work. The commander said there must have been a mistake and told her that in two hours there should be a train to Vienna. "She could leave all her valuables and documents here, have a bath, and after the bath she would receive her documents and a travel permit to Vienna," Mr. Rajzman cited the camp commander as saying. "The lady, of course, went to the bath house, from which she never returned."[38]

The cumulative impact of these deaths, even among those who survived into the 1950s and later, cannot be ignored in the history of psychoanalysis either in Europe or in the Americas. What was the impact of the Holocaust on psychoanalysis as it became a "Jewish science" in exile?

The "Jewish science" in exile

Because of considerable support for psychoanalysis and its founders within the Allied nations, close to 90 percent of the Viennese analysts did escape. Some found considerable professional success and rose quickly to leadership—bearing the authority of Freud's inner circle—in existing institutes, especially in the United States (e.g., New York, Boston, and Los Angeles), Great Britain (especially London), South America (especially in Argentina), and Palestine (cities in modern-day Israel). In addition to clinical practice and treatment, some also imported the progressive approaches to education begun in Vienna in the 1920s.[39] Only three (non-Jewish) analysts remained in Vienna, most notably August Aichhorn, who served in the Viennese outpost of the official German Institute for Psychotherapy, while conducting underground seminars in psychoanalysis. He re-established the Vienna Psychoanalytic Society after the war and chaired it until his death in 1949.[40]

In a brilliant analysis of the impact of the Holocaust on psychoanalysis, based on both documentary evidence and on interviews with émigré analysts, Emily Kuriloff describes the collisions that occurred when these refugees arrived in the U.S.[41] These new refugees joined an already established psychoanalytic community, mainly centered in the northeast but radiating out into other parts of the country as well. New York was the jewel in the crown, and tensions between the Americans and the European émigrés created a "wretched" atmosphere of mutual suspicion, in- and out-groups, and paranoia, as described by one observer.[42] As described in Chapter 4, the New York Institute had dug in its heels in opposition to lay analysts in an effort early on to obtain mainstream respectability as part of the medical profession. Many of the émigrés themselves were lay analysts, or their European medical credentials were not accepted. But those who had trained directly with Freud had the advantage of having an unrivaled psychoanalytic genealogy and were given deference.[43] Others were most often urged to join outlying institutes. The émigrés in turn tended to stick together and to look down on the Americans. The next generation of leaders in New York came from their group: Heinz Hartmann, Ernst Kris, and Rudolph

Loewenstein. These émigrés established ego psychology in the United States as synonymous with "classical analysis" for many decades.[44]

Kuriloff attributes the well-known rigidity of American ego psychology in the 1940s, 1950s, and beyond, to a subliminal drive by these wartime émigrés to establish certainty and security amidst the strains of assimilation to a new culture, and perhaps more unconsciously, as a post-traumatic re-enactment of the harsh authoritarianism they had experienced under the Nazi regime.[45] Kurt Eisold described the atmosphere of the Boston Psychoanalytic Institute as "too charged with humorless hostility ... an assemblage of cultists, rigid in thought, armored against new ideas, and ... ruthlessly rivalrous for power."[46] Kris' son told Kuriloff that psychoanalysis had not been that way before the war:

> I do know that the [postwar] orthodoxy was a stifling thing, and not neces-
> sarily was it always the case. For instance, I was later told that the analyst's
> silence was not part of the Viennese tradition. The notion of "pure" abstin-
> ence in this way was partly English and American.[47]

Otto Kernberg recalled that the Viennese émigrés "idealized what they had lost in Europe, and experienced new ideas as a threat to that idealization."[48]

Kuriloff's findings are significant, not only with regard to the institutional rigidity of the post-war psychoanalytic establishment in America, but also because this rigidity permeated "classical Freudian" *theory* as well—the vicissi-tudes of history and culture and the Nazi trauma actually had the effect of freez-ing their theorizing.[49] The émigré analysts' clinging to what they had lost resulted in a tendency to preserve Freudian concepts such as the drives, repres-sion, and resistance, as if sealing them in the hard rock of amber. As Kuriloff describes, they felt they had lost everything, and the preservation of psycho-analysis as they had first learned it at the feet of Freud had the function of a tal-isman, a denial of loss.[50]

This defensive rigidity impacted not only the training of future generations of analysts, but impacted patients as well. Kuriloff documents numerous examples of Holocaust survivor patients whose post-traumatic suffering was repeatedly interpreted in terms of oedipal dynamics and neurotic defense. Adult trauma, when it was acknowledged, was thought to be less significant than the infantile past, and patients' reactions to later trauma were interpreted through the lens of earlier developmental crises (usually oedipal).[51] Analyst Dori Laub described receiving such classical supervision in Boston:

> He was a wonderful supervisor, but even he did not see the trauma in my
> patient's life. The patient's father was lost in the Pacific during the war and
> my supervisor focused on her jealousy.... No one asked about the father, or
> the intergenerational transmission of trauma.... The analysis failed.... The
> patient would scream at me and a colleague next door heard and asked me,
> "What are you doing to her?"[52]

Laub told Kuriloff that "orthodoxy became an armor, the theory became their armor, to leave no opening for some memory, some recognition of what had happened to creep in."[53] This rigid emphasis on intrapsychic conflict and oedipal dynamics over actual external events may also help to explain the reluctance of psychoanalysts to recognize the pervasiveness of childhood sexual abuse, and the necessity of working empathically with survivors to heal from real traumatic events in their lives.

It should be emphasized that not all émigré analysts, nor all Holocaust survivors more generally, had identical reactions to the traumatic events of World War II. Kuriloff recounts analyst Anna Ornstein's insistence that not every Holocaust survivor exhibits severe pathology (as is often assumed), and that themes of resilience, imagination, and empathy characterized the lives of many survivors. In Ornstein's case, as a younger analyst and Self Psychologist, she felt she could draw on her memories—which were conscious—to form an empathic bond with her patients' suffering.[54] Nevertheless, most of the older émigré analysts seem, like many Holocaust survivors generally, to have suppressed if not repressed some of their worst memories from their homeland, and others—perhaps adaptively to some degree—compartmentalized their experiences as personal, and "essentially incompatible with their professional analytic stance—one of abstinence and neutrality—so that any published record they produced tended not to value nor elaborate on how their private pain influenced their theory or praxis."[55]

Another effect of the Holocaust on the émigré analysts was simply a lack of trust—for people or institutions. As a professor of Holocaust studies at Harvard Divinity School once told our class, "One day you are sitting with your family in a beautiful room eating a chicken dinner. The next day the rug is pulled out entirely from under you. You learn how fragile security can be." Jewish refugees, in general, understood that their welcome in America was conditional. They were not blind to many of the same strains of antisemitism that they had encountered in Europe, and sought to blend in as best they could. Many of the analysts had also been forced to flee their homes not only for being Jewish, but for being socialists—and in some cases (especially in Berlin, as with Fenichel), Marxist activists.[56] Socialists, Marxists, and "Bolsheviks" were increasingly regarded with suspicion by a majority of Americans, culminating in the McCarthy era in the 1950s, and Jews were often assumed to be in sympathy with the hated communist enemy. Post-war analysts, therefore, were not only quiet about their Jewish identity and political leanings for reasons of therapeutic neutrality, but also for fear of reprisals and—not unlike the first analysts in *fin-de-siècle* Vienna—out of a desire to assimilate.

As Russell Jacoby describes, post-war psychoanalysis lost both its philosophical and political features—losses to which a new generation of American trainees were none the wiser. By the 1950s,

> psychoanalysis became transformed, and transformed itself. The second generation of analysts witnessed, suffered, and abetted this reconstruction of

psychoanalysis; however, they only talked, often regretfully, among themselves about it. A grasp, even an inkling, of this change did not pass into the general culture. None of the second generation of analysts publicly expressed a belief that the sleek American psychoanalysis did scant justice to the original project. Oddly, while the knowledge of Freud steadily increases, knowledge of the psychoanalytic movement and its original imperatives recedes.... The psychoanalytic texts endured, but the spirit and culture vaporized. Americans who did not experience the European chapter accepted a reduced psychoanalysis, devoid of its politics and culture, the whole enterprise. For the refugees, suppression of their culture was a small price to pay. Initially they buried, adjourned or abandoned a political psychoanalysis in the name of personal survival.[57]

Jacoby observes how, in America, much depth and political complexity of psychoanalytic writing were lost in this process:

Many, including Siegfried Bernfeld and Otto Fenichel, remain familiar figures. Their oeuvre, however, survives laundered, its political and cultural vitality bleached out. The familiarity with their work is deceptive.... As psychoanalysts should know, however, the familiar is not outside history; it is drenched in the past. The familiar has been made familiar by effacing the foreign, and, perhaps, forbidden; in this sense, psychoanalysts are acceptable after their unacceptable past has been censored. In brief, the lives and oeuvre of Fenichel and a wide group of other political analysts have been sanitized and prettified, often with their own cooperation. The catastrophe of exile and their ineluctable Americanization buried their nonconformist theories, hopes, and commitments. In the end, they fit in and succeeded by sacrificing their own identities.[58]

In addition to the trauma of the Holocaust itself, there were numerous painful losses to overcome. Ernst Federn recalled

the true tragedy that befell psychoanalysis in exile. Not only did that exile mean the loss of home, but also the loss of language and the loss of philosophical bearings. This loss was all the harder to bear as language and philosophy also meant economic and social status.[59]

No one wanted to rock the boat. "[A] 'gentleman's agreement' existed among post-war analysts, wherein 'one does not discuss Jewishness'."[60] It is interesting, in light of this understandable caution, that the one member who most flouted this rule—and published volubly on Judaism and Jewishness from a psychoanalytic perspective—was Theodor Reik, whom the New York Psychoanalytic Society refused to admit. To "come out" so publicly as a Jew required both *chutzpah* (audacity), and perhaps again, as in Vienna, the perspicacity of living on the margins—even, for Reik, on the margins of psychoanalysis itself.

Lewis Aron and Karen Starr extend these historical insights to draw a further parallel between the rigid dichotomies of post-war American "classical analysis" ("analyzable/non-analyzable; phallic/castrated; depth/surface; rational analyst/ irrational patient, among many others"[61]) and the dissociation by Enlightenment-identified Jewish analysts (going all the way back to Freud) of the most denig-rated and abject aspects of Jewish identity—the stereotype of the vulgar *Ostjuden*, the Jew as racially other, and, following Gilman,[62] Boyarin,[63] Brick-man,[64] Geller[65] (among others), the antisemitic equation of the Jewish male with weakness, primitivity, femininity, and homosexuality. They critique the post-war division between psychoanalysis (intellectual, renunciatory, stoic, insight-oriented—and patriarchal/phallic) versus psychotherapy and social work (affec-tive, caring, vulnerable, relational—and feminine). They interpret this split within American psychoanalysis as arising from an unconscious bifurcating impulse at the origins of psychoanalysis, derived from unconscious defenses against antisemitism, racism, misogyny, and homophobia, and they argue com-prehensively that a full acknowledgement of what was dissociated in the anti-semitic cultural milieu of early psychoanalysis can lead to a more holistic and socially conscious practice of analysis today—"a psychotherapy for the people."[66] Such a healing of a split between analysis and therapy, "cure and care," would in fact be most compatible with the idealistic social goals of the analysts in Red Vienna between the world wars, as described in the previous chapter. They suggest that today, when psychoanalysis has once again been pushed to the margins of both the medical and the therapeutic mainstream, we should claim the position of marginality as a plus—revaluing the positive, crea-tive, and "optimally vulnerable," even "strategic"[67] side of marginality that char-acterized the earliest analysts' social location.

Social implications and free associations: (what) are we learning from the past?

Taking into consideration years of mounting fear, the eventual terror of forced migration, and an aftermath of often intense survivor guilt, psychoanalysis was riddled at its origins with an often repressed but uncanny return of an innumer-able crowd of unlaid ghosts. Beginning with Freud's Viennese circle, and con-tinuing on from the first generation of analysts in Europe across the globe, psychoanalysis bears a multi-generational wound—antisemitism and the Holo-caust are its deepest scar and stain, a persistent, still largely unmetabolized trauma at the heart of the discipline.

One consequence of all this unmetabolized trauma may be that of all the psychotherapeutic disciplines, psychoanalysis has been among the slowest to recognize the impact of *context* on the psyche—both at the level of individual patients' sufferings, and at the level of society. This has finally been accomp-lished largely by relational psychoanalysts through the insistence on intersubjec-tivity and mutual psychic influence, via the recuperation of formerly exiled thinkers such as Sándor Férenczi. Lewis Aron and Karen Starr,[68] Stephen Mitch-ell,[69] Neil Altman,[70] Jessica Benjamin,[71] Gilbert Cole,[72] Philip Cushman,[73] Adrienne Harris,[74] Dorothy Evans Holmes,[75] Kimberlyn Leary,[76] Melanie Suchet,[77] Cleonie White,[78] and other relationalists have begun to bring the attention of psychoanalysis as a field to issues of race, class, gender, sexuality, and politics. This turn toward context is also apparent in the long overdue admission in 2015 of the William Alanson White Institute—the interpersonalist school founded by Harry Stack Sulli-van and his colleagues—into the American Psychoanalytic Association.[79] Increas-ing attention is paid to race, gender, and power by the "Tavistock" school of unconscious group relations based originally in London on the work of Wilfred Bion.[80] This (re-)turn toward context begs the question how context really did matter to the first historic generation of psychoanalysts, and should recall that his-toric, immersive reality of antisemitism into our present awareness.

Holocaust survivor Elie Wiesel, who died in the summer of 2016, was known for his passionate exhortation that we must never forget the horrors of the Holo-caust, lest we repeat them. Wiesel's words were powerful, but only a little over seventy-five years after *Kristallnacht*, few Americans, especially those outside the Jewish community, know or remember what that was, much less how it might still be relevant today. We appear to be immersed in a period of history in both the United States and Europe that feels eerily similar to the emergence of hate speech, violence, and demagoguery that preceded the Holocaust in Europe. (How) can psychoanalysis with its deep appreciation for the impact of history—especially buried history—help facilitate Wiesel's project of staying awake in the face of rising terror?

The decades between world wars

It is perilous to compare any other era in the modern western world to Nazi Germany. Such comparisons can all too easily turn into a form of arguing from extremes, and history never repeats itself exactly. History is nevertheless a source of wisdom, with cautionary tales that can point out new dangers based on past evils—especially when those evils were of human design. Stephen Frosh notes that

> … anti-Semitism is not "hard-wired" into the psyche, but rather is the cultur-ally available vehicle for the expression of certain psychic conflicts that are themselves more likely to occur under some social circumstances (such as those which prevailed in Germany after the First World War) than others.[81]

With all due caveats in mind, then, let us consider certain parallels between the years between the two world wars, and the decades leading up to our present time.

At the end of World War I, the Germans, Austrians, and their allies were pun-ished by the terms of the Treaty of Versailles.[82] They had lost over three million soldiers during the war, and by the end of the war the people were impoverished by a destroyed economy, many literally starving, and further ravaged by the Spanish flu that swept the continent in 1918. There was a profound, global economic depression, already preceded by the 1873 market crash. In Austria in particular, the arrival of thousands of eastern European Jewish settlers after the new constitution of 1867 caused native Gentile Austrians to regard the immigrants as interlopers who would steal their jobs.[83] As Frosh notes,

> young men saw their fathers go to war and come back defeated, and then saw these same fathers as unable to protect them against the ravages of the economic depression of the early nineteen-twenties, with the concomitant impact on mothers who would be in a state of long-term heightened anxiety. Under such conditions, the mother's anxiety and the father's weakness produces an internal state of boundary loss and fragile identity, which is kept at bay only by increasingly strong defensive operations, specifically splitting and projection. It also made these youngsters (specifically young men) ... prone to regression and sado-masochism, so when the renewed troubles of the nineteen-thirties arose, and with it the Nazi promise of safety and revenge in the mass, the response was immediate and powerful.[84]

So it was that ordinary people who were neither politicians nor military leaders, but simply ground up by the consequences of economic depression and war, found it easy to view themselves as victims. Hitler's rhetoric of nationalism and making Germany a great imperial power again filled a vacuum that felt irresistible. People blamed the liberal German Weimar Republic and Austrian government—along with Jews, socialists, and communists—for collaborating with the Allied Powers and betraying the German cause. Whipped up by Hitler's charismatic racial rhetoric, many individuals found permission in this rhetoric to release their previously more private racist words and deeds as public hate speech and overt violence.

Hitler's bizarre blend of pseudo-Christianity, paganism, and *Volkskultur* (with Wagnerian opera as its grand art form) invoked a shared cultural narcissism on a massive scale. Gradually a popular consensus was fostered until it seemed less and less shocking (all the while rationalized by the scientists, the lawyers, the anthropologists, and Hitler's brand of psychologists) to "purify" the Aryan nation by gathering together, then deporting, and then killing, all Jews, along with the also long-hated Roma ("Gypsies"), homosexuals, persons with disabilities, Marxists, and resistance fighters. For Jewish upper-class professionals and intellectuals, this seemed impossible to comprehend. Like the proverbial frog in the pot of water, as the heat was turned up, all too few—including Freud himself—realized the extremity of the inferno beneath their cultured feet.

Into the twenty-first century

During the Vietnam War and subsequent wars in the Persian Gulf, Iraq, and Afghanistan, Americans have sent millions of young family members overseas. The specter of 9/11, the first major attack on U.S. soil, persists as a trauma in the national psyche—especially among those whose previous sense of security and privilege was not tested (e.g., by racism and the often "invisibilized" violence in non-white neighborhoods). While not rising to the numbers of soldiers lost during the two world wars, poor and working-class families seeking economic security from the military have sent their loved ones off to war and received back a disproportionate number of flag-draped coffins and wounded warriors. Countless families cope with the invisible damage of PTSD and moral injury.

We have lived economically through a "great recession," job loss, and a widening gap between rich and poor. There have been resounding complaints on both the right and the left. Many around the globe consider us, like the empires of the early twentieth century, to be the modern imperial aggressors—yet conservative political rhetoric, especially beginning with President George W. Bush's speech after 9/11, frames us as innocent victims hated by forces of evil abroad. Our common public discourse glorifies war and warriors, while at home, oppressed groups including both persons of color and women, have fought for their rights, threatening white middle-American complacency and sense of entitlement. Racist backlash has resulted in growing violence.

As historian Richard Hofstadter stated decades earlier during the Goldwater era, American politics has been prone to a "paranoid style" (quoting sources as early as the 1700s).[85] "American political life ... has served again and again as an arena for uncommonly angry minds."[86] From a psychoanalytic perspective, whether drawing on Freud's still salient description of group psychology[87] or Melanie Klein's conceptualization of the "paranoid schizoid position"[88] (especially as applied to group dynamics by Bion[89]), Hofstadter precisely describes the paranoid-schizoid character of political groups who see themselves as targeted by a demonized Other. "The central image is that of a vast and sinister conspiracy, a gigantic and yet subtle machinery of influence set in motion to undermine and destroy a way of life."[90] Demagogues are exceptionally adept at exploiting this sense of threat and projecting it outward on entire groups as an "axis of evil."[91]

So in the U.S. today, as in Europe between the world wars, many who view themselves as ordinary people who are neither politicians nor military leaders—nor Wall Street financiers—also feel ground up by global political, economic, and military trends far beyond their personal control. It is easy for middle Americans to view themselves as victims, and President Donald Trump's rhetoric of nationalism and "making America great again" has seemed irresistible to many white, working-class voters and others who have felt disenfranchised by those in power. A growing number of Americans blame the liberal democratic government, Wall Street (again invoking the specter of antisemitism against Jewish financiers), and immigrants, for taking away their jobs and destroying the comfortable white, middle-class America, the myths of white picket fences, apple pie, and Horatio Alger—and white supremacy—on which they thought they could rely.

American extremists wrap themselves in Swastikas (outlawed in Germany and Austria), and borrow from Gobineau's racial playbook.[92] The upper echelons of Trump's administration include individuals with ties to the fascist "Alt-Right" movement in the U.S., and even to an earlier twentieth-century Nazi "knighthood."[93] Early in the Trump presidency, White House press secretary Sean Spicer asserted that Hitler had never used chemical weapons "against his own people," astonishingly ignoring the gassing of 6,000 Jews a day at Auschwitz alone at the height of the deportations,[94] and revealing an unconscious assumption about who the "real" German, Austrian, and Polish people were (and were not).

Still others who would never identify themselves as neo-Nazis were also whipped up during the 2016 presidential election by racist, Islamophobic, and antisemitic[95] propaganda. As in the 1930s, many individuals have found permission in this rhetoric to release their previously more private racist words and deeds as public hate speech and overt violence. Anti-Muslim hate groups tripled from 34 in 2015 to 101 in 2016.[96] In July 2016, the chilling specter of crowds of jubilant Republican convention-goers chanting "Lock her up! Lock her up!" and even "Hang that bitch!"[97] at a summer rally in Raleigh, North Carolina, transmuted a traditional democratic process into a witch trial against Democratic candidate Hilary Clinton. Following Trump's inauguration as president, the Southern Poverty Law Center, a longstanding civil rights organization in the U.S., recorded over 1,000 hate incidents against immigrants, Blacks, LGBTQ people, Muslims, and women, with over one-third making direct reference to Trump or his campaign.[98] In addition to antisemitic hate crimes that had been rising for several years (including before the election), close to 300 Jewish graves were desecrated in St. Louis and Philadelphia around one month after the inauguration,[99] and the Anti-Defamation League documented 161 bomb threats against Jewish institutions between January and early March, 2017, including many directed at Jewish Community Centers with children in daycare.[100]

It should be noted that the situation of American Jews is demonstrably different from more vulnerable Jewish communities in Europe, either during World War II or now—the Jewish community has relatively more political power and numbers.[101] Melanie Suchet cautions against simply conflating the peril of Jews in Austria-Germany in the 1930s to antisemitism in America today. Citing Gilman's[102] theory that by rejecting a feminized racial depiction of the Jewish male and shifting the attention of psychoanalysis from race onto gender and sexuality, she notes that Freud effectively excised race from the professional psychoanalytic discourse from very early on.[103] It follows then, in Suchet's words, that

> anti-Semitism may have played an influence in the U.S. not only around wishes to assimilate professionally, but wishes to remain whitened. So racial

inferiority may have been repressed, or dissociated and the forefathers could not allow themselves to feel inferior.... Jews in 20th century Vienna were regarded as racially denigrated, but that identification has been disavowed in the U.S., through the passing and assimilating into Whiteness. The trauma of that denigration and subsequent extermination of Jews may not have been able to be fully recognized in the years following the Holocaust, adding to the difficulty of acknowledging victimization. Perhaps that would explain, in some part, the limited ability we have cultivated to make psychoanalysis a hospitable home for African-Americans. It may dredge up for us, whitened Jews, the traumatized, dissociated identification of the oppressed, degraded other. Psychoanalysis, as a predominantly Jewish institution in the U.S., may have needed to stay whitened.[104]

At the same time, Jews do continue to function as a convenient scapegoat and Other in the U.S.,[105] along with—and with differing historical antecedents and levels of violence—African Americans, Latinos, Asians, Native Americans, women, sexual minorities, and increasingly in our own time, Muslims. To quote Frosh again,

Fenichel (1946), in one of the last papers he wrote, offers a powerful account of both the social and personal dynamic of anti-Semitic feeling. Fenichel takes the common psychoanalytic position that anti-Semitism arises in periods of social stress: the anti-Semite, immersed in confusion and led astray by ideological forces "sees in the Jew everything which brings him misery—not only his social oppressor but also his own unconscious instincts, which have gained a bloody, dirty, dreadful character from their socially induced repression." Why the Jew? Because "with his unintelligible language and incomprehensible God" the Jew appears "uncanny" to the non-Jew, yet recognizable in continuing to hold to "archaic" customs that were once part of the non-Jew's repertoire: "rejected instincts and rejected ancient times are revived for them in these incomprehensible people who live as strangers in their midst." Jews are the ideal object for projection of disturbing unconscious urges "because of the actual peculiarities of Jewish life, the strangeness of their mental culture, their bodily (black) and religious (God of the oppressed peoples) peculiarities, and their old customs," which remind the anti-Semite of "old primeval powers" which non-Jews have given up. Linked to this is a more profound identification between the Jew as foreign and uncanny, and the site of foreignness within: "It can be expressed in one sentence: one's own unconscious is also foreign. Foreignness is the quality which the Jews and one's own instincts have in common." ... [R]acist hate is magnified by the anti-Semite's terror of [his own] inner urges.[106]

To quote Julia Kristeva, "How could one tolerate a foreigner if one did not know one was a stranger to oneself?"[107] And as Melanie Suchet has noted, for white persons, this means coming especially to accepting "the parts of the self that feel abhorrent" in order to "find our way to a more settled whiteness. This is not a whitewashed space, not a conflict-free space, but a complex racialized web."[108]

The United States is not unique in its (re-)turn to xenophobic and nationalistic conservatism (nor did Hofstadter consider American politics to be unique in its paranoia).[109] Throughout Europe, right-wing movements have continually gained political leverage since the turn of the twenty-first century. Austria's near-victory by the Freedom Party signals a strong rise in the popular appeal of fascism after long frustration with the stasis within the center-left and center-right coalition. The longstanding denial of Austria's complicity in the Holocaust—"the myth that it had been the first 'victim' of the Third Reich"[110]—holds sway among increasing numbers of Austrians, in spite of a (long-delayed) public admission by Chancellor Franz Vranitzky in 1991,[111] and an even more recent public acknowledgement by Chancellor Christian Kern in 2017.[112]

Austria's near neighbor Hungary has the largest right-wing majority in Europe, but Poland, France, Great Britain ("Brexit"), and even Denmark and Sweden have also seen growing support for nationalist, anti-immigrant parties— some right-wing, others approaching a kind of left-wing fascism. Jeffrey Goldberg, Editor-in-Chief of *The Atlantic*, wrote, "Is it time for the Jews to leave Europe?"[113] While cautioning against comparing contemporary events directly to the Holocaust, Goldberg states,

> It is not 1933. But could it be 1929? Could Europe's economic stagnation combine with its inability to assimilate and enfranchise growing populations of increasingly angry Muslims in such a way as to clear a path for volatile fascist-style populism? ... Will European Jews again be faced with choosing between "a coffin and a suitcase?"[114]

Conclusion: a final plea for prophetic witness

Children are burning all over the world in wars waged in the name of religion and "ethnic cleansing." Refugees are exploited and endangered by human smugglers, desperate migrants are turned back at national borders by soldiers at barbed wire fences, and over three million children die each year of starvation.[115] Children are washing up dead on the shores of western democratic nations. For modern liberals, perhaps especially in America, all of this may have seemed impossible to predict or comprehend. Yet throughout the fall of 2016 we witnessed rallies and conventions that looked and sounded like lynch mobs. Like the proverbial frog in the pot of water, how high will the heat be turned up beneath *our* feet? Who will, like the father of the burning child,[116] continue to sleep through forebodings of destruction in order to preserve the illusion of safety, and who will notice the flickering of the flames? Who will wake up "when the most rapid awakening is called for"?[117]

Rather than heeding Elie Wiesel's warning to remember, it seems in our century that we are re-enacting the trauma of the twentieth century in a fresh instance of the uncanny and a "return of the repressed." In David Meghnagi's words,

> Certain pages of the brief and densely written "*Das Unheimliche*" ["The Uncanny"] seem almost to have sprung from Freud's mind to give an explanation for the logic of antisemitism and the sinister feeling of anguish and paralysis of many German Jews about an event that was so familiar to them but which they deluded themselves into thinking belonged to the past.[118]

Freud's prescient 1921 book, *Group Psychology and the Analysis of the Ego*,[119] written between world wars, should be on every American's and European's reading list now. In it, Freud shows how individuals' longing for a protective father can all too readily lull them into surrendering their own capacity for reason when presented with a charismatic strongman who is willing to think and act—supposedly—on their behalf. And all too often religion itself, especially in its fundamentalist forms, is recruited in the service of this brainwashing.

As American psychoanalysis has gradually been opening the door to validating religious experience and viewing spirituality as something more than purely regressive or pathological,[120] might the capacity to live in the tension between psychoanalysis and religion help us to resist the dichotomizing, pathological splitting, and "othering" tendencies so prevalent in twenty-first-century America? Relational analyst Lewis Aron recently affirmed that psychoanalysis "may be envisioned as a religious practice, a form of worship, in which contact is made with the Almighty through immersion in the richness and depth of the inner life and in communion with the Other."[121] Philip Cushman has also argued that the in-depth and multi-layered process of midrash has relevance both for relational psychoanalysis and for "resistance to fundamentalist movements," through its interrogation of singular readings of scripture, traditional narratives, or politics.[122] He draws on the relational psychoanalytic concept of the multiplicity of the self to argue for complexity of interpretation as equally necessary in religious study, in the practice of psychoanalysis, or in political life.[123]

If psychoanalysis is the "talking cure" for individuals who find themselves acting irrationally against their own best interests, what "talking cure" will we find to help us resist the blind repetition of the horrors of xenophobic nationalism/irrationalism in the America and Europe of today? What language(s) can we borrow from the highest and best of our multiple psychological and religious traditions (whether as believers or as secular descendants claiming a longstanding ethical culture and heritage) to resist violence, and to restore justice and the rule of love of the neighbor, the stranger, and the sojourner? In the words of the prophet Micah (6:8), "The Holy One has told you, O mortal, what is good; and what is required of you but to do justice, and to love kindness, and to walk humbly with your G-d?"

Notes

1 Greenberg, 2000: 27. Used by permission, Perseus Books, 2017.
2 I am using this term not only in the literal sense, but as relational analyst Donnel Stern (2009) describes recognition that helps bring "unformulated experience" into new narrative awareness (pp. 110ff.).
3 Freud, 1955a/1919.
4 E.g., Davoine and Gaudillière, 2004; Kuriloff, 2014; Laub, 2015.
5 Ibid.
6 Especially, see Kuriloff, 2014; cf. Fisher, 2004; Prince, 2009.
7 Bettelheim, 1943.
8 See Chapter 6.
9 The postcolonial literature is vast, and still expanding. A classic text is Bhabha, 1994. Other foundational texts include Fanon, 2004/1961, 2008/1952; Said, 1979; Spivak, 1988. For overviews, see Young, 2003; Chakrabarty, 2015. Said (2003) reads Freud's *Moses and Monotheism* through a postcolonial lens in relation to the Israeli–Palestinian conflict.
10 Contra Gay, 1987: 146–147. Contemporary historians of psychoanalysis have used the term "optimal marginality" to describe the acuity and creative genius from a marginal status, which has arisen within psychoanalysis from Freud to the present (summarized in Aron and Starr, 2013: 8–9, 29, *et passim*).
11 Deutscher, 1968: 26–27.
12 Reijzer, 2011: 25, also citing Deutscher, 1968: 25–41.
13 See Chapter 1.
14 Freud, 1955a/1919.
15 Mühlleitner and Reichmayr, 1997: 79.

16 Ibid.
17 About a dozen had emigrated earlier, and some had died.
18 Mühlleitner and Reichmayr, 1997: 94.
19 Launer, 2015.
20 Mühlleitner and Reichmayr, 1997: 100. Dokumentationsarchiv des österreichischen Widerstandes, n.d.
21 Ibid., 80, 97. Dokumentationsarchiv des österreichischen Widerstandes, n.d.
22 Ibid., 80, 95.
23 Ibid., 101.
24 Ibid.
25 Ibid., 80, 98.
26 Ibid., 74.
27 Ibid., 80, 95.
28 Ibid., 80, 101.
29 Wesenauer, 2008–13.
30 Jeseník oficiálni stránky, 2016 (https://www.jesenik.org).
31 Kaufhold, 2009. His daughter Else was also an analyst, who emigrated to New York.
32 Kaufhold, 2014.
33 E.g., Sterba, 1982: 39.
34 M. Freud, 1957: 16. Freud's older half-brothers, Emmanuel and Philipp, had emigrated to England in 1860, and his elder sister Anna Freud Bernays to the United States in 1892, and therefore were not in immediate peril (Gay, 2006: 649n). Freud's younger brother Alexander escaped to Switzerland in 1938, and subsequently to Canada. Freud's sons, Oliver and Ernst, emigrated from Berlin to France and England in 1933, and the remaining children and their families left Vienna over a period of months in 1938, settling in the U.S., England, and France. For more details on the Freud household's emigration, see Schur, 1972; Cohen, 2012: 193. On Freud's last year in London, cf. Fry, 2009.
35 Freud, 1996.
36 Gay, 2006: 619. Wistrich (1991: 90–91) records:

21 synagogues were burnt down, dozens of prayer-rooms were destroyed, 4,083 Jewish shops were plundered and closed down, 1,950 Jewish homes were ransacked, 7,800 Jews were arrested, 680 committed suicide and 91 were murdered. Indeed, in some areas, Austrian antisemitism was showing itself to be a few steps ahead of Germany in the persecution of Jews

and demonstrating early support for what would eventually become systematically genocidal in Eichmann's "Final Solution."
37 Kershner, 2016: n.p.
38 Ibid.
39 Kaufhold, 2003.
40 Kaufhold, 2014; Bronner, 2008: 16–17.
41 Kuriloff, 2014.
42 Kirsner, 2000, cited in Reijzer, 2011: 4–6.
43 Ibid., 9.
44 A similar story of disruption occurred in London. The arrival of Anna Freud in the British Psychoanalytic Society precipitated an infamous power struggle between "classical" Freudians in London and the already-established Melanie Klein (Kohon, 1986).
45 Cf. Fisher, 2004; Prince, 2009; Reijzer, 2011: 4–6.
46 Eisold, as quoted in Prince, 2009: 188.
47 Aron and Starr, 2013, and Aron, personal communication, August 3, 2017.
48 Ibid., 42.

49 Ibid., and Kuriloff, personal communication, February 3, 2017.
50 Kuriloff, 2015.
51 Prince, 2009: 190.
52 Kuriloff, 2014: 43; cf. Laub, 2015: 302–306.
53 Ibid.
54 Ibid., 30–31.
55 Ibid., 23.
56 Jacoby, 1983: 12.
57 Ibid., 5–6, 7.
58 Ibid., 9; cf. Fenichel, 1946.
59 Federn, 1988: 158. Also cited in Prince, 2009: 186.
60 Kuriloff, 2014: 11, citing Prince, 2009: 190 and Ostow, 1982: 150.
61 Aron and Starr, 2013: 254, and Aron, personal communication, August 3, 2017.
62 Gilman, 1993.
63 Boyarin, 1997.
64 Brickman, 2003.
65 Geller, 2007.
66 Aron and Starr, 2013.
67 Citing Stepansky, 2009.
68 Aron and Starr, 2013.
69 E.g., Mitchell, 1988, 2004.
70 E.g., Altman, 2009.
71 Numerous writings, e.g., Benjamin, 1988, 2017.
72 E.g., Cole, 2005.
73 E.g., Cushman, 1996, 2015.
74 E.g., Harris, 2009.
75 E.g., Holmes, 2016, 2017.
76 E.g., Leary, 2000.
77 E.g., Suchet, 2007.
78 E.g., White, 2002, 2004.
79 Smaller, 2015.
80 Bion, 1961.
81 Frosh, 2010: 357.
82 See Chapter 7.
83 D. Klein, 1985: 9.
84 Frosh, 2010: 353, also citing Wangh, 1964. Cf. Ostow, 1996.
85 Hofstadter, 1963: 9.
86 Ibid., 3.
87 Freud, 1955b/1921.
88 M. Klein, 1975/1952.
89 Bion, 1961.
90 Hofstadter, 1963: 29.
91 George W. Bush, in State of the Union address, January 29, 2002 and thereafter.
92 In his self-published reprint edition of Gobineau's 1853 *Inequality of the Human Races*, Tyson (2016) writes:

  To place Man above the laws of nature by declaring that every race is equal is a fallacy, and does not in any way celebrate diversity.... The quality of Gobineau's work is beautiful. Despite too high a view of the white race in particular, Arthur's style and thought, is manly.
      (www.amazon.com/Essay-Inequality-Human-Races-lawlessness/dp/1535241179/
          ref=sr_1_2?ie=UTF8&qid=1473033461&sr=8–2&keywords=Gobineau+
              inequality+of+the+human+races. Accessed September 4, 2016.)

93 Smith and Banic, 2017.
94 U.S. Holocaust Museum, 2017.
95 E.g., Flegenheimer and Haberman, 2016.
96 SPLC, 2017.
97 https://newrepublic.com/article/134892/will-blood.
98 Potok, 2017: 35.
99 Ellis and Levenson, 2017.
100 Anti-Defamation League, 2017.
101 Goldberg, 2015.
102 Gilman, 1993.
103 Suchet, 2004: 423–424. Cf. Frosh, 2010: 362–363.
104 Suchet, 2016, and personal communication, March 27, 2017.
105 E.g., Frosh, 2010.
106 Ibid., 352, citing Fenichel, 1946: 18, 20, 22, 29. Cf. White, 2002, on racial hate and its disavowal in the countertransference.
107 Kristeva, 1991: 182.
108 Suchet, 2017: 47, also citing Suchet, 2007.
109 Hofstadter, 1963: 6.
110 Wistrich, 1991: 92. The revelation that the high-ranking Austrian official Kurt Waldheim was implicated in the death camps prompted a renewed wave of Austrian antisemitism rather than outrage, believing that Waldheim had been slandered, and during World War II had merely been doing his duty as a loyal Austrian citizen (pp. 88–97). Cf. Wistrich, 2010: 213–235.
111 Wise, 1991.
112 Associated Press, 2017.
113 Goldberg, 2015.
114 Ibid.; cf. Browning, 2017.
115 World Hunger, 2016.
116 See Chapter 7.
117 Freud, 1953: 510.
118 Meghnagi, 1993: 65.
119 Freud, 1955b/1921.
120 E.g., Aron, 2004; Aron and Henik, 2010, 2015; Aron and Starr, 2013, especially Chapters 7, 12–16; Eigen, many publications, e.g., 1998, 2014; Epstein, 1995; Finn and Gartner, 1992; Hoffman, 2011; Safran, 2016. Brickman (2010) observes a positive shift in psychoanalytic writing on religion from "seek[ing] after the evolutionary origins of religion … ([as in] *Totem and Taboo*); rather, it asks what elements of religion … function in sustaining the stability and vitality of the self" (p. 37).
121 Aron, 2004: 450.
122 Cushman, 2007: 47.
123 Ibid. Cf. Flax, 1993: 93; in a more theological vein, see Cooper-White, 2011.

References

Aische, Gregor, Pearce, Adam, and Rousseau, Bryant (2016). How far is Europe swinging to the right? *New York Times*, December 5. Online at www.nytimes.com/interactive/2016/05/22/world/europe/europe-right-wing-austria-hungary.html?_r=0. Accessed January 20, 2017.
Altman, Neil (2009). *The analyst in the inner city: Race, class, and culture through a psychoanalytic lens*, 2nd ed. New York: Routledge.

Anti-Defamation League (2017). Anti-Semitism in the U.S./6th wave of bomb threats targeting the Jewish community. Online at www.adl.org/news/article/6th-wave-of-bomb-threats-targeting-the-jewish-community. Accessed March 14, 2017.

Aron, Lewis (2004). God's influence on my psychoanalytic vision and values. *Psychoanalytic Psychology, 21* (3): 442–451.

Aron, Lewis and Henik, Libby (Eds.) (2010). *Answering a question with a question: Contemporary psychoanalysis and Jewish thought.* Brighton, MA: Academic Studies Press.

Aron, Lewis and Henik, Libby (Eds.) (2015). *Answering a question with a question: Contemporary psychoanalysis and Jewish thought, Vol. II.* Boston: Academic Studies Press.

Aron, Lewis and Starr, Karen (2013). *A psychotherapy for the people: Toward a progressive psychoanalysis*. New York: Routledge.

Associated Press (2017). Austria's chancellor invokes country's role in Holocaust. January 26, 2017. Online at www.atlanticbb.net/news/read/category/Europe%20News/article/the_associated_press-austrias_chancellor_invokes_countrys_role_in_holoc-ap. Accessed May 4, 2017.

Benjamin, Jessica (1988). *The bonds of love: Psychoanalysis, feminism, and the problem of domination*. New York: Pantheon.

Benjamin, Jessica (2017). *Beyond doer and done to: Recognition theory, intersubjectivity, and the third.* New York: Routledge.

Bettelheim, Bruno (1943). Individual and mass behavior in extreme situations. *Journal of Abnormal and Social Psychology, 38*: 417–452.

Bhabha, Homi (1994). *The location of culture*. London: Routledge.

Bion, Wilfred R. (1961). *Experiences in groups and other papers*. London: Hogarth.

Boyarin, Daniel (1997). *Unheroic conduct: The rise of heterosexuality and the invention of the Jewish man*. Berkeley: University of California Press.

Brickman, Celia (2003). *Aboriginal populations in the mind: Race and primitivity in psychoanalysis*. New York: Columbia University Press.

Brickman, Celia (2010). Psychoanalysis and Judaism in context. In Lewis Aron and Libby Henik (Eds.), *Answering a question with a question: Contemporary psychoanalysis and Jewish thought* (pp. 25–54). Brighton, MA: Academic Studies Press.

Bronner, Andrea (Ed.) (2008). *Vienna Psychoanalytic Society: The first 100 years.* Vienna: Christian Brandstätter Verlag.

Browning, Christopher (2017). Lessons from Hitler's rise. (A review of Volker Ullrich, Hitler's Ascent 1889–1939.) *New York Review*, April 20: 10–14.

Chakrabarty, Jaydeep (2015). *Postcolonialism: A critical introduction.* Booktango/Amazon kindle.

Cohen, David (2012). *The escape of Sigmund Freud*. New York: Overlook Press.

Cole, Gilbert (2005). Categories as symptoms: Conceptions of love in the psychoanalytic relationship. *Psychoanalytic Quarterly, 4* (4): 977–987.

Cooper-White, Pamela (2011). The "other" within: Multiple selves making a world of difference. In *Braided selves: Collected essays on multiplicity, God, and persons* (pp. 156–170). Eugene, OR: Cascade.

Cushman, Philip (1996). *Constructing self, constructing America: A cultural history of psychotherapy*. Boston: Da Capo Press.

Cushman, Philip (2007). A burning world, an absent God: Midrash, hermeneutics, and relational psychoanalysis. *Contemporary Psychoanalysis, 43* (1): 47–88.

Cushman, Philip. (2015). Relational psychoanalysis as political resistance. *Contemporary Psychoanalysis, 51*: 423–459.

Davoine, Françoise and Gaudillière, Jan-Max (2004). *History beyond trauma*. Susan Fairfield (Trans.). New York: Other Press.

Deutscher, Isaac (1968). The non-Jewish Jew. In *The non-Jewish Jew and other essays*. Tamara Deutscher (Ed.) (pp. 25–41). New York: Hill & Wang.

Dokumentationsarchiv des österreichischen Widerstands ([n.d.]). Online at https://doew.at. Accessed October 6, 2017.

Eigen, Michael (1998). *The psychoanalytic mystic*. London: Free Association Books.

Eigen, Michael (2014). *Faith*. London: Karnac.

Ellis, Ralph and Levenson, Eric (2017). Jewish cemetery in Philadelphia vandalized; 2nd incident in a week. CNN, February 27, 2017. Online at www.cnn.com/2017/02/26/us/jewish-cemetery-vandalism-philadelphia.

Epstein, Mark (1995). Thoughts without a thinker: Buddhism and psychoanalysis. *Psychoanalytic Review, 82*: 391–406.

Fanon, Frantz (2004). *The wretched of the earth*. Richard Philcox (Trans.). New York: Grove. (Orig. French publ. 1961.)

Fanon, Frantz (2008). *Black skin, white masks.* Richard Philcox (Trans.). New York: Grove. (Orig. French publ. 1952.)

Federn, Ernst (1988). The fate of a science in exile. In Edward Timms and Naomi Segal (Eds.), *Freud in exile: Psychoanalysis and its vicissitudes* (pp. 146–162). New Haven, CT: Yale University Press.

Fenichel, Otto (1946). Elements of a psychoanalytic theory of anti-Semitism. In E. Simmel (Ed.), *Anti-Semitism: A social disease* (pp. 11–32). New York: International Universities Press.

Finn, Mark and Gartner, John (Eds.) (1992). *Object relations theory and religion: Clinical applications.* Westport, CT: Praeger.

Fisher, David James (2004). Towards a psychoanalytic understanding of fascism and anti-Semitism: Perceptions from the 1940's. Online at www.hagalil.com/2009/12/fisher.

Flax, Jane (1993). *Disputed subjects: Essays on psychoanalysis, politics, and philosohy*. New York: Routledge.

Flegenheimer, Matt and Haberman, Maggie (2016). Donald Trump's Star of David Tweet. *New York Times*, July 3. Online at www.nytimes.com/2016/07/04/us/politics/donald-trumps-star-of-david-tweet-came-from-a-fringe-website-a-report-says.html. Accessed January 20, 2017.

Freud, Martin (1957). *Glory reflected: Sigmund Freud—Man and father*. London: Angus & Robertson.

Freud, Sigmund (1953). *The interpretation of dreams*. In J. Strachey (Ed.), *Standard edition of the complete works of Sigmund Freud*, Vol. 4–5 (entire). (Orig. German publ. 1900.)

Freud, Sigmund (1955a). *The uncanny*. In J. Strachey (Ed.), *Standard edition of the complete works of Sigmund Freud*, Vol. 17: 217–256. (Orig. German publ. 1919.)

Freud, Sigmund (1955b). *Group psychology and the analysis of the ego.* In J. Strachey (Ed.), *Standard edition of the complete works of Sigmund Freud*, Vol. 18: 65–144. (Orig. German publ. 1921.)

Freud, Sigmund (1996). *Kürzste Chronik*. Michael Molnar (Ed.). Basel: Stroemfeld/Roter Stern. (Orig. unpubl. MS 1938, at the Freud Museum, London.) Excerpts online at www.wpv.at/geschichte/emigration-sigmund-freud/kuerzeste-chronik. Accessed January 14, 2017.

Frosh, Stephen (2010). "Foreignness is the quality which the Jews and one's own instincts have in common": Anti-semitism, identity and the other. In Lewis Aron and Libby

Henik (Eds.), *Answering a question with a question: Contemporary psychoanalysis and Jewish thought* (pp. 345–368). Brighton, MA: Academic Studies Press.

Fry, Helen (2009). *Freud's war*. Stroud, UK: History Press.

Gay, Peter (1987). *A godless Jew: Freud, atheism and the making of psychoanalysis*. New Haven, CT: Yale University Press.

Gay, Peter (2006). *Freud: A life for our time*. New York: W.W. Norton.

Geller, Jay (2007). *On Freud's Jewish body: Mitigating circumcisions*. New York: Fordham University Press.

Gilman, Sander L. (1993). *Freud, race, and gender*. Princeton, NJ: Princeton University Press.

Goldberg, Jeffrey (2015). Is it time for the Jews to leave Europe? *The Atlantic*, April 2015. Online at www.theatlantic.com/magazine/archive/2015/04/is-it-time-for-the-jews-to-leave-europe/386279.

Greenberg, Irving (2000). The Shoah and the legacy of antisemitism: Judaism, Christianity, and partnership after the twentieth century. In Tivka Frymer-Kensky, David Novak, Peter Ochs, David Fox Samuel, and Michael A. Singer (Eds.), *Christianity in Jewish terms* (pp. 25–48). Boulder, CO: Westview/Perseus.

Harris, Adrienne E. (2009). The socio-political recruitment of identities. *Psychoanalytic Dialogues*, 19: 138–147.

Hoffman, Marie (2011). *Toward mutual recognition: Relational psychoanalysis and the Christian narrative*. New York: Routledge.

Hofstadter, Richard (1963). *The paranoid style in American politics and other essays*. Cambridge, MA: Harvard University Press.

Holmes, Dorothy Evans (2016). Come hither, American psychoanalysis: Our complex multicultural America needs what we have to offer. *Journal of the American Psychoanalytic Association, 63* (3): 569–586.

Holmes, Dorothy Evans (2017). Culturally imposed trauma: The sleeping dog has awakened. Will psychoanalysis take heed? *Psychoanalytic Dialogues, 26* (6): 664–672.

Jacoby, Russell (1983). *The repression of psychoanalysis: Otto Fenichel and the political Freudians*. New York: Basic Books.

Jeseník oficiální stránky (2016). Online at www.jesenik.org. Accessed October 6, 2017.

Kaufhold, Roland (2003). Spurensuche zur Geschichte der in die USA emigrierten Wiener Psychoanalytischen Pädagogen. *Luzifer-Amor: Zeitschrift zur Geschichte der Psychoanalyse, 31*: 37–69.

Kaufhold, Roland (2009). Else Pappenheim. Psyalpha Wissenplatform für Psychoanalyse. Online at www.psyalpha.net/biografien/else-pappenheim/roland-kaufhhold-else-pappenheim. Accessed January 28, 2017.

Kaufhold, Roland (2014). Trauma der Psychoanalyse? Vertreibung der Psychoanalyse aus Wien und die Folgen … Online at http://buecher.hagalil.com/2014/11/trauma-der-psychoanalyse. Accessed July 13, 2016.

Kershner, Isabel (2016). Mapping the Holocaust: How Jews were taken to their final destinations. *New York Times*, May 6: A6. Online at www.nytimes.com/2016/05/06/world/middleeast/mapping-the-holocaust-how-jews-were-taken-to-their-final-destinations.html?_r=0.

Kirsner, Douglas (2000). *Unfree associations: Inside psychoanalytic institutes*. London: Process Press.

Klein, Dennis B. (1985). *Jewish origins of the psychoanalytic movement*. Chicago: University of Chicago Press.

Klein, Melanie (1975). Notes on some schizoid mechanisms. In *Envy and gratitude and other works 1946–1963*. Masud Khan (Ed.). London: Hogarth. (Orig. publ. 1952.)

Kohon, Gregorio. (1986). *The British school of psychoanalysis: The independent tradition*. London: Free Association Books.

Kristeva, Julia (1991). *Strangers to ourselves*. Leon Roudiez (Trans.). New York: Columbia University Press.

Kuriloff, Emily A. (2014). *Psychoanalysis and the Third Reich: History, memory, tradition*. New York: Routledge.

Kuriloff, Emily A. (2015). Interview on *Psychoanalysis and the Third Reich*. Christopher Bandini, interviewer. New Books Network. Online at http://newbooksnetwork.com/emily-kuriloff-contemporary-psychoanalysis-and-the-third-reich-routledge-2013. Accessed January 15, 2017.

Laub, Dori (2015). The testimonial process as a reversal of the traumatic shutdown of narrative and symbolization. In Lewis Aron and Libby Henik (Eds.), *Answering a question with a question: Contemporary psychoanalysis and Jewish thought, Vol. II* (pp. 301–321). Boston: Academic Studies Press.

Launer, John (2015). *Sex vs. survival: The life and ideas of Sabina Spielrein*. London: Overlook Duckworth.

Leary, Kimberlyn (2000). Racial enactments in dynamic treatment. *Psychoanalytic Dialogues, 10*: 639–653.

Meghnagi, David (1993). A cultural event within Judaism. In *Freud and Judaism* (pp. 57–71). London: Karnac.

Mitchell, Stephen A. (1988). *Relational concepts in psychoanalysis*. Cambridge, MA: Harvard University Press.

Mitchell, Stephen A. (2004). *Relationality: From attachment to intersubjectivity*. New York: Routledge.

Mühlleitner, Elke and Reichmayr, Johannes (1997). Following Freud in Vienna. *International Forum for Psychoanalysis, 6*: 73–102.

Ostow, Mortimer (1996). *Myth and madness: The psychodynamics of antisemitism*. New Brunswick, NJ: Transaction.

Potok, Mark (2017). The Trump effect. *Southern Poverty Law Center: Intelligence Report, 162*: 32–35.

Prince, Robert (2009). Psychoanalysis traumatized: The legacy of the Holocaust. *American Journal of Psychoanalysis, 69* (3): 179–194.

Reijzer, Hans (2011). *A dangerous legacy: Judaism and the psychoanalytic movement*. Jeannette Ringold (Trans.). London: Karnac.

Safran, Jeremy D. (2016). Agency, surrender, and grace in psychoanalysis. *Psychoanalytic Dialogues, 33* (1): 58–72.

Said, Edward (1979). *Orientalism*. New York: Pantheon/Random House.

Said, Edward (2003). *Freud and the non-European*. London: Verso/Freud Museum.

Schur, Max (1972). *Freud, living and dying*. New York: International Universities Press.

Smaller, Mark (2015). Historic moment for the APsaA: The William Alanson White Institute. *The American Psychoanalyst, 49* (1): 1, 3.

Smith, Alexander and Banic, Vladimir (2017). Sebastian Gorka made Nazi-linked Vitezi Rend "proud" by wearing its medal. *NBC News*, April 8, 2017. Online at www.nbcnews.com. Accessed April 14, 2017.

Spivak, Gayatri Chakravorty (1988). Can the subaltern speak? In Cary Nelson and Lawrence Grossberg (Eds.), *Marxism and the interpretation of culture* (pp. 271–313). Urbana, IL: University of Illinois Press.

SPLC (Southern Poverty Law Center) (2017). Hate groups rise, fueled by Trump campaign. *SPLC Report, 47* (1): 1.

Starr, Karen (2008). *Repair of the soul: Metaphors of transformation in Jewish mysticism and psychoanalysis.* New York: Routledge.

Stepansky, Paul (2009). *Psychoanalysis at the margins.* New York: Other Press.

Sterba, Richard (1982). *Reminiscences of a Viennese psychoanalyst.* Detroit: Wayne State University Press.

Stern, Donnel (2009). *Partners in thought.* London: Routledge.

Suchet, Melanie (2004). A relational encounter with race. *Psychoanalytic Dialogues, 14* (4): 423–438.

Suchet, Melanie (2007). Unraveling whiteness. *Psychoanalytic Dialogues, 17* (6): 867–886.

Suchet, Melanie (2016). Facing our racialized selves. NYU Postdoctoral Program in Psychoanalysis and Psychotherapy Diversity Conference, New York, January 2016.

Suchet, Melanie (2017). Reclaiming a mind: Commentary on paper by Yvette Esprey. *Psychoanalytic Dialogues, 27* (1): 47–51.

Tyson, Mark Guy Valerius (2016). Introduction to Arthur de Gobineau. *The inequality of the human races: The hidden causes of revolutions, bloody wars, and lawlessness* (Reprint edition). CreateSpace Independent Publishing Platform. (Orig. French publ. 1853.)

U.S. Holocaust Museum (2017). Gassing operation. *Holocaust Encyclopedia.* Online at https://ushmm.org/wlc/en/article.php?ModuleId=10005220. Accessed April 12, 2017.

Wangh, Martin (1964). National Socialism and the genocide of the Jews: A psychoanalytic study of a historical event. *International Journal of Psycho-Analysis, 45*: 386–395.

Wesenauer, Gabriela (2008–13). Stefanie Bornstein-Windholzova—Chronologie. Psyalpha Wissenplatform für Psychoanalyse. Online at www.psyalpha.net/biografien/ stefanie-bornstein-windholzova. Accessed January 28, 2017.

White, Cleonie (2002). Surviving hate and being hated: Some personal thoughts about racism from a psychoanalytic perspective. *Contemporary Psychoanalysis, 38*: 401–422.

White, Cleonie (2004). What dare we (not) do? Psychoanalysis: A voice in politics? *Psychoanalytic Perspectives, 2* (1): 49–55.

Wise, Michael Z. (1991). Austria admits role in Holocaust. *Washington Post*, July 10, 1991. Online at www.washingtonpost.com/archive/politics/1991/07/09/austria-admits-role-in-holocaust/a7485c1c-3a82-4558-852e-b222983a386a/?utm_term=.696e6a942b76. Accessed March 20, 2017.

Wistrich, Robert S. (1991). *Antisemitism: The longest hatred.* New York: Pantheon.

Wistrich, Robert S. (2010). *A lethal obsession: Anti-semitism from antiquity to the global Jihad.* New York: Random House.

World Hunger (2016). World hunger child facts. Online at www.worldhunger.org/world-child-hunger-facts. Accessed April 14, 2017.

Young, Robert J.C. (2003). *Postcolonialism: A very short introduction.* Oxford, UK: Oxford University Press.

Index

9/11 attacks 269

Abraham, Karl 21, 22, 27, 30, 152, 153, 154, 201, 238
Adler, Alfred 21, 23, 25, 27, 28, 29, 31, 32, 40, 45, 67, 74, 170; feminist ideas 62; and Freud 24, 25, 33–4, 40; organ inferiority concept 25, 33
Adler, Ernst 240
Adler, Ida Bauer ("Dora") 240–1
affect 58–9
Agape 170, 171, 172, 174
aggressive drive 24, 33, 111, 135, 136, 164, 195, 198, 226, 260
Aichhorn, August 262
Albright, W.F. 138
Altman, Neil 267
Ambulatorium 242
American Psychiatric Association 94
American Psychoanalytic Association (APsA) 156, 267
analytical psychology 4, 39, 45
Andreas of Rinn 227
animism 58, 135
"Anna O." (Bertha Pappenheim) 241
Anschluss 5, 6, 73, 243–4
antiquities, Freud and 2, 113, 114
Antisemitic League 232
antisemitism 4, 7–13, 25, 26, 73–6, 77, 140, 172, 219–24, 228, 231–4, 235, 237, 239, 258–60, 266; Christian 220–1; definitions of 219–20; Freud on 74–6; internalized 69–71, 81, 172, 222; and politics 73–4; pre-Christian 219, 220; racialized 221–3, 231, 233; as a "total context" 8, 219–24, 258, 260; in United States 222, 264, 269–71; in Vienna 7–8, 9–10, 11, 79, 132, 220, 222, 223, 230, 233

anxiety 61, 98, 103, 104, 135, 153
archetypes 3, 35, 193, 194, 195, 198, 199
Archiv für Rassenbiologie 69
Arendt, Hannah 220, 224
Arnstein, Fanny 228
Aron, Lewis 236, 266, 267, 273
"Aryan" race 39–40, 76, 77, 132, 188, 196, 198, 201, 202, 204, 232, 234, 239, 242, 243, 268
assimilation, Jewish 71–3, 74, 78, 138, 222, 227, 230–2, 235, 236, 237–8, 259, 260, 264
Association of Professional Chaplains 94
atheism 22, 36, 63, 78, 136, 162, 174, 187, 234; of Freud 2, 3, 35, 76, 93, 102
Austria 3, 9, 10, 13, 41, 42, 57, 58, 72, 73, 138, 184, 219, 220, 222–4, 225–35, 238–40, 243, 244, 259, 260, 267–8, 270, 272; *Anschluss* (annexation) by Hitler 5, 6, 73, 103, 130, 243–4; Babenberg monarchy 225; Christian Social Party 10, 72, 223, 232, 233, 239, 240; Constitution (1861) (February Patent) 229; Constitution (1867) 72, 229, 268; election (2016) 10; Freedom Party (FPÖ) 10, 272; Habsburg monarchy 57, 225, 226, 228, 235; Parliament 9, 42, 229; Revolution of 1848 228–9, 241; Social Democrats 239

Bach, David 21, 34
Bair, Deirdre 26
Bakan, David 227
baptism 25, 27, 72, 75, 165, 171, 241, 241–2
Barth, Karl 104
Bass, Alfred 260
Bassevi, Jacob 225

Bauer, Ida ("Dora") 240–1
Bauer, Otto 239, 240
Bauman, Zygmunt 219–20
Becker, Ernest 149
Beer-Hoffman, Richard 140
belief, religious 13, 35, 45, 57, 58, 61, 63, 67, 78, 95, 100, 106–7, 109–10, 111, 112, 114, 131, 133, 135, 137, 139, 165–9, 174, 189, 221, 222, 237
Bellen, Alexander van der 10
Beller, Steven 71, 77, 219, 222, 229, 232–3, 236–7
Benjamin, Jessica 267
Berggasse 19 3, 6, 223, 244–5
Berlin 30, 102, 128, 129, 201, 238, 264
Berlin Psychoanalytic Society 243
Bernays, Isaac 231
Bernfeld, Siegfried 265
Bettelheim, Bruno 258
Bible 64, 108, 109, 112–13, 113, 114, 137, 161; Exodus 130; Genesis 162; Job 130; John 110; Matthew 22; Micah 273
Biedermann, Alois Emanuel 95
Bildung 238
Billig, Michael 224, 240–1
Binswanger, Ludwig 21, 24, 25, 26, 28, 36, 37–8, 42, 96
Bion, Wilfred 267, 269; unconscious group relations 43, 81, 267
Bleuler, Eugen 27, 30, 103, 186, 187
Blum, Harold 240
B'nai Brith 76, 79–80
Böddinghaus, Martha 32
Bohemia 126, 228, 240
Bonaparte, Marie 261
Bornstein-Windholzova, Stefanie 261
Boston Psychoanalytic Institute 263
Boyarin, Daniel 220, 221, 231, 266
Breasted, James Henry 138
Brecher, Guido 261
Brentano, Franz 76
Breuer, Josef 186, 241
Brickman, Celia 266
Brill, A.A. 21, 67, 130, 156
British Psychoanalytical Society 4
Buber, Martin 138, 169
Budapest 21, 30, 126, 128, 151, 242
Buddha/Buddhism 94, 107
Bullitt, William 244
Bultmann, Rudolf 99
Burghölzli clinic, Zürich 185–6
Bush, George W. 269

Calvin, John 35, 94, 104, 108
Calvinism/Calvinists 35, 93, 226
case study, religion as material in 58, 65, 67–8, 73, 199
castration 131
castration complex 68, 74, 75
Catholic Church/Catholicism 57, 65, 66, 67, 77, 108, 135, 136, 199, 225–6, 227, 230; hegemony of 57, 238; normalizing of in Austria 58; repressiveness of 35, 64, 81, 93; see also Christianity
Charcot, Jean-Martin 68
Chassidism 227
childhood/children 61, 63, 65, 67, 156, 157
Christ/Jesus 63, 107, 108, 134, 135, 139, 161, 165, 171, 172, 194, 195, 196, 197, 198, 220, 221
Christian Social Party, Austria 10, 72, 223, 232, 233, 239, 240
Christianity 57–8, 63–6, 72, 75, 76–7, 107, 108, 135, 139, 163, 165, 166, 171, 172, 173, 188, 219, 220, 221, 228; Jewish conversion to 72–3, 78, 230; masochistic character of 65–6; see also Calvinism/Calvinists; Catholic Church/ Catholicism; Protestantism
circumcision 68, 74, 75, 131
civilization 57, 61, 107, 108, 125, 132, 136, 173, 174, 198, 232
Clinton, Hillary 270
Cole, Gilbert 267
collective unconscious 3, 35, 134, 193, 194
Committee, (Secret) 151, 152, 154
communion/eucharist 65, 135–6
communism/communists 172, 231, 239, 264, 268
complex/complexes 193; Oedipal 33, 127, 155, 157, 236
confession 65
Confucianism 135
Congress of Vienna (1815) 227, 228
conscience 72, 107, 132, 133, 155; social 242
conscious/consciousness 157, 159, 160, 218
context 266–7; "total context", antisemitism as 8, 219–24, 258, 260
conversion, religious 25, 59, 72, 73, 76, 78, 80, 98, 99, 152, 170, 222, 225, 227, 230, 232, 241; symptom 185
Coudenhove-Kalergi, Count 75
countertransference 26, 125, 191
Covington, Coline 205

creativity 7, 12, 44, 45–6, 58, 81, 98, 156, 157, 158, 161, 162, 163, 165, 167, 168, 170, 172, 174, 191, 192, 194, 199, 203, 204, 229, 237, 242, 266
criminology 22, 61, 130
Cubelic, Marija 130
Cuddihy, John Murray 236
culture 4, 5, 6, 8, 9, 22, 33, 36, 56–8, 61, 62, 63, 108, 125, 127, 130, 133, 134, 138, 158, 162, 165, 167, 173, 222, 224, 227, 229, 231, 232, 235, 236, 239, 259, 263, 265, 273; dominant 173, 222, 231, 259, 260; European 69, 185; German 71, 76, 138, 187, 204, 224, 227, 234, 238; Jewish 25, 27, 75, 77, 78, 171, 188, 219, 221–2, 224, 227, 231, 237, 238, 259–60, 271; Viennese 9, 57, 81, 224, 227, 229, 230, 236
Cushman, Philip 236, 267, 273
Czernowitz, Bukowina 260

Danto, Elizabeth 242
Darwin, Charles 108, 133, 150, 199
Davidowicz, Lucy 244
death 58, 64, 66, 67–8, 127, 160, 162, 164, 165, 166, 170
death instinct 184, 191–9
Decker, Hannah S. 240
Demnig, Gunter 8
democracy/democratic 21, 139, 171, 172–3, 174, 228, 229, 237, 269, 270, 272
depth psychology 103, 138, 149, 157
Deutsch, Adolf 260
Deutsch, Helene 32, 43
Deutscher, Isaac 259
devil 64, 163, 166
Dilthey, Wilhelm 95
dogma 108, 135, 136–7
Dolfuss, Engelbert 243
"Dora" (Ida Bauer) 240–1
dreams 34, 35, 36, 65, 78, 80, 97, 98, 100, 161, 164, 190, 193, 200, 202, 203, 205, 217–19, 241; dream of the burning child 217–19, 245–6
Dreyfus, Alfred 234
drive theory/drives 24, 33, 56, 61, 64, 96, 100, 105, 107, 111, 113, 131, 1334, 136, 157, 164, 191, 192, 197, 198, 263
Dühring, Eugen 232
Dürig, Walter 129

Ebner, Margaretha 94

economic inequality/poverty 69, 108, 129, 220, 223, 224, 226, 230, 233, 235, 239, 240, 268
Edict of Toleration 227
education 22, 56, 57, 72, 93, 96, 106, 168, 185, 224, 227, 228, 229, 230, 234, 237, 238, 240, 241, 262
ego 33, 156–7, 173, 193, 194, 195, 198
ego ideal 157, 163
ego psychology 125, 263
Eisold, Kenneth 43
Eisold, Kurt 263
Eissler, Kurt 25–6
Eitington, Max 21, 22, 68
Ellenberger, Henri 172
Engelmann, Edmund 223
Enlightenment 79, 112, 220, 227, 230, 233, 236, 237, 238, 266
envy 8, 41, 57–8, 75, 219, 220, 225, 231
equality 173, 237
Eros 101, 134, 170, 171, 172, 194; and Thanatos 127
ethics 4, 101, 104, 110, 168, 237
Eucharist 135, 136
Europe 138, 225, 226, 228, 237, 238–9, 266, 267, 272

faith (religious) 36, 45, 61, 63, 65, 72, 93, 94, 95, 99, 100, 101, 104, 106, 108, 111, 112, 114, 135, 136, 138, 170, 171, 174, 187, 199, 227
Fall, myth of, the 162
Fanon, Frantz 173
fate 159, 162, 168, 192
father 63, 64, 67, 68–9, 153, 161, 165
fear 104
Federation of Jewish Women 241
Federn, Ernst 73, 261, 265
Federn, Paul 7, 21, 24, 29, 31, 32, 59, 61, 62, 66, 68–9, 129, 154
femininity 169, 266
feminism 62, 169
Fenichel, Otto 264, 265, 271
Ferdinand I, Emperor 227–8
Ferdinand II, Emperor 226
Ferenczi, Sándor 21, 27, 28, 30, 34, 35, 37, 64, 96, 152, 153, 154, 235, 243, 267; conflict with Freud 40
Feuerbach, Ludwig 107
Flaubert, Gustave: *Temptation of Saint Anthony* 126, 127
Fliess, Wilhelm 57, 60, 114

Forel, Auguste 186
Franz I, Emperor 227, 228
Franz Josef I, Emperor 72, 228–9, 233
Frazer, James 4, 138
Freedom Party of Austria (FPÖ) 10, 272
Freud, Adolfine ("Dolfi", sister) 224, 261
Freud, Amalie (mother) 224
Freud, Anna (daughter) 3, 24, 32, 96, 242
Freud, Jakob (father) 78, 112, 113, 114
Freud, Marie ("Mitzi", sister) 261
Freud, Martha Bernays (wife) 231
Freud, Martin (son) 24, 78, 152, 223, 224
Freud, Sigmund 1–2, 3, 6, 7, 12, 31, 64,
    66, 67, 157, 169, 170, 173, 186, 221,
    222, 226, 235, 236–7, 238, 242, 259,
    269; and Adler 24, 25, 33–4, 40;
    antiquities collection 2, 113, 114; on
    antisemitism 74–6; atheism of 2, 3, 35,
    93, 102; and B'nai Brith 76, 79–80; on
    Catholicism 65, 66, 67; and death
    instinct 198; death of 130, 160, 174;
    "Dora" case 240–1; drive theory 100,
    105, 131; exile in London 24, 103, 204,
    261; and Ferenczi 40; on guilt 61; views
    on Jewish conversion to Christianity
    72–3; and Jewish enlistment 234–5; and
    Jewish identity 76, 77, 78–9; and Jung
    3, 24–7, 28, 34–6, 37–40, 45, 97, 98,
    199; and Pfister 45, 93, 96, 97–8, 100–3,
    105–14 (correspondence with 3, 93, 94,
    100, 101–2, 103, 106, 110–11);
    professorship of 57, 79–80; and Rank
    40, 149, 151, 152, 153–4, 155, 160, 161;
    seduction theory of 79, 241; and
    Spielrein 76, 184, 188, 190–1, 192, 198,
    199, 200–1, 204–5, 234; and Stekel
    36–7, 40; structural model of 156, 193;
    topographical model 218; and Vienna
    Society (deference of members to 22–3;
    disdain for members 28; and dissenting
    opinions 40–1, 42–3; leadership role 43,
    44; and women's membership 32); on
    status of women 62; and Zionist
    movement 234
Freud, Sigmund, published writings of:
    "Analysis of a Phobia in a Five-Year
    Old Boy ('Little Hans')" 46; An
    Autobiographical Study 233–4; Beyond
    the Pleasure Principle 184; "A
    Comment on Anti-Semitism" 75–6;
    Civilization and its Discontents 59, 111;
    The Ego and the Id 156; The Future of
    an Illusion 2, 59, 102, 103, 106, 114,
    126, 133, 136, 168; Group Psychology
    and the Analysis of the Ego 100–1, 273;
    Inhibitions, Symptoms, and Anxiety 154;
    The Interpretation of Dreams 25, 79,
    126, 153 (Dream of burning child
    217–19, 245–6); Jokes and their
    Relation to the Unconscious 226; Moses
    and Monotheism 2, 45, 59, 74, 138, 161;
    "The Natural Position of Women" 62;
    "Obsessive Actions and Religious
    Practices" 2, 35, 60; On the History of
    the Psycho-Analytic Movement 40; "On
    the Question of Lay Analysis" 102, 129;
    "On the Two Principles of Psychic
    Happenings" 61–2; Psychopathology of
    Everyday Life 60; "The Question of Lay
    Analysis" 22, 102; "A Religious
    Experience"; Totem and Taboo 2 4, 35,
    40, 58, 59, 62, 126, 131, 221; "The
    Uncanny" ("Das Unheimliche") 128,
    273
Freud, Sophie (daughter) 239
Fromm, Erich 159, 173
Frosh, Stephen 267, 268, 271
Furtmüller, Carl 21, 31, 34, 59, 66

Gadamer, Hans-Georg 169
Gay, Peter 2, 26, 28–9, 34, 39–40, 70–1,
    77, 113, 132, 155, 223, 235, 243
Geller, Jay 78, 221, 266
Gentiles 25, 26, 38, 68, 78, 80, 97, 132,
    139, 222, 224, 225, 230, 234, 240, 259,
    268
German culture 71, 224, 227, 238
Germany 238, 239, 267–8; Weimar
    Republic 239, 268
Gilman, Sander 69, 77, 169, 219, 220, 221,
    235, 266, 270
Gincburg, Mira [Oberholzer-] 32
Gnosticism 135
Gobineau, Josef Arthur de 232, 270
God 57, 58, 64, 104, 107, 112, 133, 135,
    139, 163, 167; -imagoes 59, 95, 112;
    -"Logos" 110, 114, 140; faith in 63
Goldberg, Jeffery 272
Graf, Max 21, 22, 23, 29, 45, 46, 68, 72, 73
Graf, Rosa Freud 261
Greek mythology 161, 162, 163
Greenberg, Irving 258
Grollman, Earl 225, 227, 231
Gross, Frieda 32

Gross, Otto 32
Guatarri, Felix 173
guilt 60, 61, 64–5, 104, 134, 157, 158, 159, 162, 163, 164, 167, 171
Gymnasien 71, 223, 232

Habsburg (monarchy) 57, 71, 138, 225, 226, 227, 228, 229, 230, 232, 233, 235; Catholic alliance 6, 57, 239
Harnack, Adolf von 95, 136
Harris, Adrienne 183, 267
Hartmann, Dora 243
Hartmann, Heinz 262
Haskalah 237
hate speech 10, 267, 268, 270
Hebbel, Christian 63
Heisenberg principle 167
Heiwehr 239
Heller, Hugo 21, 64, 128
Heller, Yom-Tov Lipmann 226
Henick, Libby 236
hero/heroism 78, 80, 131, 159, 161, 162, 163, 166, 170, 171, 186, 187, 188, 192, 196, 198–9, 201–5, 233, 236, 242
Herzl, Theodor 234
Hilferding, Margarete 21, 32, 34, 69, 190, 260
Hinkle, Beatrice 32
Hirschfeld, Elfriede 97
Hitler, Adolf 9, 10, 73, 103, 112, 129, 130, 140, 200, 204, 222, 232, 234, 243–4, 268, 270
Hitschmann, Eduard 21, 29, 31, 65, 67–8, 71, 80
Hofer, Norbert 10
Hofstadter, Richard 269, 272
Holmes, Dorothy Evans 267
Holocaust 8–9, 12, 138, 140, 184, 200, 220, 221, 244, 258–9, 260–2, 266, 267, 271, 272; impact on psychoanalysis 262–6; psychoanalysts murdered in 4, 184, 244, 260–1; survivors 261, 263, 264, 266, 267
homosexuals/homosexuality 266, 268
Hug-Hellmuth, Hermine 32
Hummel, Johann Nepomok 10
humor, Jewish 137, 226
Hungary 238, 243, 272
hysteria/hysterical 60, 69, 79, 94, 185

Ibsen, Henrik 150
id 156, 162, 193, 198

Imago 3, 5–6, 56, 59, 98, 103, 126, 133, 151, 162
immigration: anti- 10; Jewish 227
immortality 149, 162, 164–5, 166, 167, 168, 169, 170, 172, 173, 174
individuation 173, 193, 195, 205
inferiority complex 24, 25, 33
Innocent III, Pope 225
International Journal of Psychoanalysis 4, 106
International Psychoanalytic Association (IPA) 30, 35, 39, 98, 102
international psychoanalytic congresses: 1908, Salzburg 30, 32; 1910, Nürnberg 30; 1913, London 39; 1918, Budapest 126, 128, 151, 242
Internationale Psychoanalytische Bibliothek 128–9
Internationale Zeitschrift für Psychoanalyse 37
Internationaler Psychoanalytischer Verlag 152, 154
Islam 10, 135
Islamophobia 10, 270, 271

Jacoby, Russell 32–3, 264–5
Jahrbuch für Psychoanalyse und Psychopathologische Forschungen 5, 30, 39
James, William 80
Jaspers, Karl 94, 104–5
Jewish/Jewishness (as identity) 25, 58, 76–9, 169, 235–8, 259, 265; in America 222, 264, 269–71; assimilation 71–3, 74, 78, 138, 222, 227, 230–2, 235, 236, 237–8, 259, 260, 264; in Austria 229; bourgeoisie 78, 223–4, 230–1; and conversion to Christianity 72–3, 78, 230; culture 171, 227, 231, 237, 238; discrimination (*see also* antisemitism); distinctiveness 237, 238; émigrés 260, 262–6; in Europe 138, 225, 228, 237; humor 137, 226; "Jewish Problem" 222; and obsessional neurosis 68–9; *Ostjuden* 70–1, 78, 81, 222, 236, 266; as "Other" 8, 70, 231–2, 259, 266, 271; and race 69, 73, 78, 266; and *Selbsthass* 69–71, 172; stereotypes 68, 69, 230, 231, 266; in Vienna 8, 70, 71, 78, 222, 225–35
Jones, Ernest 4, 21, 22, 28, 30, 34, 36, 37, 46, 152, 153, 154, 184, 244

Jonte-Pace, Diane 113
Joseph II, Emperor, and Edict of
    Toleration 227
Judaism (as religion) 58, 68, 77, 107, 125,
    131–2, 135–9, 163, 165, 166, 167, 171,
    172, 219, 220, 221, 235–8, 265;
    Chassidic 227; Conservative movement
    231; and education 237; and ethics 237;
    law 226; Orthodox 227, 231; rabbis in
    221; Reform movement 231
Judentum 77, 78
Jung, C.G. 3–4, 30, 45, 67, 105, 134, 156,
    170, 238, 260; analytical psychology of
    4; archetypes 3, 35, 195; collective
    unconscious 3, 35, 134, 193; complexes
    193; and Freud 3, 24–7, 28, 34–6,
    37–40, 45, 97, 98, 199; and Pfister 97,
    98; and Spielrein 25, 183, 184, 186–7,
    188–90, 192, 196, 198–9, 201–3, 204–5;
    and the Vienna Society 3, 4, 21, 27
Jung, C.G., published writings of: *Red
    Book* 4, 195, 199; *Symbols and
    Transformation of the Libido* 184, 199
Jung, Emma 24, 32, 186, 188
Jung Wien movement 21

Kabbalah 141, 236
Kafka, Franz 236
Kahane, Max 21
Kempner, Salomea 261
Kern, Christian 272
Kernberg, Otto 263
Kerr, John 184, 199
Khatyaturyan, Margarita 204
Kierkegaard, Søren 125
Klein, Dennis 223, 230–1, 235, 237
Klein, Melanie 155, 269
Kohn, Edmund 79
Kohut, Heinz 70
Kohut, Thomas 70
Kraus, Karl 21
Kris, Ernst 262
Kristeva, Julia 271
Kuriloff, Emily 262–4

Lamarckism 77, 134
Landauer, Karl 260
Laub, Dori 263–4
Launer, John 183, 186, 199, 200
"lay/non-medical analysis" 21, 22, 97, 98,
    99, 102, 105, 129, 130, 149, 151, 156,
    262

Leary, Kimberlyn 267
Leo XIII, Pope 72
Leopold I, Emperor 71, 227
Leopold V, Babenberg Duke of Austria
    225
Leopoldstadt (Vienna) 8, 12, 71, 149, 227,
    228
Lessing, Theodor 70, 171, 172
Lewis, C.S. 111–12
libido 33, 35, 98, 100–1, 133, 156, 187;
    and death instinct 191–7, 198, 199
Lieberman, E. James 172
Liebknecht, Karl 203
Liechtenstein, Prince 232
"Little Hans" (Herbert Graf) 21, 46, 68, 72
Loewenstein, Rudolph 262–3
London 30, 39, 262, 267; Freud's exile in
    24, 103, 204, 261
Loos, Adolf 229–30
love 40, 43, 46, 59, 63, 66, 67, 71, 91,
    93, 94, 95, 98–9, 100–1, 103–5, 107,
    108, 110, 113–14, 134, 163, 173,
    194–5, 223, 231; *Agape* 170, 171, 172,
    174, 273; -hate 27, 80; of fate 159;
    romantic 99, 128, 163–4, 166, 186,
    188–9, 192, 194–9, 204; self- 171; *see
    also Eros*
Löwenfeld, Leopold 69
Lueger, Karl 10–11, 72, 79, 221, 232, 233,
    234
Luria, Alexander 183, 204
Luther, Martin 66, 226
Lutherans 226

Maday, Stefan von 34
Maeder, Alphonse 39
mana 166–7
Marcuse, Herbert 137
marginality 77, 236, 259, 265, 266
Maria Theresa, Empress 227
Maritain, Jacques 172
Marr, Wilhelm 232
Mary (Mother of Jesus)/Madonna 63, 64,
    65, 139, 171, 240–1
masculinity 169
masochism 27, 128, 129, 130, 134, 169,
    184, 195, 198, 268; Christian 65, 66,
    134
masturbation 37, 61, 65, 67, 68
matriarchy 165–6
May, Rollo 172
medicine/medical profession 21, 22, 42,

71, 76, 79–80, 95, 102, 126, 127, 129, 130, 185, 186, 187, 188, 189, 191, 199, 204, 223, 262, 266; care 242, 261; *see also* lay/non-medical analysis; women, in medicine
Meghnagi, David 236, 273
Meisl, Alfred 260
Menaker, Esther 156, 158, 161, 170
Mendelssohn, Moses 237
Merkur, Dan 173–4
Metternich, Klemens von 228
midrash 236, 273
Miller, Henry 155
Mincer, Beata "Tola" 152, 155
Mitchell, Stephen 267
Moltzer, Lou Maria 32
monotheism 75, 107, 138, 139
moral injury 128, 269
moral/morality 21, 22, 24, 61, 69, 70, 72, 99, 100, 101, 107, 109, 110, 114, 125, 133, 135, 136, 140, 157, 162, 163, 167, 168, 172, 174, 227, 230–1, 236, 237, 241
moralism 41, 109–11, 158, 162–3, 192
Moravia 228
Moravian church movement 93
Moses 78, 137 138, 139, 161, 236, 245
mother 63, 65, 67, 68, 95, 111, 112, 114, 128, 137, 150, 153, 155, 161, 164, 171, 185, 187, 193, 195, 196, 199, 201, 203, 217, 231, 240, 241, 245, 268; "Church" 97; divine/Great 139, 167, 183, 195; Earth 197, 205; principle 163
Müller-Braunschweig, Carl 132–3
multiple-self theory 193
Murphy, Newton 129
mystical/mysticism 25, 67, 77, 94, 99, 170, 187, 199, 202, 236
myth/mythology 3, 5, 22, 35, 40, 56, 60–2, 67, 78, 126, 127, 135, 137, 138, 139, 149, 151, 161–5, 194, 195–7, 199, 200; Biblical 161, 162; Greek 161, 162, 163; Siegfried 187, 196–7, 198–9, 202–3, 204, 205

Nase, Eckart 97
National Psychological Association for Psychoanalysis (NPAP) 130
Nazi/Nazis 3, 9, 105, 140, 172, 184, 200, 204, 220, 224, 239, 242, 244, 268; concentration camps 8, 105, 244, 245, 260–2; neo-Nazis 9, 270

neo-fascism 272
neo-Nazis 270
Neue Freie Presse 224, 234
neurosis 25, 33, 40, 56, 58, 61, 64, 65, 73, 79, 98, 133, 134, 135; inverse proportion with religion 68, 101; Jews as prone to 68–9; obsessional 35, 60, 67–8, 68–9, 107, 133; war 128–9
New York 30, 102, 262–3
New York Psychoanalytic Society and Institute 7, 130, 154, 262, 265
Nietzsche, Friedrich 44, 125, 149, 150, 155, 158, 159, 162, 167, 168, 169, 194, 195
Nin, Anaïs 155, 156
Nordau, Max 233
Noth, Martin 138
Nothnagel, Hermann 79
Nunberg, Herman 23–4, 56, 62

Oberholzer, Emil 98, 102
obsession/obsessional 35, 60, 67–8, 68–9, 107, 133
Oedipus/oedipal 62, 63–4, 131, 161, 162, 164, 263, 264; complex 33, 127, 155, 157, 236; conflict 40, 43, 153; crisis 23, 35
Offer, Daniel 44
Oppenheim, David Ernst 260
Oppenheim, Hermann 31, 34
Oratsch, Ella 128
original sin 65, 66, 112, 165
Ornstein, Anna 264
Ostjuden 6, 70, 71, 78, 81, 222, 230, 236, 237, 266
Ostow, Mortimer 69, 236
"Other" 170, 173, 269, 273; Jews as 8, 70, 231–2, 259, 266, 271
Oxaal, Ivan 235

Palestine 233, 234, 260, 262
Pappenheim, Bertha ("Anna O") 241
Pappenheim, Martin 261
paranoia/paranoid 34, 38, 60, 226, 231, 262, 269, 272
paranoid schizoid position 269
Paris, Jewish population in 233
patriarchy 163, 165
patronage 57
Paul (Apostle) 94, 101, 139, 171, 172
Peace of Westphalia (1648) 226
personality types (Rank) 158, 163

Pfister, Oskar 2, 3, 39, 40, 59, 93–124, 223; biography of 95–105; and Freud 45, 93, 96, 97–8, 100–3, 105–14; correspondence with 3, 93, 94, 100, 101–2, 103, 106, 110–11; and Jung 97, 98; and Swiss Society for Psychoanalysis 98, 102; and theology 94, 95, 103, 104, 105

Pfister, Oskar, published writings of 6, 93–4; "Analytic Pastoral Care" 99–100; "Analytic Soul-care" 94; "Calvin's Intervention in the Peney Witch Trial in 1545" 104; *Christianity and Fear* 103–4; "Free Will" 96; "Health and Religion" 105; "The Illusion of a Future" 94, 103, 106–11; "The Inner Judge and its Pastoral Treatment" 103; "Karl Jaspers as Sigmund Freud's Adversary" 104; *Love in Children and Its Aberrations* 98; "Marital Love and Its Developmental Failure" 98–9; "New Testament Pastoral Care and Psychoanalytic Therapy" 103; *The Psychoanalytic Method* 94, 98; "Sins of omission of theology compared to modern psychology" 96; "Social development as struggle for human dignity" 96

Pfister, Oskar Robert 95

Phanes 195

philosophy 5, 37, 56, 60, 76, 94, 95, 96, 101, 104, 105, 108, 109, 125, 137, 149, 155–6, 159, 161, 162, 166, 167, 169, 171, 173, 174, 227, 264, 265

Piaget, Jean 3, 183, 203

piety 58, 61, 127

Pinsker, Leo 233

pleasure principle 59, 62

pogroms 132, 204, 228, 233, 234

postcolonial theory 259

poverty/economic inequality 69, 108, 129, 220, 239

preconscious 218

procreation 165

Protestantism 25, 59, 93, 95, 97, 103, 105–6, 108–9, 136, 188, 199, 226, 230; *see also* Calvinism/Calvinists; Christianity

Protocols of the Elders of Zion 234

Prussia 228

psychiatry 5, 22, 26, 27, 56, 94, 97, 102, 105, 129, 186, 238

psychoanalysis, "applied" 5, 97, 125, 126, 131, 133, 134, 137, 138, 149, 152; classical 46, 125, 167, 263, 266; contemporary 258, 266–7; impact of Holocaust on 262–6; Jewishness of 39, 76–9, 235–8; origins of 21–2, 76, 265, 266; post-war 258, 262–6; relational 125, 266–7, 273; as a "science of culture" 22; and social reform 240–3; as subculture 24

psychology 96, 97, 104, 125, 150, 151, 158, 162, 165–73; analytical 4, 39, 45; depth 103, 138, 149, 157; ego 125, 263; group/mass 171, 269, 273; and/of religion 3, 4, 22, 35, 95, 104, 106, 111, 114, 126, 127, 133–4, 258; Self 70, 264; social 170; "surface" 23, 33; "two-person" 125

psychosis 60, 104

race: Jews as a 69, 73, 78, 221–3, 231, 233, 266; *see also* whiteness

racism 9, 10, 69, 81, 221–3, 266, 268; in United States 222, 269, 270–2

Rajzman, Samuel 261–2

Rank, Estelle 172

Rank, Otto 2, 3, 31, 34, 37, 56, 65–6, 128, 129, 149–82, 191, 219; biography of 149–60; on death 160, 162, 164, 165, 166, 170; on democracy 172–3, 174; and Ferenczi 152, 153, 154; and Freud 40, 149, 151, 152, 153–4, 155, 160, 161; on guilt 157, 158, 159, 160, 162, 163, 164, 167, 171; on immortality 162, 164–5, 166, 167, 168, 169, 170, 172; and Jessie Taft 160, 172; personality types of 158, 163; and religion 161–74; as Secretary of Vienna Society 4, 5, 28, 29, 73, 151; self-analysis 150; on the soul 164, 165, 166–7, 168, 169; Ten Commandments 150; on will 156–60, 162–3, 164, 165, 167–8, 169, 170, 171

Rank, Otto, published writings of: 6, 149, 152–3, 161–2; *Art and Artist* 149, 158; "The Artist" 151, 161; *Beyond Psychology* 160, 169–74; *The Development of Psychoanalysis* 153; *Der Doppelgänger* 162, 164, 165, 169; "The Essence of Judaism" 242; "The Myth and Birth of the Hero" 161; *Outlines of a Genetic Psychology* 155; *Psychology and the Soul* 164–9; *The*

Trauma of Birth 149, 153–4; *Truth and Reality* 156, 157, 158–9, 160, 162–4, 166, 167; *Will Therapy* 156, 160
rationality 108, 237
reality principle 59, 99, 108, 136, 162, 245
Reformation 66, 225–6
Reijzer, Hans 259
Reik, Theodor 2, 3, 40, 44, 46, 66, 102, 125–48, 149, 226, 235, 265; biography of 126–30; dissertation on Flaubert's *Saint Anthony* 126, 127; and Freud 127–8, 130; "Listening with the Third Ear" 141; on religion 63, 131–40; and trauma 128
Reik, Theodor, published writings of 6, 126, 127, 128, 129, 130, 131–3, 134–40; *The Compulsion to Confess* 128, 130; "Couvade" 131; *The Creation of Woman* 137; *Dogma and Compulsion* 135–7; *Fragments of an Analysis* 128; *From Thirty Years with Freud* 133; *Jewish Wit* 137; "The Mark of Cain" 131; *Masochism and Modern Man* 129, 134–5; *Mystery on the Mountain* 137–40; *A Psychologist Looks at Love* 134; *Ritual* 131–2; "The Strange God and One's Own God" 132
Reinhold, Josef 261
Reitler, Rudolf 21, 31, 63, 67
relational psychoanalysis 125, 266–7, 273
religion 1, 2–4, 45–7, 56–81; as affective phenomenon 58–9; anthropological study of 58, 131, 135; in clinical case material 67–8; as "crooked cure" 60; as cultural product 61; Eastern 62; as enemy 2, 60; as guardian of civilization 108; as hostile to thought 108; inverse proportion with neurosis 68, 101; as neurotic compulsion 107; as obsessional neurosis 35, 60, 68, 107; Pfister and 93–114; prehistoric/"primitive" 35, 58, 62, 77, 131–40; 162, 164, 166; as protection against neurosis 60–1; psychology of 3, 35, 133–4, 258; Rank and 161–74; Reik and 63, 131–40; Spielrein and 188–9, 191, 194, 196, 199–200; as a wishful construct 107–8; women and 58, 62; *see also* Buddha/ Buddhism; Christianity; Judaism; Protestantism
repression 38, 61, 63, 69, 103, 107, 136, 156, 184, 199, 271; "Return of the

Repressed" 7–10, 132, 133, 139, 140, 273
Richebächer, Sabine 184
Rie, Oskar 80
right-wing movements, twenty-first century 272
Riklin, Franz 30, 97
Rizzuto, Ana-Maria 111, 112, 113, 114, 237
Roazen, Paul 24, 36, 40, 46, 155
Robert, Marthe 78
Roheim, Geza 138
Rolland, Romain 113, 223
Rose, Louis 21–2, 72
Rothschild, Baron Edmond de 233
Rudolf I, Emperor 225
Rudolf II, Emperor 225
Russia 228, 233, 234

Sachs, Hanns 5, 21, 27, 41–2, 56, 57, 128, 152, 155
Sadger, Isidor 21, 22, 23, 28, 31, 32, 63–4, 68, 69, 260
St. Germain, Mark 112
Salberg, Jill 218, 233
Salomé, Lou Andreas 32, 44, 154
Scheftel, Pavel (Paul) 200, 201, 204
Schindel, Robert 226
Schleiermacher, Friedrich 95, 162
Schnitzler, Arthur 57, 219, 231
Schönerer, Georg Ritter von 232, 233
Schopenhauer, Arthur 125, 150, 158, 162, 167, 169
Schorske, Carl 72
"Schreber" case (Freud) 67, 184
Schulchan Aruch 226
Schur, Max 24
Schuschnigg, Kurt von 243
Schweitzer, Albert 105
science/scientific 108–9, 134, 168
seduction theory 79, 241
Seelsorge 93, 94, 96, 99, 103, 104, 105, 106
Seipel, Ignaz 239
self-analysis 125
"Semitic" (term) 232
Servitenkirche 12
sex/sexuality 33, 34, 57, 58, 64, 65, 66, 111, 127, 135, 136, 157, 167, 260; *see also* libido
sexual abuse 64, 79, 264
sexual intercourse 165

sexual symbolism 63
Sherman, Murray 131
Siegfried myth 187, 196–7, 198–9, 202–3, 204, 205
Sigmund Freud Museum, Vienna 2, 6, 8, 12
sin 58, 64, 104, 162, 167, 171; original 65, 66, 112, 165
Singh, Sundar 99
Slavet, Eliza 77, 221
social change/reform 72, 80, 96, 108, 170, 228, 231, 237, 240–3
social construction 221, 222
Social Democrats, Austria 239
social justice 80, 99, 237, 260
social psychology 170
social work 95, 99, 105, 160, 266
socialism/socialists 21, 33, 74, 136, 230, 236, 239, 240, 264, 268
Society for Free Psychoanalysis 34
Society of Physicians 79
Sombart, Werner 69
soul 94, 109, 110, 114, 149, 150, 156, 162, 164, 165, 166–7, 168, 169, 189, 201
Spicer, Sean 270
Spielrein, Renate 201, 202, 203
Spielrein, Sabina 3, 32, 127, 183–214; biography of 185–91, 200–5; death in holocaust 4, 184, 205, 260; on death instinct within the libido 184, 191–9; and Freud 76, 184, 188, 190–1, 192, 198, 199, 200–1, 204–5, 234; and Jung 25, 183, 184, 186–7, 188–90, 196, 198–9, 201–3, 204–5; and Luria 183, 204; and Piaget 183, 203; and religion 199–200; and Siegfried myth 187, 196–7, 198–9, 202–3, 204, 205; and symbolism 195–6, 200, 204; and Vygotsky 183, 204
Spielrein, Sabina, published writings of 199–200; "Contributions to and Understanding of the Child's Mind" 200; "Destruction as a Cause of Coming into Being" 191–7, 199; "On the Psychological Content of a Case of Dementia Praecox" 191, 199–200
Sprengnether, Madelon 113
Stach, M. von 32
Starr, Karen 266, 267
Steiner, Maximilian 21, 31
Stekel, Wilhelm 21, 22, 23, 24, 27, 28, 31, 36–7, 40, 44, 58, 61, 64, 65, 67, 68, 129, 223

Stephansdom (cathedral) 6, 57
Stolpersteine ("Stumbling Blocks") 8
Strache, Heinz-Christian 10
Strozier, Charles 44
structural model (Freud) 156, 193
sublimation 56, 59, 60, 61, 65, 93, 97, 98, 101, 136, 157, 194, 198, 201
Suchet, Melanie 267, 270–1, 271–2
Sugar, Nicola 260–1
suicide 24, 61, 160, 164, 185, 186, 188, 244
Sullivan, Harry Stack 267
Sulloway, Frank 235–6
superego 133, 156, 193
superstition 46, 57, 61, 65, 99, 109, 133, 220
"surface psychology" 23, 33
Swiss Society for Psychoanalysis 98, 102
symbols/symbolism 3–4, 6, 12, 35, 60, 97, 131, 155, 174, 197, 200, 201–3, 204, 205, 229, 231, 245; dream 36, 97, 218, 245; religious 57, 58, 63, 64, 67, 133, 135, 137, 139, 163, 165, 166, 172, 187, 194, 195–6, 198; sexual 25, 63
synagogues 127, 139, 225, 226, 227, 233, 241
Szasz, Thomas 173

taboo 64, 136, 165
Taft, Jessie 152, 160, 172
Talmud 8, 22, 132, 231, 236, 237
Tausk, Victor 21, 24, 28, 31, 37, 44, 65
"Tavistock" school 267
Teller, Frida 261
theology 134, 135; Pfister and 94, 95, 103, 104, 105
Thirty Years' War (1618–48) 225, 226
Thurneysen, Eduard 97, 104
Tillich, Paul 139
topographical model (Freud) 218
Torah 226
totalitarianism 173
totemism 58, 107, 135, 138, 165, 166, 170
transference 5, 26, 59, 60, 100, 101, 186–7, 199
Treaty of Versailles (1919) 238, 267
Trump, Donald 269, 270
truth 162
"two-person" psychology 125

uncanny 218–19, 258, 271, 273
unconscious 33, 64, 65, 76, 77, 98, 100, 125, 163, 193, 194, 218, 259; collective 3, 35, 134, 193, 194

unconscious group theory 43, 267
United States/America 262–6, 267, 269–72;
9/11 attacks 269; antisemitism in 222,
264, 269–71; election (2016) 270; "Great
Recession" 269; Jewish emigration to
233, 260; Jewishness in 222, 264,
269–71; racism in 222, 269, 270–2

Vienna: antisemitism in 7–8, 9–10, 11, 79,
132, 220, 222, 223, 224, 233; Catholic
hegemony in 57, 81; Congress of (1815)
227, 228; culture 9, 57, 81, 224, 227, 229,
230, 236; districts 71, 228; Holocaust
memorials 8–9, 12; Jewish population in
8, 70, 71, 78, 222, 225–35; *Jung Wien* 21;
Leopoldstadt district 8, 11, 71, 149, 227,
228; as patronage society 57; "Red
Vienna" 240, 241, 266; *Ringstrasse* 223,
229–30; *Unterer Werd* 226
Vienna Psychoanalytic Society 2–3, 6, 98,
129, 219, 241, 242–3; conflict and
conformity in 40–3; disbanded (1938)
244; executive committee 31, 32;
expansion and rivalries (1908–10)
27–32; members murdered in Holocaust
4, 184, 244, 260–1; minutes of 4, 5, 28,
29, 56, 64–5, 73; oedipal dynamics
within 40, 43; Rank as secretary of 4, 5,
28, 29, 73, 151; re-established (1949)
262; unconscious group dynamics 43,
81; women in 32–3, 242; *see also*
Wednesday Night Psychological Society
Votivkirche 6
Vranitzky, Franz 9, 272
Vygotsky, Lev 183, 204

Waal, Edmund de 230
Wagner, Richard 150, 160, 187, 196–7, 268
Wagner-Juaregg, Julius 129
war neuroses 128–9
Wednesday Night Psychological Society
2–3, 6, 7–8, 21–3, 125–6; deference to
Freud among members 22–3; members
21; rising tensions (1907–08) 23–4; *see
also* Vienna Psychoanalytic Society

Weimar Republic 239
Weininger, Otto 65, 169
Westerink, Hermann 95, 98
White, Cleonie 267
Whitehead, Alfred North 159
whiteness 271–2; *see also* race; racism
Wiesel, Elie 267, 272
will 96, 156–60, 162–3, 164, 165, 167–8,
169, 170, 171
will to power 24, 33, 161
William Alanson White Institute 267
Winternitz, Pauline Freud ("Pauli") 261
Winterstein, Alfred von 21, 64, 71
Wistrich, Robert 243–4
Wittels, Fritz 21, 24, 27, 29, 31, 32, 62, 65,
66, 68, 72, 242
Wolff, Toni 32, 192
women 24, 62, 74, 113, 166, 169; feminist
views on 62, 74, 169; and Freud 113;
Jewish 185, 188, 224, 241; and Jung
188; in medicine 21, 185, 186, 187, 189,
191, 199, 204; and Rank 172; and
religion 58, 62, 165–6; rights of 62, 241,
269, 270, 271; and sexuality 24, 191,
193, 198; as soul-bearers 165–6; in
Vienna Psychoanalytic Society 2, 32–3,
191, 242
World War I 224, 234–5, 238–9, 267–8
World War II 132, 264
Wortis, Joseph 28, 41, 73
Wunderli, Erika 95

Yad Vashem 261
Yiddish 39, 71, 223, 227, 231

Zeitschrift für Religionspsychologie 60,
154
Zentralblatt für Psychoanalyse 31, 34, 37
Zinzendorf, Ludwig von 93, 97
Zionism/Zionist 76, 78, 128, 138, 198,
233, 234, 236
Zuckmayer, Carl 244
Zuppinger-Urner, Martha 103
Zürich 4, 27, 30, 31, 97, 100, 185, 199;
Burghölzli clinic 185–6

Made in the USA
Middletown, DE
30 January 2020